Modernist Authorship and Transatlantic Periodical Culture

Historicizing Modernism

Series Editors

Matthew Feldman, Professorial Fellow, Norwegian Study Centre, University of York, UK; and Erik Tonning, Professor of British Literature and Culture, University of Bergen, Norway

Assistant Editor: David Tucker, Associate Lecturer, Goldsmiths College, University of London, UK

Editorial Board

Professor Chris Ackerley, Department of English, University of Otago, New Zealand; Professor Ron Bush, St. John's College, University of Oxford, UK; Dr. Finn Fordham, Department of English, Royal Holloway, UK; Professor Steven Matthews, Department of English, University of Reading, UK; Dr. Mark Nixon, Department of English, University of Reading, UK; Dr. Julie Taylor, Northumbria University, UK; Professor Shane Weller, Reader in Comparative Literature, University of Kent, UK; and Professor Janet Wilson, University of Northampton, UK.

Historicizing Modernism challenges traditional literary interpretations by taking an empirical approach to Modernist writing: a direct response to new documentary sources made available over the last decade.

Informed by archival research, and working beyond the usual European/American avant-garde 1900–45 parameters, this series reassesses established readings of Modernist writers by developing fresh views of intellectual contexts and working methods.

Series Titles

Arun Kolatkar and Literary Modernism in India, Laetitia Zecchini
British Literature and Classical Music, David Deutsch
Broadcasting in the Modernist Era, Matthew Feldman, Henry Mead, and Erik Tonning
Charles Henri Ford, Alexander Howard
Chicago and the Making of American Modernism, Michelle E. Moore
Christian Modernism in an Age of Totalitarianism, Jonas Kurlberg
Ezra Pound's Adams Cantos, David Ten Eyck
Ezra Pound's Eriugena, Mark Byron

Ezra Pound's Washington Cantos and the Struggle for Light, Alec Marsh
Great War Modernisms and The New Age Magazine, Paul Jackson, Gerri Kimber, and Janet Wilson
Historical Modernisms, Jean-Michel Rabaté and Angeliki Spiropoulou
Historicizing Modernists, Edited by Matthew Feldman, Anna Svendsen, and Erik Tonning
James Joyce and Absolute Music, Michelle Witen
James Joyce and Catholicism, Chrissie van Mierlo
Jean Rhys's Modernist Bearings and Experimental Aesthetics, Sue Thomas
John Kasper and Ezra Pound, Alec Marsh
Judith Wright and Emily Carr, Anne Collett and Dorothy Jones
Katherine Mansfield and Literary Modernism, Edited by Janet Wilson
Katherine Mansfield: New Directions, Edited by Aimée Gasston, Gerri Kimber, and Susan Reid
Late Modernism and the English Intelligencer, Alex Latter
The Life and Work of Thomas MacGreevy, Susan Schreibman
Literary Impressionism, Rebecca Bowler
The Many Drafts of D. H. Lawrence, Elliott Morsia
Modern Manuscripts, Dirk Van Hulle
Modernist Authorship and Transatlantic Periodical Culture, Amanda Sigler
Modernist Lives, Claire Battershill
Modernist Wastes, Caroline Knighton
The Politics of 1930s British Literature, Natasha Periyan
Reading Mina Loy's Autobiographies, Sandeep Parmar
Reframing Yeats, Charles Ivan Armstrong
Samuel Beckett and Arnold Geulincx, David Tucker
Samuel Beckett and the Bible, Iain Bailey
Samuel Beckett and Cinema, Anthony Paraskeva
Samuel Beckett in Confinement, James Little
Samuel Beckett and Experimental Psychology, Joshua Powell
Samuel Beckett's German Diaries 1936–1937, Mark Nixon
Samuel Beckett's "More Pricks Than Kicks," John Pilling
Samuel Beckett and the Second World War, William Davies
T. E. Hulme and the Ideological Politics of Early Modernism, Henry Mead
Virginia Woolf's Late Cultural Criticism, Alice Wood

Modernist Authorship and Transatlantic Periodical Culture

1895–1925

Amanda Sigler

BLOOMSBURY ACADEMIC
LONDON • NEW YORK • OXFORD • NEW DELHI • SYDNEY

BLOOMSBURY ACADEMIC
Bloomsbury Publishing Plc
50 Bedford Square, London, WC1B 3DP, UK
1385 Broadway, New York, NY 10018, USA
29 Earlsfort Terrace, Dublin 2, Ireland

BLOOMSBURY, BLOOMSBURY ACADEMIC and the Diana logo
are trademarks of Bloomsbury Publishing Plc

First published in Great Britain 2022
Paperback edition published 2024

Copyright © Amanda Sigler, 2022, 2024

Amanda Sigler has asserted her right under the Copyright,
Designs and Patents Act, 1988, to be identified as the Author of this work.

For legal purposes the Acknowledgments on pp. x–xiii constitute
an extension of this copyright page.

Cover design: Eleanor Rose

All rights reserved. No part of this publication may be reproduced or transmitted in any form or by any means, electronic or mechanical, including photocopying, recording, or any information storage or retrieval system, without prior permission in writing from the publishers.

Bloomsbury Publishing Plc does not have any control over, or responsibility for, any third-party websites referred to or in this book. All internet addresses given in this book were correct at the time of going to press. The author and publisher regret any inconvenience caused if addresses have changed or sites have ceased to exist, but can accept no responsibility for any such changes.

A catalogue record for this book is available from the British Library.

A catalog record for this book is available from the Library of Congress.

ISBN:	HB:	978-1-3502-3540-3
	PB:	978-1-3502-3544-1
	ePDF:	978-1-3502-3541-0
	eBook:	978-1-3502-3542-7

Series: Historicizing Modernism

Typeset by Integra Software Services Pvt. Ltd.

To find out more about our authors and books visit www.bloomsbury.com
and sign up for our newsletters.

Contents

List of Illustrations	viii
Editorial Preface to *Historicizing Modernism*	ix
Acknowledgments	x
Introduction	1
1 Deceiving Appearances in James's Fiction: The Illustrated *Turn of the Screw*, Advertisements, and *Collier's* U.S.S. *Maine* Coverage	17
2 Reconsidering Kipling's Imperialism: Kim in *McClure's* and *Cassell's*	65
3 Contextualizing *Ulysses*: Collaboration and Competition in the *Little Review*	125
4 A New Look for Mrs. Dalloway: Consumer Activity and Artistic Production in the *Dial*	179
Coda	235
Bibliography	241
Index	249

List of Illustrations

1 Masthead by John La Farge, which prefaced all installments of *The Turn of the Screw* except for the Easter issue 24
2 Eric Pape's illustration of the governess and ghost on the stairs in *Collier's* 34
3 H.R. Millar's illustration of the letter-writing scene in *Cassell's* 89
4 John Lockwood Kipling's illustration of Kim and the letter-writer in *Cassell's* 91
5 E.L. Weeks's portrayal of the letter-writing scene in *McClure's* 92

Editorial Preface to *Historicizing Modernism*

This book series is devoted to the analysis of late nineteenth- to twentieth-century literary Modernism within its historical contexts. *Historicizing Modernism* therefore stresses empirical accuracy and the value of primary sources (such as letters, diaries, notes, drafts, marginalia, or other archival materials) in developing monographs and edited collections on Modernist literature. This may take a number of forms, such as manuscript study and genetic criticism, documenting interrelated historical contexts and ideas, and exploring biographical information. To date, no book series has fully laid claim to this interdisciplinary, source-based territory for modern literature. While the series addresses itself to a range of key authors, it also highlights the importance of non-canonical writers with a view to establishing broader intellectual genealogies of Modernism. Furthermore, while the series is weighted toward the English-speaking world, studies of non-Anglophone Modernists whose writings are open to fresh historical exploration are also included.

A key aim of the series is to reach beyond the familiar rhetoric of intellectual and artistic "autonomy" employed by many Modernists and their critical commentators. Such rhetorical moves can and should themselves be historically situated and reintegrated into the complex continuum of individual literary practices. It is our intent that the series' emphasis upon the contested self-definitions of Modernist writers, thinkers, and critics may, in turn, prompt various reconsiderations of the boundaries delimiting the concept "Modernism" itself. Indeed, the concept of "historicizing" is itself debated across its volumes, and the series by no means discourages more theoretically informed approaches. On the contrary, the editors hope that the historical specificity encouraged by *Historicizing Modernism* may inspire a range of fundamental critiques along the way.

Matthew Feldman
Erik Tonning

Acknowledgments

My early thinking on this project began at the University of Virginia, where, during my doctoral studies, colleagues and mentors collectively created a vibrant intellectual atmosphere that shimmered with brilliance, energy, and reciprocity. I am grateful to UVA and its English Department for funding research trips that laid my project's foundations, and even more grateful for the conversations that enhanced the value of that research. Special thanks are due to Steve Arata and Alison Booth for their detailed comments on my doctoral dissertation, upon which this book is based. Though the project has evolved considerably since then, the imprint of their editorial guidance is still palpable. My heart is overwhelmed with awe and gratitude for the intellectual generosity of Michael Levenson, who directed my dissertation and the shape of my life. He has been there every step of the way, from my project's infancy to its maturity as a book. I could not have asked for a better guide.

The third chapter of my book was conceptualized at the Zürich James Joyce Foundation, whose two-month summer fellowship enabled my first forays into the *Little Review*. During that initial research trip in 2007 and the many that followed, my work was informed by lively intellectual exchanges with such perceptive scholars as William Brockman, Michelle Witen, Scarlett Baron, David Vichnar, Erika Mihálycsa, Vike Plock, and Sabrina Alonso. Of course, the Zürich James Joyce Foundation would not be what it is without the curatorial hands of Ursula Zeller, Ruth Frehner, and Frances Ilmberger, or the watchful eyes of Fritz Senn.

My book's transatlantic focus was forged during many trips between America and Europe, with Joycean cities such as Zürich, Dublin, and Trieste serving as hubs. I am especially grateful to Anne Fogarty and John McCourt for first giving me fellowships to, and later inviting me to speak at, the Dublin James Joyce Summer School and the Trieste James Joyce Summer School, respectively. These summer schools, in combination with the Bloomsday symposia and activities of the Zürich James Joyce Foundation, ushered me into the cross-cultural exchanges that define Joyce studies. Within this at once intimate and expansive world, Sean Latham has served as a guiding touchstone for my periodical-based research, and Clare Hutton provided useful pointers as the manuscript neared completion. I extend my fondest affection to the broader Joycean community, whose many gracious members have welcomed me, and so many other young scholars, with warm hearts and generous minds. To name them all, and thank them adequately, would require another book.

Much appreciation is due to my editors at Bloomsbury, particularly Laura Cope and Ben Doyle, for their professional guidance throughout the publication process, including their patience and understanding when medical issues pushed back deadlines. Having faced a major surgery as well as separate injuries that limited typing and the work I love, I thank God for a strong medical team, particularly my family physician, whose prayerful and compassionate care underwrote a strategic plan to manage health challenges alongside teaching and writing imperatives. There is a reason Philippians 4:13 has been my favorite verse since I was a little girl, and, in times like these, it gains deeper resonance with every keystroke. Likewise, I am thankful for my colleagues at Baylor University, both those who supported me during medical challenges and those who were involved in more direct ways with my book. Richard Rankin Russell provided feedback that sharpened the book's argument, and Julia Daniel helped see the manuscript through to its final revisions. For quote-checking, citation formatting, proofreading assistance, and research support, my thanks go to my graduate students Grace McCright and Savannah Chorn.

Collectively, UVA and Baylor have served as bookends to this project. Sandwiched in between those bookends are many conferences, research trips, and scholarly exchanges that contributed to the intellectual trajectory of my work. I am grateful for lecture invitations from the Modernist Versions Project and other venues that gave me opportunities to share my research, as well as for the collegial feedback provided along the way. Additionally, the following libraries graciously opened their collections to my inquisitive spirit: the Beinecke Rare Book and Manuscript Library at Yale University, where I consulted the *Dial*/Scofield Thayer Papers; the University of Wisconsin-Milwaukee Libraries, Archives Department, which houses the *Little Review* Records, 1914–64; the Zürich James Joyce Foundation, which owns original issues of the *Little Review*; the University of Delaware, which holds the Florence Reynolds Collection related to Jane Heap and the *Little Review*; the Library of Congress, where I consulted editions of *Cassell's*; the Albert and Shirley Small Special Collections Library at the University of Virginia, where I viewed original copies of the *Egoist*; and the Harry Ransom Center at the University of Texas at Austin, which furnished access to original issues of *McClure's* and other turn-of-the-century magazines.

The following institutions and organizations have kindly supplied images: the Fenimore Art Museum Library, Cooperstown, New York, which provided original illustrations of Henry James's *The Turn of the Screw* in *Collier's*, bringing to light new visual details that were lost in microfilm processing; the Herman B. Wells Library of Indiana University Libraries, which supplied illustrations of Rudyard Kipling's *Kim* in *Cassell's*; and the Modernist Journals Project, which supplied an illustration of *Kim* from *McClure's*.

Additionally, portions of this monograph have appeared in earlier publications, and I am grateful to the presses and editors for permission to reproduce.

My book's first chapter builds upon the following article:

Sigler, Amanda. "Unsuspecting Narrative Doubles in Serial Publication: The Illustrated *Turn of the Screw* and Collier's *U.S.S. Maine* Coverage." Copyright © 2008 Johns Hopkins University Press. This article first appeared in *The Henry James Review*, Volume 29, Issue 1, Winter 2008, pages 80–97. Published with permission by Johns Hopkins University Press.

My book's third chapter contains portions of the following article:

Sigler, Amanda. "Archival Errors: *Ulysses* in the *Little Review*." *European Joyce Studies* 20 (2011): 73–87. Material is reused with the permission of Brill and *European Joyce Studies*.

My book's fourth chapter builds upon the following article:

Sigler, Amanda. "Expanding Woolf's Gift Economy: Consumer Activity Meets Artistic Production in *The Dial*." *Tulsa Studies in Women's Literature* 30, no. 2 (Fall 2011): 317–42. Material is reused with the permission of the journal editors.

I would also like to acknowledge the Estate of Richard Aldington for permission to quote from the following unpublished letter:

Letter from Richard Aldington to Scofield Thayer, May 24, 1920, *Dial*/Scofield Thayer Papers, Beinecke Rare Book and Manuscript Library, Yale University. © Estate of Richard Aldington. Excerpts from Richard Aldington's letter of May 24, 1920, to Scofield Thayer (Beinecke Rare Book and Manuscript Library, Yale University) reproduced by kind permission of the Estate of Richard Aldington c/o Rosica Colin Limited, London.

The author and publisher gratefully acknowledge the permission granted to reproduce the copyright material in this book. Every effort has been made to trace copyright holders and to obtain their permission for the use of copyright material. The publisher apologizes for any errors or omissions and would be grateful if notified of any corrections that should be incorporated in future reprints or editions of this book. The third party copyrighted material displayed in the pages of this book are done so on the basis of "fair dealing for the purposes of criticism and review" or "fair use for the purposes of teaching, criticism, scholarship or research" only in accordance with international copyright laws, and is not intended to infringe upon the ownership rights of the original owners.

Introduction

As the editors of the Modernist Journals Project note, little magazines emerged at the beginning of the twentieth century in reaction to the mass magazines. Whereas commercial magazines carried many pages of advertisement (often over 100 pages of ads in a single issue), boasted large circulation numbers (in the tens or hundreds of thousands), were essentially money-making enterprises, and printed easily accessible literature that appealed to a broad, popular audience, the little magazines were devoted to art for art's sake, ran comparatively few pages of advertising, published works that were more experimental in nature, and appealed to a small coterie audience of intelligent readers. Little magazines, in accord with their name, were often physically small, and their circulation numbers usually amounted to a few hundred or a few thousand. Ushering in the era of high Modernism, they began appearing around the year 1910, as Ezra Pound notes in his essay "Small Magazines," and they were often short-lived. Typical little magazines had a lifespan of about five or ten years, often less; *Blast* famously ran for only two issues. For editors of little magazines, art came before commerce, but, crucially, they were still interested in advertisements and in how the tools of the commercial world could be used for their benefit. As Sean Latham and Robert Scholes note, a so-called "hole in the archive" was created when libraries rebound periodicals, fatally eliminating the advertising pages, which were judged unliterary and hence inconsequential.[1] Yet these advertisements, and their original magazine issues, represent the only format that can be trusted to preserve a full record of literary and cultural intersections.

In the chapters that follow, I seek to describe and delineate the precise ways in which Modernism was engaged with the commercial world. In order to understand Modernism fully, it is necessary to re-open the original periodicals that housed Modernist texts, whether they were little magazines or mass-market journals. While scholars such as Jennifer Wicke, Mark Morrisson, and others have already made the case for Modernism's engagement with the commercial sphere, many of Modernism's more intricate engagements still remain uncovered, hidden between the covers of periodicals or in the largely unmined editorial files of dusty archives. For instance, Morrisson notes that "Margaret Anderson's quintessential little magazine [the *Little Review*] borrowed directly from mass market publications and advertising rhetorics to style a popular periodical that would, however, eschew mass appeal as the basis of its editorial decisions."[2] But the *Little Review* and other little magazines like the *Dial*, as I show, did more than to borrow from the mass-market press: they also allied themselves commercially with these larger periodicals by producing joint subscriptions. This was a vexed relationship, as Morrisson notes, but it went beyond borrowing to incorporate mutual advertising.

Returning to the magazines unveils more, however, than Modernism's intimate commercial investments. The image of Modernism, and the interactions that brought it into being, assume a different shape. These magazines dislodge the notion of the autonomous work of art and show that Modernism's hallmark texts reached the public as interdependent artifacts, stories shaped not only by authorial intention but also quite forcefully by editorial prerogative and by surrounding material—including advertisements, illustrations, and readers' letters. In the magazines, Modernism becomes more collaborative, more interactive, more closely tied to commercial culture, and more dependent upon chance juxtapositions and accident.

Modernist Authorship

Henry James meticulously arranged his multi-volume New York Edition, for which he selected and framed his works with "lengthy prefaces" and exercised "control" over the accompanying illustrations.[3] Similarly, James Joyce "played a significant role in determining the physical shape of the first edition" of *Ulysses*, fastidiously selecting such details as the font (Elzevir) and the color of the cover (Greek blue).[4] Virginia Woolf, too, is known for the artistic self-fashioning she enjoyed when she and her husband Leonard set up the Hogarth Press in 1917, such that she could present her novels to the public as she wished them to appear. Even an author as commercially popular as Rudyard Kipling, who is less frequently associated with a Modernist milieu (though Henry James attended his wedding), filed a lawsuit against publishers who used book bindings and packaging of which he disapproved.[5] In many ways, these writers conform to the iconic image of the self-fashioned turn-of-the-century author who rigorously defended artistic autonomy. These writers, evidently, desired to have a fairly heavy hand in the public dissemination of their works.

And yet there is another side to the story. Each of these authors, like many of their contemporaries, agreed to give up a certain amount of autonomy in exchange for publishing their writing in magazines, where the presentation and packaging of their works would be determined by outside forces. Aaron Jaffe's notion of authorial imprimatur, a significant component of which is derived from textual autonomy and authorial self-fashioning, must be counterbalanced by a consideration of the collaborative forces that shaped authors' public image and their texts' impact—a point upon which Jaffe himself insists. Furthermore, an author's signature style, or imprimatur, may look quite different depending on which version of the text one consults—a (frequently earlier) magazine version, or a (later) book version. It is notable that when Jonathan Goldman applies the concept of authorial imprimatur developed by Jaffe, the examples he gives of Joyce's signature style are drawn mostly from the book version of *Ulysses*. Joyce's stylistic trademarks, Goldman says, "include the 'Aeolus' headlines, the overture that commences 'Sirens,' the script format in 'Circe,' the questions and responses that make up the catechistic style of 'Eumaeus,' and the nearly unbroken block of continuous text that comprises the forty-odd pages of 'Penelope.'"[6] Of these examples, only the "Sirens" overture occurs in the *Little Review*, and even then it is not called "Sirens." Original magazine readers would have known it as Episode XI. In the *Little Review*, "Aeolus" (Episode VII) occurred without its now-famous headlines, and, since the *Little Review* was facing obscenity charges in 1921, and Joyce's novel was incomplete, "Circe," "Eumaeus," and "Penelope" were never published serially.

What this points to is that Joyce, in spite of his reputation for fastidious oversight of production, was willing to subject his work to a much less stable publication process as he was developing what Jaffe and Goldman would call his imprimatur. In other words, to become a self-fashioned Modernist icon, Joyce first allowed his seminal work to undergo an important developmental stage in journal issues, where much of the fashioning (especially including such paratextual elements as font, colors of the cover, surrounding material, etc.) would be determined by editors. Joyce himself was also still deciding how he would like his final text to look—the "Aeolus" headlines, for example, were a later invention. This surrendering of his work to the market, the evidence suggests, influenced his composition of *Ulysses* as a complete novel. As Clare Hutton asserts, "the process of serialization was of formative and fundamental significance to the genesis of *Ulysses*."[7] In the *Little Review*, alterations to his text enraged Joyce, but, more importantly, these errors and departures influenced the composition of Joyce's ever-evolving work. As David Weir notes, "Joyce actually added material to *Ulysses* that was directly inspired by" the *Little Review* censorship trials.[8] Were it not for the original periodical publication of *Ulysses*, and the scandal it inaugurated, the mock obscenity trial in Joyce's "Circe" chapter may have looked substantially different. Furthermore, even before the government ruled *Ulysses* to be obscene, letters to the editor stirred up numerous debates about *Ulysses* and its artistic merits (or demerits, according to some readers). This innovative column allowed for a Modernism that was more participatory, since readers were responding to each other and watching their letters appear alongside installments of Joyce's novel.

One could make similar arguments for Henry James, Rudyard Kipling, Virginia Woolf, and their contemporaries. While the specifics of each case will vary, the works they published in journals were differently inflected and resulted in fundamentally different experiences for magazine as opposed to book readers. In the magazines, Modernist authorship is more collaborative, and Modernist readership is more participatory. As Margot Norris writes, "The degree of reader participation is inevitably much greater for a virgin than a veteran reader, thereby producing not only more extensive speculation, and greater risk, but also a wider and more interesting range of interpretation."[9] This effect is only magnified in the magazines, for several reasons: (1) In the event of serialization, Modernist works usually appeared in magazines before they appeared in book form, such that periodical readers are by definition first-time readers; (2) Modernist magazines embedded literary works alongside other items—such as illustrations, advertisements, or (un)related articles—that opened up an even greater "range of interpretation" than might be realized in Norris's study, which focuses on book versions as opposed to periodicals; (3) Modernist magazines had the infrastructure, and employed the machinery, to encourage reader participation—whether in the form of letters to the editor, advertisement cut-outs, or editorial announcements and insertions that urged subscribers to take action; (4) Unlike a one-time book purchase, a magazine subscription (usually for a year's time) involved a long-term, cyclical commitment—an agreement if not to read, at least to receive a publication on a monthly (or weekly or quarterly, etc.) basis.

Although my book's title leads with "Modernist Authorship," the book is less about authorship *per se* than it is about the mediation of authorship through the collaborative and circumstantially contingent work of periodicals. In tracing the influence of surrounding periodical artifacts, my chapters at times directly engage with, and at other times implicitly build upon, Gérard Genette's concept of "paratext," as articulated in his influential and oft-cited study entitled *Paratexts: Thresholds of Interpretation*. Genette defines paratext as "accompanying productions" such as "an author's name, a title, a preface, [or] illustrations" that adorn the text.[10] At one point, Genette categorizes magazines as being part of a "*prior* paratext"—as, for example, when they issue announcements heralding a forthcoming book, with books being the form of publication that gains primacy in Genette's analysis.[11] Elsewhere, however, Genette admits that he has given periodicals short shrift when he identifies three lacunae in his study: translation, serial publication, and illustration.[12] Although my monograph does not deal with translation, it does take up serial publication and illustration.

While the concept of "paratext" is still relevant to magazines, its theoretical conceptualization must be significantly altered to account for the kind of unpredictable circumstances and community forces (whether mass-market or coterie) that characterize periodical production. In the magazines, readers encountered Modernist and proto-Modernist texts not as packages meticulously arranged by the author, but as one part of a larger product whose shape and design were largely beyond the author's control. Thus when Genette writes that the "main issue for the paratext" is "to ensure for the text a destiny consistent with the author's purpose," we must qualify that remark by remembering that he is speaking of a book's paratext.[13] In a book, the paratext may very well be a "conveyor of a commentary that is authorial or more or less legitimated by the author."[14] In a magazine, by contrast, the paratext will serve a communal purpose: it reflects the design of the editors, but it also reflects the desires of the community members (advertisers, artists, other authors, readers), and these communal designs and desires are in turn inflected by fortuitous as well as planned events and correspondences.

It should be noted that, while my project may find useful intersections with cultural studies and critical theory (including paratextual considerations, reader-response theory, and, in the Woolf chapter, gift theory), it is primarily an act of historical recovery. Even in our cyber-conscious age, when efforts to digitize Modernist periodicals abound, valuable clues remain buried in the physical archive. That is why my book goes back to the archives, turning to original issues of magazines and rarely consulted editorial correspondence to describe the emergence of Modernism. Though this project involved travel to a range of libraries, the collections cited most frequently are the *Dial*/Scofield Thayer Papers at Yale's Beinecke Rare Book and Manuscript Library and the *Little Review*'s editorial records at the University of Wisconsin-Milwaukee. These editorial files, viewed in combination with original magazine issues, underscore how factors beyond Modernist authors' control powerfully influenced the packaging and reception of their works. In this way, the argument that follows unearths archival evidence to describe a collaborative, consumer-oriented Modernism that developed out of both intentional and serendipitous groupings in periodicals. These periodicals adjust our perceptions of authors elsewhere known to be "in charge" and reveal the central role that compromise and chance played in the emergence of Modernism.

Transatlantic Periodical Culture

In particular, the argument that follows returns to the archive in order to trace the serialization and advertisement of four key texts: Henry James's *The Turn of the Screw* in *Collier's* (1898), Rudyard Kipling's *Kim* in *McClure's* and *Cassell's* (1900–1), James Joyce's *Ulysses* in the *Little Review* (1918–20), and Virginia Woolf's "Mrs. Dalloway in Bond Street" in the *Dial* (1923). While all of these authors lived largely and in some cases exclusively in Europe, their texts were making transatlantic journeys to American magazines, where they were received by American audiences: *Collier's*, *McClure's*, the *Little Review*, and the *Dial* were all published in New York (the *Little Review* made its own transatlantic relocation to Paris, but only after serialization of *Ulysses* was complete). Thus, while we tend to think of James as an American who became a British citizen, of Kipling as a British author with strong colonial ties to India (who also briefly lived in Vermont), of Joyce as an Irish author who spent his adult life on the European Continent, and of Woolf as a solidly British author, the publication of their texts on the opposite side of the ocean underscores the strong transatlantic component to their identity.

While these authors may have been writing from a European perspective, American magazines were presenting them to the public. In many ways, these authors became (as the periodicals publishing them claimed) central to American culture. As an American living in Europe, James could elucidate both cultures; Kipling influenced American imperial policy; and Joyce's scandalous works challenged American moral standards and legal precedent. Even Woolf, who lived all her life in London, and seems so quintessentially English, was paraded by the *Dial* as essential reading for Americans who desired to be intellectually cultured. Indeed, during this time, magazines themselves were becoming more international, intent upon publishing authors from other continents, bringing multiple nationalities together between their covers, and establishing channels for transatlantic dialogue. While *fin-de-siècle* magazines contained seeds of transnationalism,[15] it was the Modernist magazines that saw these seeds grow to maturity.

My first two chapters, on James and Kipling, treat prominent authors who were writing at a crucial turning point in literary history, at the juncture between Victorianism and Modernism. Both James and Kipling published in mass-market periodicals, making their debuts before the advent of little magazines, but they were writing at a time when aesthetic and production climates were changing and magazines were acquiring a more international scope. While both James and Kipling are often associated with nineteenth-century literature (and rightly so, given the substantial body of work they produced in that period), their turn-of-the-century works employ many stylistic features, such as unreliable narrators and ambiguous endings, that would become integral to high Modernist aesthetics.

James and Kipling represent two sides of the late Victorian era. They are both strongly transatlantic authors with a wide body of works—a point underscored in Christopher Benfey's recent biography of Kipling's American years—but James's sophisticated, intellectual prose and comparatively palatable ideological stance have proven more appealing to academics over time. Likewise, his concern with narratology and consciousness has informed literary theory and proven pivotal in studies of the Novel as a genre. Although both writers admired each other's work, James's formal, at times snobbish, focus on style and society contrasts with Kipling's focus on plot and backstreet adventure. Kipling, who won the Nobel Prize in 1907, was content to be an at once prestigious and popular author, while James's anxiety about the marketplace foregrounds many high Modernists' concerns about the mixing of elite and low cultures.

In terms of transatlantic historical events, the serialization of *The Turn of the Screw* unwittingly brings the Spanish-American War into focus, just as later Modernist works including Woolf's *Mrs. Dalloway* and T.S. Eliot's *The Waste Land* would, on an intentional level, bring the First World War into focus.[16] Whereas James composed *The Turn of the Screw* before the U.S.S. *Maine* dramatically exploded in Havana Harbor, making any parallels between fiction and history a matter of coincidence, Kipling's political impact on the Spanish-American War and its aftermath (especially the war in the Philippines) can be directly traced through such poems as "The White Man's Burden." As a result of this notorious poem and related statements on imperial duty, Kipling is often taught and studied with some degree of political embarrassment or intellectual dismissal today: Even while asserting that from "1890 to 1920, Rudyard Kipling was the most popular and financially successful writer in the world," Christopher Benfey acknowledges that "Kipling has never quite joined the ranks of unquestioned canonical writers, like Joseph Conrad and Virginia Woolf"; and in certain circles, writing on Kipling is considered "potentially career-killing."[17] Nevertheless, Kipling performs the important work of bringing British and American imperialism into focus. His views on race are as essential to study as they are uncomfortable to behold. And it is important to recognize, as this book argues, that Kipling's image as a voice of Empire was at once forged in and tempered by periodicals on both sides of the Atlantic.

While my first two chapters concentrate on turn-of-the-century commercial magazines, the last two chapters treat two prominent and frequently paired (albeit antagonistically in some cases) authors of the high Modernist period, Joyce and Woolf. These final chapters turn toward the little magazines that created a separate space, or, as several scholars have termed it, a "counter-public sphere" for artistically ambitious works. Within this experimental coterie, Joyce is arguably the most influential male Modernist, and Woolf arguably the most influential female Modernist. Both authors are known for having pioneered a daring stream-of-consciousness style, and their stylistic innovations are central to the definition of Modernism. On the one hand, *Ulysses* and *Mrs. Dalloway* function as stylistic masterpieces in each writer's canon, representing their authors at a stage of artistic maturity; on the other hand, the early versions of these works in magazines elucidate the process of a maturing artistic consciousness that coincided with a newly emergent Modernist sensibility. These works helped define the Modernist era, but the magazines shaped, packaged, and defined these works for audiences in the first place.

As with the commercial magazines publishing James and Kipling, the little magazines publishing Joyce and Woolf give us a new perspective on transatlantic literary-historical intersections. *Ulysses*'s serialization overlaps with the First World War, and its publication in the United States on brittle wartime paper reminds us how the war's impact stretched far beyond European trenches. Unlike *Collier's*, which extensively covered the build-up to the Spanish-American War during the serialization of James's work, the *Little Review* chose largely to ignore the Great War during the serialization of *Ulysses*, a novel which likewise sidesteps the military conflict, namely by being set in 1904. The *Little Review* viewed the war as a distraction from the weightier concerns of art. But not all little magazines approached the Great War in the same way. If we turn to Woolf in the *Dial*, we see that the presence of the war is palpable yet muted in "Mrs. Dalloway in Bond Street," at least in comparison to its more extensive, and profoundly tragic, development in the full-length novel. Most remarkably, the war veteran Septimus Smith does not yet surface in the short story. But, as if by proleptic synchronicity, surrounding articles in the July 1923 *Dial* fill in these gaps, creating a heightened sense of desperation and loss even before Woolf added Septimus's postwar trauma and suicide to the narrative.

These observations carry implications for our pedagogy, which I will return to in the coda. For now, it is sufficient to observe that James, Kipling, Joyce, and Woolf are all frequently taught authors, and it may be helpful for readers of this book to think about the ways these authors' periodical archives, as unearthed in each chapter, could be brought into the classroom. In fact, in recent years, two serial-based editions of the texts treated here have been published, with each being marketed for classroom use. Their re-publication is suggestive of the rich pedagogic potential latent in periodical studies. Instructors may wish to pair Chapter 1 of this book with Peter G. Beidler's *The Collier's Weekly Version of Henry James's The Turn of the Screw*; and Chapter 3 with *The Little Review Ulysses*, edited by Mark Gaipa, Sean Latham, and Robert Scholes. Chapter 1, which discusses the Spanish-American War alongside James's ghost story, will help students understand how historical contexts intersect with literary production. The chapter provides an in-depth consideration of historical-literary intersections, rather than merely printing a side-by-side timeline of "historical events" and "literary publication dates." Chapter 2, with its documentation of imperialistic advertisements and racially inflected illustrations, could be used to introduce students to the British Empire. Chapter 3, which covers one of the most famous trials in literary history, uses archival evidence to give students added context to censorship debates during Modernism. Chapter 4, on *Mrs. Dalloway*, could enhance classroom discussions of feminine gift economies or the cultural impact of the First World War. Instructors looking for more advanced applications could ask students to search original periodical issues to see what other connections— or notable points of dissonance—they find between the literature and nearby periodical artifacts.[18] Indeed, this sort of activity is common in periodical studies courses, and it is my hope that *Modernist Authorship and Transatlantic Periodical Culture: 1895–1925* will provide another model for promoting this type of contextual work. Ultimately, by reading the following chapters alongside original periodical issues (and modern reprintings of serialized texts), students and their instructors may be prompted to ask, "How intentional was Modernism?"

It is this book's argument that Modernism emerged largely through unintended pathways and convergences. This picture comes into focus when we choose prominent authors as focal points, yet it should be noted that magazines open up avenues for exploring marginalized authors as well—a point to which I will briefly return in the coda. While the coda focuses on major authors, it simultaneously proposes ways that periodical-based pedagogy may serve to bring marginalized authors and media, including advertisements, into dialogue with mainstream course materials. Indeed, with the growing curricular interest in diversity and inclusion, instructors may wish to organize courses such that these marginalized authors and media claim the spotlight.

Overview of Chapters

The first chapter examines three simultaneously occurring serial artifacts that shaped *The Turn of the Screw* in *Collier's*: the illustrations accompanying James's tale, news coverage of the U.S.S. *Maine* explosion that sparked the Spanish-American War, and advertisements that eerily suggest cures for the very ailments plaguing James's characters. The Spanish-American War, often overlooked in favor of more prominent Modernist military conflicts such as the First World War, shows strong corollaries with James's story, and the *Maine* controversy functions as the historical predecessor to Modernist ambiguity. By an accident of historical convergence, the *Maine* exploded in Havana Harbor while *The Turn of the Screw* was being serialized, such that James's mysterious story with its unanswered questions (who is responsible for the story's evil events: the governess, the children, or the ghosts?) was paired with *Collier's* coverage of a real-life mystery (who is responsible for the *Maine*'s explosion: conspiring Spaniards, or misfortunate American seamen?). I argue that Eric Pape's illustrations of *The Turn of the Screw*, while initially seeming to authenticate the governess's narrative, are more complex than traditionally thought. They function similarly to the photos of the *Maine* wreckage, which initially seemed to support the theory of Spanish sabotage but were later revealed to be consistent with the theory of internal combustion. Similarly, advertisements used visual images to support questionable claims. This chapter shows that initial impressions, whether of historical disasters, commercial products, or fictional events, are often as misleading as James's professed antipathy for the market.

The second chapter shows how the fiction of Kipling, an author often associated with jingoism, is placed in a periodical context that questions the extent of *Kim*'s imperialism. *Kim*'s relationship to Empire depends on which magazine—British or American—readers happen to pick up. In significant ways, meaning becomes an accident of geographic location and adjacent periodical artifacts. In the New York-based *McClure's*, support for imperialism is gently tempered by muckraking series and by articles reflecting on America's rebellion from colonial rule. In the London-based *Cassell's*, however, *Kim* is intricately linked to the magazine's investment in British imperialism. This chapter unearths advertisements, fiction, and news articles that glorify Empire, as well as promotional materials for *Kim* that equate literary with imperial success. But even in *Cassell's*, the illustrations of three competing visual artists unwittingly threaten to undermine the stability of the magazine's editorial position. While John Lockwood Kipling's images of Kim reinforce the boy's seemingly effortless ability to pass as Black or White, the images by H.R. Millar and E.L. Weeks present Kim as alternately British (in Millar's case) and Indian (in Weeks's case). The visual evidence alone leaves readers wondering which version of Kim to believe in, making it unclear whether he remains loyal to the British secret service or ultimately rejects imperial games in favor of India and the lama. Colonial urgency gives way to Modernist ambiguity. Ultimately, the periodical archive suggests that Kipling's novel should be read as being suspicious of imperialism, not unabashedly complicit with it.

The third chapter examines how Joyce, who would later achieve near-complete authorial control of *Ulysses* in its 1922 book publication, exercised virtually no influence over the packaging of his novel in serial form. Revisiting the censorship that altered Joyce's text, this chapter capitalizes on the *Little Review*'s editorial archives at the University of Wisconsin-Milwaukee, thereby revealing how the suppression of the *Little Review* was tied not only to *Ulysses* but to other materials, both written and visual, published by the magazine. In letters composed by censors and by Joyce's advocates, *Ulysses* is paired with drawings of nude figures, with other artistically daring fiction, and with risqué First World War articles. From this evidence, we learn that the Post Office censors were anxious not merely about Joyce's scandalous fiction, but also about the harmful magnifying effect created when this fiction was placed alongside similarly scandalous material. Furthermore, even before the government censors confiscated episodes of *Ulysses*, the *Little Review*'s own devoted readers objected to Joyce's work. In the *Little Review*, *Ulysses* falls short of becoming an autonomous work of art and instead becomes an interdependent artifact that was shaped through the collaborative and competitive interplay among editors, censors, and readers.

The fourth chapter explores how "Mrs. Dalloway in Bond Street," which focuses on a shopping trip, unexpectedly intersects with the *Dial*'s secret, uneasy negotiations between commercial and gift economies in the 1920s. In terms of Woolf's career, the 1920s would seem to mark a point when Woolf turned from journalism to the Hogarth Press, where she exercised more control over her fiction. And yet this is only half the picture. In reality it was the time when she was beginning to place more of her fiction in magazines. "Solid Objects" appeared in *The Athenaeum* (October 20, 1920); "An Unwritten Novel" appeared in the *London Mercury* (July 1920); "In the Orchard" appeared in *Criterion* (April 1923) and *Broom* (September 1923); next came "Mrs. Dalloway in Bond Street," in the July 1923 *Dial*.[19] I have chosen to focus on "Mrs. Dalloway in Bond Street" because, as Susan Dick notes, this story marked an "important stage in Woolf's development, for it was in writing 'Mrs. Dalloway in Bond Street' that she first found a way to place her narrator within her character's mind and to present that character's thoughts and emotions as they occur."[20] In addition, however, its publication in an American magazine represents Woolf's transatlantic reach, thus augmenting Brenda Silver's studies of Woolf's later appearances in the American press. These appearances came to be marked by a certain celebrity status, even as magazines' promotional tactics brought Woolf's writing and iconic image into dialogue with commodity culture and consumer marketing. "Mrs. Dalloway in Bond Street" is of particular interest because it is a work of literature that centers about a consumer-oriented shopping trip; it is also a story that was first published in a magazine that struggled to balance its firm commitment to art with the inevitable pressures of business. In the midst of this struggle, the *Dial* sought to carve an alternative path through the discourse of gift-giving, which is coincidentally a theme taken up by Woolf's fiction as well. These fortuitous points of convergence and marketplace negotiation are captured in the *Dial*'s very revealing editorial archives at the Beinecke Library, which this final chapter unpacks.

Periodical Studies

With the rise of the New Modernist Studies and its materialist turn, scholars have increasingly highlighted the important role that periodicals played in the dissemination of Modernist works. There is now within the field a growing recognition of the way physical artifacts shaped aesthetic ambitions. One could point to any number of studies—Mark Morrisson's *The Public Face of Modernism* (2001); Suzanne W. Churchill and Adam McKible's *Little Magazines and Modernism: New Approaches* (2007); Ann Ardis and Patrick Collier's

Transatlantic Print Culture, 1880–1940 (2008); the three-volume *Oxford Critical and Cultural History of Modernist Magazines* (2009–13); Robert Scholes and Clifford Wulfman's *Modernism in the Magazines* (2010); or Eric Bulson's *Little Magazine, World Form* (2016), to name a few. And this list does not include studies of single authors, such as Clare Hutton's *Serial Encounters: Ulysses and the Little Review* (2019), or newly issued editions of Modernist texts based on their serial form, such as Peter G. Beidler's *The Collier's Weekly Version of Henry James's The Turn of the Screw* (2010) or Yale's *The Little Review Ulysses* (2015), edited by Mark Gaipa, Sean Latham, and Robert Scholes. Further adding to the growing field of periodical studies, digital humanities projects such as the Modernist Journals Project (at Brown and the University of Tulsa) and the Princeton Blue Mountain Project are undertaking the decades-long task of digitizing hundreds of magazines.

But these ambitious undertakings, as monumental as they are, do not tell the full story. Previous scholarship tends to present Modernism as a movement emerging from intentional collaboration between authors and editors, while in reality Modernist texts were distinctly dependent upon accident, printing constraints, and surrounding artifacts that competed with and often distorted authorial intention. One recent (2019) study, Clare Hutton's *Serial Encounters*, briefly alludes to the way literary historians tend to be tempted toward an intentional fallacy:

> [Journal editors] bring geographically dispersed authors, texts, concepts, and ephemera into a kind of momentary cultural synergy. While literary historians may come to identify that synergy as a fact of significance, it is important to bear the moment of origin in mind, and not to over-determine the significance of a journal, given that it is multi-authored, contingent, expedient, and ultimately social, both in origin and intention. In other words, it is important to note that a journal, viewed as a document within literary history, is, to an important degree, a document of happenstance.[21]

It is not merely, then, that authors were giving up control to editors; it is also that they were ceding part of that control to random occurrences and chance. Hutton makes this observation in passing, but this question of happenstance is a central thread that my argument takes up.

While in tune with recent innovations, my chapters also comment upon older, established scholarship, such as Lawrence Rainey's *Institutions of Modernism* (1999) and Jennifer Wicke's *Advertising Fictions* (1988). Whereas Wicke discusses advertisements that surface within fiction, I discuss actual advertisements that were published alongside literary works, between the same magazine covers. This interplay between literature and advertisement happened in little magazines as well as mass-market periodicals. It was not merely that little magazines engaged in coterie publishing that became its own market force, as Rainey describes, but that they also sparked ongoing relations with commercial periodicals and national advertisers while cultivating that image of high culture.

The first two chapters of my book, on the proto-Modernists James and Kipling, whose work I study in commercial periodicals, set the stage for the last two chapters, on the high Modernists Joyce and Woolf, whose work I study in literary magazines. Returning to the archive for a thorough investigation of the journals that shaped Modernism, my project resituates this revolutionary literary event as a movement not only consolidated geographically in cities like London, Paris, or New York but also consolidated textually and materially between the covers of periodicals, which brought various literary and cultural artifacts together even as they disseminated them to a global audience. As the evidence suggests, the success of this "consolidate and disseminate" enterprise depended as much on extrinsic as on intrinsic factors. Once we approach Modernism through periodicals, we realize that Modernism's first engagements with the public were to a significant extent based on chance. Released from isolating book covers, literary works receive surprisingly different inflections, and the historical recovery of Modernism takes on a new density.

Notes

1 Sean Latham and Robert Scholes, "The Rise of Periodical Studies," *PMLA* 121 (March 2006): 520.
2 Mark Morrisson, *The Public Face of Modernism: Little Magazines, Audiences, and Reception, 1905–1920* (Madison: University of Wisconsin Press, 2001), 15.
3 Kirsten MacLeod, "Material Turns of the Screw: The *Collier's Weekly* Serialization of *The Turn of the Screw* (1898)," *Cahiers Victoriens et Eduoardiens* 84 (2016): 10, https://doi.org/10.4000/cve.2986.
4 Clare Hutton, *Serial Encounters: Ulysses and the Little Review* (Oxford: Oxford University Press, 2019), 1.
5 See "Kipling Sues Publishers: Wants $25,000 Damages from Several Leading American Houses," *New York Times*, April 23, 1899: 2, *ProQuest Historical Newspapers*. The lawsuit was "brought primarily against" G.P. Putnam's Sons (2).
6 Jonathan Goldman, *Modernism Is the Literature of Celebrity* (Austin: University of Texas Press, 2011), 63.

7   Hutton, *Serial Encounters*, 126.
8   David Weir, "What Did He Know, and When Did He Know It: The *Little Review*, Joyce, and *Ulysses*," *James Joyce Quarterly* 37, nos. 3–4 (Spring–Summer 2000): 390.
9   Margot Norris, *Virgin and Veteran Readings of Ulysses* (New York: Palgrave Macmillan, 2011), 10.
10 Gérard Genette, *Paratexts: Thresholds of Interpretation*, trans. Jane E. Lewin (Cambridge: Cambridge University Press, 1997), 1.
11 Genette, *Paratexts*, 5.
12 Genette, *Paratexts*, 405–6.
13 Genette, *Paratexts*, 407.
14 Genette, *Paratexts*, 2.
15 Peter Brooker and Andrew Thacker, eds., *The Oxford Critical and Cultural History of Modernist Magazines*, Vol. 1 (New York and Oxford: Oxford University Press, 2009), 75.
16 In tandem with my argument about the Spanish-American War in *Collier's*, Daniel Hannah has recently made a similar case for a "surprising interrelationship" between James's *The Awkward Age* and "coverage of the Spanish-American War" in *Harper's Weekly*. See Hannah, "'Inevitable irruption': Henry James's *The Awkward Age*, *Harper's Weekly*, and the Spanish-American War," *American Periodicals: A Journal of History & Criticism* 31, no. 1 (2021): 19, muse.jhu.edu/article/793760.
17 Christopher Benfey, *If: The Untold Story of Kipling's American Years* (New York: Penguin, 2019), 3, 4, 10. While Benfey dismisses the idea that writing on Kipling is career-ending, the statements made to him as he was writing indicate that some scholars hold this perception.
18 *McClure's* and the *Little Review* have been digitized by the Modernist Journals Project, an open-access scholarly database; both runs are incomplete, but they do cover the years during which *Kim* and *Ulysses* were serialized, respectively. At the time of press, they are the most easily accessible of all the magazines studied in my book. Issues of *Cassell's* may be found on HathiTrust. Additional magazines may become available online as the process of digitization proceeds.
19 See Susan Dick, ed., *The Complete Shorter Fiction of Virginia Woolf* (Orlando: Harcourt, 1989), 299–302.
20 Dick, ed., *The Complete Shorter Fiction*, 3.
21 Hutton, *Serial Encounters*, 44.

1

Deceiving Appearances in James's Fiction

The Illustrated *Turn of the Screw*, Advertisements, and *Collier's* U.S.S. *Maine* Coverage

Framing James's Tale: Douglas's Opening Section, Surrounding Stories in *Collier's*, and La Farge's Masthead

When in 1898 Robert J. Collier assumed editorship of the journal founded by his father, he faced declining circulation numbers and a legacy of "hard times."[1] Freshly emerged from Harvard and relatively inexperienced in journalism, Collier needed a way to revitalize the weekly periodical, which had once enjoyed a circulation of a quarter-million.[2] Two ground-breaking events occurred in the year he began editing *Collier's Weekly*: the journal secured rights to publish Henry James's *The Turn of the Screw*, and the U.S.S. *Maine* exploded in Havana Harbor, providing rich possibilities for news coverage. As Frank Luther Mott records, Collier made two significant statements explaining the decisions he made during his first year at the journal: "I showed my judgment of the public taste by ordering a serial story by Henry James. [...] It was at that time [...] that the *Maine* blew up and Jimmy Hare [sent to Havana to cover the story] blew in."[3] Although Mott mentions these two events on the same page of his *History of American Magazines*, he does not draw any further connection between them, and even scholars analyzing *The Turn of the Screw* as a serialized work have frequently bypassed the surrounding articles in favor of focusing on James's vexed relationship to the marketplace or on his general distrust of periodical illustrators. This chapter returns to the first publication of *The Turn of the Screw* in *Collier's*, examining not only how the journal's seldom-reprinted illustrations interact with the tale but also how *The Turn of the Screw* itself both anticipates and complicates its relationship to surrounding visual images, advertisements, and articles.[4] Specifically, I will discuss how Eric Pape's illustrations are more ambiguous than traditionally thought, how the advertisements promote an equation between visuality and truth that is troubled by James's tale, and how the coeval emergence of the *Maine* story at the outbreak of the Spanish-American War uncannily yet appropriately intersects with *The Turn of the Screw*, reflecting and reifying anxieties about narrative reliability. Collectively, this constellation of issues—ambiguity, deceptive appearances, unreliable narration, and an international impulse—sets the stage for Modernism and suggests that its hallmark traits emerged coevally and serendipitously with unpredictable market forces and unforeseen historical events.

As Sean Latham and Robert Scholes write, periodicals are "rich, dialogic texts" that "create often surprising and even bewildering points of contact between disparate areas of human activity."[5] By examining these contexts—the physical positioning of James's story in *Collier's* and the historical moment in which the serialized tale was published—we can not only begin to appreciate more fully how the story's first readers would have encountered and responded to the tale but also find grounds for rethinking our own twenty-first-century approaches to the text. Although most scholars responding to *The Turn of the Screw* work from the text as it appeared in book form—*The Two Magics* (1898), the New York Edition of *The Novels and Tales of Henry James* (1908), or modern reprintings of these editions—the original readers of *The Turn of the Screw* encountered it in a radically different form, one that has significant implications for our understanding of the tale's publication and reception history—and indeed, for our understanding of reading itself. When the tale appeared in *Collier's*, it had not only textual variants that differentiated it from later book versions but also a whole range of neighboring texts and images that gave it different inflections.[6] By interrogating the relationships between the disparate artifacts that first readers encountered, we can begin to develop a more nuanced account of reading as an experience that extends beyond processing words on a page (the aspect of reading emphasized by historical collation, by reader-response theory, and by other approaches), and we can better evaluate how that processing is mediated and conditioned by illustrations, advertisements, and other material artifacts in the text's immediate vicinity.

This kind of strong contextualization will also show the extent to which accident and chance compete with or, in some cases, complement, authorial intent. To the extent that James did not control the illustrations, the advertisements, or the surrounding news stories, these paratextual elements (to borrow Gérard Genette's term) de-centralize authorial power. In some cases, the relationship becomes competitive: Advertisements insist on their own veracity, whereas James's narrative casts doubt on its own reliability. But in other cases, the competing messages tip into complementary ones: The coverage of the *Maine* story in the popular press, which James elsewhere bemoaned, in retrospect serves to reinforce some of his points about untrustworthy narrative reports. Similarly, Pape's illustrations, while initially seeming to promote a superficial reading of James's tale as a literal ghost story, in retrospect call into question the governess's perception of events. A closer examination of these illustrations shows how they could be viewed as mirroring James's artistic ambiguity in much the same way that John La Farge's masthead does. However we interpret these illustrations, the fact remains that they were not commissioned by James himself. In sum, the periodical paratext positions proto-Modernist works like *The Turn of the Screw* as texts governed by careful editorial planning (such as the deliberate pairing of illustrations with James's text), by marketplace contracts uncontrolled by authors and only partially controlled by editors (insofar as magazine editors solicited advertisements and reserved space for them but did not fully determine their content), and by pure coincidence beyond either author's or editor's foresight (such as the explosion of the *Maine*). In all three cases, we see how in the magazines, Modernist and proto-Modernist authorship becomes subsumed under the banner of outside controlling forces.

These surrounding elements with bearing upon the text may be thought of as "paratext." Genette writes that the paratext is by definition "characterized by an authorial intention and assumption of responsibility," but he later qualifies this remark by stating that "the degree of responsibility may vary," and still later he observes that some types of paratext do "not always involve the responsibility of the author in a very meaningful way"; when it comes to promotional materials, for example, the author is, according to Genette, "satisfied just to close his eyes."[7] Here we see authorial intention being gradually eroded from the equation. In *Paratexts: Thresholds of Interpretation*, Genette is dealing mostly with book as opposed to serial publication, but if his study had included serialization, we would see this trend toward erosion of authorial intention borne out even more fully. James—like Kipling, Joyce, and Woolf in later chapters—agreed to hand over his story to magazine editors, mirroring the way that the governess in *The Turn of the Screw* hands over her manuscript to Douglas. The governess's manuscript is then passed along (as would happen to an author's manuscript in an editorial office), re-transcribed (as would happen when the magazine's typesetters got hold of a manuscript), and framed for the audience by an unnamed narrator (who substitutes as a kind of editor who introduces the story). In this way, James signals that the presentation of his own work, before his own (magazine) audience, is largely out of his hands.

In light of the large body of critical commentary that analyzes James's tale as a frame narrative, it is important to resituate *The Turn of the Screw* within its original context as a serialized tale—especially since the outermost frame within the story gestures toward an audience of magazine readers. The narrator's comparison of the holiday gatherers' "last story" to "the mere opening of a serial"[8] gains even greater significance when we consider that this comment first appeared not between the covers of a book but between the covers of a periodical that had a tradition of publishing short stories, including ghost and sensation fiction. In his oft-cited formulation, T.S. Lustig notes, "The introductory chapter of *The Turn of the Screw* begins just after a story has been told and ends just before a story is about to begin."[9] Thus when the narrator states that Douglas's story is told in the context of other tales, we may wish to think of it not only as adding "another turn of the screw"[10] to the Christmas Eve stories related within James's narrative but also as adding another turn of the screw to the stories published in *Collier's*. In 1897, the year leading up to the publication of *The Turn of the Screw*, *Collier's* frequently serialized stories suggestive of horror and intrigue, including "The Curious Corpse" by Louis Zangwill and "Monseigneur: Unfolded in Eleven Mysteries" by Samuel Freedman. That same year it also published "Eat Not Thy Heart" by Julien Gordon, advertised as the "author of 'A Diplomat's Diary,' 'A Successful Man,' 'Vampires,' etc. etc." When it published Richard Dowling's "Old Corcoran's Money," the journal reminded readers that the author had also penned "The Mystery of Killard," "Sweet Inisfail," "Catmur's Caves," and "The Dark Intruder." Alongside writers who have largely faded into obscurity, well-known authors such as Sir Walter Besant, Robert W. Chambers, George Gissing, Sarah Grand, and Stephen Crane also published fiction in the twelve months immediately preceding and succeeding the appearance of James's famous ghost story. Collectively, these stories frame James's tale, even as the frame of his own story also gestures toward a larger audience of magazine readers.

The story's serialization in *Collier's* not only embeds it within the magazine's tradition of publishing popular fiction and mysteries, but also alters readers' understanding of the tale on its own terms. In *The Victorian Serial*, Linda K. Hughes and Michael Lund have shown that authors used the serial structure to parallel themes of pause and progression in their works, and their observations can easily be extended to James's tale. In "the extended time of serial publication," periods "of expectation" experienced by characters within fiction (the example given by Hughes and Lund is that of Emily's pregnancy in Trollope's *The Prime Minister*) are mutually experienced by readers.[11] These forced interruptions both unite readers with characters and accentuate the divide between periodical and book publication. Thus, even a reader picking up *Collier's* for the first time in January 1898, or a reader who had ignored the previous fiction, would undergo a substantively different reading experience than later readers who purchased the tale in a book form that allowed for uninterrupted reading. Readers of the book, in other words, could choose to read *The Turn of the Screw* in a single sitting, or, if they preferred to divide their reading time, could decide when to start and stop reading the text. Readers of the serialized version did not have these options but were instead held in suspense as they waited for the next weekly installment.[12]

This unique characteristic of serial publication was one James was familiar with and took advantage of in composing *The Turn of the Screw*. Because the first installment ends precisely when the governess's tale begins, James withholds the story from his reading public in much the same way that Douglas delays its telling. When the auditors exclaim over the proposed story with enthusiasm, Douglas tells them, "I can't begin. I shall have to send to town."[13] His announcement is followed by "a unanimous groan,"[14] but his audience, like James's, must wait for the story's arrival. In the interim, the ladies depart, much to the narrator's relief.[15] The resulting male audience, "more compact and select,"[16] enables James (as Anne T. Margolis parenthetically notes) "to make the opening frame self-reflexive in regard to the dubious propriety of telling such a tale before *his* own sexually-mixed magazine public."[17] Margolis's parenthetical observation deserves to come out of its parentheses. The frame, I wish to suggest, is all the more evocative because of its existence as a serialized frame, and this recognition compounds the ways in which James is interacting with his audience as readers of periodicals. He was, as June Howard notes, "intensely aware of his potential and actual audiences."[18]

And Collier, who approached James in 1897 to secure a story from him, was well aware of James's particular literary appeal, as reflected in his decision to place James at the head of other "well-known novelists" in an early January 1898 advertisement. The *Collier's* ad shows how mass-market magazines recognized the appeal of "high" literature; later, as high Modernism witnessed the proliferation of little magazines, the reverse would also become true: coterie magazines recognized the appeal of mass-market advertising techniques. In the 1898 *Collier's* ad, which uses James's artistic credentials to distinguish *Collier's* from the "ordinary news journal,"[19] *Collier's* announces its plans to become not only more visual but also more highbrow:

> Beginning with Vol. XX., No. 17, dated January 27, 1898, COLLIER'S WEEKLY will INCREASE the number of its ILLUSTRATED PAGES from SIXTEEN to TWENTY-FOUR. The Illustrations will not only be more NUMEROUS, but they

will be the work of such FAMOUS ARTISTS as—FREDERIC REMINGTON, HOWARD PYLE, JOHN LA FARGE, A. B. WENZELL, T. DE THULSTRUP, W.J. SMEDLEY, ERIC PAPE, PETER NEWELL, [AND] ALICE BARBER STEPHENS.[20]

In the second column of this advertisement, *Collier's* announced that it would begin "the publication of HENRY JAMES'S great serial, 'THE TURN OF THE SCREW,'" in the same number. The story would be "illustrated by John La Farge and Eric Pape" and "followed by stories by 'Julien Gordon,' I. Zangwill and other well-known novelists." Significantly, then, the announcement casts James's tale as part of its effort to reinvent the magazine, and it places *The Turn of the Screw* specifically within the contexts of contemporary fiction and illustration. The announcement's subhead, repeating the cover's formulation of *Collier's Weekly* as "AN ILLUSTRATED JOURNAL OF ART, LITERATURE AND CURRENT EVENTS," further reminds readers that James's tale forms part of a larger narrative in which visual art, fiction, and historical events (as disparate as they may otherwise be) are brought together under cover of the magazine.

The magazine, which had changed its name in 1895 from *Once a Week* to *Collier's Weekly: An Illustrated Journal*,[21] frequently used visual images to complement and substantiate the truth claims of its news coverage, but James's tale implicitly challenges this equation between visuality (a representation of events) and truth (the actual facts of the case). Whereas the familiar proverb "seeing is believing" seems to underwrite the magazine's decision to publish multiple illustrations and photographs, James's tale argues that readers in fact cannot trust the visual evidence presented before their eyes. In *Collier's*, photographs of the U.S.S. *Maine* disaster and events in Cuba are offered to readers as proofs validating reporters' written accounts. Similarly, for James's governess, "*to see ghosts = to see letters*" (to borrow Shoshana Felman's equation[22]), but, by making the governess a questionably reliable narrator (indeed, she is the prime example of the "unreliable narrator" in Wayne C. Booth's landmark study, *The Rhetoric of Fiction*), James also questions whether any visual evidence (of ghosts, of a Spanish mine, etc.) can substantiate verbal claims or translate into seeing words on the page.

In history, a faulty equation between visuality and truth can have tremendous consequences: The Spanish-American War was at least partly justified on the grounds of visual evidence that later historians find suspect. The 1898 official report—judging on the basis of crew testimony, naval expertise, artifacts recovered by divers, and "drawings" of the ship "exhibited before the court"[23]—concluded that a Spanish mine had been responsible for the explosion of the

Maine. This conclusion was "a major factor in the origins of the war."[24] As James's tale illustrates, an assumption that the truth and the visual are closely aligned can also have significant implications for our interpretation of fiction. When we resituate *The Turn of the Screw* within its original periodical context, we can see how the predicament of James's governess has a corollary in the 1898 events actually being experienced by *Collier's* readers, and how the stakes of interpretation are intensified within this highly visual medium.

When we examine *The Turn of the Screw* in *Collier's: An Illustrated Journal*, we can discern how James's tale not only engages generally in aesthetic debates about the pictorial but also carries specific implications for *Collier's* readers in America, where newspapers were urging war through a combination of verbal and visual appeals.[25] The Spanish-American War and James's *The Turn of the Screw* anticipate Mark Wollaeger's claims about the First World War propaganda and Joseph Conrad's *Heart of Darkness*: "[R]eliable information has always been hard to come by in wartime," Wollaeger writes,[26] but "with World War I, when newly invented propaganda techniques first harnessed the considerable power of the advertising industry to the political aims of the nation-state, the most telling saying emerged: the first casualty of war is truth."[27] Wollaeger's argument about how *Heart of Darkness*, serialized in *Blackwood's* 1899–1900, anticipates and critiques the First World War propaganda that "fill[ed] heads with pictures"[28] can be extended to *The Turn of the Screw*, published just one year earlier in *Collier's*. But whereas Wollaeger argues that *Heart of Darkness* has strong corollaries in a war that happened fifteen years after its publication, I will show how *The Turn of the Screw* has strong corollaries in a war that occurred in the same year of the tale's publication, and that received significant coverage in the same periodical. In this way, James's critique of the press and the pictorial prefigures the problematics surrounding the Conradian "desire 'to make you see,'"[29] just as the Spanish-American War, described by the *Saturday Evening Post* as a "newspaper-made war,"[30] anticipates the amplified proliferation of propaganda in the First World War.

As someone familiar with the author and his views, John La Farge, a lifelong friend of James,[31] produces ambiguous artwork that reinforces James's critique of narratives that all too quickly align perception with fact. Because the ghost in his masthead is strategically positioned so that only the governess can see him, La Farge effectually questions her reliability in much the same way James does (see Figure 1). Far from illuminating or simplifying James's tale, La Farge's dark masthead, which preceded every installment except the Easter issue of April 9, generated so much perplexity that even the editor claimed he never understood "what either the story or the pictures were about."³² Perhaps because of the masthead's intriguing ambiguity, perhaps because of La Farge's prominent presence in the nineteenth-century artistic scene, or perhaps because of his close relationship with James, his masthead has received more critical commentary than all the individual illustrations of Eric Pape combined.³³ As I will discuss in greater detail below, however, the same kinds of questions critics have posed about intentionality in the masthead might also usefully be asked with respect to Pape's illustrations of individual scenes. But the masthead carries special significance because it was reproduced repeatedly, almost like a familiar advertisement attached to a product, thus perpetually unnerving or assuring readers (depending upon one's orientation) with its perplexing yet familiar scene: In the center of the illustration, the governess places her right hand on Miles's shoulder, drawing him into an embrace, while a shadowy figure in the background evokes the ghost of Peter Quint. The scene is formally framed between symmetrical, decorative monsters that echo each other in the fashion of Gothic doubling.

Positioned above James's tale, the masthead itself acts as a frame to a frame story. Notably, when it first appeared on January 27, the masthead "represented the governess and Miles before James's story introduced them."³⁴ Readers opening the journal of January 27 would encounter the image before hearing from Douglas of "my sister's governess,"³⁵ who is never named, and before learning from the frame tale's narrator that she had in her charge two children by names of "Miles" and "Flora."³⁶ But so little information is given about the governess

Figure 1 Masthead by John La Farge, which prefaced all installments of *The Turn of the Screw* except for the Easter issue. The reproduced image is taken from *Collier's Weekly*, Volume 20, 1898, Courtesy of the Fenimore Art Museum Library, Cooperstown, New York.

in the first installment (which concludes before her first-person narration begins) that it would be difficult for readers to label the figures in La Farge's masthead with any degree of confidence until later issues, when the governess's affection for Miles becomes explicit. Moreover, the triangulation between Quint, Miles, and the governess is more reminiscent of the novella's closing scene—with Quint's "white face of damnation,"[37] the boy's "missing wholly" the ghost,[38] and the governess's desperate effort "to press him" to herself[39]—than of its opening. The masthead, then, by virtue of its physical positioning above the title, not only presents James's characters before they are verbally described in the first installment but also appears to summon the final installment's climactic encounter before the narrative even begins.

Adam Sonstegard argues that the masthead "regulates the tale for the magazine's readers as it attempts to provide a definitive interpretation of characters and events,"[40] but critical interpretations of the illustration have proven it far more ambiguous than definitive. It raises more questions than it answers. As Sonstegard himself notes, "Miles's childish countenance" gives readers "little reason to see him as defiant or disobedient, but at the same time, a shadowy set of features in the upper-left corner of the painting recreates Peter Quint as an opposing influence" who threatens to extract the boy from his governess's protective and affectionate embrace.[41] The masthead, far from offering a "definitive interpretation" of the characters, suggests that they are precariously poised between security and disaster—which is, coincidentally, the same uncertain state in which the United States found itself, as *Collier's* frequent articles on national security and the nation's growing tensions with Spain underscore. The illustrated characters are surrounded visually by darkness and vaguely defined, ominously lurking evil influences, which, whether imagined or real, threaten to rob them of the apparent bliss they find in each other's arms.[42]

Another oddity, compounding the puzzling nature of the image for *Collier's* readers, is a mysterious dark hand that cradles Miles's head. Adeline R. Tintner concludes that the hand, contrary to any realistic logic, must "belong to the governess, who, strangely, has already been equipped with a white right hand."[43] Applying a Freudian reading to the illustration, she suggests that the "white right hand expresses the governess's protective, motherly relation to Miles," whereas the "dark right hand expresses the destructive, mind-clutching, sexually repressed part of her nature."[44] But if Tintner can propose an elucidative yet anatomically impossible interpretation attributing the hand to the governess, there is little to prevent other anatomically impossible interpretations attributing the disembodied hand to Quint, to Miles himself, or to the conspicuously absent

Miss Jessel, who may be making her only appearance in the form of the dark, skeletal fingers that grip Miles's childish locks.

La Farge's masthead, like the tale it illustrates, defies conclusive interpretation. As S.P. Rosenbaum concludes, "La Farge's illustration preserves something of the ambiguity of the ghosts" and expresses "something of James's own intention [...] to encourage the reader to summon up his own vision of terror."[45] Of course, with James, the question of whether the paratext reflects his intention is made complicated by the fact that we do not know what his intention was. Upon publishing a 2010 edition of *The Turn of the Screw* that sought to recapture the 1898 serialized text, Peter Beidler wrote: "After my analysis of the more than five hundred differences in wording between the first and the last *Turn of the Screw*, I am convinced that James's revisions reveal nothing of his 'intentions' about whether the ghosts are real or merely the hallucinations of a neurotic governess."[46] Yet, as an intimate acquaintance of James, La Farge could be expected to know "something of James's own intention"; the two artists had enjoyed a lifelong friendship, and the illustrator had been instrumental in shaping James's career as a writer. When James in his teenage years was "still undecided between palette and pen," the older La Farge advised him to become a writer.[47] Although James in general despised the popular magazine illustrations that threatened to push literature off the page, he admired La Farge's work[48] and even sat for a portrait painted by La Farge.[49] "La Farge, in turn, served as the model" for the protagonist of James's story "A Landscape Painter,"[50] serialized in the *Atlantic Monthly* of February 1866. James also portrayed La Farge in *The American Scene*, where he described the artist's celebrated mural *The Ascension*.[51] By supplying the masthead for *The Turn of the Screw*, then, La Farge emerges from James's fiction to illustrate it. And in this case, the paratext does seem to reinforce authorial intention and to operate with some degree of authorial sanction.

Significantly, both La Farge and James interacted closely with the periodical world, and both did so with a sense of periodicals' international reach and implications. As Henry Adams writes, La Farge, who wrote as well as illustrated, developed a "practice of using newspapers to gain publicity or promote his views,"[52] just as James manipulated the periodical market to his own advantage, as Michael Anesko has eloquently and meticulously described in *Friction with the Market*. Anesko writes: "By securing English copyright for his wares and often selling them to English as well as American periodicals for serial use, James effectively doubled his income as a writer."[53] And La Farge's practice of using periodicals as vehicles to espouse his critical views began with an international artistic controversy in 1878, one sparked when he "proposed that

American wood engravings should be sent to the world's fair in Paris."[54] When the landscapist George Inness opposed this idea, a lively "exchange of letters" erupted in New York newspapers, including the *New York Tribune*, the *New York World*, and the *New York Evening Post*.[55] In these debates, La Farge wrote as a New York-born American with European roots (his parents were émigrés from France). Conversely, when James composed *The Turn of the Screw* for serialization in the New York-based *Collier's*, he wrote as a resident of England with American roots. Just as La Farge merged French and American cultures, traveling frequently between both continents,[56] so James brought American and European sensibilities together in his writing. In 1888 he wrote to his brother William,

> I have not the least hesitation in saying that I aspire to write in such a way that it would be impossible to an outsider to say whether I am at a given moment an American writing about England or an Englishman writing about America (dealing as I do with both countries,) and so far from being ashamed of such an ambiguity I should be exceedingly proud of it.[57]

Thus, the publications of La Farge and James, as well as their actual movements between continents, underscore the transatlantic component inherent in both of their careers. And this transatlantic sensibility is further reflected in James's calculated decision to publish in periodicals on both sides of the Atlantic.

The friendly relationship between La Farge and James is well-documented in the biographies and critical works addressing each respective artist; what is perhaps less frequently noted in James scholarship, however, is La Farge's own fascination with horror, which paralleled James's forays into the supernatural realm. S.P. Rosenbaum, for example, merely describes him as "an accomplished landscape and portrait painter, magazine illustrator, worker in stained glass, and religious muralist,"[58] omitting his perhaps lesser-known but equally important professional identity as an illustrator of ghost and horror stories. La Farge's grandson reports that the illustrator had a "pre-occupation with the metaphysical, psychic forces that control human existence" and that his "interest in the occult" can be traced back to his early book illustrations for *The Wolf Charmer*, "the creepy Breton legend."[59] La Farge's interest in "hallucinations and subliminal consciousness," his grandson suggests, can best be observed in his *The Uncanny Badger*, published in 1897—the year before La Farge illustrated James's story.[60] This interest in subliminal consciousness and the uncanny is also evident in the masthead La Farge designed for *The Turn of the Screw*. While the masthead does provide "visual continuity for a tale that spanned four months of serial publication and grew increasingly mysterious during that time,"[61] it complicates rather than resolves the mysteries.

Though James could not have anticipated it, the ambiguity upon which his story relied would also become a central theme in *Collier's* coverage of events in Cuba. Of course, much of the uncertainty surrounding the Cuban events would eventually be resolved, but for nineteenth-century periodical readers the initial sense of chaos, heightened by unreliable reports emerging from Cuba, would have been felt just as strongly as James's permanent, deliberate ambiguity. When the second installment of *The Turn of the Screw* appeared on February 5, 1898, it was preceded by an article speculating on the reasons for the *Maine's* recent departure for Havana Harbor. "The Situation in Cuba" began by unveiling the unreliability of previous stories: "Most news reports from Cuba consist in denials of earlier news reports," the writer observes, and even "official" stories cannot be trusted.[62] Rioting in Cuba, military tensions with Spain, and the protection of American citizens abroad are all cited as possible reasons for the *Maine's* summons to Havana Harbor. The emphasis on protecting innocent Americans and aiding abused Cubans, an issue to which the press would repeatedly return, uncannily mirrors the governess's conviction in James's tale that she must guard the innocent children who are threatened by evil of unknown magnitude. At the same time, the suspense and fear experienced by James's governess would have been felt by *Collier's* readers as the political climate became increasingly unstable and unpredictable.

Collier's reporters, searching desperately for explanations, realized that the truth could not always be so easily uncovered. Like James's governess, they are frequently forced to admit speculations rather than certainties. As the writer of "The Situation in Cuba" concludes, "Probably no single explanation of the sending of the *Maine* tells the entire truth."[63] The reporter's assertion unwittingly echoes Douglas's insistence (delivered in the first installment) that his own "story *won't* tell, [...] not in any literal vulgar way."[64] Douglas is of course literally referring to the governess's love affairs, but interpreted in the more nuanced understanding which he advocates, the claim that the "story won't tell" can be read in the same sense as Poe's assertion in "The Man of the Crowd": "'*er lasst sich nicht lesen*'—it does not permit itself to be read."[65] Like the elusive "man of the crowd," James's governess also defies strict classification; she does not permit herself to be read. She is alternately interpreted as a victim and as a predator, as a matronly protector and as a corrupted governess, as a sane person and as a madwoman. For her as for *Collier's* reporters, no single explanation will tell the entire truth. This uncertainty is reflected in La Farge's ambiguous masthead; and, I will argue, it is also reflected in Pape's art, though scholars have often insisted that his illustrations simplify James's story, and though James himself complained about the practice of periodical illustration. Upon closer inspection, however, we can see that Pape's images add another layer of complexity to the tale, presenting yet another version of the many documents to which the frame narrator alludes.

Pape's Portrayal of the Governess and the Ghosts

It is interesting to note that the illustrations, like the governess's story itself, have been accused of obscuring information and of communicating inaccurate descriptions. While James appreciated sophisticated visual art, he generally despised the commercial art appearing in popular serials, and in his critical preface to *The Golden Bowl* he described the frustrations of "the author of any text putting forward illustrative claims" who finds his text "elbowed" by the "competitive process" of visual illustration.[66] The preface echoes sentiments he expressed earlier in his essay on "American Magazines." That James wrote this essay the year in which *The Turn of the Screw* was serialized indicates that the unfortunate proliferation of illustrated periodicals was at the forefront of his mind in 1898. In the essay, James laments the surrender of the "golden age of familiar letters" to the "reign of the picture":[67]

> That the magazines are, above all, copiously "illustrated," expresses portentously, for better or worse, their character and situation [...]. There was never, within my recollection, a time when the article was not, now and then, to some extent, the pictures; but there was certainly a time when it was, at the worst, very much less the pictures than today.[68]

As James composed his tale, he was self-consciously aware of and reflecting upon the venue in which it would appear. As Sonstegard writes, "James knew as he wrote the tale that an editor of a popular periodical would take his turn serializing it" and "commercial artists would take their turns illustrating it."[69] James, then, sees his tale as competing with the illustrations that would accompany it.

Unlike La Farge's mysterious masthead, which does not represent any particular moment in the narrative, Pape's illustrations of individual scenes express a "particular thing in the text," clashing with James's preference for art "the reference of which to Novel or Tale should exactly be *not* competitive and obvious, should on the contrary plead its case with some shyness."[70] Keyed to particular textual moments by their captions, the Pape illustrations are "obvious" in the way they correspond to James's tale, but, I argue, they do *not* take an obvious interpretative position with respect to the governess's narrative. Their representation of events is far more ambiguous than past critical assessment would lead us to believe.

Little is known about Eric Pape, except that he "was a pupil of Emil Carlsen and studied at the École des Beaux-Arts, Paris" and "lived and worked in Manchester, Massachusetts."[71] He illustrated "several books,"[72] including the fairy-tales of James's acquaintance Hans Christian Andersen—and in this regard it is notable that James's governess compares her initial experiences at Bly to "story-books and fairy-tales."[73] Like fairy-tales, *The Turn of the Screw* is also a children's story—though less in the sense of being for them than being about them. Though Pape did not know James intimately the way La Farge did, he was working in a genre evoked by James's fiction. In his groundbreaking essay, Edmund Wilson in fact describes the tale as belonging "to a small group of fairy tales whose symbols exert a peculiar power by reason of the fact that they have behind them, whether or not the authors are aware of it, a profound grasp of subconscious processes."[74] In effect, then, Wilson converts James's description of his story as a "fairy-tale pure and simple"[75] into a fairy-tale that is purely complex. Because Pape illustrated fairy-tales—stories that derive their power from their dual delivery of "simple" readings enjoyed by children and "complex" readings with underlying symbolism perceived by adults (as Jack Zipes, Maria Tatar, and other folklorists have shown)—he is in some ways an ideal illustrator for *The Turn of the Screw*.

But because he did not collaborate with James, Pape has been seen as producing reductive interpretations of *The Turn of the Screw* that would have displeased its author. Observing how the ghosts are visually manifested in Pape's illustrations, Rosenbaum wryly notes, "The ambiguous nature of James's ghosts clearly presented no challenge."[76] Similarly, Sonstegard accuses Pape of painting "in black and white what James's story keeps dimly, ambiguously shrouded. He accepts [...] what the governess sees as truth."[77] The question these critics do not ask, however, is exactly *which* of the story's many layers Pape is actually illustrating: Is he illustrating from the governess's point of view, from Douglas's interpretation, from the frame narrator's perspective, or as a reader-critic outside the frame? Sonstegard and Rosenbaum both assume that Pape is illustrating the story from the reader's point of view—that is to say, he is functioning as another reader-critic, albeit a naive one, telling *Collier's* audience how the story ought to be interpreted. That Pape visually represents the ghosts does not necessarily mean that he credits the governess's story, however; he could be representing the ghosts as hallucinations, not as actual presences. Even if he is presenting the story from the governess's point of view, as Douglas does when he turns over the manuscript, or as James does when he grants the governess a first-person narration, he is not necessarily endorsing that point of view. In the argument that follows, I do not mean to refute the validity of Sonstegard's detailed and provocative reading, insofar as he suggests that Pape's art seems to authenticate the governess's story—indeed, it is plausible if not probable that Pape's 1898 audience would have interpreted the illustrations as depicting actual ghosts (as opposed to hallucinations of the governess). What I do mean to question is the *necessity* of reading Pape's illustrations in this way.

A closer examination of Pape's illustrations may reveal that they, like James's story, can be interpreted more richly and ambiguously than first readings will allow. As Terry Heller notes, *The Turn of the Screw* was at first "read as a literal ghost story," though a few reviewers objected,[78] and the first readings of Pape's illustrations have also interpreted them as telling a literal ghost story. But as time passed, "more intricate responses" to James's tale "began to emerge,"[79] and under the school of New Criticism debates raged between "apparitionist" and "non-apparitionist" readings until the 1960s, when the dichotomy began to dissolve, yielding to a new "stress on ambiguity."[80] Ironically, a century after the Pape illustrations' first publication, we are still in the early stages of the art's reception history, since so few critics have actually commented on it, and most of them do so only in passing. I would like to suggest, however, that we can use the trajectory of the tale's reception history to ask whether its illustrations might also be viewed as "apparitionist" from one perspective and "non-apparitionist" from another. We can then ask whether this dichotomy suggests that the *Collier's* illustrations achieve greater ambiguity than previously credited.

Pape's illustration accompanying the third installment (issued on February 12) inaugurates the series of drawings that depict images of the ghosts. In the illustration, the governess, with her back to the readers of *Collier's*, stands in a long dress between the foliage surrounding Bly and peers upward at a shadowy figure in the distant tower. The caption, quoting the governess's astonished reaction, reads, "He did stand there!—but high up, beyond the lawn and at the very top of the tower."[81] Perhaps influenced by this caption, Sonstegard argues that Pape makes Quint's shade "even more substantive, even more 'realistic,' than the governess herself."[82] Significantly, however, only Quint's silhouette can be discerned in the illustration, and he is so far removed from the governess's point of view in the foreground of the painting that he measures proportionately about a tenth of her size. Since his waist and legs are obscured by the crenellations, only his upper body is visible, whereas the governess's entire body is portrayed. He seems from this perspective at least to garner less "substance" than the governess.

For Sonstegard, the illustration commands that *Collier's* readers understand an "apparitionist" interpretation of the story, in which the ghosts are rendered all the more prominent by virtue of their visual appearance on the pages of the magazine. As he notes, Quint "stand[s] out in a bold contrast of black and white that seems to authenticate" the ghost's presence.[83] Visually, he is at the center of the painting, hovering above the vanishing point where the lines of perspective would meet. But it is possible to give another interpretation to the illustration in which the governess's gaze does more than the artist's brush to bring Quint into existence. Because she is looking directly at him, she may be thought to be summoning the shade by her own will; he could be, in other words, a projection of her desires. In the tale itself, the man's image follows shortly upon the governess's internal visualization of it. When the governess is walking in the gardens surrounding Bly, she thinks to herself, "it would be as charming as a charming story suddenly to meet some one,"[84] and almost as if in response to her internally expressed desire a man appears in the battlements of the house. It is as if her imagination summons Peter Quint into existence. Although she claims that "the man who looked at me over the battlements was as definite as a picture in a frame,"[85] Pape's art interrogates just how "definite" this pictorial appearance is. The illustration, which fails to grant Quint any of the definitive facial attributes the governess later describes,[86] calls the governess's story into question, suggesting that she later added details that were never there or at least could not, at so great a distance, have been observed.

Moreover, the tale itself anticipates its accompanying visual illustrations. When in the fourth installment the governess relates her encounter to Mrs. Grose, she effectively reconstructs the painting that accompanied the previous (third) installment. Telling Mrs. Grose that he had "no hat,"[87] the governess both confirms readers' visual memory of Pape's illustration in the previous issue (in which Quint does indeed appear hatless) and draws a "picture" for the housekeeper.[88] Realizing the power of her visual descriptions, the governess "quickly added stroke to stroke" to complete the picture of Quint.[89] While the governess, by the time of her conversation with Mrs. Grose, has received a "better" view of Quint through the window,[90] she asserts that he did not appear there with any "greater distinctness, for that was impossible,"[91] and she tells Mrs. Grose that she "saw him [on the tower] as I see you."[92] This clear image of

Quint, with "close-curling" red hair, "a pale face," "little rather queer whiskers," "particularly arched" eyebrows, "sharp, strange" eyes, a "wide" mouth, "thin" lips, and a basically "clean-shaven" appearance,[93] was not what readers of *Collier's* encountered. In *Collier's*, Quint's shadowy appearance stands in stark contrast to Pape's previous illustration, which had depicted Douglas relating the tale to house guests with clearly defined features.

When they are illustrated, James's characters are rendered much more real than the ghosts that haunt them. In the sixth installment, Pape again displays the governess in far greater detail than the ghosts she either sees or imagines (see Figure 2). Encountering Quint on the staircase, she appears fully illuminated by her candle in the upper left-hand corner, while the shadowy ghost appears so shrouded in the opposite corner that microfilm copies even fail to reproduce him. Sonstegard, for example, does not detect the ghost that can be seen in original copies of *Collier's*, such as those held by New York's Fenimore Art Museum Library, or in other reproductions of the illustrations, such as those reprinted in Terry Heller's *The Turn of the Screw: Bewildered Vision* and in Peter G. Beidler's *The Collier's Weekly Version of The Turn of the Screw*. As Sonstegard himself notes, the microfilmed images from which he works suffer from regrettable "obscurity."[94]

Relying on microfilm, which effectively erases the ghost from the scene, we may be inclined toward this analysis:

> Readers' imaginations, and their recollections of Quint's previous appearances, evoke more imagery than Pape's paintbrush is required to supply. The candle illuminates only a small corner of an otherwise dark rectangle, as if Quint's frightening presence occupies more space than the dimly illuminated governess. [...] [R]eaders squint into black spaces to verify the story's visions, as Pape sacrifices detail to enhance opaque suggestiveness.[95]

This reliance on microfilm has significant consequences for our assessment of Pape's intention: Here, Pape appears to refrain from painting the ghost spied by the governess, in favor of inviting readers to "supply" their own image. He "sacrifices detail" to increase the periodical user's sense of horror. But if we return to original copies of *Collier's*, we unearth a different view: The apparition is airy, to be sure, and surrounded in darkness, but he is unquestionably present. Pape, then, does not intend to suggestively magnify Quint by encasing him in shadows, and he does not intend for readers to conjure up their own images of the ghost. Without actually authenticating the governess's narrative, Pape—like Douglas, the frame narrator, or James himself—nonetheless faithfully leaves the alleged apparition in the scene.

Figure 2 Eric Pape's illustration of the governess and ghost on the stairs in *Collier's*. The reproduced image is taken from *Collier's Weekly*, Volume 20, 1898, Courtesy of the Fenimore Art Museum Library, Cooperstown, New York.

Restoring the ghost to this scene on the staircase, we can now more accurately juxtapose the ghostly illustrations with those illustrations that actually do not contain ghosts. And we can establish this principle: Whenever Pape illustrates a scene in which the governess claims she sees a ghost, the ghost is always present, even if it is shadowy or faintly defined. But whenever Pape illustrates a scene that does not involve ghosts, he does not take the liberty of sketching them in (which might suggest that they were present without the governess being aware of it). The presence or absence of the illustrated ghosts remains consistent with the governess's account, even if certain details introduce interpretive difficulties (as with the tower illustration, which fails to grant Quint the facial attributes the governess claims for him).

The image accompanying the next illustrated installment, of March 19, does not portray the ghosts at all—because they are not mentioned.[96] Miles and the governess are in the garden outside the church, in a peaceful landscape that evokes spring as easily as "autumn"[97] and suggests a mood of "cherubic, rural innocence."[98] At the same time, there is something unsettling about the way the governess averts her eyes from the boy, casting her gaze at the ground in the painting's lower left corner even as he, pushing his body against the stone slab upon which she sits, stares directly at her. The apparently peaceful image, which stretches across two pages and carries the caption "He presently produced something that made me drop straight down on the stone slab,"[99] carries ominous undertones and subtly raises questions about the innocence of the story's purportedly angelic children. Little Miles forces the governess to cast herself down upon a stone in the church graveyard; little Flora, who does not appear in any of the illustrations, becomes almost more ghostly than the visually embodied Quint and Jessel.[100]

The final illustration, portraying the governess sprawled on the ground after her climactic dispute with Flora at the lake (but again, omitting Flora), shifts the focus back to the conflict between the governess and the ghosts. Depicting Miss Jessel for the first time, the illustration gives material form to the apparition that readers would have needed to imagine for themselves in her three previous appearances: once at the first lake incident, once on the stairs, and once in the schoolroom. Significantly, the governess's downcast gaze, recalling her averted eyes in the previous scene with Miles, prevents her from making eye contact with the apparition, who appears as a shadowy figure in the upper right corner of the illustration.[101] Like Quint's ghost in the tower, her dark, indistinct form is thrown into relief against a white background. This last illustration seems to present the most persuasive evidence for reading Pape as an "apparitionist" who believed in the ghosts' actual presence, since Miss Jessel's hovering in the background seems independent of the prostrate governess's gaze. But if the governess is not looking at Miss Jessel, no one else is either. In Pape's illustrations, the governess is the only one ever shown as definitively seeing the ghosts. Despite the visual representation of ghosts on the page, the veracity of the governess's account is still called into question. Pape's viewers as much as James's readers are left to decide for themselves whether they can credit her story.

Still, however, an argument for Miss Jessel's actual presence seems the more obvious if not the strongest interpretation of Pape's final illustration, and it is worthy of note that James, too, initially regarded *The Turn of the Screw* as a "real" ghost story with "actual" ghosts. In his January 12, 1895 notebook entry, James records his memory of the horror story told to him by the Archbishop of Canterbury, in which the "servants *die* (the story vague about the way of it) and their apparitions, figures, return to haunt the house *and* children [. . .]. It is all obscure and imperfect, the picture, the story, but there is a suggestion of strangely gruesome effect in it. The story to be told—tolerably obviously— by an outside spectator, observer."[102] Notably, James refers to his "story" as a "picture," suggesting that in spite of all his diatribes against magazine illustrations he still imagined his story visually (and in fact this preference for his own art explains why he disliked competing visualizations). Writing about *The Turn of the Screw* to Louis Waldstein, James stated, "It is the intention so primarily, with me, always, of the artist, the *painter*, that *that* is what I most, myself, feel in it—and the lesson, the idea—ever—conveyed is only the one that deeply lurks in any vision prompted by life."[103] Equating the "artist" with the "painter," James suggests not only that the tale itself is a kind of painting but also that its meaning "lurks" deeply and may not be immediately detected.

Interestingly, early reviews of James's tale also characterized it as an eerie story with visual propensities.[104] In a November 1898 review in the *Bookman*, James's tale of "corruption" is described as a "picture," "[e]very inch" of which "seems an outrage in our first heat."[105] In "Henry James as a Ghost Raiser," *Life* describes *The Turn of the Screw* in literary language that begins with a grammatical analysis but quickly slips into art metaphors: "Seldom does he make a direct assertion, but qualifies and negatives and double negatives, and then throws in a handful of adverbs, until the image floats away upon a verbal smoke. But while the image lasts, it is, artistically, a thing of beauty."[106] Here "assertions," "negatives," and "adverbs" in prose become translated into an artistic "image" that can fade like "smoke," a substance at once visual and ephemeral. Similarly, the *Literary World* in Boston notes, "If we can call 'What Maisie Knew' a picture of purity in the midst of pollution, so we might call this story of poor little Miles and his sister Flora a picture of corruption in the midst of rare loveliness."[107] These metaphors comparing *The Turn of the Screw* to an "image" and a "picture" suggest on the one hand that a story so visually suggestive would not need illustrations to accompany it, and perhaps in some cases *could not* be adequately illustrated (if the picture it implies is as elusive as *Life* avers); on the other hand, these metaphors suggest that James's language naturally evokes visual images that an illustrator could then transfer to paper.

When the last installment of *The Turn of the Screw* appeared on April 16, it was unaccompanied by any of Pape's illustrations, whereas the emerging naval story was copiously illustrated. As Sonstegard writes, "The political reality of the looming Spanish-American War intruded upon the imaginative unreality of the story [...]. Without dwelling on the governess's mental condition, without illuminating her pupil's demise, *Collier's* carried on with the next article, subsuming James's carefully obscured conclusion to the magazine's business."[108] That "next article," titled "Spain's Vulnerable Seaports," seems at first glance like a story "utterly unrelated" to *The Turn of the Screw*.[109] I would like to suggest a few ways, however, in which the story *is* related. Of course, the connection is unwitting, made possible by what contemporary readers would have been encountering contiguously. This thematic and contextual relation, forged by coincidence rather than causality, marks an uncanny way in which the "increasingly mysterious" James story[110] mirrors escalating international tensions between America and Spain.

The U.S.S. *Maine* Crisis, *Collier's* Use of Visual Images, and Narrative Reliability

We usually do not associate *The Turn of the Screw* with imperialism,[111] but *Collier's* locates it in a historical context that forces it to share space with international controversies over European colonial practices and US intervention in foreign conflicts. Situated thus, *The Turn of the Screw* can be viewed as a transatlantic text on multiple levels: though set in England, it is written by an American-born author; though composed in Europe, it is first published in New York; though concerned with local events at Bly, it is printed in a medium that locates it firmly within a larger, international context—specifically, the context of the Spanish-American War. By pairing an examination of *Collier's* highly visual coverage of events in Cuba with the original illustrations accompanying James's story, we can explore how *The Turn of the Screw*'s publication in *Collier's* provides us with one model for reconsidering both James's relation to the periodical world and his tale's relation to the pictorial. Significantly, the issues of narrative reliability attached to the U.S.S. *Maine* disaster, to James's governess, and to visual images foreground concerns that became central to the Modernist movement.

James's unreliable governess is emblematic of the fragmentation and uncertainty accompanying the end of the nineteenth century as modernization disrupted traditional socioeconomic structures and Victorian realism gave way to Modernist ambiguity. Although instances of narrative unreliability certainly existed before Modernism, the tendency toward unreliable narration becomes more pronounced in the Modernist period, which has produced some of the most widely discussed problematic narrators: F. Scott Fitzgerald's Nick Carraway, Ford Madox Ford's John Dowell, the array of competing voices in William Faulkner. As Terry Eagleton notes, the Modernist novel is characterized by "the break-up of language, the collapse of narrative, the unreliability of reports, the clash of subjective standpoints, the fragility of value, the elusiveness of overall meaning."[112] Similarly, Stephen Kern, a professor of history, proposes that the "weak plots, stream of consciousness, unreliable narrators, and unresolved endings" in *fin-de-siècle* and Modernist texts can be related to substantive historical developments of the period "such as urbanism, imperialism, and World War I."[113] Yet if the First World War is the defining military conflict of Modernism, in many ways the Spanish-American War ushered in the era. Many of the Modernist techniques Kern identifies, such as "unreliable narrators" and "unresolved endings," were already emerging in literature when the Spanish-American War broke out in 1898.

Perhaps it is not so surprising, then, that one of the strongest ties between the *Maine* story and *The Turn of the Screw* is the issue of narrative reliability. Even as James was presenting a narrator whose reliability would come under suspicion, *Collier's* was covering a story that was also significantly distorted by unreliable reports. On March 12, for example, the journal observed that "news reports" of events in Cuba "are eagerly read, even if their veracity is suspected."[114] Nonetheless, *Collier's* continued to pursue its own dramatic coverage of the *Maine* disaster, surrounding James's tale with photos portraying starving Cubans, paintings illustrating the explosion on the *Maine*, and documentary stories of the disaster accompanied by artistic and photographic representations, sometimes consuming half an issue. On February 26, it published a dramatically illustrated two-page spread depicting the destruction of the battleship. Like James's tale, *Collier's* coverage of the *Maine* mystery was deeply invested in visual forms. In the same March 12 article, *Collier's* reported that pictures of the *Maine* were selling "better than those of noted beauties and other celebrities," and the journal claimed that photographs, far from performing a merely commercial function, could even be used to resolve disputed stories about the disaster.[115] The idea that visual images could authenticate certain narratives while derailing others mirrors the governess's assertion in *The Turn of the Screw* that her precise visual descriptions confirm her story's authenticity. She defuses Mrs. Grose's suspicions by asking her "how, if I had 'made it up,' I came to be able to give, of each of the persons appearing to me, a picture disclosing, to the last detail, their special marks—a portrait on the exhibition of which she had instantly recognised and named them."[116] For James's governess as for *Collier's* reporters, visual images act as compelling articles of evidence, capable of persuading readers that sensational stories have basis in reality. James himself denounced the journalistic coverage, writing to his brother William on April 20, "I see nothing but the madness, the passion, the hideous clumsiness of rage, or mechanical reverberation; and I echo with all my heart your denouncement of the foul criminality of the screeching newspapers."[117] He felt sure that Spain had been wrongly accused and "savagely assaulted."[118] Yet the American public was as unsure about the source of the *Maine*'s explosion as readers would be about the source of evil in James's story.

Even as debates about James's tale would later rage over where to locate the source of evil—in the apparitions, the governess, the children, or elsewhere—so debates in *Collier's* raged over who was to blame for the *Maine*'s disaster. Some thought spontaneous internal combustion had caused the ship to explode, whereas war hawks and certain *Collier's* reporters insisted that a Spanish mine was responsible. *Collier's* position and the complicated question of assigning blame can be seen, for example, in the way the magazine began its March 5 issue:

> At the hour when we write, which is less than a week after the catastrophe which befell the United States battleship *Maine* in the harbor of Havana, there is a widespread and sincere effort on the part of the American people to comply with her commander's request for a suspension of judgment. To take for granted, however, that the disaster was the outcome of an accident occurring [...] within the vessel itself is not to suspend judgment, but to pronounce it. It is to lay, by implication, the blame for the catastrophe on the constructors of the ship or on her commander, Captain Sigsbee, and his fellow officers. [...] We have but little patience, therefore, with those who [...] profess to consider it a duty, in the absence of conclusive evidence to the contrary, to attribute the loss of the *Maine* to accident, and to assume that the Spaniards are innocent of a dastardly crime.[119]

Several pages later, the March 5 installment of the James story recapitulates a similar debate over the virtues of withholding judgment when the governess and Mrs. Grose discuss Miles's reported misconduct. Mrs. Grose reprimands her interlocutor for her suspicions:

> "Surely you don't accuse *him*— "
> "Of carrying on an intercourse that he conceals from me? Ah remember that, until further evidence, I now accuse nobody." Then before shutting her out to go by another passage to her own place, "I must just wait," I wound up.[120]

Though James had completed his story in 1897 and thus could not be responding directly to the *Maine* inquiry, his fictional tale nevertheless provides readers with a character who occupies a position analogous to theirs. Both are plagued by an indeterminate yet not unsuspected source of evil, forced to wait painstakingly on evidence, and instructed to reserve judgment.[121]

As both *Collier's Maine* coverage and James's tale show, those who find themselves in such positions are tempted to draw premature conclusions, even while extending courtesy to suspected parties. For example, in a March 5 article appraising the Spanish vessel *Vizcaya* (originally sent to New York as a way of reciprocating the *Maine*'s visit to Cuba), *Collier's* notes with suspicion that the *Vizcaya* has been ordered to "hasten" to Havana with other Spanish vessels.[122] The article's concluding observation tips praise of the "fine" ship into criticism of its country: "as the meaning of 'haste' depends upon the nation using the word, the movements of these cruisers cannot be anticipated, except that on reaching Havana not one of them will be assigned to moorings over a mine."[123] Though the reporter's allusion to the *Maine*'s sinking implicates Spain, the article does not specify whether Spanish negligence or design should be blamed, consistent with the assertion in "The Destruction of the *Maine*" that "deliberate complicity" and "criminal neglect" must both be investigated as possibilities.[124] In either case, *Collier's* insists, the United States should demand an indemnity from the Spanish government "should the destruction of the *Maine* be ascribed to an outside agency, even though it should prove impossible to trace the crime to its perpetrators and accessories."[125]

Just as the extent of Spain's involvement with the alleged terrorists is impossible for reporters or investigators to document with assured accuracy, so in James's story the extent of the children's interaction with the ghosts remains frustratingly ambiguous. In the March 19 installment, for instance, James's governess notes that "whether the children really saw" the ghosts who possessed them "was not yet definitely proved."[126] Melanie Dawson's apt description of *The*

Turn of the Screw as "a tale of the horrors of the unclassifiable" with "an elaborate creation of inconclusive alliances"[127] could also apply to the *Maine* mystery simultaneously being covered in *Collier's*. In both cases, the investigators find themselves frustrated in their attempts to clearly delineate links between horrific events (international naval explosions, or domestic haunting), the underlying source of evil (a possible Spanish mine, or supposed ghosts), and those closely associated with the assumed source of evil (the suspected Cuban accomplices, or the possessed children).

Although *Collier's* censured the yellow "penny journals that pander to a class of readers unthinking or perverse,"[128] the weekly's own copious illustrations of the *Maine* and Havana repeatedly reminded Americans of the unavenged naval loss, and its pictures of poverty-stricken Cubans argued the case for humanitarian intervention. The magazine's coverage of the story and its cover illustrations predicted "WAR" even before the United States officially declared it on April 25, 1898, nine days after the last installment of *The Turn of the Screw*; in smaller type, the April 16 cover qualifies its banner: "AWAITING THE WORD." What the *Maine* story demonstrates, then, is the urge to find a villain even in stories where the evidence is insufficient to do so. As heightened international tensions at the *fin de siècle* compelled individuals to declare their national loyalties and political positions, James's first readers may have been all the more inclined to search within his story for a central locus of good which they could then juxtapose against a definitive source of evil. This urge to assign blame, underwriting interpretations of events at Bly on the one hand and in Cuba on the other, would be consistent with the first readings of *The Turn of the Screw*, which interpreted it as a literal ghost story and, for the most part, did not question the governess's reliability. Yet, like the competing interpretations of *The Turn of the Screw* which have since emerged, investigations of the *Maine* in the nineteenth, twentieth, and twenty-first centuries have produced conflicting conclusions about the true cause of the battleship's explosion. Its story remains as elusive as the fiction appearing alongside it.[129]

Whatever the coincidence of James's mysterious ghosts and the *Maine's* mysterious explosion, a strong material association persists between these two mysteries. James could not have predicted the explosion of the *Maine* on February 15, in the midst of his story's serialization, but he would have been familiar with the reputation *Collier's* had for journalism that highlighted disasters and used dramatic visual images to attract readers. Martha Banta describes *Collier's* as "a popular periodical" marked by "crudity" (in contradistinction to *Life's* "sophistication") and "filled with battle-front photography, inches-high headlines, celebrity journalists, and cheap thrills."[130] Although Banta is describing the *Collier's* of 1914, the journal had an established history of focusing on battle scenes, explosions, and catastrophes. In its September 16, 1897 issue, for example, *Collier's* prominently displayed "THE TERRIBLE WRECK ON THE SANTA FE RAILROAD NEAR EMPORIA, KANSAS" (as the caption screamed) in a two-page spread that dramatically threw darkly colored train cars into relief against the brilliant light from the explosion. In the April 30, 1898 issue, two weeks after the last installment of *The Turn of the Screw*, another two-page spread illustrated a similarly explosive scene, again with brilliant flashes of light that highlighted the battleship's outlines, and a caption that exhorted Americans to "REMEMBER THE MAINE!"

The magazine's reporting on the Spanish-American War "made its position secure as a great national weekly by what was probably the best 'picture coverage' given any war by a magazine up to that time."[131] Illustrations "made" its reputation, as *Collier's* itself recognized. Its March 19 issue, for instance, was saturated with images of the Cuban crisis, ranging from photographs of sugar plantations and city streets to the more devastating images of Captain Sigsbee overseeing the coffins of the lost crew, the *Maine*'s wounded sailors receiving medical attention, divers descending under the wreckage, and artifacts being recovered from the sunken ship. In some cases, *Collier's* would embed photographs or illustrations within the columns of prose on the page, thus solidifying the link between the written text and the visual images. In the issue of March 12, the two-page article on "The Havana Tragedy" included eight photographs that surrounded or jutted into the prose. Like Mrs. Grose, who frequently instructs James's governess to look at the children in order to absolve doubts, *Collier's* told readers that they could arrive at the truth by viewing the visual images it produced for them:

> Among the pictures sent from Havana by our artist, the first on this page sets at rest the story, oft-reprinted though oft-denied, that when the *Maine* entered Havana Harbor she enraged the Spaniards by being "stripped for action." From the photograph it appears that while passing Morro Castle she did not differ outwardly in any respect from her customary appearance when in harbor; stripped for action her boats would have been in the water and all movable top hamper would have been placed out of sight.[132]

The picture is accordingly displayed at the top of the article, so that readers may view it to verify the journal's written interpretation of events. Because readers of *Collier's* would be accustomed to the expressed symmetry between prose and image, whereby each representation mutually enforces the other, it would be natural to assume that the visual images accompanying James's fiction would also authenticate it. But as we have seen, *The Turn of the Screw* and its artists complicate this association.

Visuality, Narrative, and Truth in Advertising: How Ripans Tabules and Other Products Inflect James's Tale

There is yet another arena in which written words are brought into equation with the pictorial, which is in turn brought into equation with the truth: and that arena is advertising. Notably, installments of *The Turn of the Screw* often concluded just before the advertisements began; even when a short column immediately followed the tale, an advertisement or two often occurred on the same page as James's tale. And if James's readers continued to read after his installment concluded, they would be peppered with advertisements inviting them to wash themselves with Pears' Soap, to write with the Lincoln Fountain Pen, to sharpen their razors with a "Keen-Edge" block, to decorate their walls with a US map, to take scenic trips on the Denver and Rio Grande Railroad, to cure constipation with Cascarets, to chew Beeman's Pepsin Gum, and to update their homes and offices with "Electric Novelties" such as bicycle lights, necktie lights, dollar motors, and battery table lamps manufactured by the Ohio Electric Works. Some of these ads are illustrated; others make their appeals solely in words.

In late nineteenth-century *Collier's*, we encounter a diverse display of advertisements promising cures to various medical ailments, offering solutions to household and business problems, and unfolding technological advances that will improve readers' daily lives. Health concerns, national themes, business matters, and domestic subjects all come to the fore as various discourses, ranging from the medical to the literary, the legal to the popular, the financial to the scientific, are evoked. Readers are pulled out of the fictional, supernatural world of James's ghost story to enter into the seductive world of advertising, a kind of fantasy world that offers to fulfill readers' desires. Here (that is to say, somewhere between pages 22 and 24 of *Collier's*) readers become consumers. But the presence of the advertising pages, attractively displaying their goods, also reminds us that readers of James's story were already in some sense consumers— people who, at any rate, had bought *Collier's* for the goods *it* had to offer: reports on escalating tensions with Spain, updates on the Zola trial, advice on fashion, and the thrill, pleasure, leisure, or inspiration found in its poetry and fiction.

The advertisements present in miniature the diverse array of subjects addressed in this self-described "journal of art, literature, and current events"—which at the time of *The Turn of the Screw*'s serialization boasted new departments devoted to books, drama, fads and fashions, athletics, art, and music. The magazine's news articles, its literature, and its fashion columns are mirrored in advertisements for wall maps (echoing the maps in *Collier's* that accompanied articles about Spain, Cuba, and the United States), advertisements for writing utensils ranging from typewriters to fountain pens (underscoring the tools with which literature is produced), and advertisements for various beauty creams and medicines (reinforcing fashion articles with the products that are necessary to purchase if one is to appear fashionable). Moreover, the illustrations authenticating the advertisements also recall the visual images that accompanied news articles, fiction, and feature columns. And these are just a few of the many parallels that could be drawn between the magazine items and its advertisements.

Although there exists a "distinctly modern bias against the commercial aspects of aesthetic production," a bias that Modernists shared with us and that is in part responsible for the elimination of advertising pages in the library rebinding process,[133] it is important to realize how closely the fields of reporting and advertisement, literature and commercialism, art and the popular market were operating within periodicals at the turn of the century. As Lawrence Rainey notes, "Modernism's interchanges with the emerging world of consumerism, fashion, and display were far more complicated and ambiguous than often assumed."[134] For Rainey, Modernism

> is a strategy whereby the work of art invites and solicits its commodification, but does so in such a way that it becomes a commodity of a special sort, one that is temporarily exempted from the exigencies of immediate consumption prevalent within the larger cultural economy, and instead is integrated into a different economic circuit of patronage, collecting, speculation, and investment.[135]

But even as Modernists carved out a counter-public sphere, they still engaged with the commercial mass market in significant ways. James, like many Modernists following him, not only arranged for special volumes of his works but also published frequently in mass-market periodicals. Similarly, Gertrude Stein had by 1922 "contributed more often to *Vanity Fair* than to the *Little Review*."[136] But even the *Little Review* advertised mass-market periodicals like *Collier's* within its pages, as I discuss in later chapters. Thus, it is not merely that Modernists adopted or co-opted certain mass-market techniques or technologies, but that they participated—directly or indirectly, willingly or resistantly—in the promotion and articulation of popular culture.[137]

In spite of his literary pretensions, James himself was distinctly aware of the financial rewards that could be reaped by appealing to the emerging mass market—a market that many other authors were already entering successfully:

> He was an inveterate newspaper and magazine reader and would have read contemporary serializations and book reviews [...]. Many of his friends and acquaintances were extraordinarily successful with the new mass market: E.F. Benson, Frances Hodgson Burnett, F. Marion Crawford, Rudyard Kipling, Robert Louis Stevenson, and Mrs. Humphrey Ward all wrote best sellers. [...] For all of James's scorn, he maintained a strong interest in the popular market in England and America.[138]

James was not only interested in the mass periodical market, he was also dependent upon it. His letters to friends and requests to publishers for advances document his financial dependence upon periodical publication. As Michael Anesko notes, having a "perpetual serial running" was a "financial necessity" for James, and these phrases were employed in the author's letters.[139] Furthermore, Anesko writes,

> The rapid rise and expansion of the reading public, the proliferation of periodicals, and the development of the modern publishing firm all contributed to the making of Henry James [...]. Even though James was among the first observers to recognize the commercialization of literature that, by the end of the century, was so widely deplored, his own behavior in the marketplace effectively demonstrates the changing nature of the literary vocation. [...] [I]ts ranks were swelled in James's lifetime by [...] writers for whom the written—better still, the published—word was not merely an intellectual diversion but primarily a source of income and status.[140]

This account by Anesko underscores how closely intertwined were the worlds of intellectualism and finance. Developing this line of thought in *Marketing Modernisms*, Kevin Dettmar and Stephen Watt aptly claim that "*marketing*" embraces "both material *and* intellectual" practices.[141] And the interaction between these worlds becomes especially evident when we return to the advertisement-saturated periodicals in which many Modernist and proto-Modernist works were initially published.

Although the practice of eliminating advertising pages in the library rebinding process reflects the temptation to draw a sharp divide between the aesthetic artifact and the commercial product, in fact these seemingly opposed realms not only engaged in discourse with each other but were in many ways dependent upon each other: to attract customers and advertisers, *Collier's* had to offer "art, literature, and current events" to readers. Presumably, it was these articles—not the ads—that enticed readers to buy *Collier's*. (Note that it is not called a journal of "art, literature, current events, and advertising," even though the ads take up a significant portion of space.) But in order to publish "art, literature, and current events," magazines like *Collier's* needed funding, and that funding came from advertisement. At the end of the nineteenth century, as scholars such as Richard Ohmann and Mark Morrisson have pointed out, the proliferation of advertisement made it possible for periodicals to lower their subscription prices even below printing cost, "thereby vastly increasing circulation" and "reaping fantastic profits from advertisers."[142] The vastly increasing circulation numbers made possible by advertising revenue thus also increased the circulation of literary works like James's *The Turn of the Screw*.[143] Advertisement funded periodicals and, by extension, also funded the spread of Modernism.

Furthermore, as artists realized, publication itself could act as a mode of advertisement. Anesko relates that James "deliberately chose not to register copyrights for some of his work (especially nonfiction) that was first published in Great Britain" in order to maintain "good relations with English publishers and men of letters."[144] But more than that, James realized that piracy functioned as a form of free publicity. Without emphasizing this realization of James's, Anesko quotes an unpublished James letter that does:

> "I lately published an article (The Art of Fiction) in *Longman*," he told Benjamin Ticknor, "without appending a warning as to the U.S. copyright. But I did this on purpose, as the paper was not a story. I don't like to flaunt that American claim here for anything but stories, & consider that the reproduction (partial or entire) of that article in the U.S. will have done me more good than harm—as it will have advertised my fictions!"[145]

Anesko quotes this letter in order to elucidate James's perspectives on international copyright, but the letter is also interesting for the way James casts his own writing not merely as literature but also as promotional material. Here, "The Art of Fiction" is transformed from an essay about fiction to an advertisement for it.

The line between advertisement and fiction is not always sharply defined. Just as magazine articles could further a cause or promote a product, so, in a reverse formulation of this principle, did advertisements in *Collier's* sometimes appear as short fictions. By their very nature, advertisements occupy an ambiguous space, wavering between several different genres of classification: "Are ads text or image?" Latham and Scholes ask, referencing the "special problems of periodical advertising" that "have scarcely been addressed by theoreticians of metadata."[146] Advertisements, like literary texts, have narratives of their own, and the advertisements for Ripans Tabules within the pages of *Collier's* are particularly telling for the way that they combine visual story-telling with verbal story-telling, using illustrations to authenticate narrative and borrowing from the conventions of fiction to craft advertising copy into personal testimonial.

The implications for *The Turn of the Screw*—a personal narrative that was also accompanied by illustrations understood to serve an authenticating function—may be surmised. As with the *Maine* story, the similarities between the Ripans Tabules and *The Turn of the Screw* are coincidental and unintentional but nonetheless significant. In the February 26 issue of *Collier's*, when James's governess was relating her concerns about the girl in her care to Mrs. Grose, another female narrator—this time in the advertising pages—was expressing concerns for her daughter. In James's tale, the governess has just observed six-year-old Flora at the lake, supposedly communing with Miss Jessel; the governess relates that she then "got hold of Mrs. Grose as soon after this as I could" in order to discuss the terrible affliction that plagues Flora.[147] At the end of their emotional interview, the governess experiences an overwhelming sense of "miserable defeat" and bursts out in despair, "I don't save or shield them! It's far worse than I dreamed. They're lost."[148] The installment ends here, with the governess's tearful declaration that she cannot cure the children of the evil that has fallen upon them.

This particular installment of *The Turn of the Screw* was not illustrated by Pape, but on the page after the installment ends the Ripans Tabules advertisement includes a picture of two females holding an interview with each other. A young girl stands next to the seated figure who is presumably her mother, who in turn appears to be addressing another seated lady. Because of the child's presence, the image, even if taken out of context, could not be taken as an illustration for *The Turn of the Screw*, but it comes close to suggesting the confessional scene between Mrs. Grose and the governess. Moreover, the text of the Ripans Tabules ad communicates similar feelings of exhaustion and hopelessness, though, as one might expect, it does not end on this note of despair. In the advertisement, a mother relates her desperate and initially fruitless attempts to help her afflicted daughter:

> My little girl, eleven years old, has had all her life a very serious and stubborn constipation. I had given everything I could think of, and still once in about two or three weeks she would wake at night crying pitifully with pain, and for two or

three hours would suffer intensely until finally relieved by frequent enemas. All this was very wearing.[149]

At this moment of distress and exhaustion, similar to the governess's despair in James's tale, a solution to the "serious and stubborn" condition presents itself:

> My brother insisted I should try Ripans Tabules and finally he got them for me. I tried them, giving her two every night for awhile, then two every other night, then she took them herself when she felt like it. It is now about three months since she has had any trouble, and her bowels are in a very healthy condition. Her color is good and she is gaining flesh. As I have given her no other medicine I ascribe her improved condition wholly to Ripans Tabules.[150]

The visual image above the ad appears to verify this story, since the girl is presented as evidence to her mother's friend, who stands in for the magazine audience. The presence of this other lady, who is not mentioned in the text of the ad, implies that the mother is verbally relating her story to a friend, much as the governess voices her concerns to a confidante in the form of Mrs. Grose. James's tale, to be sure, is far more complicated than the Ripans ad strategy: the governess records her narrative—including her conversations with Mrs. Grose—in manuscript, and the full story is shared many years after its occurrence and only through many layers of remove. But the comparatively simplistic ad defines in miniature the situation that James's tale demarcates in intricate detail: a written narrative combined with an oral account, a scene of distress over a child resulting in a female-to-female conference, and words reinforced by visual images.

The story does not end here, however, for, if we proceed to later issues, we discover that the eleven-year-old girl is unfortunately not the only one who suffers from medical ailments that cast their victims and caretakers into states of despair. We also learn that bodily ailments are not the only sort afflicting the populace. Like serialized fiction, the Ripans Tabules ads provide new narratives with new issues of *Collier's*. The ad of March 26, 1898 is particularly telling in this regard, insofar as it portrays a woman who suffers from mental illness, a diagnosis non-apparitionist critics from Edmund Wilson onward have given to James's governess. In the March 26 installment, the governess has just declared to Mrs. Grose that the children have tricked her into allowing them to escape with the ghosts, Miles in the schoolroom with Quint, Flora outside with Miss Jessel—an idea that non-apparitionist critics would call delusional. At the end of the installment, Mrs. Grose and the governess depart for the lake to find Flora. Two pages later we receive this story from Ripans Tabules:

> A young lady in New York City relates the curious case of her sister who suffered from a sort of nervous dyspepsia—that was what the doctor called it. She was despondent, low-spirited, inclined to imagine all sorts of things.[151]

The reference to a female who "imagine[s] all sorts of things" curiously matches critics' descriptions of James's hallucinating governess, who imagines that the children are arranging secret meetings with evil apparitions. Though this connection may not have occurred to 1898 *Collier's* readers, who were inclined to read James's tale as a literal ghost story, the uncanny connection is readily apparent after 100 years of *Turn of the Screw* criticism.

The ad continues, reflecting on the odd nature of the patient's affliction, placing an emphasis on strangeness that early reviewers would also evoke in their descriptions of James's "queer" mood and "sickening" tale that communicated something "peculiarly against nature":[152]

> One thing especially seemed to be in her mind: that was the idea that abscesses were forming in different parts of her body. The sister who tells the story had found Ripans Tabules a specific for headache, and generally had a supply on hand. One day, more in joke than in earnest, she said to the afflicted one: "Try these: they'll cure you." Well, she did try them, and strangely enough the Tabules did cure her. The despondency left her. This was nearly a year ago. She took less than a dollar's worth in all, and has not taken one for over eight months now.[153]

If such a story can be believed, one cannot help feeling that James's governess would have benefited from learning about this product. But increasing mystery and prolonged suffering are as central to James's tale as a miraculous cure is to a Ripans Tabules ad.

Despite the similarities in narrative, the ad and James's tale also operate at cross-purposes, insofar as each aims for a different end (clarity and success in the ad, ambiguity and tragedy in the tale). And this sense of disparity is generally reflected when we compare any *Collier's* advertisement to James's tale. As Ohmann notes, newspaper ads at the turn of the century often "stood in sharp contrast to the dire news they accompanied,"[154] and the same sort of relationship exists between *Collier's* advertising pages, which were generally enthusiastic and soothing, and the stories (both news and fiction) that the magazine published. In James's story, mysterious horrors grip readers; conversely, in the ads, their problems are diagnosed, clarified, and cured. In the traumatic U.S.S. *Maine* story, an undiscovered source of evil causes a massive battleship to explode; conversely, in the ads, readers are soothed by vehicles of transportation that run smoothly, taking passengers to faraway destinations without incident, and by technology that works properly or can be easily repaired. Ohmann quotes a charming 1909 *New York Evening Post* editorialist who aptly describes the "happy" advertising world, so starkly juxtaposed to the world of news:

> What a reconstructed world of heart's desire begins with the first-page advertisement. Here no breakfast food fails to build up a man's brain and muscle. No phono records fail to amuse. No roof pane cracks under cold or melts under the sun. No razor cuts the face or leaves it sore. Illness and death are banished by patent medicines and hygienic shoes. Worry flies before the model fountain pen. Employers shower wealth upon efficient employees. Insurance companies pay what they promise. Trains always get to Chicago on time. Babies never cry; whether it's soap or cereal, or camera or talcum, babies always laugh in the advertising supplement. A happy world indeed, my masters![155]

Of course, this is not to say that ads never alluded to tragedy or disaster. As we have seen from the Ripans Tabules ad, serious ailments threaten the welfare of both adults and children in advertising pages. But, as Ohmann notes, such "vile diseases" in the ads around 1900 are "always instantly curable."[156] In *Collier's*, advertisements following *The Turn of the Screw* counterbalance the unresolved puzzles of James's strange story by offering readers solutions to problems. Whereas the home appears as a haunted, terrifying place in *The Turn of the Screw*, the products advertised in *Collier's*, like those in other magazines of the period, "ease the transition from home as a site of production to home as a site of consumption and leisure."[157] Advertisements, as Ohmann notes, instruct "us in seeing and understanding the made objects that surround us, which is to say, most of the perceived and touched world that most people inhabit most of the time."[158] James's story, by contrast, instructs readers in the supernatural world of elusive apparitions and in the intangible world of the mind.

Although the advertisements act differently and reach for different ends than either sensational news stories like the U.S.S. *Maine* disaster or terrifying ghost fiction like *The Turn of the Screw*, these various genres nevertheless employ strikingly similar techniques to achieve their rather divergent goals. In *Collier's*, news stories as well as fiction and advertisement use illustration as an ostensible means of authenticating narrative. The March 26 Ripans Tabules ad discussed above, for instance, includes a picture of two women—presumably the sisters discussed in the advertising copy, though it could also be the narrator-sister explaining the cure to a lady friend—positioned next to a table in a scene that is at once domestic and personal. This illustration of an intimate, friendly conversation reinforces the written story, which employs the sort of "[w]riting style" Ohmann would classify as "represent[ing] one-to-one communication."[159]

This mode of providing "testimony" was used by advertisers to "personalize" their copy,[160] and the visual image further underscores the sense of individualized communication.

But the ad is, of course, produced for mass-market consumption, not for a distinct individual; moreover, the claims made by the ad are so far-reaching that readers might very well question their truth value. Likewise, in James's story we have the fiction of Douglas presenting a personal narrative to an intimate circle of friends—an image that is reinforced by Pape's fireside illustration in the January 27 installment—when in actuality the governess's story is being sold to a mass-market audience and being read by thousands of strangers scattered across the nation. These similarities between the Ripans Tabules ad and James's story may be unwitting, but, whether or not *Collier's* editors anticipated these specific connections, they did at least intend to achieve a sense of cohesion in the way they selected and assembled the various periodical items. As Mark Morrisson writes, "A set of tastes in commodities, literature, entertainment, and so forth, was intended to cohere into a recognizable ensemble, and that ensemble appealed to and organized a very large audience."[161] Thus when *The Turn of the Screw* was first published, it was conceived of as part of an integrated, albeit diverse, whole that also included advertising.

Illustration, as I have discussed, provides one way of achieving a sense of cohesion among arenas that may be as disparate as fiction, history, and commerce. We have seen that *The Turn of the Screw*, stories about the *Maine*'s explosion, and advertisements for commercial products were all illustrated components of *Collier's*. Although we tend to separate literary work from commercialization, it is important to remember that, historically, magazine editors have "worked carefully to solicit, craft, and organize the material" they receive into "an autonomous print object."[162] At the same time, the equally important impulse to variety found in periodicals—an impulse that is absent from, or only present in a greatly reduced degree in anthologies and books—opens up room for new interpretive possibilities and carves out space both for forging connections between disparate artifacts and for appreciating the startling juxtapositions that are created when separate spheres of discourse clash, compete, and merge between the covers of a single volume. The accidental explosion of the *Maine* could not have been anticipated by either author or editor, yet *The Turn of the Screw* comes to function as a fictional corollary that raises similar questions about perception, visuality, and narrative reliability. When chance and accident intrude upon both authorial intent and editorial design, they produce not only frustration but also opportunity. In this way, the unwitting connections between periodical artifacts in *Collier's Weekly* mentally prepared readers for high Modernism's more pronounced engagements with narrative perspective, stylistic ambiguity, and wartime anxiety.

Conclusion

While the journal's other illustrations often serve an explanatory, authenticating function, the illustrations accompanying James's tale frequently do more to provoke questions than to provide answers. Because they visually represent the ghosts, Pape's illustrations at first seem to authenticate the governess's story. In a more nuanced reading, however, Pape's art challenges the governess's interpretation of events, since he never gives the shadowy apparitions the sharp definition reserved for James's other characters and since he never shows anyone but the governess looking at the ghosts. Finally, we can conclude that the artwork—not only by La Farge, but also by Pape—yields ambiguity rather than certainty and represents events without delivering firm judgment. James's illustrators show that there is no easy equation between truth and visuality, a link that was simultaneously being explored by investigators of the U.S.S. *Maine* explosion and that was being promoted by advertisers. As the 1898 court of inquiry relied on visual evidence to determine the cause of the battleship's sinking, so Robert J. Collier relied on photographs and artists' illustrations to document the disaster in a way that emphasized the magnitude of the catastrophe and conveyed a sense of impending war to readers. This evidence leading to the investigators' eventual verdict and the Spanish-American War was later re-examined by a 1911 board of inspection, which drained the harbor and took multiple photographs of the wreckage before concluding that a mine and a subsequent magazine explosion were jointly responsible for the damage. This evidence was in turn questioned and re-interpreted by researchers in 1974, who concluded from the same 1911 photographs used to substantiate the 1898 inquiry's conclusion that the explosion was caused not by the alleged Spanish mine but rather by internal combustion alone. Similarly, as I have argued, Pape's illustrations deserve another evaluation, one that interrogates whether they actually portray the allegedly culpable ghosts as the source of evil or instead locate responsibility with the protagonist.

Additionally, by reminding ourselves of the richly illustrated periodical context in which *The Turn of the Screw* was first published, we are forced to think more deeply about the way that James's story itself persistently questions the reliability of the visual, interrogating not only the governess's vision but also "the magazine's visual propensities."[163] By returning to *Collier's*, we can view *The Turn of the Screw* not only as a solitary book published between its own covers, as a companion to *Covering End* (with which it was published in 1898), or as an anthologized work published alongside other fiction, but also as a serialized story that critiques the practice of periodical illustration within that medium—a medium that, moreover, places James's story about narrative reliability alongside a news story similarly plagued by questionable visual evidence and unreliable reporting. Within this context, James's governess becomes a figure for the reporter, someone sent to Bly to collect a story that will later be transmitted to Douglas and then redistributed to the holiday gatherers. Like the periodical articles, her narrative is a "written" document[164] with visual components, suggested by the governess's frequent appeals to the pictorial and her famous claim that "I saw him [Quint] as I see the letters I form on this page."[165] Although James's governess asserts the authenticity of the visual, James himself questions it, showing that the other characters do not see (or at least do not admit they see) what the governess claims she sees.

The multiple layers of transmission raise further questions about the story's integrity. As the frame narrator notes, the governess recorded her tale in a manuscript which she then gave to Douglas, who then gave it to the narrator, who made "an exact transcript" with his "own" hands "much later."[166] Its publication in *Collier's* represents another transmission of the narrative, and the accompanying illustrations tell the story once more, presenting visual evidence that, as in the case of the *Maine* investigation, opens itself up to multiple interpretive possibilities. Although James may have been intending a general critique of the magazine's popular journalism and abundant illustration, as critics such as Adam Sonstegard and Melanie Dawson have insightfully argued, his tale finds itself positioned in a medium that allows it to address a very particular story in *Collier's*. Alongside the *Maine* story, James's tale is differently inflected and comes to sound a subtle note of warning not only against irresponsible reporting but also against authority figures who, like the governess, adopt overly drastic measures in their impulsive efforts to "battle" forces of evil and protect the innocent.[167] Resituated within its original periodical context, *The Turn of the Screw*'s critique of sensational reports that were further dramatized by visual art becomes all the more evident.

Although particular relations between the U.S.S. *Maine* explosion and James's ghostly story may be coincidental, the evolving historical conditions (increasing distrust of Spain, coupled by the proliferation of periodicals and "yellow" journalism) and the parallel trajectory of literary developments (increasing distrust of narrators, coupled by the proliferation of voices and narrative fragmentation) make a convergence logical, even if not readily predictable. By reading for these unwitting connections that carry literary and historical resonance, we see that the development of Modernism is determined not only by formal authorial and editorial decisions but also by chance convergences beyond either the author's or the editor's control.

Returning *The Turn of the Screw* to *Collier's* enables us to posit an all-scanning reader, a thorough digester of "art, literature, and current events" who would have encountered the naval story and the ghost story simultaneously. This reader, unlike a book reader, might well have recognized the similarities I have pointed out; or he—or she—might have turned to James's fiction as a means of escaping the present reality, a way of replacing escalating tensions in the real world by sensational events contained within the fictional world. In any case, *The Turn of the Screw* provides a fictional ground for readers to negotiate and contemplate the compounded levels of uncertainty plaguing their own historical moment—the very immediate crisis unfolding on adjacent pages. And an all-scanning reader sensitive to points of connection as well as to divergences between the many artifacts that confronted him or her in *Collier's* would have arrived at a more subtle and more (historically and materially) inflected analysis than is possible when we encounter the tale in book form. This leads to a new type of "reader response" analysis that goes beyond close reading of the text at hand (the kind espoused by Stanley Fish and others) to insist that the articles occurring alongside a fictional (or poetic) work also be taken into consideration when evaluating the reader's response to a given serialized text. In other words, there is much to be gained by merging reader-response theory with Genette's concept of paratext.

But this is not to say that questions of authorial intention should be dismissed. The material conditions of publishing in periodicals were, after all, something of which James was himself acutely aware. Rather, we need to pay closer attention to the ways readers' experience and interpretation of a text—and by "readers" here I mean not only contemporaneous readers but also twenty-first-century critics—are shaped by a diverse combination of factors that include chance alongside authorial intention; likewise, questions of a text's historical and social position should be examined alongside considerations of the text's physical position vis-à-vis visual images and other works surrounding it in serial form. These surrounding works in *Collier's*—in particular, the illustrations, the U.S.S. *Maine* story, and the advertisements—not only inflect James's tale in 1898 but should also prompt us to consider how our own twenty-first-century readings are conditioned by the text's more recent surrounding artifacts: book covers, introductions, and reprinted reviews and scholarly articles in a critical edition, or surrounding articles and prefatory material in an anthology.

In Henry James we encounter an author who frowned upon ardent nationalism nevertheless publishing his work in a venue that devoted extensive coverage to the precise international controversies he felt were exaggerated; an author who vocalized his discontent with illustrations nevertheless handing over a piece he knew would be illustrated; an author who despised the commercial serials nevertheless sending his articles to "screeching" periodicals;[168] an author who denigrated potboilers nevertheless writing one (indeed, by his own count, several) and admitting openly to it. If these were mere contradictions, they would be uninteresting; but they are less contradictions than articulations of a nuanced position, and what they point to is the fact that James's relation to the market, as Marcia Jacobson, Michael Anesko, and others have shown, is far more vexed than initial assessments reveal and than even he himself wished to disclose. When we combine this evidence with a strong contextualization of *The Turn of the Screw* within the covers of *Collier's*, we receive a sharper picture of James's place in the periodical world. To Jacobson's and Anesko's accounts of James's careful, oft concealed, calculations, we can add the complementary role that coincidence played in the serialization of James's tale. The *Maine* story James did not anticipate, the illustrations he did not control, the advertisements he did not order—all of these point toward the way periodicals uniquely bring together disparate artifacts, extending beyond authorial intention to present their audiences with an array of combinations and possibilities that would not otherwise be imagined.

Notes

1 Frank Luther Mott, *A History of American Magazines* (Cambridge: Harvard University Press, 1957), 4:454.
2 Mott, *A History of American Magazines*, 4:454.
3 Qtd. in Mott, *A History of American Magazines*, 4:455.
4 It is interesting to note, for example, that the editors of the Norton critical edition of *The Turn of the Screw*, Deborah Esch and Jonathan Warren, choose under their "Illustrations" heading to mention only the Charles Demuth illustrations, which they reprint (130–2). La Farge and Pape are ignored, although the editors do note

that the serialized version was "illustrated" (88). Demuth's paintings, executed in 1917 and 1918, were published separately, not alongside the text of James's story. The La Farge and Pape illustrations, appearing alongside the first publication of *The Turn of the Screw*, seem to provide the more immediate context. See Esch and Warren, eds., *The Turn of the Screw* (New York: Norton, 1999).

5   Sean Latham and Robert Scholes, "The Rise of Periodical Studies," *PMLA* 121, no. 2 (2006): 528.

6   This is not to discount the necessary editorial tasks of textual comparison and collation, but it is to suggest that additional kinds of comparison are needed and deserve more scholarly attention than they currently receive. When Deborah Esch and Jonathan Warren, editors of the Norton *Turn of the Screw*, compare the periodical version to later editions of the tale, they focus on substantive departures that surface in collation, though they also mention accidentals and allude to some of the surrounding structure: "The periodical version, in addition to being divided into a frame and twenty-four chapters, has twelve installments and five 'Parts.' In the *Two Magics* version, these parts are removed, small inconsistencies are cleared up, an early naming of Miss Jessel is suppressed, the ending of one chapter is deleted, the atmosphere of suspense is heightened, Flora's age is raised, and more focus is placed on the governess. But the major revisions appear in the 1908 New York version" (89). Esch and Warren then list James's removal of commas, increased use of the possessive pronoun "my," and modifications of verb choice (shifting from "verbs of perception and thought" to "those of feeling and intuition") as evidence that the New York edition "draws us intimately into" the governess's narrative (89). Selected results of their textual collation, printed in the Norton edition, record "mostly various major changes which James made in wording," although "some variant spelling and punctuation" have been listed (89). For ease of reference, I have cited from the Norton edition, but I also make note of any changes from the periodical version.

7   Gérard Genette, *Paratexts: Thresholds of Interpretation*, trans. Jane E. Lewin (Cambridge: Cambridge University Press, 1997), 3, 9, 347, 347.

8   Henry James, *The Turn of the Screw*, ed. Deborah Esch and Jonathan Warren (New York: Norton, 1999), 3.

9   T.J. Lustig, "Blanks in *The Turn of the Screw*," in *The Turn of the Screw and What Maisie Knew*, ed. Neil Cornwell and Maggie Malone (New York: St. Martin's, 1998), 100.

10 James, *The Turn of the Screw*, ed. Esch and Warren (New York: Norton, 1999), 1.

11 Linda Hughes and Michael Lund, *The Victorian Serial* (Charlottesville: University Press of Virginia, 1991), 119.

12 This is not to imply, however, that readers of the serialized version all approached the text in the same way. Some may have casually browsed the journal and skimmed James's tale, while others may have scrutinized every word; some may have read each installment out loud with frequent breaks, while others might

have read each installment silently and without ever putting the paper down. Undoubtedly, reading experiences and practices vary even among those who possess "identical" copies of a literary work, but my point is that James's periodical readers do not have the same options open to them as later readers who encounter the tale in book form. Reversing this formulation, we can also see how we as twenty-first-century book readers do not have the same interpretive avenues open to us as the periodical readers of 1898, who encountered James's tale amid a rich assemblage of surrounding artifacts, ranging from illustrations of ghosts to sensational news stories to advertisements that mirrored fiction.

13 James, *The Turn of the Screw*, ed. Esch and Warren, 2.
14 James, *The Turn of the Screw*, ed. Esch and Warren, 2.
15 James, *The Turn of the Screw*, ed. Esch and Warren, 4.
16 James, *The Turn of the Screw*, ed. Esch and Warren, 4.
17 Anne T. Margolis, *Henry James and the Problem of Audience* (Ann Arbor: UMI Research Press, 1985), 128.
18 June Howard, *Publishing the Family* (Durham: Duke University Press, 2001), 262.
19 Melanie Dawson, "The Literature of Reassessment: James's *Collier's* Fiction," *Henry James Review* 19, no. 3 (1998): 230.
20 Advertisement in *Collier's*, January 6, 1898.
21 Frank Luther Mott, *A History of American Magazines* (Cambridge: Harvard University Press, 1957), 4:454.
22 Shoshana Felman, "Turning the Screw of Interpretation," *Yale French Studies* 55/56 (1977): 151.
23 H.G. Rickover, *How the Battleship Maine Was Destroyed* (Washington, DC: Naval History Division, Dept. of the Navy, 1976), 68.
24 Rickover, *How the Battleship Maine Was Destroyed*, vii.
25 See Mott, *A History of American Magazines*, 4:241; and Richard F. Hamilton, *President McKinley, War and Empire* (New Brunswick: Transaction Publishers, 2006), 1:149–69.
26 Mark Wollaeger, *Modernism, Media, and Propaganda: British Narrative from 1900 to 1945* (Princeton: University of Princeton Press, 2006), 13.
27 Wollaeger, *Modernism, Media, and Propaganda*, 13.
28 Wollaeger, *Modernism, Media, and Propaganda*, 26.
29 Wollaeger, *Modernism, Media, and Propaganda*, 30.
30 Qtd. in Mott, *A History of American Magazines*, 4:241.
31 Adam Sonstegard, "'A Merely *Pictorial* Subject': *The Turn of the Screw*," *Studies in American Fiction* 33, no. 1 (2005): 59.
32 Mott, *A History of American Magazines*, 4:455.
33 Pape provided illustrations for the installments of January 27, February 12, March 5, March 19, and April 2; seven of the twelve installments were unaccompanied by illustrations of specific scenes.

34 Sonstegard, "'A Merely *Pictorial* Subject,'" 66.
35 James, *The Turn of the Screw*, ed. Esch and Warren, 2.
36 James, *The Turn of the Screw*, ed. Esch and Warren, 5.
37 James, *The Turn of the Screw*, ed. Esch and Warren, 84.
38 James, *The Turn of the Screw*, ed. Esch and Warren, 85.
39 James, *The Turn of the Screw*, ed. Esch and Warren, 84.
40 Sonstegard, "'A Merely *Pictorial* Subject,'" 65.
41 Sonstegard, "'A Merely *Pictorial* Subject,'" 65.
42 Oddly enough, Leon Edel refers to La Farge himself as a "distant ghost" of James's youth (*Treacherous Years* 50), as if the artist had become like one of the vague apparitions he paints. Though Edel's expression is of course metaphorical, the idiom—on the one hand highly appropriate, on the other hand unwittingly conflationary—nonetheless compounds the sense of the uncanny surrounding the illustrator and his ghostly art. In a further coincidence, James himself refers to La Farge as an "apparition" as he recalls memories of his friend. See *Notes of a Son and Brother* (New York: Charles Scribner's Sons, 1914), 86.
43 Adeline R. Tintner, *The Museum World of Henry James* (Ann Arbor: UMI Research Press, 1986), 223.
44 Tintner, *The Museum World of Henry James*, 223.
45 S.P. Rosenbaum, "A Note on John La Farge's Illustration for Henry James's *The Turn of the Screw*," in *The Turn of the Screw*, by Henry James, ed. Robert Kimbrough (New York: Norton, 1966), 258.
46 Peter G. Beidler, ed., *The Collier's Weekly Version of Henry James's the Turn of the Screw* (Seattle: Coffeetown Press, 2010), 159.
47 Henry Adams, "The Mind of John La Farge," in *John La Farge* (New York: Abbeville Press, 1987), 17.
48 Adams, "The Mind of John La Farge," 64.
49 Adams, "The Mind of John La Farge," 15.
50 Adams, "The Mind of John La Farge," 17.
51 Adams, "The Mind of John La Farge," 64.
52 Adams, "The Mind of John La Farge," 68.
53 Michael Anesko, *"Friction with the Market": Henry James and the Profession of Authorship* (New York: Oxford University Press, 1986), 36.
54 Adams, "The Mind of John La Farge," 67.
55 Adams, "The Mind of John La Farge," 67, 77.
56 Adams, "The Mind of John La Farge," 69.
57 Henry James, *The Letters of Henry James*, ed. Percy Lubbock (New York: Charles Scribner's Sons, 1920), 1:141–2. James also praised La Farge for his transatlantic fluidity, calling him "the 'European'" in *Notes of a Son and Brother*, 88.
58 Rosenbaum, "A Note on John La Farge's Illustration," 255.

59 Henry La Farge, *John La Farge* (New York: Kennedy Galleries, 1968), n.p.
60 La Farge, *John La Farge*, n.p.
61 Sonstegard, "'A Merely *Pictorial* Subject,'" 66.
62 "The Situation in Cuba," *Collier's*, February 5, 1898, 5.
63 "The Situation in Cuba," 5.
64 James, *The Turn of the Screw*, ed. Esch and Warren, 3. The serialized tale contains a comma between "literal" and "vulgar."
65 Edgar Allan Poe, "The Man of the Crowd," in the *Norton Anthology of American Literature*, vol. B, ed. Nina Baym, 6th ed. (New York: Norton, 2003), 1561. This edition does not give an umlaut to the "a" in "lässt."
66 James, *The Art of the Novel* (New York: Charles Scribner's Sons, 1962), 331.
67 James, "American Magazines; John Jay Chapman," in *Henry James: The American Essays*, ed. Leon Edel (Princeton: Princeton University Press, 1989), 235.
68 James, "American Magazines; John Jay Chapman," 234, 235.
69 Sonstegard, "'A Merely *Pictorial* Subject,'" 61.
70 James, *The Art of the Novel*, 333.
71 Emmanuel Bénézit, ed., *Dictionary of Artists*, 14 vols., English ed. (Paris: Gründ, 2006), 10:878.
72 Bénézit, ed., *Dictionary of Artists*, 10:878.
73 James, *The Turn of the Screw*, ed. Esch and Warren, 9.
74 Edmund Wilson, "The Ambiguity of Henry James," in *The Turn of the Screw*, ed. Esch and Warren, 172.
75 James, "Preface to the New York Edition," in *The Turn of the Screw*, ed. Esch and Warren, 124.
76 Rosenbaum, "A Note on John La Farge's Illustration," 258.
77 Sonstegard, "'A Merely *Pictorial* Subject,'" 75.
78 Terry Heller, *The Turn of the Screw: Bewildered Vision* (Boston: Twayne, 1989), 8.
79 Neil Cornwell and Maggie Malone, eds., *The Turn of the Screw and What Maisie Knew* (New York: St. Martin's, 1998), 2.
80 Cornwell and Malone, eds., *The Turn of the Screw and What Maisie Knew*, 3.
81 James, *The Turn of the Screw*, ed. Esch and Warren, 15; James, "The Turn of the Screw," *Collier's*, February 12, 1898, 21.
82 Sonstegard, "'A Merely *Pictorial* Subject,'" 71.
83 Sonstegard, "'A Merely *Pictorial* Subject,'" 71.
84 James, *The Turn of the Screw*, ed. Esch and Warren, 15.
85 James, *The Turn of the Screw*, ed. Esch and Warren, 16.
86 James, *The Turn of the Screw*, ed. Esch and Warren, 23.
87 James, *The Turn of the Screw*, ed. Esch and Warren, 23.
88 James, *The Turn of the Screw*, ed. Esch and Warren, 23.
89 James, *The Turn of the Screw*, ed. Esch and Warren, 23.

90 James, *The Turn of the Screw*, ed. Esch and Warren, 20.
91 James, *The Turn of the Screw*, ed. Esch and Warren, 20.
92 James, *The Turn of the Screw*, ed. Esch and Warren, 22.
93 James, *The Turn of the Screw*, ed. Esch and Warren, 23.
94 Sonstegard, "'A Merely *Pictorial* Subject,'" 83.
95 Sonstegard, "'A Merely *Pictorial* Subject,'" 75.
96 This image is the only Pape illustration which Heller does not reproduce, perhaps because it was not embedded within James's story like the other illustrations, but rather occurred as a full-page spread several articles after James's installment had ended.
97 James, *The Turn of the Screw*, ed. Esch and Warren, 52.
98 Sonstegard, "'A Merely *Pictorial* Subject,'" 71.
99 James, *The Turn of the Screw*, ed. Esch and Warren, 55; James, "The Turn of the Screw," *Collier's*, March 19, 1898, 12–13. In the Norton edition, "he" is lowercase.
100 Beidler speculates that a "miniature sketch" accompanying Pape's signature may be intended to represent Flora, but he also suggests that it could be the governess (*The Collier's Weekly Version*, xxvi).
101 Beidler points out an inconsistency with this illustration: Pape's artwork "shows the governess being observed by the ghost of Miss Jessel, whereas it had long since disappeared" (*The Collier's Weekly Version*, xxviii).
102 James, *The Notebooks of Henry James*, ed. F.O. Matthiessen and Kenneth B. Murdock (New York: Oxford University Press, 1970), 178–9. But his view of the ghosts, as Edel has argued, was to change in subsequent years. In the preface to the New York edition, James writes that the ghosts "*were believed* to have appeared" (James, Preface, 124; Edel, Introduction to *The Turn of the Screw* in *Stories of the Supernatural*, 427; Edel's emphasis). By 1908, then, James had altered his vision of the tale and its apparitions—at least according to Edel. But others have claimed that James's changes are more or less stylistic and do not essentially alter the nature of the tale.
103 James, *Henry James Letters*, ed. Leon Edel (Cambridge: Harvard University Press, 1984), 4:84. James's italics.
104 These reviews, it should be noted, are responding to *The Turn of the Screw* as it was published within *The Two Magics* in 1898, following its serialization in *Collier's*.
105 "Mr. James's New Book," *Bookman*, November 1898, 54, rpt. in *Henry James: The Contemporary Reviews*, ed. Kevin J. Hayes (Cambridge: Cambridge University Press, 1996), 304.
106 "Henry James as a Ghost Raiser," *Life*, November 10, 1898, 368, rpt. in *Henry James: The Contemporary Reviews*, 306.
107 "The Two Magics," *Literary World*, November 12, 1898, 367–8, rpt. in *Henry James: The Contemporary Reviews*, 306.

108 Sonstegard, "'A Merely *Pictorial* Subject,'" 66–7.
109 Sonstegard, "'A Merely *Pictorial* Subject,'" 66.
110 Sonstegard, "'A Merely *Pictorial* Subject,'" 66.
111 A few critics, however, have made this connection, noting that the uncle's relatives live in India, thus giving the tale a "colonial subtext" (Cornwell and Malone, eds., *The Turn of the Screw and What Maisie Knew*, 7).
112 Terry Eagleton, *The English Novel* (Malden, MA: Blackwell, 2005), 19.
113 Stephen Kern, "Changing Concepts and Experiences of Time and Space," *The Fin-de-Siècle World*, ed. Michael Saler (London and New York: Routledge, 2015), 74.
114 "The Havana Tragedy," *Collier's*, March 12, 1898, 4.
115 "The Havana Tragedy," 4.
116 James, *The Turn of the Screw*, ed. Esch and Warren, 33. The periodical version reads "recognized" for "recognised" in this passage.
117 James, *Henry James Letters*, ed. Leon Edel, 4:72.
118 James, *Henry James Letters*, ed. Leon Edel, 4:73.
119 "The Destruction of the *Maine*," *Collier's*, March 5, 1898, 2.
120 James, *The Turn of the Screw*, ed. Esch and Warren, 36. The serialized text inserts commas after "Ah," "Then," "go," and "passage." It also reads "my" for "her" in the phrase "to her own place."
121 The periodical format in which the U.S.S. *Maine* story and *The Turn of the Screw* emerged further compounded the sense of prolonged anticipation, since readers would have to wait a week before receiving updates from *Collier's*.
122 "The Spanish Flag in New York Harbor," *Collier's*, March 5, 1898, 5.
123 "The Spanish Flag in New York Harbor," 5.
124 "The Destruction of the *Maine*," 2.
125 "The Destruction of the *Maine*," 2.
126 James, *The Turn of the Screw*, ed. Esch and Warren, 50.
127 Melanie Dawson, "The Literature of Reassessment: James's *Collier's* Fiction," *Henry James Review* 19, no. 3 (1998): 233.
128 "A Monument to the *Maine*," *Collier's*, April 2, 1898, 2.
129 The 1898 official report concluded that the explosion was a result of terrorist action. Thirteen years later, a second investigation reached the same conclusion, largely based on the evidence of a plate which had been pushed inside the ship's hull, implying that an outward force was to blame. In 1974, a third investigation concluded that the explosion was the result of an internal accident, not of Spanish terrorism. The argument for internal combustion is based on the close proximity of the coal bunkers to the ship's magazines and on evidence that the distorted plate could have been pushed inside the ship by the force of inrushing water following the explosion. See Rickover for a detailed discussion of the *Maine* explosion and investigations.

130 Martha Banta, *Barbaric Intercourse: Caricature and the Culture of Conduct, 1841–1936* (Chicago: University of Chicago Press, 2003), 321.
131 Mott, *A History of American Magazines*, 4:235–6.
132 "The Havana Tragedy," 4.
133 Latham and Scholes, "The Rise of Periodical Studies," 521.
134 Lawrence Rainey, *Institutions of Modernism: Literary Elites and Public Culture* (New Haven: Yale University Press, 1998), 7.
135 Rainey, *Institutions of Modernism*, 3.
136 Kevin Dettmar and Stephen Watt, eds., *Marketing Modernisms: Self-Promotion, Canonization, Rereading* (Ann Arbor: University of Michigan Press, 1996), 5.
137 At the end of the nineteenth century, modernization made popular culture even more visible than before: "Cheap paper, the rotary press, the Linotype machine—at the most mundane level, these inventions led to the explosion of mass market print publications and advertising at the end of the nineteenth century in Britain and America," as noted by Mark Morrisson, *The Public Face of Modernism: Little Magazines, Audiences, and Reception, 1905–1920* (Madison: University of Wisconsin Press, 2001), 3. These technological developments, and the growth of mass-market periodicals, created both opportunities and anxieties for authors at the *fin de siècle*. Rita Felski notes that "Modernist texts bore a highly ambivalent and often critical relationship to processes of modernization" in *The Gender of Modernity* (Cambridge: Harvard University Press, 1995), 13. Yet, in the midst of their critical stance, Modernists were also tempted by the various advantages modernization offered.
138 Marcia Jacobson, *Henry James and the Mass Market* (Alabama: University of Alabama Press, 1983), 14.
139 See Anesko, *Friction with the Market*, for a thorough discussion of James's letters in this regard. The quotations are on p. 52 of Anesko's book.
140 Anesko, *Friction with the Market*, 33.
141 Dettmar and Watt, eds., *Marketing Modernisms*, 2.
142 Morrisson, *The Public Face of Modernism*, 4.
143 As early as 1886, *Cosmopolitan* realized the importance of periodicals to the circulation of literary works: "The reputation of American authors has been spread abroad in England largely by the great American illustrated magazines, which have now an enormous circulation on the other side of the Atlantic" (qtd. in Mott, *A History of American Magazines*, 229).
144 Anesko, *Friction with the Market*, 164.
145 Anesko, *Friction with the Market*, 164.
146 Latham and Scholes, "The Rise of Periodical Studies," 524.
147 James, *The Turn of the Screw*, ed. Esch and Warren, 29.
148 James, *The Turn of the Screw*, ed. Esch and Warren, 32. The serialized tale reads "protect" for "shield" and contains an exclamation point after "lost"—

thereby intensifying the governess's despair. A dash replaces the period after "dreamed," giving a further sense of breathlessness to the exclamation.

149 Advertisement for Ripans Tabules, *Collier's,* February 26, 1898, 23.
150 Advertisement for Ripans Tabules, *Collier's,* February 26, 1898, 23.
151 Advertisement for Ripans Tabules, *Collier's,* March 26, 1898, 24.
152 "Mr. James's New Book," *Bookman,* November 1898, 54, rpt. in *Henry James: The Contemporary Reviews,* 304; Rev. of *The Two Magics, Illustrated London News,* December 3, 1898, 834, rpt. in *Henry James: The Contemporary Reviews,* 308; H.W. Lanier, "Two Volumes from Henry James," *American Monthly Review of Reviews,* December 1898, 732–3, rpt. in *Henry James: The Contemporary Reviews,* 308.
153 Advertisement for "Ripans Tabules," *Collier's,* March 26, 1898, 24.
154 Richard Ohmann, *Selling Culture: Magazines, Markets, and Class at the Turn of the Century* (London: Verso, 1996), 210.
155 Qtd. in Ohmann, *Selling Culture,* 210.
156 Ohmann, *Selling Culture,* 210.
157 Ohmann, *Selling Culture,* 91.
158 Ohmann, *Selling Culture,* 212.
159 Ohmann, *Selling Culture,* 187.
160 Ohmann, *Selling Culture,* 187.
161 Morrisson, *The Public Face of Modernism,* 204.
162 Latham and Scholes, "The Rise of Periodical Studies," 528–9.
163 Sonstegard, "'A Merely *Pictorial* Subject,'" 61.
164 James, *The Turn of the Screw,* ed. Esch and Warren, 2.
165 James, *The Turn of the Screw,* ed. Esch and Warren, 16.
166 James, *The Turn of the Screw,* ed. Esch and Warren, 4.
167 James, *The Turn of the Screw,* ed. Esch and Warren, 84.
168 James, *Henry James Letters,* ed. Leon Edel, 4:72.

2

Reconsidering Kipling's Imperialism

Kim in *McClure's* and *Cassell's*

Introduction

As a novel set in India, centered about the British Empire, written by an author with Irish roots, and first serialized in America, *Kim* embodies the many cross-cultural currents and voyages taking place at the *fin de siècle*. When the New York-based *McClure's* was serializing *Kim* from December 1900 through October 1901, the London-based *Cassell's* was following closely, with installments of *Kim* appearing between January and November 1901. Published at the end of Queen Victoria's reign—indeed, in the midst of serialization when the change in monarchy took place—Kipling's novel occupies a unique place both physically and historically. *McClure's* editors refer to it as "a masterpiece of literature which will make notable in the intellectual world the last year of the Nineteenth Century,"[1] and I wish to ask how this culminating historical and literary moment provides us with an opportunity to reflect on several key intersections—between Victorianism and Modernism, between text and image, between technology and Empire, and between advertising and art.

On the one hand, flashy covers and extensive illustrations in *McClure's* and *Cassell's*, two popular turn-of-the-century magazines, serve as a sharp contrast to the generally monochromatic covers and more text-heavy content of Modernist little magazines such as the *Dial* and the *Little Review*. On the other hand, the marketing of Kipling as a celebrity author foreshadows the way coterie and middle-brow magazines would present high Modernist authors such as James Joyce and Virginia Woolf as celebrities. Even as artistic magazines rejected many aspects of commercial culture, they learned from mass-market magazines that advertising content could strengthen and validate literary content. Kipling's fiction and poetry, like Henry James's work, witnessed striking connections to advertisements sharing the same magazine covers. In Kipling's case, some of these overlaps with commercial products were serendipitous; other parallels were misleading; and still other intersections witnessed overt allusions to Kipling, using his reputation to promote merchandise as diverse as soap and shingle stains. A closer look at Kipling and periodical culture, then, unveils how the circumstances of *Kim*'s serialization could give rise to Modernist anxieties about popular culture and aesthetic pursuits.

Moreover, periodicals on either side of the Atlantic show how chance factors of geography—whether someone happened to subscribe to an American or a British magazine, for example—shaped readers' impressions of Kipling's popular appeal, literary merit, and imperialist discourse. Ultimately, these periodical markers, which Gérard Genette would term paratext—the geographic imprint, the type and number of illustrations, the advertisements, and the surrounding articles—suggest that Kipling's adventure story, while more episodic and plot-driven than a psychoanalytic Jamesian ghost tale, may be just as ambiguous. Even as readers of James's *The Turn of the Screw* debate its protagonist's mental state (is the governess sane or insane?) and its author's intention (is this supposed to be a literal ghost story?), readers of Kipling's *Kim* debate whether his protagonist ultimately sides with the British secret service or with the lama. Kipling's authorial intention also comes into question: Does he mean to endorse or shake off imperialism? Particularly in the London-based *Cassell's*, surrounding ads and articles metonymically pull *Kim* into an adamant pro-imperialist stance. However, widely divergent illustrations—some that emphasize Kim's British affiliations, others that portray Kim as belonging to India—suggest there may be many competing ways of interpreting the novel. Its form and narrative structure follow Victorian conventions, but its ambiguous ending points us toward Modernism.

Although critics such as Edward Said and Zohreh T. Sullivan have contextualized *Kim* both historically and culturally, the mass-market periodicals in which history and literature unfold side by side have not been studied comprehensively enough. Scholars who examine *Kim*'s relation to imperialism usually mention *Cassell's* and *McClure's* only in passing, if they mention them at all. This failure to consider *Kim*'s periodical origins has led some to unfair evaluations of Kipling's novel. In his 1978 biography of Kipling, Lord Birkenhead criticizes *Kim*, citing its episodic structure as evidence for Kipling's weakness as a novelist. *Kim*, Birkenhead insists, "is not by any normal standards a novel at all, but a series of linked episodes in the progress of the Lama and Kim, most of which could be prised from their neighbors without disturbing the symmetry of the whole."[2] But the very episodic nature that Birkenhead dismisses was largely responsible for the novel's success as a serial: readers digesting monthly installments would need a novel that could be easily continued after a thirty-day hiatus, and magazines eager to attract new subscribers (as *McClure's* and *Cassell's* were) would need novels that could seize readers' attention even in the midst of serialization. In fact, in its promotional campaigns, *Cassell's* eagerly insisted that *Kim* could be "*taken up at any point.*"³ To be sure, *Cassell's* aided new readers by publishing short summaries of previous installments and issuing additional copies of previous magazine issues, but *Kim* was successful largely because its individual episodes could attract readers by standing alone, even while forming part of a longer and more intricate narrative structure.

Like Lord Birkenhead, Kipling's other biographers neglect *Kim*'s serialization, even as they document Kipling's role as a journalist in India. Yet when *Kim* first met a public audience it appeared alongside a diverse set of imperialist narratives and historically inflected artifacts, ranging from fictional stories to character sketches and from scientific forums to advertisements. Ironically, for all of their emphasis on Kipling's imperialism, none of the major biographies discusses the very imperial context of *Kim*'s serial publication. In a relatively early biography (1966), J.I.M. Stewart asserts that *Kim* charts the tension between Kipling's two identities, one as "son of the raj" and the other as "Lockwood Kipling's son [...] and therefore [...] a man deeply reverencing the immemorial spirit of India."⁴ Stewart does not discuss *Kim*'s serialization, but his assertion about Kipling's relationship to his father—as I show below—could be strengthened by a discussion of how Lockwood Kipling's illustrations augment the novel in its serial form, just as his assertion about Kipling's role as "son of the raj" could be further explored by considering how *Cassell's* and *McClure's* situate *Kim* alongside imperialist propaganda and celebrations of British rule. Of course, other magazines during the *fin de siècle* would similarly have aligned Kipling with imperialism. For instance, Kipling's works were situated amongst imperialist-themed items in *Macmillan's Magazine*, *Strand Magazine*, the *Pall Mall Gazette*, *Windsor Magazine*, *The Morning Post*, *St. James's Gazette*, and the *Illustrated London News*, among others. Some periodicals that worked with Kipling, such as *Century*, took an ambivalent stance and published "an array of articles for and against expansionism and imperialism."⁵ That is to say, *Cassell's* and *McClure's* are not unique in terms of the company Kipling kept, but rather emblematic of a societal trend. The historical emphasis on Britain's (and America's) right and duty to rule may not surprise us any more than it retroactively appalls us, but the periodical archive does help explain why Kipling became so closely connected with imperialism—and it underscores that this association was built not on

Kipling's works alone, but in conjunction with surrounding periodical artifacts that presented a collective impression. Similarly, as we will see in later chapters, James Joyce's reputation as a scandalous author was formed not on the basis of *Ulysses* alone, but in conjunction with surrounding artifacts in the *Little Review* that caught censors' eyes. The reputations of Modernist and proto-Modernist authors were made in the magazines.

Other Kipling biographers give readers more details about *McClure's*, but large gaps still remain. Biographies, of course, are neither bibliographies nor, necessarily, critical assessments. But their tendency to omit mention of serialization reflects the general scholarly tendency to emphasize book publication over periodical publication. Angus Wilson's 1977 biography declares that "Sam McClure, the magazine editor" numbered among Kipling's close friends,[6] yet we are never told that he serialized *Kim*—or any other works by Kipling, for that matter. While Harry Ricketts mentions that *McClure's* offered Kipling $10,000 for the serial rights to *Captains Courageous*,[7] he curiously omits mention of *Kim*'s serialization. In doing so, he follows a pattern established by Charles Carrington in 1955, who similarly neglects *Kim* when mentioning *McClure's*.[8] But when Carrington states that "the reader is left with the assurance that Kim [...] will find reality in action, not in contemplation,"[9] his interpretation could be reinforced by discussing how the stories serialized alongside *Kim* frequently emphasized action and adventure. Readers of the serialized *Kim*, accustomed to adventure stories in the magazine issues, would arguably have been inclined toward Carrington's verdict. In his 1999 biography, Andrew Lycett finally states that *McClure's* serialized *Kim*, offering £5,000 for the serial rights. Lycett, however, mentions *McClure's* only to show how periodical publication delayed book publication: "Although *Kim* was finished in August [1900], and Rudyard would have liked to have published it before the end of the year," the magazine "schedule had to be accommodated. This meant that, though the serialisation began in December 1900, the book did not appear until the following October."[10] And Lycett's otherwise impressively thorough book, extending to 659 pages, follows other biographies when it neglects to mention that *Kim* was also serialized in *Cassell's*, from January to November 1901.

Curiously, *Cassell's* seems to have fallen off the radar of Kipling biography. *McClure's* fares slightly better, but not by much. More recently, in his 2002 biography, David Gilmour records that *McClure's* published "The White Man's Burden" in February 1899, but, like Ricketts and Carrington before him, he does not mention that *McClure's* followed with *Kim* in 1900–1, even though Kipling's novel is often thought of as a corrective to his poem. As Ricketts himself notes, *Kim* marked "his swansong to India and was a delighted celebration of cultural and racial difference—in the strongest contrast to his White Man bluster."[11] One might ask how these two seemingly divergent works came to be published in the same periodical within the space of two years. Did the editorial aims of *McClure's* change? Was *McClure's* simply indiscriminate about the works it published? Or do critics such as Ricketts interpret *Kim* and "The White Man's Burden" as opposites where *fin-de-siècle* readers would have read them as complementary pieces?

A more subtle, strongly contextualized reading may be conducted when we return to the magazines, examining Kipling through the periodical pages that introduced his first readers to his work. In this reading, we will see how *McClure's* and *Cassell's*, magazines that have been sidelined in Kipling criticism, packaged *Kim* (like "The White Man's Burden") both as an anthropological work supplemented by illustrations and as a story with strong ties to Empire. This reading is reinforced by surrounding advertisements for imperial products, by fiction and news articles that glorify Empire and adventure, by illustrations that highlight the difference between British citizens and colonial subjects, and by the magazines' promotions of *Kim*, in which the novel's influence is brought into equation with the Empire's success. This, at least, is the immediate impression that first readers would have received.

A closer inspection, however, unveils anxiety, ambiguity, complexity: While the line drawings by H.R. Millar clearly distinguish British men from "Orientals," Lockwood Kipling's photographed sculptures make it difficult to differentiate between colonizer and colonized. Although most surrounding articles celebrate the Empire, a few subtly question the legitimacy of British imperial practices. While *Cassell's* most strongly promotes the association between *Kim* and the British Empire, *McClure's* articles on the Declaration of Independence and American fights for freedom remind New York readers that the United States, like India, was once a British colony. While *McClure's* promoted patriotism, its muckraking articles nevertheless exposed government injustices, calling large institutional structures into question as undercover reporters exposed the corruption of the ruling force. Without ever denouncing imperialism explicitly, both *Cassell's* and, to an even greater extent, *McClure's* contain subtle undercurrents that challenge the dominant (critical, but also editorial) tendency to align *Kim* with imperialist agendas. Furthermore, these periodicals also trace how *Kim* formed part of the magazines' larger editorial interests, such as technological advances, anthropological descriptions, geographic explorations, criminal investigations, and military conflicts—all of which are both recorded in *Kim* and reflected in surrounding material.

These magazines worked to promote a guided heterogeneity of material within their covers, even as they placed themselves in instructive roles, announcing hierarchies of importance to readers. Thus, the magazines' many advertisements for *Kim* would reinforce readers' perceptions of Kipling as an author of consequence. For both magazines, but especially for *Cassell's*, Kipling was a celebrity author, and *Kim* was presented as something like a major attraction in a circus. Although both *Cassell's* and *McClure's* published much adventure fiction, readers were instructed to view *Kim* as the hallmark of excellence in both adventure narratives and in the broader genre of serialized fiction. Thus, *Kim*'s first periodical readers not only were bombarded with the above-mentioned historical, technological, anthropological, geographic, legal, and military contexts, but were also urged to consider Kipling's fiction as a matter of first importance within this diverse assemblage.

Turn-of-the-century periodical readers found themselves in a position very different from that of the modern reader who casually fishes *Kim* out of bookstore shelves crammed with many competing titles. Nor did periodical readers find themselves in a position similar to the twenty-first-century student who studies *Kim* in a course that includes other literature the professor has judged to be of comparable, or perhaps even greater, value. Indeed, *Kim* is usually included on syllabi because of its imperial themes, not because of its literary value. Unlike these later readers, early twentieth-century magazine consumers were urged to view *Kim* as something special, an artifact that stood out from its surrounding contexts even while sharing certain characteristics with them. By featuring *Kim* on almost every cover, and always printing installments of *Kim* next to the frontispiece, *Cassell's* placed Kipling's serial in a position of primacy. While *McClure's* did not consistently make *Kim* its lead item, the American magazine did embark on striking advertising campaigns for Kipling's novel, promoting *Kim* more heavily than other fiction it was simultaneously serializing. The modern-day equivalent would be similar to entering a bookstore and encountering copies of *Kim* on a prominently positioned display shelf, or browsing books online and being bombarded with ads for *Kim*.

Serialization in *Cassell's*: Imperial Discourse and Surrounding Stories

Between the original periodical covers of *McClure's* and *Cassell's*, Kipling's novel emerges as a text that not only brings the "mystery of the East" to the West[12] but that also participates in transatlantic dialogue between Queen Victoria's Empire and the emerging American one. As Edward Said notes, "*Kim* is central to the quasi-official age of empire," and "[w]hen we read it today" we recognize how it forms "a very illuminating part" of Anglo-Indian history.[13] But the historical context Said outlines acquires even greater resonance when we position *Kim* in the English journal *Cassell's*, where the novel's first readers were repeatedly exposed to imperialist, militaristic, and nationalist discourse. From the moment of its first appearance in print, *Kim* was embedded both culturally and materially in the context of imperialism.

References to the British Empire not only surfaced repeatedly in surrounding articles but also occurred in promotional material for the novel. Even before serialization began, readers were encouraged to think of *Kim* in an imperialist context. In December 1900, *Cassell's* announced that *Kim* would soon begin serialization:

> [T]he Editor has now secured a feature for the new year which will undoubtedly cause an immensely increased demand for the Magazine throughout the British Empire.
>
> In securing the rights of Mr. Rudyard Kipling's brilliant serial, "Kim," for "CASSELL'S MAGAZINE," Messrs. Cassell & Co. have effected an arrangement which will mark an epoch in the history of a periodical which has a unique record.
>
> [...] already a largely-increased demand for "CASSELL'S MAGAZINE" has followed as a natural consequence. Mr. Kipling's readers are to be counted by tens of thousands in every corner of the British Empire.[14]

Here, *Cassell's* casts *Kim* as a novel that goes beyond documenting the British Empire, which by 1900 had expanded to include 420 million subjects,[15] and proceeds to become itself a powerful entity destined to spread to "every corner" of the Earth. On the next page, the article "In the Arena" describes Kipling as "the writer who has voiced, more than any other, that note of British Imperialism which has been the mark of recent years."[16] Thus when Said observes that the "ultimate analogy is between the Great Game and the novel itself,"[17] he suggests a parallel that *Cassell's* was already eager to promote at the turn of the century.

Furthermore, *Kim* was not the only story in *Cassell's* that used the game as a metaphor for Empire. Other fictional works, such as "The Christmas Present" by James Workman, similarly encouraged this association between playing games and practicing imperialism. In "The Christmas Present," set north of Cape Colony, a British officer named Montgomery brings a gift of toy soldiers to his sweetheart's younger brother.[18] The story's central motifs—the love interest between Montgomery and Mary, the role reversal between captor and captive, the intrigue behind colonial conflicts, the clever characters who utter words with secret double meanings—were fairly simple and predictable plot devices for stories serialized in *Cassell's*, but (with the possible exception of romance) they anticipate themes that *Kim* would later develop on a more complex level. As the plot of "The Christmas Present" thickens, sly references to toy "soldiers" that later materialize as actual Mounted Infantry encapsulate the correlation between children's games and the British Empire. Hence this short story, published in December 1900, prepares the way for *Kim*, which began serialization in the next issue and opened with the memorable description of a young boy playing on "the gun Zam-Zammah."[19] The subsequent pages inform readers that Kim "executed commissions by night on the crowded housetops for sleek and shiny young men of fashion. It was intrigue, of course—he knew that much, as he had known all evil since he could speak, —but what he loved was the game for its own sake."[20] Thus, the child's play on top of imperial weaponry, which Kim defends "since the English held the Punjab and Kim was English,"[21] metamorphoses into an adult game of political intrigue. This move from child's play to imperial Great Game is also inscribed in Workman's story. But whereas the young boy of Workman's story remains largely invisible, the young boy in Kipling's story becomes the central focus, as well as an actual player in—not just a miniature re-enacter of—the imperial Great Game.

In later chapters, the "Jewel Game"[22] that Kim plays with Lurgan Sahib's Hindu boy once again reinforces the correlation between playing children's games and working for the British secret service. Jewels could be readily linked to the British occupation of India, and readers of *Cassell's* would have quickly identified jewels as the spoils of colonial conquest. One article in *Cassell's* even describes the Taj Mahal as an "inimitable jewel," thereby magnifying innumerable little stones into one gigantic, embodied symbol of imperial dominion.[23] India itself, of course, was commonly referred to as the "crown jewel" of the British Empire. In the Jewel Game, Kim and his companion first begin by reciting which jewels have been displayed in each round, but they later play this memory game "with piles of swords and daggers" and with "photographs of natives."[24] The game thus becomes progressively more realistic and militaristic, as the objects of play switch from jewels, which function as symbols of British imperial wealth, to the actual weapons (swords and daggers) enabling conquest and the documentary photographs of conquered colonial subjects. *Kim* can thus be read as a novel that trains British boys for the imperial mission *Cassell's* was simultaneously promoting. By integrating references to jewels in both its fiction and nonfiction articles, *Cassell's* strengthens its propagandistic message with promises of wealth.

As part of this imperializing mission, *Cassell's* would use anthropological articles to document the manners and habits of colonized people in other lands. Far from being neutral in these reports on colonies, customs, and technologies, *Cassell's* also informed readers of deceptive tricks that natives had developed. Interestingly, one of these tricks involved jewels. As the first episode of *Kim* was being serialized in January 1901, *Cassell's* informed readers that

> X-rays were recently called in to detect a diamond thief in Calcutta. "Pouching" is a native art of swallowing valuables, or rather hiding them in the "sac" of the throat. In this case a small object was observed in the sac of the supposed thief, but its nature was uncertain. The method would be more useful with metal objects, which give a sharp photograph.[25]

This article almost reads like an intelligence report, evaluating the efficacy of new technology in detecting and subduing deceptive natives. The article also evinces an urge to describe the "native art[s]" that *Kim* was simultaneously documenting. The first chapter of *Kim* introduces readers not only to many Hindi words (such as *"bilaur"* [crystal], *"chela"* [disciple], and *"maya"* [illusion]) but also to the museum Curator, himself a symbol of the Empire's anthropological, documenting impulse. As the Curator smiles "at the mixture of old world piety and modern progress that is the note of India today,"[26] the reader is suddenly brought out of the fiction by the adverb "today," which reminds readers that *Kim*, far from being a purely fictional tale, also serves a contemporary, documentary function. Like the news articles and nonfiction reports in *Cassell's*, Kipling's novel introduces readers to the customs and manners of the Indian colonials. Within this historical and material context, Kipling's beloved descriptions of majestic India, so often praised by critics, acquire not only aesthetic beauty but also anthropological significance.

Despite occasional references to the subversive tactics of colonial subjects, *Cassell's* by and large painted a glowing image of the British Empire, one that emphasized the loyalty of natives, the generosity of monarchs, and the mutual benefits of colonial rule. The writer of "Living Women Sovereigns," Marie A. Belloc, concludes with a paragraph resounding in praise for Queen Victoria and her Empire:

> As to our own beloved Sovereign, her position is in many ways so completely unique that she cannot be compared with any female Sovereign of old or modern times. To say that on her kingdom the sun never sets is a truism. During her

reign the Anglo-Saxon race has learnt, as it never did before, to rule the world, and in a great measure the splendid example set by Queen Victoria has taught the race its lesson.[27]

Belloc's article, with its race-based claims to British superiority, occurs in the same issue as Chapter I of *Kim*. As Kim plays his "king-of-the-castle game with little Chota Lal and Abdullah,"[28] kicking them off the gun on which he perches, Belloc's article reinforces Anglo-Saxon superiority. According to the logic of Belloc's article, it is Kim's destiny "to rule the world"; thus her declarations support the fictional narrator when he observes that there "was some justification for Kim."[29] As Said notes some ninety years later, Kipling "is writing not just from the dominating viewpoint of a white man in a colonial possession, but from the perspective of a massive colonial system whose economy, functioning, and history had acquired the status of a virtual fact of nature."[30] Although Said does not mention them, the articles in *Cassell's* would certainly have given turn-of-the-century readers the impression that the Empire was "a virtual fact of nature." And, for *Cassell's* readers, even those who paused when recognizing that "some justification"[31] did not mean *full* justification, *Kim* would have seemed part of the magazine's pro-imperialist discourse.

Indeed, the magazine packaged *Kim* alongside many imperialist articles and travel narratives that confirm in news reports what Kipling articulates through fiction. One especially glowing representation of Empire, which contains strong parallels to *Kim*, was published in July 1901, when Chapter IX of *Kim* was being serialized. It is in this installment that Kim receives his training from Lurgan Sahib and attends school at St. Xavier's in preparation for his entry into the Great Game. *Cassell's* parallel news article, "The King's Travels," traces the growth and imperial education of Edward VII. As Lurgan Sahib tells Kim, "God causes men to be born—and thou art one of them—who have a lust to go abroad at the risk of their lives and discover news,"[32] *Cassell's* reporters inform readers that the "young Prince [Edward]" also traveled extensively as a youth, visiting lands that he would one day be "called upon to rule."[33] *Kim's* reference to "God" and the article's use of "called upon" evoke religious language used as a justification for Empire. In *Cassell's*, both fiction and news stories allude to the White Man's divine destiny to rule.

Additionally, both *Kim* and "The King's Travels" create narratives of imperial dominion that chart a boy's growth into manhood, showing how becoming a man translates into becoming a ruler of colonial subjects. Both narratives also move from scenes of conflict to scenes of peace, showing how initial resistance to colonial rule can be overcome, resulting in harmony. *Kim* opens with the boys fighting over Zam-Zammah, yet it concludes with the lama smiling, "as a man may who has won salvation for himself and his beloved."[34] In *Cassell's*, the word "Salvation" is capitalized, further emphasizing victory over evil and delivery from strife. Like *Kim*, "The King's Travel's" similarly documents a transition from strife to harmony as it records the king's adventures as a prince:

> From Italy the young Prince passed to Malta and Gibraltar, realising for the first time the extent and greatness of the Empire he would some day be called upon to rule; he found the British flag flying over distant territories, British guns, British troops defending British places of arms planted defiant upon foreign soil.[35]

By the end of the article, however, "defiant" arms have vanished, as the prince grows into a king and natives transform into loyal subjects:

> Here [in Bombay] began that exuberant welcome that greeted him [King Edward] throughout India, shown in such a great wealth of passionate enthusiasm and unrivalled gorgeous display as is possible only in the "shiny" East. From Bombay to Ceylon, from Ceylon to Madras, and finally to Calcutta, at all the coast-wise stations which had grown from trading posts to rank with the richest cities of any time or people, it was the same; the same gathering in of princes and potentates, the descendants of historic enemies, now the most loyal fellow subjects of the Great Empire.[36]

Interestingly, the reporter's word choice, "as is possible only in the 'shiny' East," closely mirrors Kipling's own phrasing, when he repeatedly asserts that certain poses, expressions, or sensations are possible only in India. By asserting India's unique traits, both Kipling and the *Cassell's* reporter amplify the land's exotic appeal.

But the writer of "The King's Travels" does not stop here; instead, his glowing description of King Edward's journeys through India continues, building upon the already-established racial discourse and emphasizing the happiness achieved through Empire:

> The progress up country will be remembered in India for all time; the halt at holy Benares, the visit to Cawnpore and Lucknow, the great durbar at Delhi, where the heir of the Anglo-Saxon kings took his seat upon the throne of the Great Mogul; [...] the cities of the North-West, once scenes of unceasing unrest, all happily at peace now under the strong aegis of the British dominion.[37]

Notably, the reporter evokes many of the landscapes and cities also described in *Kim*; Lucknow is the site of Kim's formal education, and Benares is the site of Kim's reunion with the lama. For Kim, however, Lucknow is the place "where they teach nothing—at the long price,"[38] and Benares strikes him "as a peculiarly filthy city."³⁹ Thus the glowing images in the travel article come into conflict with the more temperately painted cityscapes in *Kim*. Descriptions in news and fiction did not always coincide in their details, even if their overarching message was essentially the same. As this example shows, *Cassell's* was willing to accommodate some variety in its authors' positions, as long as stories and articles adhered to the general editorial policies, including the magazine's imperial disposition.

While the reporter's declarations seem grandiose and exaggerated, as India is carried in one sentence from "unceasing unrest" to "peace [...] under the strong aegis of the British dominion," his assertions reflect the prevailing attitude of the time, evincing an approach to imperialism that Kipling seems to have shared. In his correspondence, Kipling would frequently refer to the civilizing mission of the "White Man." In an August 1898 letter to George Cram Cook, for example, he referred to "the White Man's destiny," describing how "administering alien races who have no rights" would "educate" America, the emerging imperial power.⁴⁰ Implicitly, this letter suggests why serialization of *Kim* on both sides of the Atlantic would, in a few years, be desirable: one could argue that the imperial message Kipling wishes to impart is not just about affirming British dominion but also about providing an instructive model for the United States. As a *Bildungsroman* that also ties education to Empire, *Kim* functions as a particularly suiting vehicle for articulating Kipling's views (even if a subtler reading may begin to unravel the extent of his convictions).

As a boy's adventure tale, the novel also fits in easily with other stories in *Cassell's*, which tapped into a youth market even as it primarily targeted adult readers. Stories such as "The Mill on the Kop" by Robert Barr (December 1900), "The Battle of Forty Fort" by Stephen Crane (April 1901), and "From Sunset to Sunrise" by E. Spender (September 1901) all included teenage boys who, like Kim, prematurely enter skirmishes and battles against foreigners. In "The Mill on the Kop," Hans, the German miller's son, must engage in acts of bravery to defend his father's mill, much like Kim must also take risks for the Empire. To be sure, Barr's story presents the battle from the perspective of the defending Germans, as opposed to the attacking British soldiers, but the lesson of a young boy courageously rising to action remains the same. In "The Battle of Forty Fort," the landscape shifts from Africa to America, where Crane's sixteen-year-old narrator joins an 1878 battle against the Indigenous peoples of North America. In Crane's tale, however, the white settlers lose the battle, and the narrator is forced to admit defeat. This story may at first seem counter to *Cassell's* pro-imperial tendencies, but it may also be taken as a realistic portrayal of the sacrifices and lost battles that inevitably become part of any quest to subdue native populations (scholars have argued this is also the message of "The White Man's Burden"). Furthermore, as a story removed in both time and space from the majority of *Cassell's* English readers, "The Battle of Forty Fort: A Tale of Wyoming Valley" does not directly threaten the British right to rule natives. As a magazine that sometimes made fun of Americans, mocking their accents or their provincialism, *Cassell's* could afford to publish Crane's story of defeat without jeopardizing its pro-imperialist agenda. In fact, Crane's story may even have helped to solidify the magazine's notion that the British, unique among the White Men, were most capable of colonial management. Whereas Crane's American boy fails in battle, Kim and the British secret service succeed in stealing the documents from the Russian agents who invade India.

At the same time, the equation between nationality and imperial success cannot be formulated so simply. This equation is problematized both in *Kim*, where the hero is at once Irish, English, and Indian, and in "From Sunset to Sunrise," where a seventeen-year-old boy is "an Austrian by birth, but an Italian in heart"—a colonial situation in effect.[41] In contemporary criticism, much has been made of Kim's conflicted identity, but the novel's serial appearance alongside similar stories like "From Sunset to Sunrise" shows how even a magazine as seemingly nationalistic as *Cassell's* recognized the troubled complexities behind claims to racial purity and national superiority. Both Kipling's novel and Spender's short story map the inner struggle that takes place when blood ties come into conflict with cultural ties. Within the context of *Cassell's*, however, these works do less to undermine nationalistic assumptions than to promote the necessity of courage and loyalty in the face of conflict. Kim is praised for being "fearless,"[42] and Spender's seventeen-year-old protagonist gives his "life for Italy" even while tragically meeting "his death at the hands of Italians."[43] Although Kim is Irish, he serves the British imperialists; though Spender's protagonist is Austrian, he remains loyal to his Italian comrades even when they betray him.

Advertisements and the Technologies of Empire

Cassell's ongoing consideration of nationality and race extended to the advertising section, where frequent references to imperialism, colonial wars, and conquered territories were made. In December 1900, for example, Cerebos Table Salt published an ad that superimposed its label ("Cerebos") upon a soldier's letter, written during the Boer War. Underneath the headline, "A Letter from the Front," the ad's subhead explains, "The ONLY notepaper available near VAAL RIVER being the **'CEREBOS SALT'** advertisement from the 'Strand Magazine.'"[44] The text at the bottom of the ad concludes, "CEREBOS TABLE SALT is always 'at the front' in Good-class Houses." This ad strategically guides the reader through several movements: at first, it purports to be a "Letter from the Front," and the overarching headline almost makes it look like a news item or possibly a letter to the editor. But then the readers' eyes are drawn toward the bolded word "CEREBOS," the largest word on the page, strategically positioned in the middle of the soldier's "letter." The word "CEREBOS" is, in fact, repeated three times—in the top, middle, and bottom of the full-page advertisement. Likewise, the word "front" is repeated in the copy at the top and bottom, and in the middle the letter from the front is reproduced. Here, as the discourses of advertising and imperialism are literally intertwined (the soldier's ink even comes into contact with the word "CEREBOS" from the ad), we witness a series of recycled texts: An ad for Cerebos Salt is written upon by a soldier, and this letter is then reproduced as part of another ad for Cerebos Salt.

This palimpsest advertisement is interesting for several reasons. First, as an ad published in the December 1900 issue, one month before *Kim*'s appearance, Cerebos Salt mentally prepares readers for the many safely guarded letters to be circulated in *Kim*. Although the connection between the letter reproduced in the ad and the letter Kim delivers for Mahbub Ali is unintentional, *Cassell's* advertising section and fiction section nevertheless operate cooperatively to underscore the centrality of written communication to imperial success. While the advertisement's letter, fully legible, takes the form of domestic correspondence—a soldier writing home to his sweetheart—Mahbub Ali's letter takes the form of a political dispatch, a spy's disguised message to a military officer. The soldier's letter can be straightforwardly written and safely reprinted, whereas Mahbub Ali's letter, ostensibly about the pedigree of a white stallion, must be protected at all costs. In both cases, however, the circulation of letters is essential to maintaining ties, whether domestic or political, between various outposts of the Empire.

Secondly, the Cerebos Salt advertisement highlights the materiality of letters; for the purposes of the ad, the contents of the soldier's letter are less important than the material (a Cerebos Salt ad from *Strand*) upon which it is written. The ad in the *Strand* thus had sufficient white space to accommodate writing, and the periodical in which it is printed doubles as a source of stationery. Here Cerebos creatively reformulates business advice to include white space in advertisements. As one 1898 advertising guide advised, "Maybe that extra space is just what the ad needs to lift it out of oblivion—to make it prominent—to make it pay."⁴⁵ But, if the *Strand* advertisement contained more white space than type, the *Cassell's* ad fills that space with the soldier's handwriting. In *Cassell's*, the reproduction of the inscribed *Strand* ad is in turn framed by white space, such that one advertisement fits inside another, and the soldier's message, a very personal note to his girlfriend, becomes encased by advertising material directed toward a mass audience.

This kind of successive cocooning was also exercised in *Kim*, though on a slightly different level. When Kim writes a letter to Hurree Babu, the Woman of Shamlegh produces two walnut half-shells, and Kim slips "the piece of paper between them."⁴⁶ Thus both letters—Kim's, and the soldier's—are cocooned by surrounding material (walnut shells, or advertising copy) that on the surface have no direct relation to the enclosed contents. But the print medium forces those enclosed contents out of the shell, so to speak, such that personal letters intended for only one recipient end up being exposed to thousands of magazine readers. The soldier's letter, written in a large and legible hand, can easily be read by any consumer who cares to scrutinize the ad. Similarly, although Hurree Babu is the only character within the fiction to read Kim's letter, the boy's message is printed in the text for all of *Cassell's* readers to see: "*I have everything that they [the Russian spies] have written: their pictures of the country, and many letters. Especially the* muralsa. *Tell me what to do. I am at Shamlegh-under-the-Snow. The old man is sick.*"⁴⁷ Here, in a further recursive layer, Kim's letter refers to other letters, documents that readers of *Kim* do not actually get to read. Similarly, the Cerebos Salt advertisement hints that there are other soldiers' letters it has not printed: If the "ONLY notepaper available near VAAL River" is the Cerebos ad with its large margins, then presumably other soldiers were tearing the stationery-like ad out of the magazine, too.

The connection between the Cerebos Salt stratagem and *Kim* is a happy coincidence made possible by the conceptually expansive nature of magazines, which easily accommodate many disparate artifacts. But these seemingly dissimilar modes of representation—advertisement and fiction—both use the trope of the unveiled personal letter to appeal to readers' curiosity. Here, like the soldier in the ad or the young secret agent in *Kim*, readers are invited to become spies, as they are granted privileged access to the personal documents of others. Both ad and fiction also rely on the historical context of imperialism to heighten readers' sense of adventure and to promote a product simultaneously. By referencing the front in South Africa, the ad makes Cerebos Salt more marketable. By referencing the Great Game in India, *Kim* makes itself more appealing to readers. Hence as imperial discourse could be re-appropriated for commercial purposes, the advertisement and fiction sections of *Cassell's* in turn served to promote the Empire.

Indeed, businesses seemed eager to align their products with the discourses of Empire. One ad, for Bovril, is particularly striking in this regard. Printed in March 1902, just four months after the last installment of *Kim*, this ad shows readers "How the BRITISH EMPIRE spells BOVRIL."[48] Beneath this announcement, the geophysical shapes of the Empire's territories are rearranged in such a way that they quite literally spell "BOVRIL." The equation between product and Empire could hardly be more explicit. Every letter contains about ten territories and colonial possessions, each with a number that indicates "a separate part of the Empire."[49] The advertising copy explains, "The shapes are correct, but the sizes are not in proportion."[50] Readers are invited to identify the shapes as the ad challenges, "How many parts can you name?"[51] A "complete key," the ad promises, "will later be published in the newspapers and on the hoardings."[52] In the ad's creative arrangements of space and image, which make imperial lands the building-blocks of Bovril, the success of one becomes essential to the success of the other. The advertisement, then, strives to attract readers by aligning itself with a grand imperial mission and by using the gimmick of the puzzle. As we will see, little magazines such as the *Dial* also used the technique of the challenge question to draw readers in. Whereas the ad in *Cassell's* promotes geopolitical knowledge as a marker of intelligence, ads in the *Dial* substituted artistic knowledge as the desired intellectual distinction. By challenging readers to compete with each other, these ads not only sought to make magazine reading more participatory but also instructed readers in the types of knowledge they ought to seek and the values they ought to prize.

A similarly symbiotic relationship was set up between *Cassell's*, the magazine with a disposition toward Empire, and *Kim*, the novel that addressed colonial pressures while contributing to the magazine's success. *Kim* was consistently positioned first in the magazine's table of contents, signaling its prominence as the lead feature. In its December 1900 announcement, *Cassell's* firmly ascribed its rising subscription numbers to *Kim*, "Mr. Rudyard Kipling's brilliant serial."[53] The "immensely increased demand" for *Cassell's* "throughout the British Empire" follows as a "natural consequence" of the editors obtaining serial rights to *Kim*.[54] The advertisement, with its frequent references to Empire and the anticipated success of both the magazine and its forthcoming serial, concludes by urging readers to subscribe: "Those who wish to possess copies of **'CASSELL'S**

MAGAZINE' containing 'Kim' will have to give their orders forthwith in order to make certain that they will not be disappointed."[55]

Surrounding pages in the December 1900 issue further reinforced the magazine's alliance with Kipling, as *Cassell's* launched a strong promotional campaign in preparation for *Kim*'s first installment. On the recto of the same leaf (page 147), a portrait of Kipling by Philip Burne-Jones is displayed. Kipling is positioned in profile at his desk, a pen poised in his hand. In the context of *Cassell's*, this painted scene of writing suggests that Kipling may be in the very act of composing *Kim*. Numerous books line the shelves in the background, symbolizing volumes of literary knowledge. Smaller yet closer to Kipling's body, a globe adorns the author's desk, symbolizing politico-geographic knowledge. Both kinds of knowledge, it is suggested, will inform the composition and the success of Kipling's novel, which itself suggests that geographical and literary knowledge is essential to successful imperial enterprises.[56]

Two pages later, in the article "In the Arena" (a monthly feature of the magazine that highlighted activities of public figures in short blurbs), *Cassell's* explains its decision to publish Kipling's portrait: "As CASSELL'S MAGAZINE for January will contain the opening instalment of 'Kim,' Mr. Rudyard Kipling's new story of Indian life, there is more than the ordinary timeliness in the publication of his portrait in this number from the painting by Sir Philip Burne-Jones, which attracted so much attention at this year's exhibition of the Royal Academy."[57] *Cassell's* then proceeds to give a brief biography of Kipling, all the while asserting that the story of his career "is almost too well-known to need setting out at length."[58] *Cassell's*, it can be deduced, was drawing upon Kipling's popularity in much the same way that *Collier's* was drawing on Henry James's well-established reputation. *Cassell's* eagerly asserts that it will be publishing the author who "stands easily first as the word-painter of the soldier's life, and the writer who has voiced, more than any other," the voice of "British Imperialism."[59] Although "In the Arena" was ostensibly a collection of news stories in brief, it at times reads more like an advertisement than news copy. *Kim*, the magazine explains, will be "a story of India as the natives see it, revealing in every page the author's subtle and intimate familiarity with every phase of society in that great Empire."[60] Somewhat strangely, the editors claim that *Kim* will at once be told from the point of view of the "natives" and from that of its British author. The editors mean, of course, that Kipling's British eye will deliver a portrait of India that conveys a native's familiarity with the land and its peoples, but the floating syntax unwittingly suggests a conflation of the two national points of view and thereby unveils the central tensions inherent in Kipling's split identity (as an Anglo-Irishman born in India).

In addition to featuring Kipling in the section "In the Arena," the December 1900 issue also devotes a paragraph of "Something New" (a monthly column overviewing the latest advances in the sciences and in the arts) to Kipling:

> It is now known, wherever literature is spoken of, that CASSELL'S MAGAZINE is the fortunate possessor, for serial purposes in Britain, of Mr. Rudyard Kipling's new novel, "Kim." This story, the first Anglo-Indian novel our foremost writer has yet given us, will begin in the January number [...]. We feel sure that every friend of good literature will make this known wherever possible, and will not fail to follow this most absorbing and truly brilliant work from the first page to the last. As a great demand for the January number is looked for, we cordially invite our readers to ensure their copies by an early intimation to the newsagent.[61]

Here, the magazine not only promotes *Kim*, but also urges readers to do the same: "every friend of good literature will make this known wherever possible[.]" Once again, the magazine builds on Kipling's popularity to predict a sell-out situation. These repeated declarations of *Kim*'s brilliance, coupled by repeated warnings about the magazine's limited availability, obey the principal dictum of advertising: that repetition is key to success. (Here we may recall—or think forward to—Leopold Bloom, the ad canvasser in *Ulysses*, as he reflects, "Good idea the repetition. Same thing with ads.")[62]

Hence it should not be surprising that *Cassell's*, following this principle, continued to repeat its praise of *Kim* even as it was being serialized. In "Something New," *Cassell's* regularly published synopses of *Kim*, which it did not do for other serials (at least during *Kim*'s serialization). These blurbs not only update readers on fictional events within Kipling's story but also update readers on how *Kim* has affected the circulation of the magazine. In March 1901, for instance, *Cassell's* informed customers that "[a]dditional quantities" of issues containing installments of *Kim* had been printed "to meet the needs of readers of Mr. Kipling's story."[63] In May 1901, *Cassell's* published an ad that prominently placed *Kim* at the top of its selected contents for the forthcoming June issue. Designating *Kim* "Mr. RUDYARD KIPLING'S magnificent Serial Story," the ad reminds readers that the "*complete scenario accompanying each number permits this story to be taken up at any point*" before asserting, "*we can assure all our subscribers that Mr. Kipling has written nothing more engrossing or more worthy of his splendid reputation than this fascinating book.*"[64]

Finally, it is worthy of note that *Cassell's* chose to advertise *Kim* both in its official advertising section (numbered separately, with Roman numerals) and in its main section (with pages numbered according to the Arabic system). Interestingly, *Cassell's* typically published its table of contents in the advertising section of the previous issue. In these ads, *Kim* was always displayed prominently, in bold letters and at the top of the page. When readers received the next issue of *Cassell's*, Kipling's novel was advertised on the front cover. The advertisements for *Kim*, in other words, permeated all the major departments and spaces of the magazine. Hence, when Colonel Creighton thinks of Kim, "That boy mustn't be wasted if he is as advertised,"[65] it is hard not to read his private assessment of Kim metatextually. It is almost as if the novel anticipates and responds to the advertisements that surround it. Just as *Kim* is an advertised product within *Cassell's*, so Kim is an advertised product within Kipling's novel. Kipling's "*splendid reputation*," referred to in the May 1901 announcement quoted above,[66] acts as a corollary to his character's own "*splendid reputation*," which was simultaneously being explored in the same issue. With each installment, the advertised talents of both Kim and Kipling come under scrutiny. Judging from the enthusiastic reports in *Cassell's* and the increased demand for installments containing *Kim*, we may conclude that both author and character appear to have met expectations, coming "as advertised."

As it promoted *Kim*, the magazine also aligned the novel with the technologies and discourses of Empire. In "Something New," a regular series with short descriptions of innovations in both the sciences and the arts, *Cassell's* begins by reminding readers of *Kim*'s impending serialization, calling it "the first Anglo-Indian novel our foremost writer has yet given us."[67] Other items featured in the December 1900 "Something New" column include "a new gun camera," a US submarine, a "mammoth searchlight" in California, and a "talking foghorn" for lighthouses—all of which link *Kim* with scientific advancement, performing an equation between literary and technological innovation also made by *McClure's*. These tools for communication, surveillance, and military combat also underwrite and enable the imperial enterprises described in Kipling's novel. The magazine, I argue, materially presents the intersection between fictional imperialist narratives and what Rita Felski elsewhere describes as the "technological advances of modern nation-states" that "could be cited as a justification for imperialist invasion."[68]

An article entitled "The Greatest in the World" illustrates the link between technology and Empire that Felski describes. The article, by Pat Brooklyn, sets out "to describe and illustrate some of the principal wonders" of Man and Nature.[69] Notably, the article focuses on the Western world's accomplishments, as it records that "France possesses the largest theatre and library and the highest tower in the world,"[70] America possesses "the highest lighthouse in the world,"[71] and Switzerland possesses the "longest railway tunnel in the world."[72] In the midst of this celebration of Western technological advancement, Brooklyn writes:

> India claims the distinction of possessing the longest span of wire in the world. This is a single telegraph wire which crosses the River Kistnah. It is over 6,000 feet in length, and is 1,200 feet high, being stretched from a hill on one side of the river to one on the other.[73]

The technology of the British imperialists, in other words, makes this Indian "distinction" possible. The precise measurements also reflect the system of British surveying and surveillance that Kim was concurrently being trained to conduct in Kipling's fiction. As Kim returns to St. Xavier's, Hurree Chunder Mookerjee tells him, "Still more important [...] was the art and science of mensuration."[74] The news article on "The Greatest in the World" serves to illustrate what may be accomplished by boys going to the colonies who, like Kim, learn the art and science of mensuration.

Additionally, the "Something New" column at the end of each periodical issue further emphasized technology and invention. Synopses and updates on *Kim*, the magazine's highlighted literary accomplishment, would be followed by reports on the latest scientific advancements. Modes of transportation, such as the train, frequently surfaced alongside references to Kipling in this column. In February 1901, for instance, a synopsis of *Kim*'s first installment was immediately followed by a photograph and description of "A Director's Engine."[75] Like the author of "The Greatest in the World," the reporter covering "Something New" emphasizes precise measurements, valuing precision and size as indices of scientific value:

> The wheels are 2 feet 6 inches in diameter. The single driving wheel is 5 feet 7 inches in diameter, with an 18-inch stroke. The carriage and engine are practically in one. The former is most elaborately furnished, and is capable of holding six persons and an attendant. The total weight of the engine in working order is 37 tons. It is fitted with steam-reversing gear and can boast of the latest improvements. It is very fast, and has frequently attained a speed of 80 miles an hour.[76]

This frequent citation of numerical values—covering distance, weight, speed, and seating capacity—reinforces careful calculations Kim is taught to perform at St. Xavier's and in the Play of the Jewels.

Naturally, advertisements also participated in this discourse of innovation and progress. In the January 1901 advertising section, for example, Swan presented a diagram of its fountain pen that labeled the various parts and listed its measurements, affirming, "The Improved Sizes are unquestionably the very best Fountain Pens Money Can Buy."[77] Adjacent to the Swan Fountain Pen, a bottle of Dichroic Ink promises to be the "Best Black Ink known."[78] The ad, which is itself filled with black ink, asserts that its product is "BLACK AS NIGHT."[79] Curiously, the ink is manufactured in Dublin, Ireland, communicating an unwitting association between Irishness and blackness. It seems uncanny that, in this very magazine issue, the Irish Kim should be described as "black."[80] An ad on the same page for Aitchison Patent Eyeglasses recalls the spectacles that the museum curator gives to the lama in the same periodical issue.[81] In return, the lama gives the curator a pencase—valuable for its aesthetic, collector's value. But the gift of superior technology—in this instance, crystal spectacles that will never scratch (the lama's previous pair was badly marked)—belongs to the British, who bring and distribute civilization's wonders to the Orient. Furthermore, advertisements for encyclopedias promised to bring British citizens anthropological knowledge of foreigners. In this way, both the advertisements and Kipling's fiction contribute to the imperialist mission of *Cassell's*, which was keen to demonstrate the scientific advancements and cultural achievements of the West.

Illustrations of *Kim*

But *Cassell's* did more than surround *Kim* with articles about scientific developments and anthropological investigations; it also cast *Kim* as itself a participant in those developments and investigations. Far from being simple mirrors of textual events, the illustrations of *Kim* contribute to the magazine's commercial, technological, and anthropological agendas. In its promotional materials, *Cassell's* promises readers that Kipling's story will be accompanied by illustrations,[82] a strong selling point for mass-market periodicals (recall the ads in *Collier's* that emphasized artwork and photography). Like *Collier's*, *Cassell's* was eager to emphasize the pictorial aspects of its magazine. But, whereas visual images in *Collier's* are intended to serve a mainly authenticating function (even as they sometimes diverge from the narratives they illustrate), visual images of *Kim* extend to fulfill an important ethnological function. Illustrations for *Kim*, in other words, not only portray fictional scenes but also document India as a land outside the fiction.

In addition to serving this documentary function, the visual images were conceived of as instances of the magazine's technological innovations. When the first installment of *Kim* appeared in January 1901, it was accompanied by several visual images, including artwork by Kipling's father, John Lockwood Kipling. A caption under a picture of Kim with the lama explains, "THE ILLUSTRATIONS HAVE BEEN MODELLED IN CLAY, AND REPRODUCED BY PHOTOGRAPHY. ALIKE FOR NOVELTY OF THE METHOD AND ARTISTIC EXCELLENCE THESE PICTURES ARE LIKELY TO ATTRACT GENERAL ATTENTION."[83] Illustrations by H.R. Millar and E.L. Weeks likewise gave readers a visual encounter with the text that is lost in modern editions.[84] The serialized illustrations show how the "Orientalized India of the imagination," as described by Said and others,[85] was both evoked by Kipling's vivid prose descriptions and visually reinforced by artwork on the page. These illustrations encourage readers' fantasies of crossing racial and national boundaries. Lockwood Kipling's images of Kim most evidently reinforce the boy's seemingly effortless ability to pass as dark-skinned or light-skinned. Millar portrays Kim as European, but Weeks portrays him as a natural part of the Indian cultural landscape. Because Kim perpetually assumes different appearances depending upon which illustrator's hand creates him, readers viewing all three artists' depictions would be presented with constant visual reminders of Kim's transformative capabilities.

Moreover, the diversity of the technologies used—the line drawings by Millar, the wash drawings by Weeks, and the photographed bas reliefs by Kipling's father—engages with the magazine's anthropological mission to document and classify natives of foreign lands. At the same time, these diverse illustrations subtly suggest that visions of India, like the competing interpretations of the text itself, will vary from reader to reader. Kim's fragmented identity, as he struggles between loyalty to the lama on the one hand and to the Great Game on the other, is echoed by the varying artistic illustrations of the "poor white" Irish boy who is "burned black as any native."[86]

Like *The Turn of the Screw* in *Collier's*, Kipling's *Kim* was preceded by a recurring masthead. The masthead is drawn by H.R. Millar, who, of all three illustrators, is most keen to develop a narrative emphasizing the differences between colonizers and their subjects. This masthead was published at the head of each installment in *Cassell's*, which consistently put *Kim* first in the table of contents, but it was not used in *McClure's*, where *Kim* was frequently buried in the midst of a magazine issue. In *Cassell's*, the masthead serves as a reminder of *Kim*'s importance, and it also provides a point of continuity for readers who had to wait an entire month for a new installment. The repeated visual image thus serves to aid memory (and readers of the monthly *Cassell's*, as opposed to readers of the weekly *Collier's*, would be in greater need of a visual reminder).

But, I want to show, this masthead also introduces complications for close readers of *Kim*. First, there is the issue of time. Although several years pass over the course of the novel, as the protagonist moves from boyhood into adulthood, Kim in Millar's masthead remains a small child. Even during the concluding installment, when Kim has already overpowered a Russian agent in physical combat, he is represented as a boy whose shoulders are horizontally aligned with the lama's waist. The lama, too, is a problematic figure. Millar portrays him as a rather corpulent man, where Kipling describes him as thin. Finally, there is the issue of skin color, a problem that surfaces throughout Millar's representations of *Kim*. Although Kim is introduced as a chameleon-like figure who can pass as a native, his skin in Millar's art is clearly white. On the first page of the opening installment, when Kipling describes Kim as "burned black,"[87] Millar's line drawing directly contradicts the words on the same page. Although line drawings do not allow the kind of varied shadings used in Weeks's wash drawings, the lama's skin here is notably darker than Kim's. Hence, in both size and skin color, the lama and Kim are set apart, even though their bodily positioning, with the lama's hand on Kim's shoulder, draws them together.

The issue of Kim's identity is further problematized in April 1901, when Kim enters the camp of his father's Irish regiment and is initially mistaken for a "native" because he has dark skin and speaks Hindustani.[88] However, when Father Victor "open[s] the front of Kim's upper garment,"[89] exposing his lighter chest, Kim's Anglo-Saxon identity is revealed. "You see, Bennett, he's not very black," Father Victor tells his companion.[90] Father Victor's verdict—"he's not very black"—is in turn used as the caption for Millar's illustration on the same page. And Kim's chest is, accordingly, shown to be "not very black." Here, however, Millar's drawing translates "not very black" into completely white. Furthermore, in Millar's portrayal Kim's chest is not any whiter than his face or his neck. But for Father Victor and Bennett, it was the very contrast between Kim's exposed, sunburnt skin and his protected, cloth-covered skin that caused them to change their assessment of the little boy who had penetrated their camp. And for Kipling this duality was central to the development of Kim as a chameleon-like character.

Millar's drawings seem anxious to prove, even at the cost of violating textual integrity, that Kim is undoubtedly a sahib. Several pages later, when Kim is forced to exchange his native garments for the school uniforms, he appears, at least in Millar's illustrations, to have completely lost any traces of his native identity. Millar chooses to illustrate several key scenes of identity disguise and disclosure, but in doing so he is always careful to assure magazine readers that Kim retains his British identity. In May 1901, for instance, Millar illustrates the scene in which Kim visits a dancing-girl in order to disguise himself for a "jest."⁹¹ As she "dab[s] on the juice" that will dye Kim's skin, he cautions her, "Not too black, *Naikan*."⁹² Kim's race-inflected instructions are the words selected for the caption under Millar's drawing in *Cassell's*. Yet on this same page Kipling's narrative describes Kim as running "down the stairs in the likeness of a low-caste Hindu boy."⁹³ The caption, in other words, selectively pulls words from the text that reject identification with dark racial features and assure readers that Kim will never become "too black," even in jest. Even in this scene of transformation, Millar preserves the whiteness of Kim's skin. The dancing-girl's applicator, illustrated as a white ball even though it was presumably dipped in black dye, barely touches his nose. Millar's illustrations are consistently uncomfortable with Kim's resemblance to the natives.⁹⁴ Choosing to highlight Kim's whiteness, Millar emphasizes the importance of preserving British identity.

Yet, if we regard the illustrations by all the artists, placing Millar alongside Lockwood Kipling and E.L. Weeks, Kim does indeed appear to be very chameleon-like. Each illustrator portrays him differently. Whereas Millar emphasizes Kim's English identity, Weeks inclines to position Kim in the midst of Indian scenes as enchanting as Kipling's beautiful textual evocations, and Lockwood Kipling tends to portray his son's characters in portrait-like poses that, collectively, serve to document the various peoples inhabiting India (the Tibetan lama, the Anglo-Irish Kim, the Pathan horse-dealer, and so on). It is fitting that Lockwood Kipling, as museum curator in Lahore, should provide these sculptures that, in the context of *Cassell's*, fulfill a documentary function while also expressing admiration for their Indian subjects. As Mark Paffard notes, Rudyard Kipling describes "Indian characters so deftly that they remain in the memory, but do so explicitly as *types*, so that the reader actually recalls them by means of a label."⁹⁵ It may be added that the illustrations provided by Kipling's father, with their captions that function as anthropological labels (especially "The Jat and His Sick Child," "The Ressaldar," or "The Woman of Shamlegh"), help to reinforce Paffard's interpretation.⁹⁶

The differences between Millar, Weeks, and Lockwood Kipling are perhaps best accentuated in their varying portrayals of Kim writing a letter to the lama. Here *Cassell's* readers encounter four different versions of the same fictional event (three visual, and one textual). In the text, Kim runs from the stifling school to the liberating bazaar in order to find a letter-writer who can compose his message. The movement is one from captivity to freedom, from the military school of the sahibs to the colorful marketplace of the natives. But the letter's message concerns a return to captivity: "*In three days I am to go down to Nucklao to the school at Nucklao. The name of the school is Xavier. I do not know where that school is, but it is at Nucklao.*"⁹⁷ As the scribe records these verbally constructed sentences and offers to add instructions about the location of Xavier, Colonel Creighton unexpectedly approaches and demands an explanation from Kim, who protests that he is not running away. As proof of his loyalty, Kim offers to let Creighton read the letter. The episode concludes with the colonel questioning Kim before sending him on a mission. Each of the illustrators portrays a different segment of the scene outlined above, and their choices influence which characters receive emphasis, as well as how readers might interpret the interactions between those characters.

In Millar's illustration, as might be expected, the two sahibs—Kim, and the colonel—are illustrated in the foreground (see Figure 3). Both are standing,

"'WHY HAST THOU LEFT OUT MY NAME IN WRITING TO THAT HOLY ONE?'" (*p.* 616).

Figure 3 H.R. Millar's illustration of the letter-writing scene in *Cassell's*, May 1901, p. 615. In the caption, Colonel Creighton asks Kim, "WHY HAST THOU LEFT OUT MY NAME IN WRITING TO THAT HOLY ONE?" Image supplied by the Herman B. Wells Library, Indiana University Libraries.

while the native letter-writer kneels in the background, symbolizing his lower position both in terms of racial hierarchies and in terms of his character's value to the narrative (he is a minor character, and we do not even know his name). Creighton, dressed in a striped suit jacket, holds a cigar with one hand and Kim's letter with the other. The crouching letter-writer is almost menacing, as he observes Kim and Creighton with dark eyes. Further behind him there are sketches of an Oriental-style building with barely distinguishable human figures congregating in the passageway. By positioning the characters symbolically and taking the message out of the scribe's hands so that Creighton may hold it, Millar makes *his* message and method clear: Sahibs in the foreground, natives in the background. Sahibs enlarged at the center, natives diminutive at the vanishing point. The British control both the space on the periodical page and the actual geographic space of India.

But this is not the case in the illustrations by Weeks and Lockwood Kipling, who present a much more vibrant portrayal of Indian life (see Figures 4 and 5). Rather than presenting sahib and native in juxtaposed physical positions, Weeks and Lockwood Kipling present them in mirrored bodily postures. Rather than creating a distance between sahib and native, Weeks and Lockwood Kipling present them side by side. And Colonel Creighton, the symbol of British authority, is not even present. In Weeks's drawing, Kim and the letter-writer are shown kneeling side by side in the midst of a crowded, lively Indian bazaar. Oxen, carriages, women with children on their hips, natives with flowing robes, and an embellished Oriental building richly fill in the background. As in Millar's drawing, an archway in this building allows figures to pour into the square, but in Weeks's drawing these figures are illustrated in much greater detail. While Kim and the letter-writer are positioned in the foreground, they are close enough to be touched by the surrounding background figures. Furthermore, Kim and the letter-writer are not centered (as were Kim and Creighton in Millar's illustration); rather, Weeks locates them in the lower left corner, such that a carriage with oxen becomes the focal point of the scene. Weeks's drawing is as much a documentation of bazaar activity in India as it is an illustration of fictional events.

This bazaar activity is absent from Lockwood Kipling's sculpture, but his illustration nonetheless continues Weeks's anthropological study (Weeks's drawing was actually published in April 1901, a month before Millar's and Lockwood Kipling's appeared; the editors used it to illustrate Kim's first letter to the lama, a similar but earlier scene in the text).[98] Kim and the letter-writer

Figure 4 John Lockwood Kipling's illustration of Kim and the letter-writer in *Cassell's*, May 1901, p. 617. Image supplied by the Herman B. Wells Library, Indiana University Libraries.

are alone, in accordance with Lockwood Kipling's general tendency to focus on individual (if stereotypical) figures rather than crowds—a choice suited to the bas relief medium. Both Kim and the letter-writer are sitting down, signifying equality, at least for this present moment of collaboration. The letter-writer authoritatively raises a writing utensil in his hand as Kim looks at him intently, with one hand thoughtfully positioned underneath his chin. Each sculpted

"'COME THEN AND HELP ME, MAHBUB ALI, OR SEND ME SOME MONEY, FOR I HAVE NOT SUFFICIENT TO PAY THE WRITER WHO WRITES THIS.'"

Figure 5 E.L. Weeks's portrayal of the letter-writing scene in *McClure's*, April 1901, p. 556. The image is captioned with a quotation from page 555 of Rudyard Kipling's *Kim*, which slyly concludes the letter Kim is dictating: "COME THEN AND HELP ME, MAHBUB ALI, OR SEND ME SOME MONEY, FOR I HAVE NOT SUFFICIENT TO PAY THE WRITER WHO WRITES THIS." E.L. Weeks's illustration of this scene also occurs in *Cassell's*, April 1901, p. 513, where it is titled "KIM'S LETTER" and carries the more matter-of-fact caption, "MECHANICALLY KIM SQUATTED BESIDE HIM," a quotation from page 512 of *Kim* (in *Cassell's*). Reproduced with permission of The Modernist Journals Project (searchable database). Brown and Tulsa Universities, ongoing. www.modjourn.org.

figure occupies approximately the same amount of space, emphasizing harmony and correspondence as opposed to the hierarchy and competition of Millar's work. Kim's clothing, loose with many folds, closely resembles the letter-writer's dress. In Millar's drawing, by contrast, Kim had been portrayed in a buttoned jacket and slacks, distinctly European garb. Whereas Millar emphasizes the differences between colonizer and colonized, Lockwood Kipling, like Weeks, highlights their similarities. One additional, unique feature of the sculpting is that it eliminates distinctions in color and shading; Kim's skin is just as dark as the native's skin, and the native's skin is no lighter than Kim's. Here, unlike in Millar's art, Kim is allowed to have the same complexion as a native.

Weeks and Lockwood Kipling, then, create a picture of harmony between Britain and India, Kim and the natives. This image of harmony, of course, may not be any less imperialistic than Millar's insistence upon racial purity and British superiority. Weeks and Lockwood Kipling do, after all, appeal to exoticism and what Said terms "Orientalism," even if under the rubric of anthropological documentation. As Said writes, "*Kim* shows how a white Sahib can enjoy life in this lush complexity; and, I would argue, the absence of resistance to European intervention in it—symbolized by Kim's abilities to move relatively unscarred through India—is due to its imperialist vision."[99] In other words, the image of natives and sahibs coexisting peacefully validates the British occupation of India. If we accept Said's interpretation of *Kim*, then we may read the illustrations as an additional validation of the text's imperialist message.

Perhaps these three different illustrators, who seem to disrupt the narrative continuity with their widely varying portrayals of Indian life, actually work together in order to construct complementary narratives: While Millar's art focuses on British identity and power, the art of Weeks and Lockwood Kipling shows how a powerful British presence in India can produce a harmonious society. Like the novel, these images refuse ever to contest British rule explicitly. Taken together, these images (Millar's on the one hand, and Weeks's and Lockwood Kipling's on the other) map the tensions between the two major impulses Said detects in Rudyard Kipling's novel: "on the one hand, surveillance and control over India; on the other, love for and fascinated attention to its every detail."[100] The fact that *Cassell's* could publish such divergent illustrations of *Kim* indicates that readers at the time must have been able to balance these competing imperatives, accommodating both control and fascination in their vision of imperialism. As Zohreh T. Sullivan writes, the "contradictions in Kipling's art […] reflect those at the heart of the imperial enterprise."[101] Kipling's fiction, and its accompanying visual images, trains readers to accept these contradictions.

But the illustrations of *Kim*, like the images accompanying *The Turn of the Screw* in *Collier's*, do raise questions about narrative reliability: Just whose story is being told? If it is Kim's story, who is Kim? Which image portrays him correctly? It is suiting that Kipling's protagonist should, in this same (May 1901) installment, come to this exact crisis of identity as he asks himself this very question—"Who is Kim?"[102] This is a question to which Kim (and *Kim*) repeatedly turns. "I am to pray to Bibi Miriam, and I am a Sahib," Kim thinks to himself, desperately struggling to resolve the contradictions inscribed in his identity.[103] "He considered his own identity, a thing he had never done before, till his head swam."[104] Magazine readers, too, are forced to ponder this momentous question. As three different artists inject their varied interpretations into the pages of *Cassell's*, the question for magazine readers becomes even more vexed. In the magazine illustrations, readers are bombarded with competing interpretations of Kim's identity and, simultaneously, with competing visions of Empire in India. Yet *Cassell's* aims to show how these competing visions can be brought into harmony, even as seemingly divergent illustrations are brought together between periodical covers. The magazine illustrations by Weeks and Lockwood Kipling were also published in *McClure's*. But, as I argue below, a reader of *McClure's* would not find it quite as easy to bring these competing visions into harmony.

Serialization in *McClure's*: Technology, Adventure, Travel

In December 1900, *McClure's* published an ad promising that *Kim* would combine the adventures of Robinson Crusoe with the "mysterious religious philosophy of a land more varied than anywhere in the world."[105] While highlighting *Kim*, the ad also promotes other works that carry similar appeals to "human interest."[106] Indeed, within the space of *McClure's*, *Kim* is printed alongside illustrated stories about Indigenous Americans (such as "The People of the Buffalo") which evoke a kind of native exoticism different from yet connected to that exhibited in *Kim*; scientific articles on oceanography that include maps of India and the world's seas; technical articles such as "Great Achievements in Modern Bridge-Building" that express a desire to master turbulent waters; and historical articles on the former American Confederacy as well as illustrated articles on the British royalty (with multiple portraits of Queen Victoria). When *Kim* travels from Europe to America, then, it not only reaches a transatlantic audience but also makes new points of contact with other serialized texts and images. This transatlantic aspect of *Kim* is enhanced when we return the novel to its original periodical context, as the many forms of exchange that take place within Kipling's fiction are complemented by the magazine's articles about cultural, political, technological, and commercial modes of exchange.

A particularly illustrative example of these convergences can be found in the November 1901 issue of *McClure's*, one month after the final installment of *Kim*. Covering a wide variety of innovative technological advances, "Marvels of Modern Production" by George B. Waldron reflects on the scientific developments that have brought humans into modernity. The factory replaces the need for knitting by hand; the commercial creamery replaces the individual farmer's butter churn; the McKay sewing machine replaces the shoemaker's hammer and awl; and so forth. The last, and most interesting, example concerns the printing press. After detailing printing innovations from the fifteenth century to the present, moving from type-setting by hand to the linotype machine, Waldron's article leaps out of its historical mode to declare, in language that mirrors advertising copy, that *McClure's Magazine* is itself a "striking illustration" of society's emergence into modernity.[107] The article also links *McClure's* with improvements in transportation, appealing to magazine readers' interest in travel, locomotives, and railroads (also discussed in other articles): "Two hours after the magazine leaves the New York office it is in Philadelphia; with the stage-coach it would have taken two days. Only four days are required to deliver a copy thirty-five hundred miles away at San Francisco; before the time of the railroad it would have been twice as many months on the way."[108] As Frank Luther Mott notes, "McClure knew that America was fascinated by its own railroads—the technology of steam locomotion, the romance of railroading, the economics of railway financing and organization."[109] McClure chose to publish many stories highlighting the centrality of the railroad, both as a technological marvel and as a transportation system facilitating communication and travel—and *Kim* was among these stories McClure chose to publish. As Paffard notes, the presence of the railways "is constantly felt in the book."[110] But in *McClure's*, the railways of Kipling's fiction become part of a network of travel narratives, scientific articles, and other stories invested in the transforming power of trains.[111] The easy slippage between *Kim* and real-world reporting contributes to the sense of fiction leaping off the page and becoming reality.

To a certain extent, the new technology of train travel enables the writing of *Kim*. Many of the novel's memorable scenes and phrases would not be possible without the development of this technology.[112] In the very first chapter, Kipling describes the lama as "talking at railway speed."[113] This metaphor, an appropriation of technologically advanced transportation systems to describe the speed of language, shows how the advances of science have come to inflect literary language. Here, in Kipling's fiction, literature and technology become interlinked discourses. This interlinking was also accomplished when *McClure's* balanced scientific articles about railways with fictional stories about the same, allowing readers to obtain both the scientific facts they desired and the fantasies of railroad travel that they craved.

I want to contend that *McClure's*, imagining journalism as a field parallel to science, used its articles about new scientific inventions to position itself not only as a conveyor of the latest technological developments but also as an innovator and discoverer of literary talent. As the editors related scientific inventions to the magazine's audience, they also worked to construct an image of *McClure's* as itself an important site of discovery. When *McClure's* published a small promotional pamphlet detailing its publication history in 1901, it promised to keep its readers informed of the latest technological advances, such as "Liquid Air, X-Rays, Wireless Telegraphy, [and] Flying Machines."[114] Within this same publication, the editors claimed that the magazine had "never depended upon famous names for its fiction. [Rather, it] has been a persistent searcher for young talent."[115] *McClure's* prided itself on being the first to publish works by many now-famous authors, including Robert Louis Stevenson's "The Ebb-Tide," Sir Arthur Conan Doyle's "The Green Flag," and Anthony Hope's *Rupert of the Hentzau*. These publications, with their emphasis on adventure, create a community of works that both inflect *Kim* and reflect *McClure's* own desire to cast itself as an adventurous, innovative magazine.

Although *McClure's*, like *Cassell's*, was similarly invested in adventure stories, technological advancements, and anthropological studies, it is important to realize that the magazine edited by S.S. McClure in New York was not simply a transatlantic mirror of the magazine edited by Max Pemberton in London. Although *Kim* was published nearly simultaneously in *McClure's* and *Cassell's*, the shared historical context does not necessarily imply a shared cultural context. While both *McClure's* and *Cassell's* were patriotic magazines, *McClure's* focused on American heroes, whereas *Cassell's* focused on British ones. This division may seem self-evident and simplistic, but, as we shall see, the different national emphases also led to different views of colonial history. Although *McClure's* was on the whole a magazine with imperialist inclinations and a supporter of Theodore Roosevelt, the editors had not forgotten America's colonial history. Additionally, while *Cassell's* delivered supportive appraisals of political rulers (recall its glowing description of King Edward's reception in India), *McClure's* was more inclined to question policing forces, and it led journalism in the turn-of-the-century muckraking movement. This questioning of authority complicates interpretations of both *Kim* and its companion poem, "The White Man's Burden."

"The White Man's Burden"

Since "The White Man's Burden" is so often paired with *Kim*, as a kind of imperial philosophy underpinning Kipling's fictional narrative, I want to turn to it briefly here. The Norton critical edition of *Kim* reprints the poem as part of its "Backgrounds." But it does not mention that "The White Man's Burden" was published in the same periodical that serialized *Kim*. At the time of *Kim's* debut, the poem so often interpreted as a call to Empire had already appeared in *McClure's* (February 1899). The poem precedes, among other articles, an account of "Dewey at Manila," Captain Alfred T. Mahan's "The War on the Sea and its Lessons," and Stephen Crane's "Marines Signaling under Fire at Guantanamo." The February 1899 issue also includes photographs of "Life Masks of Great Americans" and a patriotic biography of Abraham Lincoln. The poem, then, raises the themes of military battle, adventure, and patriotism as well as manly eminence echoed in subsequent articles. I would like to suggest, however, that its placement at the forefront of these nationalistic and militaristic pieces misleadingly implies its ready endorsement of these activities while diverting attention away from the deeper, more problematic issues of colonialism that the poem communicates.

A well-traveled poem, "The White Man's Burden" is both more and less than what it pretends to be. Although it carries the subtitle "AN ADDRESS TO THE UNITED STATES" in the London *Times*, where it also appeared in February 1899, its very publication in Europe indicates that Kipling did not write his poem for America alone but actually anticipated a much broader audience. "The White Man's Burden" not only envisions the ominous future of American imperialism but also reflects self-critically on the British *Raj*. The *Times* positions the poem in the upper left-hand corner of its page; it is balanced on the right by advertisements bearing curious stylistic and visual resemblance to "The White Man's Burden." Like Kipling's verse, the ads for "Mariani Wine," "Nestle's Milk," "Nestle's Food," "Tamar Indien Grillon," and "Epps's Cocoa" map out a relatively large amount of white space to frame, and thus draw attention to, their text. Even more importantly, however, the ads repeat their slogans multiple times within this space, just as Kipling's poem begins every stanza with the message "Take up the White Man's burden." So, for example, one ad begins each line with "Epps's Cocoa," followed by various claims promoting the product: "The most nutritious," "Grateful and comforting," "For breakfast and supper," "With natural flavour only," "From the finest brands." In the cocoa ad, these messages are designed to enhance the refrain. And it would be tempting to read the claims punctuated by "Take up the White Man's Burden" in the same way, as reinforcing the refrain they modify. Here, then, we can identify an advertising distortion of Kipling's poem, a misreading enabled by consumers' familiarity with advertising copy that consistently endorses the advertised product. Readers persuaded that they must buy the oft-repeated "Epps's Cocoa," even if they did not remember the precise reasons listed underneath each mention of the product name, could also be persuaded that they must "Take up the White Man's Burden," even while forgetting the qualifications Kipling introduces after each exhortation. Because the refrain structure of Kipling's poem so closely resembles advertising structure, any apparent skepticism in the lines following "Take up the White Man's Burden" could easily be dismissed, since ads were not contradictory in this way. A misreading influenced by advertisement forces these lines into a simple, reductive imperial ascription.

Indeed, with few exceptions, Kipling's early enemies as well as his early supporters, while disagreeing on the virtues and vices of his poetry, nonetheless agreed that his writing expressed an imperialist agenda.[116] Robert Buchanan bitterly attacked the same imperial attitudes that Sir Walter Besant praised Kipling for. While observing this interpretive tendency, William Dean Howells departed from it, observing that "The White Man's Burden" "has been taken rather differently from what it was intended. To me it seems a note of warning."[117] By looking at the poem's textual environment in *McClure's* and the *Times*, we can see why it would be easy to take the poem "rather differently from what it was intended": nineteenth-century readers would be tempted to conflate the poem's meaning with that of its neighboring pieces. Readers of the patriotic *McClure's* would find it difficult to interpret the magazine's leading item in an unpatriotic way (as not supporting the American effort), and readers of the *Times* could easily read it as an advertisement for Empire directed, as the subtitle suggests, "to the United States."

But, by positioning "The White Man's Burden" alongside its sister poems, including "Recessional," we can unpack the "note of warning" which Howells detects. And we can ask how and to what extent the poem escapes its labels, subverting them even as colonial subjects subvert their imperial governments.

I will first examine how pairing the poem with "Recessional," published in the October 1897 issue of *McClure's*, elucidates its anti-imperialist moments and then discuss how the publication history of "The White Man's Burden" uncovers additional evidence for this reading.

We can detect Kipling's unease with hubristic and irreverent British imperialists in "Recessional," which he composed simultaneously with "The White Man's Burden." As David Gilmour notes, Kipling began work on both poems in June of 1897.[118] As companion poems, "Recessional" and "The White Man's Burden" express similar themes. The "show of pride"[119] in "The White Man's Burden," for example, echoes the "[w]ild tongues that have not Thee in awe" of "Recessional."[120] Kipling's famous Jubilee poem, as Gilmour observes, sounds a cautionary note:

> God [...] has made a covenant with a favoured people and, as Judge of the Nations, has granted them "dominion over palm and pine." But the modern prophet fears that his people, like the ancient Israelites, no longer hold Him "in awe." They have become boastful, arrogant and blasphemous[.][121]

The poem may deliver an even harsher critique than Gilmour suggests, for its language implies that the Empire has lost divine sanction. When Kipling writes "Beneath Whose awful Hand we hold / Dominion over palm and pine,"[122] he may not be so much implying divine sanction as he is reminding imperial lords and masters that they, too, are servants who must ultimately answer to God. Although the verse literally places "Dominion" a line beneath God's "Hand," Kipling indicates that those exercising this rule, "drunk with sight of power,"[123] have sought to rise above God with "heathen heart that puts her trust / In reeking tube and iron shard— / All valiant dust that builds on dust, / And guarding, calls not Thee to guard."[124] The "heathen heart" here mirrors the "heathen folly" of "The White Man's Burden"[125] and suggests that Kipling did not hesitate to apply the adjective to colonizers. "Recessional," then, provides a framework for interpreting "The White Man's Burden," and, while it is not necessary to place the former alongside the latter in order to perceive the anti-imperial critique of "The White Man's Burden," the Jubilee poem strengthens this reading. Although it is generally agreed that Kipling's attitudes toward Empire became negative in his later life, poems like "Recessional" and "The White Man's Burden" indicate that he was already beginning to doubt the imperial project's justice and legitimacy at the turn of the century.

A poem of imperatives, "The White Man's Burden" begins with a command which, in fact, will open every single stanza: "Take up the White Man's burden—."[126] The dash at the end of the line, however, indicates that the speaker has not finished delivering his complete command, and the subsequent text carries further injunctions:

> Send forth the best ye breed—
> Go, bind your sons to exile
>   To serve your captives' need;
> To wait, in heavy harness,
>   On fluttered folk and wild—
> Your new-caught sullen peoples,
>   Half devil and half child.[127]

Ann Parry has argued that East and West remain diametrically opposed in "The White Man's Burden,"[128] but a curious identification of "the best ye breed" with the colonial Other manifests itself in this opening stanza. Before labeling colonial subjects as "captives," Kipling casts the young colonizers in this very position by describing them as bound to exile. The young soldiers marching to the lands of Empire are, like their colonial subjects, "new-caught" under the "heavy harness" of imperialism. Certainly the stanza's final line carries religious and patronizing overtones, but Kipling does not reserve these epithets—"Half devil and half child"—for the colonial natives alone. In the final stanza, he exhorts his audience to have "done with childish days,"[129] so that the White Man, too, is figured as a child. In the third stanza, the ambiguously poised "sloth and heathen folly" suggest that the imperialists may face the same moral shortcomings as those they conquer, and "[h]alf devil" seems at times oddly more appropriate to the white man than to the Other. The same might also be said of *Kim*.

The poem's second stanza builds upon the themes of the first, and it once again resumes the refrain "Take up the White Man's burden—."[130] Instead of coupling this injunction with more commands as in the first stanza, however, Kipling softens the imperative's severity by urging "patience" and humility:

> Take up the White Man's burden—
>   In patience to abide,
> To veil the threat of terror
>   And check the show of pride;
> By open speech and simple,
>   An hundred times made plain,
> To seek another's profit
>   And work another's gain.[131]

Carrying the burden does not, as Robert Buchanan claims, necessitate a ruthless savagery in the execution of duty;[132] rather than requiring "brute courage,"[133] the lines demand a renunciation of hubris and thus a realization of humanity. In the same way that "wait" in the first stanza tempers the imperative "Go,"[134] "check" in the second stanza urges the poem's audience not to take up the White Man's burden too ostentatiously. Additionally, just as "wait" in the first stanza metamorphoses to "wait [...] On,"[135] the call to imperialism in the second stanza gradually unfolds into a call to service and sacrifice by asking the White Man to "seek another's profit" and "work another's gain." Notably, the "threat of terror" that emerges in this stanza is only veiled and not eliminated. For Kipling, the brutal realities of Empire could not be erased, but his admission of this inevitable reality does not imply his endorsement of imperialism's cruelty.

In the third stanza, the "savage wars of peace"[136] suggest the contradictions of British imperialism, while "sloth and heathen folly" undermine British rule. Critics have read savagery, heathen folly, and sloth as attributes of the colonial subject;[137] the poem, however, never makes this identification necessary, and it even suggests that these unpleasant qualities may more accurately characterize the British *Raj*. In 1899, "sloth" and "folly" appeared as lowercase words, but in the 1903 publication of the poem in *The Five Nations*, the first letter of each word is uppercase, a change preserved in the 1940 *Definitive Edition* of Kipling's verse. The new "Sloth" and "Folly" represent the only capitalization changes made to the poem, and these alterations, which occur at the same time that "God" (line 48) is pluralized, suggest that the allegorical vices have become the objects of the White Man's worship.

Whereas the fourth stanza initially writes of the "iron rule of kings,"[138] this "iron" rule becomes "tawdry" in *The Five Nations* and in the *Definitive Edition*, suggesting that there is something falsely alluring about monarchy, even if it is distinct from the "toil of serf and sweeper."[139] Rule becomes deeply problematic for Kipling, and the tension between the colonizers and the colonized is intensified in the poem's fifth stanza:

> Take up the White Man's burden,
>   And reap his old reward—
> The blame of those ye better
>   The hate of those ye guard—
> The cry of hosts ye humour
>   (Ah, slowly!) toward the light:—
> "Why brought ye us from bondage,
>   Our loved Egyptian night?"[140]

Significantly, the colonial Other receives the only lines of dialogue in the poem. Here, Kipling gives the "silent sullen peoples" he describes in the sixth stanza a voice.[141] Some argue that these lines only reinforce the strict colonial divide between white and colored, light and dark,[142] but these lines seem to be empowering the natives even while aligning them with darkness. Notably, Kipling casts the colonial subjects in the role of the Israelites, who posed the same question to Moses after their release from captivity.[143] In the simultaneously composed "Recessional," the poet casts the British colonizers in the same role. "Recessional"'s repeated line "lest we forget," as Gilmour and others have noted, derives from Deuteronomy, which cautions, "Then beware lest thou forget the Lord, which brought thee out of the land of Egypt, from the house of bondage."[144] Thus Kipling portrays both the colonizers and the colonized as in need of moral instruction and guidance.

Even if Kipling desired at times to identify himself with the white imperialists, he could never truly escape his colonial childhood, which he describes so lovingly in *Kim*. In a letter to George F. Bearns, he writes: "Like yourself, I am a colonial in that I was born in Bombay."[145] His dual identity allows him at times to adopt the voice of the colonial Other, and it is this oppressed, questioning voice which probes, criticizes, and threatens the depths of Empire in "The White Man's Burden" and *Kim*. Significantly, the Biblically derived quotation contains the only instance of the first-person plural in the poem. The colonial subjects speak in a united "cry,"[146] while the passive white audience is more spoken to than speaking. In later versions of the poem, Kipling changed "will or whisper" in line 45 to "cry or whisper."[147] By adding this similarity between colonizers and their subjects, Kipling subtly suggests that the White Man (despite the word's repeated capitalization throughout the poem) may be claiming power he does not rightfully exercise. Significantly, Kipling grants the power to judge both to colonial subjects and to imperial rulers. "The silent sullen peoples / Shall weigh your God and you," Kipling warns in the sixth stanza,[148] and in the poem's final line he asserts that his audience must anticipate the "judgment of your peers."[149] The poem itself, however, refrains from delivering a stated verdict.

The suspiciously repeated refrain—"Take up the White Man's burden"— assumes the form of an imperative, but the poem's message takes the form of a conditional, a relation of action and consequence: If you take up the White Man's burden, you can expect troubling results. Ultimately, the poem concludes in a refusal to endorse Empire. As Howells notes, "The idea that it is our destiny to assume this tremendous responsibility of governing several million savages, many thousand miles away, is not at all clear."[150] Moreover, the poem's many moves across the Atlantic as well as its appearances in multiple print media symbolize its reluctance to settle comfortably into any single position, whether physical, geographical, or ideological. Kipling refused for the entire first half of 1897 to write an ode for Victoria's Jubilee, and, I argue, "The White Man's Burden" operates similarly as a subtle form of resistance, compelling us to reevaluate the imperial product it ostensibly advertises.

The reading I have conducted is made possible by comparing multiple editions of Kipling's works—a luxury that his first readers would not have enjoyed when "The White Man's Burden" initially emerged in periodical form. The long lens of history puts us in a privileged position of evaluating Kipling's poem, as if we could watch its development with time-lapsed photography where initial readers had to be content with events unfolding in real time. From this privileged position, we can use evidence from later printings of Kipling's work, and from his complete biography, to detect his poem's cautionary message, which may not have been as readily apparent to readers in 1899. But our long historical perspective also has its disadvantages, since we are removed from the immediacy of the particular moment in which publication occurred. It is easy for us to track changes in the evolution of Kipling's poem, but it is less easy for us to absorb the sense of immediacy that Kipling's work would have generated for readers 100 years ago. It should not be surprising, therefore, if our interpretations differ from those of Kipling's initial readers, who encountered his work in both a different medium and a different historical era.

For *McClure's* readers, "The White Man's Burden" remains an imperialist poem, an interpretation that is reinforced by *McClure's* ads for Pears' Soap, as I discuss in greater detail below. I have turned to "The White Man's Burden" in part because I wish to illustrate how magazine readers of *Kim* may have remembered the Kipling of "The White Man's Burden" as a particularly imperialist author (regardless of the more subversive readings later critical perspectives make possible). But, in the remaining sections, I wish to show how this association of Kipling with imperialism becomes more complicated with *Kim*. Even *McClure's* readers who interpreted "The White Man's Burden" as a wholehearted endorsement of Empire would find it difficult to read *Kim* in the same way. As the imperialist, Victorian era gave way to the more subversive Modernist movement, *McClure's* also became more suspicious and critical of authority. This turn-of-the-century shift toward muckraking, or the "literature of exposure," creates a reading atmosphere that in turn makes *Kim*'s association with imperial authority much more tenuous. Below, I will ask to what extent we can consider Kipling's work part of this "literature of exposure."

Critiquing Authority in *McClure's*

In spite of its patriotism, *McClure's* also launched articles calling for social reform and critiquing government officials. As Frank Luther Mott notes, *McClure's* quickly became "the leader of the muckraking magazines."[151] Muckraking was used as a journalistic tool aimed toward destabilizing authority and achieving social reform. Whereas the London-based *Cassell's* exhibited great trust in British society and the country's monarchical leaders, the New York-based *McClure's* launched a much harsher critique of US society and America's governing officials. In *Cassell's*, British imperialism was strongly promoted; in *McClure's*, however, editorial opinion about capitalism and imperialism was much less cohesive. Although *McClure's* gained many readers through its famous portrait series of historical figures, it also sought to reshape historical institutions of society. As Harold Wilson notes,

> McClure and his staff were very conscious of participating in a political and economic movement intent upon reshaping many of the country's institutions. Their close ties first with Roosevelt, then with La Follette and Wilson, evidence this. [...] Criticism of a capitalistic society can, and did, emanate from a capitalistic press.[152]

This evidence from *McClure's* shows that Modernism's little magazines, which I examine in later chapters, were not the only periodicals launching critiques of capitalism.

The muckraking articles, like *Kim*, appeal to readers' desire for investigative adventure. They also build upon themes of crime and spying that Kipling's fiction employs. Kim's quest in Kipling's novel has its corollary in *McClure's* investigative reporting. As Kim was running missions for the Great Game in Kipling's fiction, Josiah Flynt was investigating crime in prominent US cities, consorting "for months together on equal terms with outcasts and criminals" and reporting their "view of various American city governments."[153] Flynt's series, "In the World of Graft," not only featured detectives and informants with criminal histories—thereby appealing to the thrills of covert missions that also captivated readers of *Kim*—but also unveiled corruption in the police force.

The first article of the "World of Graft" series was published in February 1901, when chapters III and IV of *Kim* were being serialized. Kim has already delivered the secret service message coded as a white stallion's pedigree, and he is now on the Grand Trunk Road with the lama. On the Road, they witness an exchange between a constable and a soldier:

"Who bears arms against the law?" a constable called out laughingly, as he caught sight of the soldier's sword. "Are not the police enough to destroy evil-doers?"

"It was because of the police I brought it," was the answer.[154]

This exchange between these two men, which evolves into a coded discussion about British secret service activities, gains even greater significance when read alongside Flynt's article in the same issue. Flynt's column also argues that the police are insufficient to monitor and control evil-doers; in fact, they are part of the problem of "graft," which Flynt defines as "a generic slang term for all kinds of theft and illegal practices."[155] A "grafter" (one who practices graft) may be a lower-class criminal, but he could also be "a political 'boss,' a mayor, a chief of police, a warden of a penitentiary, a municipal contractor, a member of the town council, a representative in the legislature, [or] a judge in the courts," known in the "Upper World" "only in his official capacity."[156] In other words, many grafters, or corrupt city officials, may be circulating and operating in the city without the public's knowledge. By indicting so many professions, Flynt implies that no governing or policing authority can be trusted. The soldier's comments in *Kim* thus come to echo the remarks made in Flynt's article. When asked to put their "finger on the weak spot in a city's municipal defense," Flynt's inside sources "invariably direct [him] to the authorities at the police headquarters."[157] Here, both Flynt and Kipling reinforce the idea that "corrupt police forces"[158] threaten to destabilize systems of law and protection. In Flynt's American city, as in Kipling's India, the police are a force citizens must protect themselves against.

In subsequent issues of *McClure's*, the relationship between Flynt's "World of Graft" series and Kipling's fiction strengthens. As the editors praise Flynt's groundbreaking investigative reporting, they also praise Kipling's groundbreaking literary accomplishments. Notably, Flynt's and Kipling's charming protagonists are praised for similar qualities. Spatial proximity also brings Flynt's and Kipling's work together, as the editors place their evaluation of both Flynt and Kipling on the same leaf of paper. In the two-page "Editorial Notes" at the end of the March 1901 number, *McClure's* devoted two of its three subsections to *Kim* and "In the World of Graft." The first subsection describes the opening installment of *Kim* in glowing terms. Summarizing letters they have received from subscribers, the editors describe how readers have been intrigued by Kim's secret activities and by his chameleon-like abilities:

We hear of "Kim" from all sorts and conditions of men, women, and children. [...] Some boy is agog over the mysteries of the secret service, and envious of Kim's ideal existence amid disguises, hidden messages, and rich adventures. One person says, "It is the next thing to traveling through India as a native, with command of the dialects and all the hidden things open to you[.]"[159]

Besides giving us valuable insights into the range of readers' responses to *Kim*, this paragraph also anticipates the editors' descriptions of Flynt on the verso of the same leaf. Like Kim, Flynt is also able to harness skills of shrewdness, adaptability, and versatility. Whereas Flynt is a "gentleman" who "consort[s] for months together on equal terms with outcasts and criminals,"[160] Kim is a sahib who associates freely with natives. Despite their different backgrounds (Flynt is from a respectable social class, but Kim is poor), both Flynt and Kim demonstrate an exceptional ability to range chameleon-like on various rungs of the social ladder.

Both are also able to infiltrate dangerous territories with ease, and both are remarkably able to assume new roles and disguises as they explore human relations with intensity and delight. As *McClure's* notes, "Only a beautiful feeling of fellowship with all humanity, a genuine sentiment of friendliness and a genuine absence of moral and social snobbery could put him *en rapport* with such comrades; and these traits alone would not go far without tact, shrewdness, [and] a dramatic talent for the assumption of a part."[161] These sentences refer to Flynt, but they could easily describe Kim as well. Both demonstrate exceptional interest in humanity, and exceptional talent, as they adopt various poses and identities. These were risky poses, however, and Flynt's secret investigations eventually led him into trouble. In June 1901, *McClure's* informed readers that Flynt had been "hunted" and threatened by the police because he "knew too much."[162] Similarly, Kim (who fantasizes that he may one day be great enough to have a price upon his head and be hunted like Mahbub Ali) must prevent authorities from suspecting that he knows too much. When Mahbub Ali questions him about the pedigree of the white stallion, Kim conceals his knowledge of the pedigree's significance;[163] when Creighton asks Kim to bring a cheroot-case to his house, Kim quickly asks, "Where is the house?" so that he does not appear to know too much.[164] Thus secrecy is essential to the missions of both Flynt and Kim.

For Flynt, however, disclosing secret knowledge to the public—indeed, to hundreds of thousands of readers—is crucial to the success of *McClure's* mission of social reform, not to mention sales. As the editors note in their June 1901 comments, Flynt's column "tells plainly and fully what he knows, and the telling makes a volume not only of unflagging interest, but also constitutes an exposure such as cannot but open the eyes of the great American cities to the perils of the alliance which to-day governs most of them and is daily extending its rule."[165]

In terms of disclosing secret activities to a large magazine audience, the more appropriate analogy may be between Flynt and Kipling; for while Kim delivers secret messages to one intended recipient, Kipling in turn delivers his message (and, hence, Kim's messages with it) to the same 350,000 magazine readers Flynt was targeting. If we read *Kim* alongside "In the World of Graft," we may be more inclined to register Kipling's message as one far more skeptical about imperialism and governing authorities than is generally assumed. Neither "In the World of Graft" nor *Kim* directly denounces imperialism, but both raise troubling questions about authority and societal structures of control.

Flynt's critique of ruling authorities was also reflected in historical articles. In July 1901, when *McClure's* published "The Story of the Declaration of Independence" by Ida M. Tarbell, American readers were reminded that their nation, like the India of Kipling's *Kim*, had once suffered under British colonial rule. The July 1901 article was published in celebration of America's 125th anniversary, and the editors displayed great pride in the research that informed Tarbell's article. Portraits of the signers of the Declaration of Independence lined the top of every page in this lengthy thirteen-page sketch. An editorial footnote explains, "This series of portraits of the signers of the Declaration of Independence is, we believe, the most complete ever published."[166] To be sure, Tarbell's narrative is mostly factual, and it does not read as a rallying cry, but it raises serious questions about colonial rule, and, specifically, about British colonial rule. These questions carry implications for *Kim*, since, if *Kim* is truly an imperialist narrative as so many critics claim, then *McClure's* would be asking readers to at once accept and reject British rule within the same issue. At the very least, readers of *McClure's* are prompted to consider the lama's search as a serious, and preferable, alternative to the Great Game. In the previous (June 1901) issue, Kim is finally liberated from St. Xavier's, the training ground for the Great Game; he returns to the lama, and they both discuss how they will find the River together. Shortly after Kim casts off the bonds of St. Xavier's, America casts off the bonds of Britain.[167]

Tarbell's narrative aims more to document history than to launch an argument, but at the same time her article is not very sympathetic to the British rulers. References to the colonists' "carrying on of a vigorous war against a country to which it still officially acknowledged allegiance"[168] do little to ease anxieties about supposedly loyal colonial subjects, whatever the century. Similarly, Tarbell's next claim—"It was more likely that entire separation from the mother country was imminent"[169]—does not bode well for the future of British imperialism. Tarbell also paints an unflattering picture of England when she quotes from Thomas Jefferson's memoirs. Collectively, these and other elements of Tarbell's article reveal the injustices of British colonial rule while also censuring loyal subjects who are all too reluctant to rebel. Finally, although most of Tarbell's article is concerned with history, the last paragraph brings readers from 1776 into the present, as Tarbell records the enduring importance of the Declaration of Independence. "As the years went on," Tarbell writes, "the veneration of the people for the Declaration of Independence grew."[170] As crowds flocked to see and touch the physical document, however, "great harm" came to the original.[171] Tarbell records how, over the years, signatures began to fade from the Declaration as its condition deteriorated. In 1894, however, the State Department finally took action to restore the Declaration. Eventually, after copies were made, the original was placed in a fireproof safe. Tarbell concludes her article by urging that the Declaration continue to be preserved, both as a physical and as an intellectual work: "The document itself is thus finally protected. The great truths for which it stands are not so easily preserved."[172] Her parting words further emphasize the need to spread the spirit of independence: "The eternal watchfulness of those who love liberty for its own sake is all that will secure the spirit of the Declaration of Independence. The exercise of this vigilance is the supreme and enduring concern of the nation."[173] Although the article's subject is American independence, it is hard to dismiss the implied idea that other colonies, too, might have the right to freedom from colonial rule. Placed alongside this article, Kipling's novel reads very differently. In its serialized context, the question of *Kim*'s relation to Empire becomes much more complicated and vexed.

Missing Ads: A Lost Imperial Context

If libraries' periodical departments consistently preserved the advertisements in *McClure's*, the relation between Kipling and Empire may have acquired further illuminating dimensions. But, as with bound periodical volumes in so many other libraries, the bound copies of *McClure's* that I initially consulted had eliminated the advertising pages. And, if the evidence of other scholars can be trusted, those advertising pages would have consumed half the pages in the magazine. As Frank Luther Mott notes,

> In 1898 the magazine was printing an average of 100 pages of advertising every month, and five years later the average was nearly 150, at $375 a page, and an occasional number would carry close to 200 pages of advertising. And this was in a magazine with 112 pages of text [...]. *Printer's Ink* declared that, in the

years 1895–1899, *McClure's* "carried the greatest quantity of advertising in any magazine in the world."[174]

These large numbers of advertising pages, deleted as libraries rebound periodicals, represent a tremendous loss for scholarship. Rather than discuss original issues, which are scattered across various archives,[175] for the purposes of this chapter I have instead worked from the bound volumes of *McClure's* to represent how they limit our vision.

But, what, precisely, are we missing? The bound copies obviously cannot provide the answer, but a few hints are given in other published sources. As Richard Ohmann explains in *Selling Culture*, advertisements for soap often linked personal hygiene with racial purity, and some soap ads even drew explicit links between their product and imperialism. Ohmann reprints an advertisement for Pears' Soap that occurred in the October 1899 issue of *McClure's*, just eight months after the magazine's publication of "The White Man's Burden" and fourteen months before the first installment of *Kim*. The ad portrays a distinguished man in a white, military-style uniform washing his hands in a pristine bathroom sink. Below this illustration, the text explains, "The first step toward lightening The White Man's Burden is through teaching the virtues of cleanliness. Pears' Soap is a potent factor in brightening the dark corners of the earth as civilization advances, while amongst the cultured of all nations it holds the highest place—it is the ideal toilet soap."[176] With its celebration of the white man, the Pears' Soap ad in *McClure's* serves the same function as Millar's art in *Cassell's*. The ad recalls Millar's artistic juxtaposition of superior white man to inferior colonial. Here again we see strategic use of proportion, bodily posture, and shading in the focus on the large white man at the center, who stands erect while diminutive natives crouch in the background (in the soap ad, a small native is shown kneeling outside the oval frame occupied by the principal white man, while *another* white man stands over him and offers him a bar of soap).

This ad, which prominently sets "The White Man's Burden" in large type on a line by itself, obviously recalls Kipling's poem, which readers would have been familiar with since its February 1899 publication in *McClure's*. The ad reads "The White Man's Burden" as a call to Empire, insisting that Pears' Soap is essential to civilization's spread to "the dark corners of the earth." Here, we receive not only an advertisement for Pears' Soap but also an interpretation of Kipling's work. The ad affirms that "The White Man's Burden" involves "teaching," and hence the instructive aspects both of Kipling's poem and of the nation's civilizing mission are emphasized. Presumably, natives are being instructed here in the "virtues of cleanliness," but the white magazine readers are also being instructed in these same virtues, as the ad commands them to buy Pears' Soap. Hence the ad, while juxtaposing light to dark and claiming superiority of whiteness, actually casts white readers as people who, like their darker-skinned counterparts, need to be reminded of civilization's crucial elements. In this way the ad repeats the movements of Kipling's poem, which asserts that American colonizers, like their native subjects, are in need of instruction.

This need for instruction was, curiously, reinforced in the pages of *McClure's* as *Kim* was being serialized. In June 1901, in the section labeled "Notable Books and Authors," *McClure's* reviewed *The Children of the Nations*, a handbook to imperialism written by Mr. Poultney Bigelow and addressed to the people of the United States.[177] The review begins by acknowledging America's need for this kind of instruction:

> In establishing a policy for governing our dependencies, we shall, if we are wise, be guided by the experience of nations that have wrestled for generations with such problems.
>
> The question of colonial government has in the past been one of only theatrical interest to us—it has now become one of absorbing and vital importance, and the intelligent citizen finds himself met by questions he has never been trained to consider.[178]

This acknowledgment of the challenging nature of imperialism is developed in the next paragraph, when the review informs readers that Bigelow's book is subtitled "A Study of Colonization and Its Problems."[179] While the article dismisses neither colonialism nor the value of imperial training, it also refrains from the strong pro-imperialist statements made by *Cassell's*. For *McClure's*, colonialism was a part of history and a very important part of America's political present. But it was also a vexing and problematic practice.

In the context of this book review, it is tempting to say that *Kim* could have been seen as the fictional counterpart to *The Children of the Nations*, since both Kipling's fiction and Bigelow's historical work document imperialism and teach readers how systems of colonial control operate. But *McClure's* was more inclined to see Kipling's fiction as an anthropological study than as a colonial guide. (These aims, of course, are not mutually exclusive, but one is given more weight than the other.) In the "Editorial Notes" for December 1900, when the first installment of *Kim* appeared, *McClure's* included a blurb for "Mr. Kipling's New Serial." Like *Cassell's*, *McClure's* would often use its columns as another form of advertising. The blurb is at once an advertisement for *Kim* and for the magazine, even though it masquerades as an editorial note: "Mr. Kipling stands to-day as the most forceful genius in English literature. His new story of life in India, 'Kim,' begins serial publication in this issue. It is the latest, longest, and most important work from his pen."[180] The note moves quickly from these laudatory superlatives to a more precise description of the book's subject and value:

> Sufficeth it to say here that, aside from the narrative itself, the story is rich in its illumination of the wondrous Orient. It is kaleidoscopic in its marvelous color, bringing for the first time to the Western world a realization of the life, the manners, the customs, and the philosophy of a nation that was old when Rome was a cluster of unpeopled hills.[181]

From this description alone, *Kim* appears to be as much a work of anthropology as it is a work of fiction.

This blurb also ends on a somewhat odd point for a periodical that published "The White Man's Burden" and pro-imperialist Pears' Soap ads. Although Pears' Soap uses Kipling's poem to assert the supremacy of the white race, the editorial note here uses Kipling's fiction to assert that Oriental history has deeper roots than Western history: the Oriental nations were already established when uncivilized Rome "was a cluster of unpeopled hills." *McClure's* could be inconsistent in its statements about Empire, Western civilization, and nationalism.

But what does become clear is the way *McClure's* packaged *Kim* as an anthropological work—that is to say, a novel that was less about the white man's superiority than about the Oriental's fascinating way of life. Significantly, *McClure's* contains no Millar illustrations to affirm Anglo-Saxon identity. Instead, readers only encounter the illustrations of Weeks and Lockwood Kipling, with their emphasis on Orientals. This choice of visual emphasis coincides with *McClure's* editorial view of *Kim* as a fascinating study of Indian life:

> The power of gallant courage, the mystery of the East, the fascination of strange, strong personalities, the charm of childhood, an all-pervading humor, delight in the wide spectacle of life—these are the elements of which Mr. Kipling has compounded his great stories; but not until "Kim" has he ever united all phases of his genius in one work, including high qualities hitherto reached us only through poetry.[182]

Once again, these editorial notes function as a form of advertisement. Phrases such as "the mystery of the East" appeal to exoticism and register the book's popular pulse, while phrases such as "the fascination of strange, strong personalities" curiously echo the anthropological aspirations of Colonel Creighton, the figure of the ethnologist in Kipling's novel. Creighton, as Kipling writes, has "bombarded" the Royal Society with "monographs on strange Asiatic cults and unknown customs."[183] Like *McClure's* and *Cassell's*, he is invested in the "strange" practices of foreign cultures.

As Said notes, "Of all the modern social sciences, anthropology is the one historically most closely tied to colonialism, since it was often the case that anthropologists and ethnologists advised colonial rulers on the manners and mores of the native people."[184] His late twentieth-century observation might well have been made by *Kim*'s early twentieth-century periodical readers, who could flip the pages of *McClure's* or *Cassell's* and easily arrive at articles about "Hairdressing in Many Lands" (*Cassell's*, November 1901) or "Elephant Hunting in Africa" (*McClure's*, October 1901). Said is inclined to view Creighton the ethnologist as an extremely important figure in Kipling's novel, and the character gains even further importance when we consider how the many anthropological articles surrounding *Kim* in its periodical context could well have been written by men like Creighton. Colonel Creighton, then, becomes a kind of self-reflective figure, insofar as he is a writer of anthropological articles who surfaces as a character in an anthropologically sensitive magazine. In this way, Kipling's fiction indirectly comments on the articles surrounding it.

Conclusion

In the first chapter on James, we saw how the fiction of a writer vehemently opposed to expansionist politics found itself embedded in a periodical that puts James's work in unanticipated, strong dialogue with imperialism. An author opposed to imperialism enters into an unsuspecting serial relationship with it. In this chapter, I have documented the reverse movement, showing how the fiction of Kipling, an author so often associated with jingoism and imperialism, is placed in magazines that go beyond making this alignment to modify and question the extent of *Kim*'s imperialism. In *McClure's*, the notion of benevolent imperialism is moderated by articles devoted to exposing institutional corruption and to praising the American colonies' rebellion from British rule. In *Cassell's*, however, *Kim* is, at least on the surface, closely tied to the magazine's promotion of the British Empire. Nevertheless, divergent illustrations by three distinct artists subtly undermine the stability of the magazine's stated aims. For the contemplative reader, these widely varying artistic styles suggest that there may be greater complexities to the imperial project, perhaps even unspoken contradictions.

These considerations can be tracked across several periodical numbers, or by taking an in-depth look at one issue in particular. Conducting an experiment similar to Margot Norris's speculations about virgin readers of *Ulysses*, we can imagine a *fin-de-siècle* reader picking up a copy of, say, the October 1901 issue of *McClure's* and reading it for an hour one autumn evening. For this experiment, I have posited an adult male reader with children at home. The first item in the magazine, a twelve-page illustrated article on J. Pierpont Morgan, would be hard to miss. Its first page not only introduces an economic theme, as Morgan the businessman surfaces as the embodiment of wealth, but also raises the issue of international tensions: the article asserts that Morgan controlled a yearly income "nearly as great as that of imperial Germany" and that his purchase of an English steamship company "was interpreted at first as a blow to England's supremacy on the seas."[185] The next page boldly claims, "Certain it is that the death to-day of Mr. Morgan would disturb more capital and shake more settled business institutions than the death of almost any sovereign in Europe"[186]—and this was just a few months after Queen Victoria's passing. Imagine that our *fin-de-siècle* reader now skims the remainder of this patriotic biographical sketch, making note of its rich illustrations, particularly the map showing all the major US railroads in which Morgan was interested. If the reader had purchased previous issues of *McClure's*, he would recall the parallel centrality of railroads to India and Kipling's fiction. The magazine thus serves to remind customers of very particular corollaries between fiction and reality. Far from being a mere fictional device to transport characters from one point to another, the railroad becomes an object of economic scrutiny, an index of individual purchasing power as well as international power relations, an item of immediate and pressing business concern.

These business items, however, were balanced by more light-hearted fiction, which was in turn balanced by poetry that addressed sobering themes. Coming to the end of the Morgan article, our reader would turn to "The Other Man," a fictional story by Sara Cone Bryant consisting mostly of dialogue. At the conclusion of this romantic story, a rather amusing confessional, the reader would be forced to shift gears abruptly, for the next item would transport him to the battlefield of Kipling's poem "M.I." (glossed for readers as "Mounted Infantry"). As the poem's first-person speaker describes the brutal transformations that take place during warfare, our *fin-de-siècle* reader might well begin to question Kipling's supposed jingoism. Although Clara Morris's "Staging 'Miss Mutton'" (a feature article), with its focus on the entertainment industry, might put him in a lighter mood, "The King's Visit" (historical fiction) by Robert Barr would return our reader to more serious thoughts of battle and international conflict. "The Tammany Commandment" by Josiah Flynt would remind our reader of authorities' abuse of power, further underscoring the need to expose government injustices, also a subject of Kipling's poem. Turning to the next item, a short story about Nebraska pioneers and their encounters with Indigenous Americans, our reader would be pulled along on the volcanic series of battles that erupt every few pages in this issue of *McClure's*. Significantly, the pioneer adventure, like Kipling's poem, is related in the first-person, thus strengthening the connection between the two magazine items.

Perhaps our reader would decide to skip the next item, a didactic story about young schoolgirls. This fictional piece may initially seem utterly unrelated to the surrounding artifacts, but, within the framework of the magazine's guided heterogeneity, this schoolgirl story does fit the magazine's tendency to instruct its subscribers in the value of virtue, whether exercised in the classroom, business world, or battlefield. Skipping this schoolgirl fiction, then—for, in an hour's time, our reader cannot devote full attention to all stories, and he may wish to save the didactic tale for an evening when he can read it aloud to his daughter—our reader would come to the last installment of *Kim*. Suppose our reader has been eagerly following Kim's adventures for the past ten months, and he is anxious to see whether Kim will successfully deliver the documents stolen from the Russians. He now settles more comfortably into his chair, wondering how this last adventure will end—wondering, too, perhaps, whether Kim will choose to join the lama or continue with his secret service missions. Here—unlike the modern book reader—he would encounter Lockwood Kipling's final illustration, a portrayal of the lama sitting peacefully in front of a wheel, with Kim at his feet. The caption below the image—printed ten pages before the novel's actual concluding sentence—reads, "He crossed his hands on his lap and smiled, as a man who has won salvation for himself and his beloved."[187] Encountering this same sentence some fifteen minutes later, he would reflect back on Lockwood Kipling's illustration, and he might peer slightly more closely at the image itself, to see the words the artist had carved into it: "The end of the search" (lower left corner). No other illustration is printed after this one, suggesting that this picture of the lama and his *chela* delivers a final visual verdict: Kim will remain with his holy one. And, in *McClure's*, this conclusion to the visual narrative is tied strictly to the text's own conclusion by way of the caption borrowed from the novel's final sentence. That the illustration is by Kipling's own father seems further to validate this reading of Kim as a disciple who ultimately turns away from the Great Game. At the very least, the question of Kim's loyalty to the British imperialists has been deeply undermined by the arrangement of illustrations. This, then, is the final image a *fin-de-siècle* periodical reader would have of *Kim*.[188]

Thus, our *fin-de-siècle* reader has completed a novel influenced by illustrations and its ties to surrounding material. The magazine's common threads not only link different artifacts enclosed within a single issue, but also link different issues of the magazine together, helping to form the identity of *McClure's* through reinforced points of continuity. But because magazine readers could trace many different threads—crime, war, adventure, romance, business, transportation, anthropology, imperialism, and so forth—the magazine's identity also emerged from strategic points of divergence. Furthermore, readers looking for their preferred themes might group periodical artifacts differently, sometimes cutting across genres as they did so. Those interested in transportation might connect *Kim* with scientific articles about steam engines and business articles about railroad stocks. Those with an interest in war might place *Kim* alongside fictional stories about frontier battles and Ida Tarbell's patriotic sketches of American Revolutionary heroes. And those looking for stories about childhood might group *Kim* with the very story our hypothetical *fin-de-siècle* reader skipped. But, because of Kipling's popularity and the advertising campaigns, readers would have been encouraged to consider *Kim* as a focal point in the midst of this guided heterogeneity of content.

A similar argument could be made for *Cassell's*, or, on a more general level, for the many other popular periodicals in circulation at the time: Serialized works published in these magazines were printed alongside diverse artifacts that guided readers through a range of emotions and intellectual considerations, forming a wide web of heterogeneous material that was nevertheless intricately woven together by an overseeing editor. Even as magazines set themselves up in guiding roles, however, they could not always anticipate the precise paths readers would follow on this web. Surrounding artifacts may have affected individual periodical readers differently, but in any case their experience would be substantially different from our typical twenty-first-century study of literary works in book form.

In closing I would like to suggest briefly how the issues raised by *Kim's* serialization in mass-market periodicals are echoed in Modernist little magazines. As we have seen, both *McClure's* and *Cassell's* devoted significant space in their periodicals to the promotion of Kipling's work. Similarly, both the *Egoist* and the *Little Review* embarked on quite striking advertising campaigns for James Joyce's work, using a combination of visual and print matter to promote art in ways that trouble the divide between the "counter-public sphere" and the commercial press to which it was ostensibly opposed. The divide between high art and popular culture is further troubled by an October 1901 advertisement for *Cassell's Standard Library*, in which *Cassell's* promotes works by George Eliot, Walter Scott, Jane Austen, Charlotte Brontë, and other canonical authors, declaring, "Great interest is evinced by the public at the present day in any effort to popularise by means of new and attractive forms of production the works of great writers; and it is therefore believed that the choice manner in which these books are issued will obtain for them a wide circulation."[189] Here, in the pages of *Cassell's*, we have a supposedly popular monthly expressing interest in "great writers" who practice high art, which suggests that the readers of popular periodicals could also enjoy complex novels of a sophisticated literary nature. In order for the general public to read these complex novels, however, they must (according to *Cassell's*) be packaged in "new and attractive forms." The audience a literary work reaches, *Cassell's* implies, depends not only upon that work's content and style, but also upon the way in which that work is marketed.

As *Cassell's* worked to increase the circulation of sophisticated eighteenth- and nineteenth-century authors, it demonstrated that a popular periodical could also attract, perhaps even form, highbrow readers. While *Cassell's* was undoubtedly more popular in its content and more commercial in its aims than a little magazine like the *Egoist* or the *Little Review*, it is nevertheless significant that *Cassell's*—like *Collier's* and *McClure's*—made efforts to accommodate and promote highbrow artists within its pages. Thus, when we introduce nuances and challenges to Andreas Huyssen's Great Divide, it is important that we look not only to little magazines in order to show how they engaged with commercial culture, but also to popular periodicals in order to show how they engaged with high art.

Like popular periodicals, Modernism's little magazines issued self-promotional advertisements as they worked to increase circulation numbers. For instance, the *Egoist* deployed Joyce's work as an advertising device to persuade readers to purchase back issues containing installments of *A Portrait of the Artist as a Young Man*. When *A Portrait* appeared in book form, the *Egoist* promoted the novel through advertisements that significantly culled quotations from reviews in mass-market periodicals. Similarly, when the *Little Review* advertised *A Portrait*, *Exiles*, *Dubliners*, and *Ulysses*, it drew upon quotations from the commercial press. These ads suggest that even as the little magazines constructed their own counter-public sphere and articulated anti-commercial editorial policies, they still relied upon the lessons and strategies practiced by the mass-market press.

Just as *Cassell's* and *McClure's* used *Kim* to promote the sales of magazine issues, so the *Little Review* and the *Egoist* appropriated Joyce's work for purposes that were commercial as well as artistic. These intersections suggest that

Modernism and commercial culture operate in more engaged ways than we generally assume. In order to evaluate properly the emergence and reception of Modernism, I argue, it is necessary to return to a serious study of periodicals—not only the little magazines with which Modernism is so closely associated, but also the mass-market periodicals that reviewed and published Modernist (and proto-Modernist) works while also providing advertisement and distribution models so central to Modernism's spread across national and international borders.

Notes

1   "Editorial Notes," *McClure's*, December 1900, 191.
2   Lord Birkenhead, *Rudyard Kipling* (New York: Random House, 1978), 307.
3   Advertisement for *Kim*, *Cassell's*, May 1901, 716.
4   J.I.M. Stewart, *Rudyard Kipling* (New York: Dodd, Mead, 1966), 122.
5   James Landers, "Island Empire: Discourse on U.S. Imperialism in *Century, Cosmopolitan, McClure's*—1893–1900," *American Journalism* 23, no. 1 (Winter 2006): 95.
6   Angus Wilson, *The Strange Ride of Rudyard Kipling: His Life and Works* (London: Secker and Warburg, 1977), 190.
7   Harry Ricketts, *The Unforgiving Minute: A Life of Rudyard Kipling* (London: Chatto and Windus, 1999), 225.
8   Charles Carrington, *Rudyard Kipling: His Life and Work* (London: Macmillan, 1955), 286.
9   Carrington, *Rudyard Kipling*, 362.
10 Andrew Lycett, *Rudyard Kipling* (London: Weidenfeld & Nicolson, 1999), 332.
11 Ricketts, *The Unforgiving Minute*, 271.
12 "Editorial Notes," *McClure's*, March 1901, 479.
13 Edward W. Said, *Culture and Imperialism* (New York: Vintage Books, 1993), 135.
14 Advertisement for *Kim*, *Cassell's*, December 1900, 148.
15 Sally Ledger and Roger Luckhurst, eds., *The Fin de Siècle: A Reader in Cultural History, c. 1880–1900* (Oxford: Oxford University Press, 2000), 133.
16 "In the Arena," *Cassell's*, December 1900, 149.
17 Said, *Culture and Imperialism*, 155.
18 "The Christmas Present" occurred in the *Cassell's* issue of December 1900.
19 Kipling, *Kim* (London: Penguin, 1989), 49; Kipling, *Kim*, *Cassell's*, January 1901, 163.
20 Kipling, *Kim* (London: Penguin, 1989), 51; Kipling, *Kim*, *Cassell's*, January 1901, 164. The serial version does not contain a comma after "speak."
21 Kipling, *Kim* (London: Penguin, 1989), 49; Kipling, *Kim*, *Cassell's*, January 1901, 163.

22 Kipling, *Kim* (London: Penguin, 1989), 206; Kipling, *Kim, Cassell's*, July 1901, 115.
23 "The King's Travels," *Cassell's*, July 1901, 151.
24 Kipling, *Kim* (London: Penguin, 1989), 206; Kipling, *Kim, Cassell's*, July 1901, 115.
25 "Something New," *Cassell's*, January 1901, 270–1.
26 Kipling, *Kim* (London: Penguin, 1989), 59; Kipling, *Kim, Cassell's*, January 1901, 169. The serial version hyphenates "today" (as "to-day").
27 Marie A. Belloc, "Living Women Sovereigns," *Cassell's*, January 1901, 259.
28 Kipling, *Kim* (London: Penguin, 1989), 51–2; Kipling, *Kim, Cassell's*, January 1901, 164.
29 Kipling, *Kim* (London: Penguin, 1989), 49; Kipling, *Kim, Cassell's*, January 1901, 163.
30 Said, *Culture and Imperialism*, 134.
31 Kipling, *Kim* (London: Penguin, 1989), 49; Kipling, *Kim, Cassell's*, January 1901, 163.
32 Kipling, *Kim* (London: Penguin, 1989), 209; Kipling, *Kim, Cassell's*, July 1901, 116.
33 "The King's Travels," 147.
34 Kipling, *Kim* (London: Penguin, 1989), 338; Kipling, *Kim, Cassell's*, November 1901, 576.
35 "The King's Travels," 147–8.
36 "The King's Travels," 151.
37 "The King's Travels," 151.
38 Kipling, *Kim* (London: Penguin, 1989), 206; Kipling, *Kim, Cassell's*, June 1901, 17.
39 Kipling, *Kim* (London: Penguin, 1989), 234; Kipling, *Kim, Cassell's*, August 1901, 228.
40 Kipling, *The Letters of Rudyard Kipling: 1890–1900*, ed. Thomas Pinney (London: Macmillan, 1990), 2:347.
41 E. Spender, "From Sunset to Sunrise," *Cassell's*, September 1901, 424.
42 Kipling, *Kim* (London: Penguin, 1989), 215; Kipling, *Kim, Cassell's*, June 1901, 120.
43 Spender, "From Sunset to Sunrise," 424.
44 Advertisement for Cerebos Salt, *Cassell's*, December 1900, xix.
45 Charles Austin Bates, *Short Talks on Advertising* (New York: Press of Charles Austin Bates, 1898), 56. Interestingly, this 1898 advertising guide mentions Kipling just a few pages later, when it concludes the chapter with "'But that's another story,' as Mr. Kipling says" (61). On the facing page (60), the guide prints an illustration of Kipling smoking a cigar in a beach chair. Here Kipling, an immensely popular author with great success in commercial magazines, becomes an iconic figure in an advertising guide designed to help businessmen achieve similar success by advertising in mass-market periodicals. "[A]lways keep your ad in your best papers, big enough to do you justice," Bates advises (57).
46 Kipling, *Kim* (London: Penguin, 1989), 305; Kipling, *Kim, Cassell's*, October 1901, 460.
47 Kipling, *Kim* (London: Penguin, 1989), 304; Kipling, *Kim, Cassell's*, October 1901, 460.
48 Advertisement for Bovril, *Cassell's*, March 1902, xii–xiii.

49 Advertisement for Bovril, xiii.
50 Advertisement for Bovril, xiii.
51 Advertisement for Bovril, xiii.
52 Advertisement for Bovril, xiii.
53 Announcement, *Cassell's*, December 1900, 148.
54 Announcement, *Cassell's*, December 1900, 148.
55 Announcement, *Cassell's*, December 1900, 148.
56 Compare *Kim* (London: Penguin, 1989), 211, when the Babu explains how knowledge can be gained from reading *King Lear, Julius Caesar*, and other literary works.
57 "In the Arena," *Cassell's*, December 1900, 149.
58 "In the Arena," 149.
59 "In the Arena," 149.
60 "In the Arena," 149.
61 "Something New," *Cassell's*, December 1900, 158.
62 James Joyce, *Ulysses*, ed. Hans Walter Gabler (New York: Random House, 1986), 13.1123.
63 "Something New," *Cassell's*, March 1901, 493.
64 "The New Volume of *Cassell's Magazine*," *Cassell's*, May 1901, 716.
65 Kipling, *Kim* (London: Penguin, 1989), 158; Kipling, *Kim*, *Cassell's*, May 1901, 614.
66 "The New Volume of *Cassell's Magazine*," 716.
67 "Something New," *Cassell's*, December 1900, 158.
68 Rita Felski, *The Gender of Modernity* (Cambridge: Harvard University Press, 1995), 14.
69 Pat Brooklyn, "The Greatest in the World," *Cassell's*, June 1901, 18.
70 Brooklyn, "The Greatest in the World," 23.
71 Brooklyn, "The Greatest in the World," 25.
72 Brooklyn, "The Greatest in the World," 25.
73 Brooklyn, "The Greatest in the World," 24.
74 Kipling, *Kim* (London: Penguin, 1989), 211; Kipling, *Kim*, *Cassell's*, July 1901, 118.
75 "Something New," *Cassell's*, February 1901, 382.
76 "Something New," *Cassell's*, February 1901, 382.
77 Advertisement for Swan, *Cassell's*, January 1901, vii.
78 Advertisement for Swan, vii.
79 Advertisement for Swan, vii.
80 Kipling, *Kim* (London: Penguin, 1989), 49; Kipling, *Kim*, *Cassell's*, January 1901, 163.
81 Kipling, *Kim* (London: Penguin, 1989), 59–60; Kipling, *Kim*, *Cassell's*, January 1901, 169–70.
82 "In the Arena," *Cassell's*, December 1900, 149.

83 Caption, *Cassell's,* January 1901, 207.
84 Illustrations by Lockwood Kipling and E.L. Weeks appeared in *McClure's* as well, but *McClure's* did not print the H.R. Millar drawings.
85 Said, *Culture and Imperialism,* 149.
86 Kipling, *Kim* (London: Penguin, 1989), 49; Kipling, *Kim, Cassell's,* January 1901, 163.
87 Kipling, *Kim* (London: Penguin, 1989), 49; Kipling, *Kim, Cassell's,* January 1901, 163.
88 Kipling, *Kim* (London: Penguin, 1989), 133; Kipling, *Kim, Cassell's,* April 1901, 503.
89 Kipling, *Kim* (London: Penguin, 1989), 134; Kipling, *Kim, Cassell's,* April 1901, 503.
90 Kipling, *Kim* (London: Penguin, 1989), 134; Kipling, *Kim, Cassell's,* April 1901, 503.
91 Kipling, *Kim* (London: Penguin, 1989), 175; Kipling, *Kim, Cassell's,* May 1901, 622. Kim, however, lies about the nature of the jest, pretending that he is going to visit a young girlfriend when he is in fact planning to run away from the school.
92 Kipling, *Kim* (London: Penguin, 1989), 174; Kipling, *Kim, Cassell's,* May 1901, 622.
93 Kipling, *Kim* (London: Penguin, 1989), 175; Kipling, *Kim, Cassell's,* May 1901, 622.
94 In August 1901, Millar furthers this agenda when he illustrates another transformation scene, showing how Kim disguises the imperiled agent he meets on the train. Notably, in this illustration, Kim retains his white identity; it is only the secret agent who acquires a darker skin tone. Thus, whenever Millar illustrates Kim's disguises, he does not shade his skin; but when he illustrates others' transformations, he adjusts the shading of their figures. Millar's illustrated Kim is never allowed to go native completely. It is as if Kim, as the novel's hero, must remain immune to racial "passing"—or so Millar's art would suggest.
95 Mark Paffard, *Kipling's Indian Fiction* (New York: St. Martin's Press, 1989), 81.
96 Other captions for Lockwood Kipling's images include "Zam-Zammah," "Kim and the Lama," "Mahbub Ali," "Kim and the Letter-writer," "On the Road," "Hurry Chunder Mookerjee," and "The End of the Search."
97 Kipling, *Kim* (London: Penguin, 1989), 163; Kipling, *Kim, Cassell's,* May 1901, 616.
98 Yet I read Weeks's drawing as an illustration of the second letter-writing scene, which occurs at the bazaar. The first letter-writing scene does not.
99 Said, *Culture and Imperialism,* 159.
100 Said, *Culture and Imperialism,* 161.
101 Zohreh T. Sullivan, *Narratives of Empire: The Fictions of Rudyard Kipling* (Cambridge: Cambridge University Press, 1993), 11.
102 Kipling, *Kim* (London: Penguin, 1989), 166; Kipling, *Kim, Cassell's,* May 1901, 618.
103 Kipling, *Kim* (London: Penguin, 1989), 166; Kipling, *Kim, Cassell's,* May 1901, 618.

104 Kipling, *Kim* (London: Penguin, 1989), 166; Kipling, *Kim, Cassell's*, May 1901, 618.
105 Advertisement for *Kim, Chicago Daily Tribune*, December 5, 1900, 13.
106 Advertisement for *Kim, Chicago Daily Tribune*, 13.
107 George B. Waldron, "Marvels of Modern Production," *McClure's*, November 1901, 87.
108 Waldron, "Marvels of Modern Production," 87.
109 Frank Luther Mott, *A History of American Magazines* (Cambridge: Harvard University Press, 1957), 4:593.
110 Paffard, *Kipling's Indian Fiction*, 85.
111 *Cassell's* also expressed interest in railroads and locomotives.
112 The speed of the train is needed, for example, if Kim is to deliver the white stallion's pedigree safely and efficiently.
113 Kipling, *Kim* (London: Penguin, 1989), 56; Kipling, *Kim, McClure's*, December 1900, 126.
114 *Concerning McClure's, Being a Little Book about a Big Magazine* (New York: S.S. McClure Company, 1901), 34.
115 *Concerning McClure's*, 20. The magazine was itself young, having issued its first number less than a decade earlier, in June of 1893. The magazine began with 30,000 subscribers, but by the time it was publishing *Kim* that number had increased more than tenfold. *McClure's* reported printing an average of 375,000 copies of its magazine per month during *Kim*'s distribution.
116 Elliot Gilbert, "Introduction," in *Kipling and the Critics*, ed. Elliot Gilbert (New York: New York University Press, 1965), viii.
117 Qtd. in Gretchen Murphy, *Shadowing the White Man's Burden: U.S. Imperialism and the Problem of the Color Line* (New York: New York University Press, 2010), 43.
118 David Gilmour, *The Long Recessional: The Imperial Life of Rudyard Kipling* (London: John Murray, 2002), 119.
119 Kipling, "The White Man's Burden," *McClure's*, February 1899, 290-1, line 12.
120 Kipling, "Recessional," *The London Times*, July 17, 1897, 13, line 20.
121 Gilmour, *The Long Recessional*, 121.
122 Kipling, "Recessional," lines 3-4.
123 Kipling, "Recessional," line 19.
124 Kipling, "Recessional," lines 25-8.
125 Kipling, "The White Man's Burden," *McClure's*, line 23.
126 Kipling, "The White Man's Burden," *McClure's*, line 1.
127 Kipling, "The White Man's Burden," *McClure's*, lines 2-8.
128 Anne Parry, *The Poetry of Rudyard Kipling* (Buckingham: Open University Press, 1992), 88.
129 Kipling, "The White Man's Burden," *McClure's*, line 50.
130 Kipling, "The White Man's Burden," *McClure's*, line 9.

131 Kipling, "The White Man's Burden," *McClure's*, lines 9–16.
132 Robert Buchanan, "The Voice of the Hooligan," in *Kipling and the Critics*, 26.
133 Buchanan, "The Voice of the Hooligan," 26.
134 Kipling, "The White Man's Burden," *McClure's*, lines 5, 3.
135 Kipling, "The White Man's Burden," *McClure's*, lines 5–6.
136 Kipling, "The White Man's Burden," *McClure's*, line 18.
137 See Parry, *The Poetry of Rudyard Kipling*, 89.
138 Kipling, "The White Man's Burden," *McClure's*, line 26.
139 Kipling, "The White Man's Burden," *McClure's*, line 27.
140 Kipling, "The White Man's Burden," *McClure's*, lines 33–40.
141 Kipling, "The White Man's Burden," *McClure's*, line 47.
142 See Parry, *The Poetry of Rudyard Kipling*, 88.
143 *The Bible*, Exodus 16:2-3 (King James Version). Scripture quotations from The Authorized (King James) Version. Rights in the Authorized Version in the United Kingdom are vested in the Crown. Reproduced by permission of the Crown's patentee, Cambridge University Press.
144 *The Bible*, Deuteronomy 6:12 (King James Version). Scripture quotations from The Authorized (King James) Version. Rights in the Authorized Version in the United Kingdom are vested in the Crown. Reproduced by permission of the Crown's patentee, Cambridge University Press.
145 Kipling, *The Letters of Rudyard Kipling: 1890–1900*, ed. Thomas Pinney (London: Macmillan, 1990), 2:309.
146 Kipling, "The White Man's Burden," line 37.
147 Kipling, "The White Man's Burden," in *The Five Nations* (New York: Doubleday, 1903), 79–81, line 45; Rudyard Kipling, "The White Man's Burden," in *Rudyard Kipling's Definitive Edition* (New York: Doubleday, 1940), line 45.
148 Kipling, "The White Man's Burden," *McClure's*, lines 47–8.
149 Kipling, "The White Man's Burden," *McClure's*, line 56.
150 William Dean Howells, "Opinions on 'The White Man's Burden,'" *New York Sun*, April 30, 1899, 1, *Anti-Imperialism in the United States*, ed. Jim Zwick, November 16, 2004, http://www.boondocksnet.com/ai/. These comments were also quoted in *The Literary Digest* of May 27, 1899, in an article entitled "Poetry, War, and Mr. Howells" (607).
151 Mott, *A History of American Magazines*, 4:599.
152 Harold S. Wilson, *McClure's Magazine and the Muckrakers* (Princeton: Princeton University Press, 1970), 191.
153 "Editorial Notes," *McClure's*, March 1901, 480.
154 Kipling, *Kim* (London: Penguin, 1989), 105; Kipling, *Kim*, *McClure's*, February 1901, 355.
155 Josiah Flynt, "In the World of Graft," *McClure's*, February 1901, 328.

156 Flynt, "In the World of Graft," 328.
157 Flynt, "In the World of Graft," 330.
158 Flynt, "In the World of Graft," 327.
159 "Editorial Notes," *McClure's*, March 1901, 479.
160 "Editorial Notes," *McClure's*, March 1901, 480.
161 "Editorial Notes," *McClure's*, March 1901, 480.
162 "Notable Books and Authors," *McClure's*, June 1901, 201.
163 Kipling, *Kim* (London: Penguin, 1989), 155.
164 Kipling, *Kim* (London: Penguin, 1989), 164.
165 "Notable Books and Authors," *McClure's*, June 1901, 201.
166 Ida M. Tarbell, "The Story of the Declaration of Independence," *McClure's*, July 1901, 223.
167 In the July 1901 issue, Kim returns to the Great Game, but the lama remains by his side, as a constant reminder of the alternative to the British Secret Service.
168 Tarbell, "The Story of the Declaration of Independence," 223.
169 Tarbell, "The Story of the Declaration of Independence," 223.
170 Tarbell, "The Story of the Declaration of Independence," 235.
171 Tarbell, "The Story of the Declaration of Independence," 235.
172 Tarbell, "The Story of the Declaration of Independence," 235.
173 Tarbell, "The Story of the Declaration of Independence," 235.
174 Mott, *A History of American Magazines*, 4:597.
175 The Harry Ransom Center at the University of Texas at Austin, for example, carries several original issues of *McClure's*. The run is incomplete, but the advertising sections are intact. There, we can find advertisements for a myriad array of products, including Dexter Brothers' English Shingle Stains, which uses a drawing of Kipling's house in Vermont to illustrate the product's effectiveness (*McClure's*, January 1900, 37). The ad demonstrates how authors could be used for commercial purposes, and how Kipling functioned as a transatlantic figure, or a kind of vehicle facilitating the importation of English products and ideas to America. It was not merely that Kipling's ideology carried transatlantic consequences, especially in terms of America's imperial practices, but also that Kipling's role as celebrity author influenced the transatlantic marketing and trade of at least some commercial goods in this period.
176 Qtd. in Richard Ohmann, *Selling Culture: Magazines, Markets, and Class at the Turn of the Century* (London: Verso, 1996), 203.
177 "Notable Books and Authors," *McClure's*, June 1901, 201.
178 "Notable Books and Authors," 201.
179 "Notable Books and Authors," 201.
180 "Editorial Notes," *McClure's*, December 1900, 191.
181 "Editorial Notes," *McClure's*, December 1900, 191.

182 "Editorial Notes," *McClure's*, March 1901, 479.
183 Kipling, *Kim* (London: Penguin, 1989), 223.
184 Said, *Culture and Imperialism*, 152.
185 Ray Stannard Baker, "J. Pierpont Morgan," *McClure's*, October 1901, 507.
186 Baker, "J. Pierpont Morgan," 508.
187 Kipling, *Kim, McClure's*, October 1901, 568. The words in the caption are capitalized in *McClure's*.
188 A few remaining items in the magazine may pique our reader's interest—a poem by W.E. Henley, "Elephant Hunting in Africa," "Frontenac the Savior of Canada," "The Roadmaster's Story," and "A Lament of the Country"—but our reader is tired and decides to prepare for bed.
189 Advertisement for *Cassell's Standard Library*, *Cassell's*, October 1901, x.

3

Contextualizing *Ulysses*

Collaboration and Competition in the *Little Review*

Introduction

When Leopold Bloom in *Ulysses* reflects on a meat ad's ironic placement near the obituaries, which causes him to associate Paddy Dignam's coffined corpse with potted meat, he provides a model for the sort of periodical reader who, encountering a myriad display of images and texts within a single publication, sees both intended and unintended parallels between the serialized pieces: "What is home without Plumtree's potted meat? Incomplete. What a stupid ad! Under the obituary notices they stuck it. All up a plumtree. Dignam's potted meat."[1] By causing Bloom to draw connections between two very different newspaper items, which at first glance may appear utterly unrelated—the death notices, and the food advertisements—Joyce not only uses the ad as a reflection upon events internal to *Ulysses*,[2] but also suggests that we as readers (following Bloom's example) might want to think more seriously about possible connections between his novel and the items surrounding it in its original periodical context. In this way, a text that opened itself up to competing voices and interior monologues within its pages found itself inflected by an array of competing voices and individual monologues outside its pages.

At both microscopic and macroscopic levels, readers of the *Little Review*, where *Ulysses* appeared between March 1918 and December 1920, encountered a serialized text with different complications, inflections, and contexts than those experienced by twenty-first-century readers who study *Ulysses* in book form. On a microscopic level, small alterations in the words of the text, so crucial to an author who devoted scrupulous attention to the accumulation of details, can make a difference in the way one understands and interprets the novel; on a macroscopic level, the periodical format places *Ulysses* in a radically different context, one that not only forces it to share physical space with other works between the *Little Review*'s colorful covers but that also gestures beyond the covers of the *Little Review* to locate Joyce within a larger, interconnected community of little magazines. The fastidious Modernist who would later achieve near-complete authorial control of *Ulysses* in its 1922 book publication exercised virtually no influence over the packaging of his novel in serial form. Far from being a text isolated between its own covers, *Ulysses* in the *Little Review* is cast as an element of the magazine's international, multilingual mission, as a crucial milestone in its larger battle against censorship, and as a key element of its advertising campaign. It is also a text that readers could actively and systematically engage with by contributing to the monthly "Reader Critic" column, which provided a forum for readers to express their responses to the *Little Review* and engage in debate with its editors. Collectively, these aspects of *Ulysses*'s periodical publication further complicate the divide between commercialism and Modernist aestheticism, a division that not only troubled readers but that is challenged by the text itself.

Archival evidence adds new dimensions to our understanding of the way readers negotiate the text. In particular, the following discussion draws on research conducted at the Zürich James Joyce Foundation, the Jane Heap Papers at the University of Delaware, and the *Little Review* Archives at the University of Wisconsin-Milwaukee.[3] In tracing reader responses and drawing out the implications of archival evidence, I aim to adjust the balance between the critical activities of interpretation and contextualization, showing how the text of *Ulysses*—interpreted so often by critics that more than one has asked whether anything remains to be said—needs to be more strongly contextualized through a closer examination of its often-neglected material conditions.[4]

By recontextualizing *Ulysses* within the *Little Review*, evincing a strong sensitivity to material conditions, we can unfold the multiple discourses—historical, legal, and literary—that inflect *Ulysses* as both an object of criticism and a physical artifact. For the historical context of the First World War, so often described as a major influence on Modernist work, has a telling material presence in the *Little Review*, where it surfaces in advertisements and reader–critic discussions that make its reality all the more tangible and evident. Similarly, the censorship of *Ulysses*, made famous in scholars' discussion of the "Nausicaa" trials, already had precedents in other controversial items published by the *Little Review*. Like historical conflicts and legal debates, the errors of *Ulysses* assume a new shape in the magazine. Some of the most widely discussed errors within the novel—Martha Clifford's substitution of "world" for "word," and the displaced "M" in Stephen's "Nother dying" telegram, for example—were both falsely "corrected" in the *Little Review*, thus compounding the iteration of error and transferring the responsibility for mistakes from characters within the text to readers outside the text. Furthermore, these now-famous errors inside the covers of *Ulysses*, so illuminatingly analyzed by scholars such as Tim Conley and Patrick McCarthy, were originally complemented by many now-forgotten errors surrounding *Ulysses* in the *Little Review*: spelling mistakes in advertisements for Joyce's work, errata lists that appeared alongside *Ulysses* announcements, and complaints about typographical errors in both published and unpublished letters to the editor.

As readers and contributors complained about printers' mistakes, *Ulysses* became engulfed in another and more serious set of errors: During the serialization of *Ulysses* in the *Little Review* and the "Nausicaa" trials that followed, there were accusations of moral error leveled by the New York Society for the Suppression of Vice, there were tactical errors that the lawyer John Quinn and editor Margaret Anderson accused each other of committing, and there were biographical and factual errors that surfaced in the reporting of the event. But the editors converted the scandal of error into opportunity for advertisement—a decision that carried significant ramifications for the magazine audience, already made anxious by the suspiciously similar promotional tactics of commercial periodicals. Thus, attention to the material conditions of *Ulysses*'s first publication will also show how the *Little Review*'s own engagement with advertisement, at once fascinating and suspect, modifies and enhances past scholarly analysis of ads within Joyce's novel.

As I use a method of strong contextualization to approach interpretive work, I will also probe the relationship between collaboration and competition, examining the *Little Review* as an ambitious exercise in collaborative experiment that was threatened by competing forces and claims. Even as the *Little Review* became a model of editorial, legal, and literary collaboration that encouraged dialogue between readers and contributors, between America and Europe, and among the emerging network of "small magazines," the very connections the *Little Review* facilitated were threatened by outside agencies and forces—such as the New York Society for the Suppression of Vice, the US postal authorities, or constraining publishing economics—as well as by internal divisions, including readers who argued over literature within the *Little Review*'s columns, lawyers like John Quinn who disagreed with the clients he represented, and competing editors on the masthead (especially Ezra Pound as foreign editor, and Anderson as editor/publisher) who fought for control of the magazine's direction.

But even as there were divisions, there were also connections, and a closer look at the *Little Review* shows how desperately and persistently it strove to create and maintain an international community united by daring artistic experimentation. Indeed, it may even be said that the external and internal threats to this community were also somehow essential to its success, since the *Little Review* thrived on debates and, throughout its run of fifteen years, operated on alternating cycles of collaboration and competition, unity and discord, assertions and concessions of power. Far from avoiding conflict, the *Little Review* worked to balance moments of harmony with displays of dissension, compliments with criticism, claims to strength with statements of victimization, and assertions of rectitude with admissions of error. The *Little Review* acts as a framing presenter, a further layer of agency beyond the author and narrators. When we read *Ulysses* in this context, it acquires strikingly new associations that can in turn affect our interpretation of words and events within the novel. Within the pages of the *Little Review*, representations of history, censorship, error, and advertisement—all of which have implications both within and outside the fiction—acquire additional resonance as they become part of the *Little Review*'s framing paradigms of collaboration and competition.

The Great War and International Concerns in the *Little Review*

Joyce's first readers not only lived in a different historical era, with reminders of the Great War circulating in multiple forms and in multiple media—ranging from large headlines in the mass-market newspapers to coverage in the "small magazines"—but they were also opening Joyce's novel in the pages of a magazine with boldly international ambitions. Furthermore, Joyce's own comments reveal that he also saw *Ulysses* as a literary work figuring into a broader social and historical context:

> I wrote the greater part of the book during the war. There was fighting on all fronts, empires fell, kings went into exile, the old order was collapsing with a crash; and I had, as I sat down to work, the conviction that in the midst of all these ruins I was building something for the most distant future.[5]

Significantly, advertisements and articles published alongside *Ulysses* in the *Little Review* reminded readers of the war as a very real presence. When the serialization of Joyce's novel began in March 1918, the *Little Review* printed an announcement urging readers to "remember" the "War" before complaining of late issues.[6] The editors also urged subscribers to notify them of changes of address because "it would help us keep our youth, and also save further congestion of the mail service." On the facing page, another self-advertisement announces the upcoming publication of Episodes II and III under a banner prominently describing the *Little Review* as a magazine "Respecting no vested interests, no publishers' interests, no aged magazines and reviews nor staffs of the same"—a statement of independence in tune with Joyce's sense that the "old order was collapsing" and giving way to new forms and methods that would break away from established empires, whether political or literary.

The international scope and ambition of the *Little Review* is reflected in the back cover of its March 1918 issue (the first to include *Ulysses*), which contains an advertisement for the Berlitz School of Languages, an institution boasting "over 300 branches in the leading cities of the world." This advertisement, repeated in later issues, not only bears an obvious connection to Joyce, who taught at the Berlitz School, but also subtly underscores the way in which Modernism itself was spreading to the leading cities of the world and profiting from the rich, cross-cultural exchange of ideas that took place among exiled writers who were required to communicate in new languages as they traveled between Chicago, New York, Paris, London, Zürich, and other centers of art. The growing advantages of possessing skills in international, multilingual communication are also reflected in a July 1918 advertisement for the "Multiplex Hammond Writing Machine," a typewriter that could *"Write All Languages, All Sciences, All Sizes and Style of type on ONE machine."* To write in a foreign language, one need only turn a knob ("Two types or languages always in the machine: Just turn the knob"). An October 1918 ad reiterates this easily achieved versatility: "Two styles of type or two different languages always on the MULTIPLEX: Any other two substituted in a few seconds."

As a magazine that published literary works from multiple language traditions, the *Little Review* expressed a deep commitment to internationalism. Like the Hammond Multiplex it advertised, the magazine switched easily between French and English, with occasional works in German and intermittent quotations from classical languages. In this respect it was not unlike the polylingually playful *Ulysses*. Though Pound and others would later call the *Little Review* "eccentric,"[7] it is precisely this eccentricity that provides a fitting milieu for Joyce's work. With its ads for the Berlitz School and the multilingual typewriter, the *Little Review* emphasizes the linguistic diversity that Joyce's work would also achieve. Although it is not quite true that, before *Ulysses*, Joyce's only "stylistic innovation" was "confined to the substitution of a dash for inverted commas when printing dialogue,"[8] *Ulysses* does mark a departure from Joyce's earlier works by radically experimenting with "puns, neologisms, [and] outrageous metaphors,"[9] inaugurating artistic techniques that would later reach a remarkable pitch in *Finnegans Wake*.

The linguistic possibilities evoked by the ads recall the raw material (language) and the instrument (typewriters) enabling the creation of *Ulysses*. Although Joyce could not have anticipated which ads would accompany installments of his novel, these commercial notices resonate with the linguistic experimentation of Joyce's work even as they also underscore the international commitments of the *Little Review*. It is peculiarly appropriate that the opening episode of *Ulysses* should appear within these covers. The work announces a Babel of languages, from its first lines of dialogue occurring in a foreign tongue (Mulligan's "*Introibo ad altare Dei*"),[10] to its invocation of Greek to describe the sea ("*Epi oinopa ponton*" and "*Thalatta! Thalatta!*"),[11] Mulligan's complaints about Stephen's "Paris fads,"[12] Haines's attempt to speak Gaelic with the Irish milkwoman, who mistakes it for "French,"[13] and its nation-centric debates about the "English" and "Italian" masters of Ireland,[14] followed by Haines's anxiety over "German jews."[15] As *Ulysses* connects multiple language traditions, the *Little Review* uses its advertisements and table of contents to emphasize its collaborative transatlantic enterprise. Thus *Ulysses*, from the first moments of its appearance in print, is couched in this international, multilingual milieu, in a medium of advertisement, and in the historical context of the First World War.

Because of these contexts, the comments made by characters in *Ulysses* carry different inflections for the novel's first readers than for its later scholars. When Haines observes, "It seems history is to blame" in March 1918 and Stephen,[16] one month later, declares that history "is a nightmare from which I am trying to awake,"[17] their comments carry an additional valence for *Little Review* readers, who were emerging from the most destructive war in history. Of course, Haines's and Stephen's comments are made in the fictional Dublin of 1904, and refer in the first instance to a remoter history than the immediate crises confronting the world in 1918. But, because these lines were composed during the First World War and were first published in the actual New York of 1918, they convey a transatlantic, transhistoric sense of the past as a nightmare from which the world is desperately trying to awake.[18]

By recontextualizing *Ulysses* both historically within the Great War and materially within the *Little Review*, we can engage in different kinds of literary analysis, unlocking interpretive doors that would otherwise remain closed along with the *Little Review*'s covers. But by turning to the *Little Review* and opening its covers, we see that the historical work of scholars such as Mark Wollaeger, Victor Luftig, Robert Spoo, and others[19] has a strong material counterpart that brings

Ulysses into even closer relation with the Great War. The hardships created by the war also impacted the *Little Review*, and in December 1918 it published "A Note to Our Readers" describing its financial difficulties before proclaiming, "Nevertheless, we have survived the war. [...] And won't you tell your friends that we are publishing the current works of Joyce, Yeats, Eliot, and other important men in a cheap and convenient format? They can get these writers in no other American magazine, except sporadically, and some of them not at all."[20] As we will see, the "cheap and convenient" format would later create problems for the *Little Review* when it tried to argue that its controversial material would only reach a limited, mature audience, but here the main point to be noticed is the series of connections the announcement establishes: First, the *Little Review* links itself to readers who have also "survived the war" amidst hardships; secondly, the *Little Review* links this historical, material triumph with the achievement of publishing literature by Joyce and other "important men." Finally, the *Little Review* positions these "important men" of letters within an "American" context, bringing them across the Atlantic into a New York periodical. While other periodicals' overseas correspondents sent news about the war in Europe to the US Coast, the *Little Review*'s newly appointed "foreign editor," Ezra Pound, assumed the responsibility of importing European literature to American shores. *Ulysses*, procured during the war, was judged his most important discovery.

While readers of the book in 1922 would still share the sense of history as a nightmare, for readers of 1918 the historical emergency was all the more urgent. Detailed correspondence in the *Little Review* Archive unveils how deeply affected readers as well as contributors were by the catastrophic events of 1914–18. Wyndham Lewis writes to Margaret Anderson about the impact of the war, Quinn includes meditations on the psychology of war and recognizes the heightened legal danger of critiquing the government in wartime, and Richard Aldington vividly describes his experiences in the trenches and the way it has affected his writing.[21] These letters had further reverberations: In the collection at the University of Delaware, a letter from Jane Heap describes how "we just sat and cried" upon receipt of Aldington's letter.[22] Although Heap's private letters were not published until 2000, her public letters in the *Little Review* would have made her disapproving attitude toward the war evident to her contemporaries.

Additionally, her letters in the *Little Review*, signed merely with the initials "jh," form part of an engaged dialogue with readers who were also reacting to the war. One reader wrote in to the *Little Review* demanding why it did not cover the war as other magazines and newspapers did. The letter, printed in the August 1917 number, sparked a series of responses debating the relationship between war and art. Jane Heap replied that "none of us considers this war a legitimate or an interesting subject for Art."[23] She also felt that stricter governmental controls during the war hindered literary activity, and in September 1917 she complained, "When the western nations have finished making the world safe for democracy, if it wouldn't be too satirical the Orient might wage a world war to make the world safe for Art."[24] Given Quinn's concerns that an allusion to the president in Pound's "L'Homme Moyen Sensuel" (published in September 1917) might have initially attracted unwanted government attention to the *Little Review*,[25] Heap's complaint about the war's impact on artistic freedom was not unfounded. But it angered at least one reader, who argued in October 1917 that the war could inspire great works of art: "And then Art needs something noble in it, and anything where noble self-sacrifice occurs daily is a fit subject for it."[26] In this same October issue, Wyndham Lewis's "Cantleman's Spring-Mate" describes a soldier's encounter with a young girl, a war document allegedly found on a German prisoner is reprinted, and an ad for *The Red Badge of Courage* proclaims, "This is not a story of war: It *is* War." These frequent references to war present the historical and material context into which *Ulysses* was injected, but they would ultimately prove problematic for the *Little Review* and other little magazines that took an oppositional stance to the military conflict. As the *Little Review* strove to establish transatlantic channels of artistic communication and literary exchange, reaching beyond its New York office to import contributions from Europe's experimental writers, the US government threatened to impede the *Little Review*'s dissemination of the foreign and domestic material it so provocatively assembled, and, under government monitoring, a collaborative array of transatlantic contributions often struggled to move from the initial point of collection to the end stage of circulation. Ironically, the transatlantic circuitry the magazine worked so hard to achieve was often thwarted just a few steps beyond its own front door.

Censoring the *Little Review*

As Mark Morrisson has argued, little magazines like the *Little Review*, the *Masses*, and the *Egoist* strove to create a counter-public sphere in which Modernist aesthetics could be discussed alongside social and political issues like suffrage, sex, socialism, radicalism, and anarchism. These were risky ambitions, however. In December 1917, following a controversy over its oppositional stance toward the Great War, the *Masses* (published in New York) went out of business. Just three months later, in March 1918, the serialization of *Ulysses* began in the *Little Review*, which had already been suppressed in late 1917 because of an allegedly indecent wartime story by Wyndham Lewis ("Cantleman's Spring-Mate"). Indeed, the March 1918 issue locates Joyce's *Ulysses*, its lead item, firmly within the context of censorship and current debates about obscenity. Within the same magenta covers that contain Episode I of *Ulysses*, an article by Ezra Pound protests the earlier suppression of the *Little Review* as he ruthlessly dissects section 211 of the US Criminal Code (which declared obscene literature to be "non-mailable matter"). These issues of law, censorship, and artistic expression would become urgent for *Ulysses* in 1920, when "Nausicaa" was accused of corrupting readers; what the *Little Review* shows is that from the very beginning Joyce's novel was surrounded by debates about obscenity it later became a part of.

Unlike modern books that contain single works instead of a diverse array of contributions, the *Little Review* highlights how the complex web of collaboration between authors and editors was threatened by governmental authorities competing for control of material the public received. If we return to the *Little Review*, it becomes easy to see how *Ulysses* was embedded in this ongoing competition between large government agencies and controversial little magazines, between censorship and freedom of expression, between received tradition and the daring experiments of Modernism. Pound's March 1918 article "The Classics 'Escape'" responds to a very specific act of suppression that had already taken place even before the publication of *Ulysses* began. Protesting Judge Hand's decision to keep the October 1917 issue out of the mails and calling for an amendment of the law, Pound declares, "No more damning indictment of American civilization has been written than that contained in Judge Hand's 'opinion.'"[27] Lewis's short story, and the alleged obscenity it contained, was primarily responsible for the judge's unfavorable decision. As Margaret Anderson told subscribers in the November 1917 issue:

> This story, by a distinguished man of letters, a man who at present is in the English army and is fighting in the trenches, is about a young soldier, who has a rustic encounter with a girl "in the offending fires of the spring". Also it happens to be a very good piece of prose, which was our reason for printing it. We had no hope that such a good piece of prose could gain the interest of the Postoffice for a minute.[28]

Again, in December 1917, Lewis's short story received the focus of attention when Anderson quoted Judge Hand's ruling. "The publication which is particularly objected to by the Postal Authorities," Hand had declared, "is a short story about a soldier in the British Army [...]. With satirical satisfaction he seduces a young girl and disregards her appeals when she becomes a mother."[29] Significantly, this rhetoric of the "young girl" would surface again in the trials of *Ulysses*, when the prosecution argued that "Nausicaa" would corrupt young female readers and Jane Heap countered, "If there is anything I really fear it is the mind of the young girl."[30] Hence the Lewis trial, as Mark Morrisson and others have pointed out, functions as a prelude to Joyce's later encounters with the court.[31] That the offending items by Lewis and Joyce were both published in the *Little Review* unites them bibliographically, but the magazine's continued coverage of the October 1917 suppression, extending into the months of *Ulysses*'s serialization, strengthens this connection both conceptually and materially.

While each trial primarily received attention for alleged indecency concerning human sexuality, political concerns also influenced the suppression of the *Little Review* numbers in each case. As David Weir notes, "politics had played a role" in the suppression of "Lewis's unpatriotic account of life during wartime," and later Joyce's "Lestrygonians" was "somehow read by the authorities in the context of the Espionage Act," as evinced by the Translation Bureau's concern over *Ulysses*.[32] As Weir also relates, the Translation Bureau's correspondence "adds credence" to Pound's July 1920 letter to Joyce: "The censorship was very much troubled by it [*Ulysses*] during the war. Thought it was all code."[33] Archival evidence suggests an even stronger link between the October 1917 suppression of the *Little Review* and the later suppression of episodes containing *Ulysses*. Although Lewis's story received the most attention in the October 1917 scandal, Quinn's letters to Anderson reveal that another item also provoked the authorities. In fact, Quinn believed that he could have won the Lewis court case had it not been for other offensive material in the *Little Review*. Unfortunately, an accompanying item on page 39 impeded the case.[34]

If we consult page 39 of the October 1917 *Little Review*, we discover yet another war story, yet this one purports to be factual. Ezra Pound, under the pseudonym of Abel Sanders, writes in with a "SECRET" enclosed document, allegedly taken from a German prisoner. The German document, translated and reprinted in the *Little Review*, instructs men "left behind for the sake of the Fatherland to interest themselves in the happiness of the married women and maidens by doubling or even trebling the number of births."[35] The men are directed to consult an "exhibition of photographs of women and maidens" in their district, and they are informed that their wives will not be able to seek a divorce on grounds of infidelity.[36] After "nine months," the men must submit a "full report of results."[37] This disturbing letter, although ostensibly printed to show "the true nature of the forces against which we are arrayed,"[38] carries insinuations that are less patriotically sound than morally offensive, at least in terms of prevailing early-twentieth-century mores. The letter's content, especially its encouragement of extramarital sexual relations in wartime, uncannily resembles the plot of Lewis's story—a connection that is further strengthened when we consider the headline placed above the German document: "This Approaches Literature!" Quinn's correspondence in the University of Wisconsin-Milwaukee archives suggests that this intermingling of fact and fiction, this combination of immoral content in both Lewis's story and the German war document, ultimately caused the court case for the October 1917 issue to be lost.

Arguments neither for realism nor for art as inherently above obscenity would persuade the authorities toward a favorable ruling—a result that did not bode well for the later *Ulysses* trial. When Quinn wrote to W.H. Lamar, the Solicitor for the Post Office Department in Washington, he argued that it would not "corrupt the morals" of *Little Review* readers.[39] He felt confident that Lamar would agree with him. But Lamar acted contrary to Quinn's predictions, judging the story "rather unfit for innocent young minds," as Quinn related to Margaret Anderson.[40] Yet Lamar and Quinn were not the only ones to disagree. Although Quinn presented the *Little Review*'s case in court, he also disagreed on personal and strategic grounds with the very clients he was defending. While critics have often pointed to Quinn's discomfort with Anderson and Heap's lesbian relationship, alternately glorifying or vilifying Quinn for his function in patronizing the *Little Review* (and aiding *Ulysses* in particular), comparatively little critical attention has been given to unfolding the disagreements that surfaced during the Lewis trial.[41] Yet the tensions over the Lewis case and how it should be handled are significant because they foreground later disagreements Anderson and Quinn had when it came to the defense of *Ulysses*. The conflicts between lawyer and editor may have been magnified in the 1921 *Ulysses* trial, but they already had their origins in the 1917 court case.

The connection was one identified by Quinn, who still recalled his earlier disagreements with Anderson when he prepared to defend Joyce's work. As soon as the US Post Office began confiscating issues of the *Little Review* in 1919, seizing the numbers that contained "Lestrygonians" (January 1919) and "Scylla and Charybdis" (May 1919), Quinn wrote to Anderson, reminding her of their diverging approaches to the Lewis defense and linking it to the anticipated legal battle for *Ulysses*.[42] In the Lewis case, Quinn had argued that the story taught a moral lesson.[43] Anderson, on the other hand, had argued in her *Little Review* column that there was "no warning or lesson in it."[44] Rather than defending

"Cantleman's Spring-Mate" against charges of immorality, as Quinn had done, she instead casts aside the necessity for moral argument: "I disagree even with the best arguments that could be presented in a contemporary court-room about the merits of such a story. The *Little Review* was founded in direct opposition to the prevalent art values in America. It would have no function or reason for being if it did not continually conflict with those values."[45] Because Anderson's article was published in December 1917, a month after the Lewis court case was lost, her reference to "contemporary court-room" arguments for the "merits" of literature almost certainly alludes to Quinn's unsuccessful legal defense of "Cantleman's Spring-Mate." Regardless of what Anderson hoped to achieve in her article, Quinn's correspondence confirms that he read the article as an attack on his position and as a tactical error.

Quinn's resistance to Anderson unveils deeper tensions between male lawyer and female editor, making the collaborative efforts between both parties all the more remarkable in the midst of such animated disagreement. From many perspectives, the *Little Review* trials were as much about internal tensions as external ones. Before Quinn tried to persuade outside agencies of *Ulysses*'s legal virtue, he was trying to persuade his client of the virtue inherent in his own conservative approach to legal questions and courtroom procedures. Quinn felt that Anderson was too defiant, more likely to incense judges with her vociferous arguments than to win them over to her side.[46] Quinn's June 1919 letter about Joyce closely echoes his November 1917 letter about Lewis, in which he stresses the importance of proceeding quietly rather than angrily in the courtroom.[47] Thus, although scholars have cast Quinn as a masculine authority keen to silence the unconventional female editors of the *Little Review*, his recommendation that Anderson approach authority figures with quiet respect was a policy he also applied to himself. Likewise, when he insists that defiance would be less effective than arguments made on the basis of the opposition's beliefs, he articulates a strategy that he not only recommends to his female clients but also employs in his own engagements as a prominent male lawyer. While scholars such as Adam Parkes and Bonnie Kime Scott rightly critique Quinn for forcing Anderson into a submissive role, Quinn himself was deferential to the judges. Given the outcome of both the 1917 and 1921 court cases, his deferential strategy appears to have been ineffective. But, given the mores of early-twentieth-century America, it is unlikely that Anderson's more vociferous attacks would have changed the judicial decision in either court case.

The battle over censorship was not the only one being fought. In the case of the 1921 *Ulysses* trials, Parkes argues, the fight "was as much between two deviant women and a male, heterosexual establishment as between the forces of censorship and the supporters of James Joyce."[48] As I have mentioned, the disagreements between Quinn and the *Little Review* editors sometimes had less to do with gender than critics have assumed, but differences in gender and sexual orientation certainly augmented the underlying personality conflicts. Quinn's approach to the trial of "Nausicaa," which examines the sexual transgression of Gerty MacDowell and Leopold Bloom, was "colored by his disgust" over his own sexually transgressive clients.[49] To support his point, Parkes quotes a 1920 letter from Quinn to Pound, in which Quinn refers in derogatory terms to the "aberrations" of women who deviate from traditional standards of feminine behavior.[50] But the correspondence between Anderson and Quinn reveals that the gender question, and its relation to submissive traits traditionally associated with femininity, formed the subject of a long-standing debate between editor and lawyer. Quinn not only silenced his clients in the courtroom, "unceremoniously" sending them back to their seats when they stood by his side,[51] but he also advised a policy of silence and discretion with respect to their financial situation. Just as he preferred to keep "his deviant clients out of the picture" in the courtroom,[52] so he also preferred to keep himself out of the picture when it came to the *Little Review*'s financial support. At first, however, Quinn was eager to provide funds to a magazine with ties to both Joyce and Pound.[53] But he instructed the *Little Review* editors not to broadcast his patronage, and his correspondence reveals an increasing frustration with his outspoken female clients—a frustration that eventually led him to discontinue monetary support.

The correspondence trail carries implications for *Ulysses*, not only because the early exchanges represent the start of conflicts between lawyer and client that would surface more noticeably during the "Nausicaa" trials, but also because the recurrent subjects raised in their correspondence—gender roles, aesthetic evaluation, and especially patronage—represent issues Joyce was simultaneously addressing, both biographically and fictionally. In August 1917, after Heap had told someone that Pound had "a guarantor," Quinn wrote to her, urging her not to make this fact known.[54] Quinn continues, asserting that Heap's open acknowledgment of his support ran contrary to their initial agreement. Three days later, on August 11, he wrote to Anderson, once again reiterating the need for silence and caution.[55] Interestingly, Quinn then proceeds to contrast the *Little Review*'s open statements about its financial affairs with the more reserved policies of other little magazines edited by men. For Quinn, financial matters were private matters that men knew how to keep private. His insistence upon silence also indicates his discomfort vis-à-vis his association with Anderson and

Heap, whose unconventional manners and support of anarchism had caused various anxious landlords to evict them.[56]

But Heap and Anderson did not heed Quinn's advice. Throughout the *Little Review*'s publication, they repeatedly published pleas for financial aid, often annotating such appeals with stories illustrating their poverty and printing difficulties. In December 1917, an ad titled "Will You Help?" asked readers to assist the *Little Review* financially by renewing their subscriptions "promptly" and "sending any donation that you can afford."[57] The appeal was prefaced by an explanation linking financial hardship to censorship: "The suppression of the October issue has cut into our business plans terribly. It was an especially good number, from which we hoped to get a lot of new subscribers."[58] Thus, as governmental suppression is translated into financial trouble, the editors also imply an equation between artistic merit and (missed) business opportunity, the implication being that "high" literature, not usually associated with commercial profit, would in fact attract subscribers, and profits, if the government did not interfere. Significantly, the missed business opportunity would also surface during *Ulysses*'s serialization, when book publishers who objected to Joyce refused to advertise in the magazine, as I discuss in greater detail below.

Although the *Little Review* never became a large commercial enterprise, Quinn did think that it would eventually attract enough guarantors and subscribers to become self-supporting. His correspondence reveals how optimistic he initially felt about the magazine's future prospects, both financial and literary. On February 2, 1918—Joyce's birthday—he sent a letter to Anderson with a check for $400 and a list of the generous sums other patrons had agreed to contribute, the total amount guaranteeing a supply of $200 monthly for eight months.[59] But his initial enthusiasm, expressed in the fall of 1917 and early months of 1918 (during which he sent out a flurry of letters to wealthy colleagues asking for contributions), had turned by the end of 1918 into exasperation with the magazine's perpetual financial neediness.

By the time of the 1921 *Ulysses* trial, Quinn "felt put upon as a lawyer,"[60] but it is worthy of note that in 1918, even before the suppression of *Ulysses* and prior to the major disagreements that followed, Quinn already felt "put upon" as a guarantor. In August 1917 he could still write optimistically about the *Little Review*'s literary and financial prospects,[61] but over the course of the coming year his views would gradually change. Even in his February 1918 letter (mentioned above) he had expressed disdain at Anderson's request that he approach the guarantors.[62] By December, his mild amusement had turned into extreme irritation at Anderson's financial demands.[63] Anderson had disappointed him by failing to increase circulation numbers, which he believed were needed for financial stability. Although Quinn said he did not object to her contacting the other guarantors, he informed her that he would not renew his guaranty for the coming year (he had been giving funds to the *Little Review* itself as well as allotting separate funds to Pound).

Quinn's suggestion that the *Little Review* become self-supporting by increasing its circulation not only runs counter to solid marketing advice, since profitable magazines at the time reaped profits not from subscriptions but from advertisements, but also constructs a historically unreliable equation between artistic merit and commercial success. As Edward Bishop writes, "Little magazines are by definition magazines that do not make money; they are trying to promote new ideas or forms of art, rather than sales."[64] Although Quinn obviously would not have had the advantage of hindsight that Bishop enjoys, his letters to Anderson suggest that he did not fully understand the tensions between artistic pursuits and (mass-) market dynamics. The early (pre-1920) correspondence between Quinn and the editors of the *Little Review* also shows how he often miscalculated government actions and mispredicted legal outcomes. Interestingly enough, the lawyer who would later defend the *Little Review* in court initially did not anticipate that the magazine would cause any controversy. As late as August 1917, Quinn had written to Heap that he was glad to furnish legal advice but doubted that the magazine's contents would attract the censor's attention.[65] Just two months later, however, the Post Office confiscated the *Little Review* on account of Lewis's allegedly indecent story, a prelude to the government's later suppression of *Ulysses*.

The story of the *Little Review* trial is well known and has been recounted by multiple scholars, ranging from Richard Ellmann (who takes a biographical perspective) and Jackson R. Bryer (who applauds Quinn) to Bonnie Kime Scott (who, taking a feminist approach, critiques him) and Mark Morrisson (who resituates the trials in terms of youth culture). The narrative of the "Nausicaa" episode's suppression is by now routinely recited in Joyce criticism: When the daughter of a New York lawyer received an unsolicited copy of the July–August 1920 *Little Review*, the offending "Nausicaa" episode was brought to the attention of John Sumner, Secretary of the New York Society for the Suppression of Vice.[66] Sumner, in turn, filed an official complaint, and a hearing was scheduled for October 1920. Quinn represented the *Little Review* at both the 1920 hearing and the trial that followed in February 1921. In court, Anderson and Heap were "defiant" (as Quinn described them), "exclaiming proudly that they didn't regret their action, would do it all over again, and wanted the matter prosecuted, as it would be 'the making of the *Little Review.*'"[67] As Quinn highlighted Joyce's artistic merits and argued that the "average reader would [...] be unable to understand"—and thus would not be corrupted by—the suggestive scene between Gerty and Bloom on the strand, the prosecution insisted that, "no matter how great a writer Joyce was," his works still "violated the law."[68] "Concern for the innocent young girl" was a central focus of the trial and of Heap's later editorial commentary as the opposing sides battled over the young girl "both outside and inside Joyce's text"—the merits of the fictional Gerty on the one hand, and the effect on the female reader on the other.[69] Eventually, the three district court judges ruled that *Ulysses* was obscene, and the editors were each fingerprinted and fined 50 dollars. In order to prevent his clients from being sent to jail, "Quinn had to certify" that "Nausicaa" was "the worst episode in Joyce's novel."[70]

The scandal received considerable coverage by the contemporary press, and even a century later critics continue to discuss the politics of gender relations, censorship, and pornography—albeit with varying angles and approaches—in modern-day periodicals and literary reviews. In this way the "Nausicaa" episode, originally published in a little magazine, produces a textual and social history that is in turn re-inscribed in other periodicals. Periodical publication thus forms an essential part of *Ulysses*'s reception and interpretation—not only because it initially appeared serially, but also because the critical discussions and news coverage it inspired are also frequently published in journals and magazines. In fact, it was through the agency of the press that Joyce himself learned of the overseas trial and its outcome: "Joyce did not actually find out about the *Little Review* trial until March, a month after it had ended, when he read a press cutting from the *New York Tribune* in the Parisian bookstore Shakespeare and Company."[71] Employed as vehicles for conveying messages both to and from the author, periodicals became essential to the distribution of *Ulysses* as well as news about *Ulysses*. Furthermore, the mixture of mass-market periodicals (like the *New York Tribune*) and little magazines (like the *Little Review*, the *Egoist*, and the *New Age*) involved in this system of distribution shows how the antagonistic relationship between commercial culture and elite art was mediated by a network of distribution that, paradoxically, resulted in these "high" and "low" spheres reinforcing each other, as the little magazines provided larger papers with material to convert into news items and the larger papers, in turn, provided fuel for debates in the smaller Modernist press. Controversial novels like *Ulysses*, while accentuating the differences between mass and elite cultures, nevertheless brought these two cultures into closer dialogue with each other.

The periodical format allowed for quicker dissemination than the book format, which involved a lengthier production process (though, of course, travels across the Atlantic could still result in a significant time delay), but its ability to reach mass audiences from all age groups ultimately proved problematic for Joyce. The *Little Review*'s relatively cheap price and easy availability made courts less likely to agree with arguments that the magazine's mature content would not fall into the hands of the young.[72] For these reasons, Quinn urged that *Ulysses* be published in book form before serialization could be completed. "Quinn was also certain just what kind of edition was required—a private edition" that would be expensive and be available by subscription only.[73] Quinn's reasoning was arguably based not only on his knowledge of law but also on his personal moral code, as evinced by an October 16, 1920 letter to Pound: "There are things in 'Ulysses' published in number after number of 'The Little Review' that never should have appeared in a magazine asking privileges of the mails. In a book, yes. In a magazine, emphatically no."[74] Quinn's remark suggests that, in spite of the arguments he made in court, he actually feared that *Ulysses*'s serial appearance risked corrupting the morals of the young.

Additionally, Quinn thought that a privately printed edition of *Ulysses* would bring more commercial profits for Joyce.[75] Pound, too, believed that a book would have commercial advantages—but he also saw the serialization of *Ulysses* as working symbiotically with the novel's planned book publication, not in opposition to it as Quinn believed. On October 26, 1920, Pound wrote to Anderson, "I agree with jh. that it is MUCH better [that] Ulysses shd. have appeared serially; much better. I dont, however, know that there is much use in being suppressed a fourth time. Q's plans for a private vol. now will serve. Will even improve demand for vol. if the end of the book hasn't been printed in the L.R."[76] Although Pound certainly expressed frustration with Anderson and Heap, voicing discontent over the way they "messed and muddled" *Ulysses*,[77] he also viewed the initial installments in the *Little Review* as being beneficial to Joyce. In fact, Pound had been the one to arrange for its serialization in the first place, and in the *Little Review* he found a venue where "I and T.S. Eliot can appear once a month [...] and where Joyce can appear when he likes, and where Wyndham Lewis can appear if he comes back from the war."[78] It was only when later episodes resulted in suppression of *Little Review* issues that Pound advised against publishing further installments, which would jeopardize the novel's success in the marketplace. As his correspondence suggests, Pound saw the serialization of *Ulysses* as an advertisement for the forthcoming book, and he was able to turn the serial suppression of the *Little Review* to strategic advantage: because the book would contain additional episodes that had not been serialized (since the *Little Review* was forced to cease publication of *Ulysses* after the first installment of Episode XIV), the complete book with eighteen episodes would carry additional appeal.

Before "Nausicaa": The Strategic Censorship of Anderson, Pound, and Heap

Although the "Nausicaa" episode has received the most notoriety in critical discussions of the *Little Review*, obscenity, and censorship, earlier installments already had their difficulties, and these magazine issues deserve greater attention for the way that they both foreground debates about "Nausicaa" and reveal how the first editors of Joyce's text (Pound, Anderson, and Heap) strategically exercised censorship of *Ulysses*. As Jackson R. Bryer and others have noted, Pound objected to and deleted certain "offensive" passages of Episode IV ("Calypso"), enraging Joyce when he later "discovered the corrupt nature of the text in the June, 1918, issue."[79] Pound, Paul Vanderham argues, "wanted to prevent the frankness of *Ulysses* [...] from provoking John Quinn to withdraw financial support,"[80] but he also wanted to raise Joyce's prose from its "incarnational, egalitarian tendencies" to the level of "classical decorum" he himself preferred.[81] Vanderham's informative research meticulously documents Pound's excisions, showing how he would often mask personal objections to excremental references by deleting such passages and labeling them as "bad art."[82] What Vanderham's research makes clear, however, is that Pound's objections were not merely aesthetic. They also approached alignment with Quinn's moral qualms, and they expressed a further anxiety about Joyce's tendency to "mix high and low."[83]

This anxiety was shared by other Modernists who objected to Joyce's art, such as D.H. Lawrence, Virginia Woolf, and Amy Lowell.[84] Vanderham assembles a string of quotations from these Modernists that would seem to support Andreas Huyssen's concept of the "Great Divide," insofar as these authors insist upon a kind of elitism divorced from lower concerns: Lawrence (surprisingly enough) dismissed "Penelope" as the most "obscene thing ever written," Woolf "squeamishly" objected to "the p-ing of a dog" in "Proteus," and Lowell regretted that her fellow Americans could not distinguish between "whole" life and "pure obscenities like those perpetuated by James Joyce."[85] But the fact that Joyce, as a Modernist, was viewed as dangerously crossing the divide between high and low, the erotic and the excremental, the pure and the obscene, already troubles the notion of the Great Divide, while also unveiling the complexity of "Modernism" and the difficulty of ascribing any single aesthetic to it. Furthermore, as I shall argue below, *Ulysses*'s engagement with commercial culture is also reflected by the advertisement-saturated periodical medium in which it appears. And this engagement with commercial culture was one that even Modernists like Pound could not avoid. Just as Pound was at once *Ulysses*'s "first censor" and "first notable champion,"[86] so he was also at once opposed to "low" art and forced to engage with it. And we may think of Joyce's "Calypso" episode as an initiation into the simultaneously playful and anxious space where "low" and "high" art forms intermingle, where the "erotic" blends with the "excremental,"[87] where what *Ulysses* later terms the "gentle art of advertisement"[88] appears alongside "Law, the classics," and "Literature."[89] The revised "Calypso" episode, stripped of any evident indications of Bloom's visit to the outhouse, escaped the government censor's pen, but its evasion was successful only because Pound's censorious pen had struck it first.

Despite meeting governmental approval, the episode nevertheless inaugurated a series of angry responses, demonstrating the shifting balance of control over the text from author to authority figure. As anxiety over *Ulysses* escalated from private disagreement to public scandal, the struggle for power over the words in *Ulysses* threatened to destabilize the *Little Review*'s exercise in collaborative experiment: "Calypso" first outraged Pound, and Pound's excisions in turn outraged Joyce. Then, for a few months, there was relative calm, as Bloom appeared monthly in "Lotus Eaters," "Hades," and "Aeolus." But in January 1919 it was the US Post Office's turn to be outraged. Following publication of Episode VIII ("Lestrygonians") in the *Little Review*, the government forbade "the editors' mailing any additional copies after the issues were sent to subscribers."[90] Anderson and Heap then planned a counter-attack. In May 1919, which contained Episode IX ("Scylla and Charybdis"), the editors printed allusions to homosexuality, contained in Joyce's lines "Greeker than the Greeks" and "Love that dare not speak its name," but they calculatedly omitted other problematic passages.[91] One such passage involves Stephen Dedalus's potentially offensive reply to John Eglinton's suggestion that Shakespeare, as an Englishman, loved a lord. Responding to Eglinton, Stephen begins, "It seems so" and then trails off in a string of ellipses,[92] ending in an asterisk which allows Anderson to explain: "The Post Office authorities objected to certain passages in the January installment of 'Ulysses,' which prevents our mailing any more copies of that issue. To avoid a similar interference this month I have ruined Mr. Joyce's story by cutting certain passages in which he mentions natural facts known to everyone."[93] Characterizing the Post Office's objections as "interference" and claiming that she has been forced to "ruin" Joyce's prose, Anderson, it seems, strategically censors *Ulysses* in a move designed not only to protect her magazine from further suppression but also to highlight the government's irrational objections to artistic freedom. The government's argument, she implies, is illogical, since the "natural facts" which the *Little Review* has been forced to omit are "known to everyone." While Anderson's own censorship seems to imply compliance with the authorities, the diction of her footnote reverses whatever protection capitulation might have obtained and, instead of appeasing the authorities, provokes them.

As with the Lewis story in the October 1917 number, the Joyce episode in the May 1919 issue was not, in fact, the only offending item—though it of course has received the most press. W.H. Lamar, the Post Office Solicitor, told Quinn that he had examined the May issue thoroughly and found multiple grounds for forbidding its mailing: Lamar explicitly states that the judgment was "not based solely" upon Joyce's work, but "upon the magazine as a whole," including its images as well as its words.[94] The objectionable visual material was probably the four drawings of nudes by James Light—drawings which, moreover, immediately follow the "Scylla and Charybdis" installment. In this respect, it is as if Joyce's line "Offend me still," occurring on the page immediately preceding the drawings,[95] somehow summons the offensive images that provoked the authorities. Although Joyce does not intend his line to refer to the images, Lamar's statement nonetheless indicates that he and other censors were reading the "magazine as a whole," piecing together the visual images and printed matter—however unrelated these items might otherwise be—in order to determine the overall character of the periodical.

Strangely, Lamar's insistence upon reading the magazine as a whole parallels Pound's assertion, made the same year, that *Ulysses* must be read as a whole in order for its effect to be rightly judged: "The excuse for parts of *Ulysses* is the WHOLE of *Ulysses*."[96] Although Lamar's and Pound's statements appear to mirror each other, they also diverge: Lamar insists upon reading the whole of the magazine issue (which consists of many different works brought together), whereas Pound insists upon reading the whole of the novel (which consists of a single work's scattered serial installments being brought together). These statements, highlighting the difference between book reading and periodical reading, show that *Ulysses*'s first serious readers were acutely aware of its physical format. Whereas books can be self-contained works, periodicals always position works alongside other material, both visual and printed, that inflects them.

Lamar argues that the *Little Review* as a whole is unmailable, while Pound argues that *Ulysses* is validated as a whole. But, even though they reach different conclusions about Joyce's novel, both agree that the periodical format places works in a larger context that has to be considered.

For *Ulysses*, this larger periodical context means that Joyce's novel is cast as part of a broad-based mission to unveil the Post Office's injustices and attack the strict governmental controls hindering the spread of independent ideas, the frank expression of sexuality, and the open discussion of natural bodily functions. Not only was the *Little Review* still recovering from the government's attack on the Wyndham Lewis story it *had* daringly printed (in October 1917), but it was also boldly showcasing its own, deliberate omission of "obscene" passages it *had not* printed, mimicking the government's censorial hand in a way that created a sense of intrigue surrounding the omissions (since readers were left to guess for themselves which scandalous words filled the ellipses). In the same May 1919 issue that pointedly eliminated two sensual passages from *Ulysses*, an asterisk explains that certain erotic lines in Elsa von Freytag-Loringhoven's love poem "King Adam" have been *"Donated to the censor."*[97] This "donation" is not silent but vocal and public, announced and printed for all to see in place of the scandalous lines which everyone but the editors, authors, and censor cannot see. The financial register of "donated" also ironically reflects upon the *Little Review*'s monetary troubles, which were in part caused by the controversial serializations that alienated donors (Pound, for example, was concerned that excremental references in Joyce's work would alienate Quinn, and Quinn eventually did stop supporting the magazine financially). The magazine that repeatedly issued appeals for monetary donations from subscribers, patrons, and advertisers now in turn offers a "donation" of literature to the censor. This "donation," of course, is offered ironically, not with appreciation but with resentment. Anderson's acts of prior censorship, then, far from complying with the government's wishes, are actually converted into platforms for protest.

And the censors were, predictably, provoked. In spite of the passages which had been omitted to avoid suppression, the May 1919 issue was confiscated, prompting the editors to publish an ad in June 1919 which blamed the government for readers' undelivered copies: "THE LITTLE REVIEW for May has been declared unmailable by the P. O. Department. Ask the Government to reimburse you for your loss." But the government censors were not the only ones who were provoked by Joyce's work and the *Little Review*'s policy of "making no compromise with the public taste." By the end of the year, in December 1919, Margaret Anderson was forced to admit that the publication of *Ulysses* was causing book publishers to think twice about advertising in her magazine. Some even refused altogether:

> Of those whose names are conspicuously absent two promised to take pages and then changed their minds; several promised to advertise in future numbers; several felt they had no books that would interest our readers; some refused for purely conventional reasons; some objected so strongly to our policy and to Mr. James Joyce that nothing would induce them to appear.[98]

Anderson then admits that the *Little Review* may contain objectionable material, but she insists that "objectionable" does not translate into "non-printable": "The subject matter chosen by the men who write today may be objectional. The war was objectionable, but it occurred to me that I couldn't stop it. And I haven't yet attempted to control the mind of the times."[99] Sneering at the "censor that suspects the worst of any effort dedicated to the best,"[100] Anderson concludes her article with a plea for financial support: "I ask whether you can give your support, at least once a year, to the one magazine in America in which the man of letters may obtain a hearing among his peers, ungarbled in editorial rooms to suit the public taste."[101]

The magazine's financial difficulties, however, were to magnify rather than decrease, compelling it to publish combined issues instead of monthly numbers and to raise its subscription price from $2.50 to $4.00 per year (beginning in 1921). Joyce's *Ulysses* was intimately wrapped up in these changes, as the magazine's "Advance in Price" announcement in the September–December 1920 issue explained: "Publication has been further complicated by our arrest on October fourth: Sumner vs. Joyce." On account of *Ulysses*, the *Little Review* not only faced a trial but also an exacerbated financial crisis that forced it to increase its subscription price by 60 percent. The financial crisis, now worsened, had been brooding for quite some time. In April 1920 the *Little Review* had pleaded, in a headline that spanned two pages, "*Are there 1000 people in America who will give $5 apiece to our fund[?]*"[102] As part of its appeal, the *Little Review* reminded readers that "*the 'Little Review' alone in America is performing a function performed by at least a dozen reviews in France and by eight or ten in England.*"[103]

Casting its mission as international, the *Little Review* claimed that it was forging important intellectual links between Europe and America, fostering a transatlantic exchange of ideas: "Oppressed at every turn by a new financial difficulty, we have been able in spite of this to establish some intellectual communication between England, France and America by presenting the best of the creative work produced in those countries today."[104] The *Little Review*, then, claimed that it uniquely brought America into the circle of intellectual activity in Europe, a claim that it reiterated in its September–December 1920 announcement of "Advance in Price": "REMEMBER": "The *Little Review* was the first magazine to reassure Europe as to America, and the first to give America the tang of Europe."[105] By reminding readers of its international scope, the *Little Review* not only sought to mollify readers dissatisfied with the climbing subscription prices but also underscored the way in which its magazine, by virtue of publishing many disparate artifacts simultaneously, put authors from many different backgrounds and with many different styles in dialogue with each other.

Ulysses Alongside Other Works in the *Little Review*

Readers who encountered *Ulysses* within the *Little Review*'s colorful covers were not reading this great Modernist novel in isolation but were encountering it alongside other pieces that editors had carefully packaged together. These other pieces, by engaging with Joyce's work either consciously or unwittingly, put *Ulysses* into a new aspect. Sketches by Ben Hecht, for example, would often give a montage or impression of a city, with protagonists wandering around the streets in much the same way as Joyce's characters. In the same number that published "Hades" (September 1918), W.B. Yeats's "In Memory of Robert Gregory" introduced the theme of elegy, and Ford's "Women and Men" column, as the number's last article, closed the issue by focusing on cemeteries and mourning. The September 1918 issue places Joyce in a male milieu, his fellow contributors being, in addition to Yeats and Ford, Edgar Jepson, T.S. Eliot, Sherwood Anderson, Ben Hecht, John Rodker, and Ezra Pound. But this collection of exclusively male contributors on the contents page, with Margaret Anderson surfacing as the sole female name in her capacity as editor, was the exception rather than the norm.

Although Wyndham Lewis classed Joyce among the "Men of 1914," he frequently appeared in the *Little Review* alongside female writers, including those whom Bonnie Kime Scott terms the "Women of 1928" (Virginia Woolf, Rebecca West, and Djuna Barnes). As Scott notes:

> Stories by Djuna Barnes and poetry by Mina Loy and Amy Lowell (following Lowell's repudiation by Ezra Pound) appeared alongside *Ulysses*. Indirectly, this affected Joyce's experience of the courts and the reception of his work by a wider set of readers. Knowing of Barnes's *Little Review* connection, Joyce sought her

out for news of the trial when Barnes first arrived in Paris, mentored her in an exceptional manner, and entered her accounts of Modernism.[106]

In the *Little Review*, then, Joyce is situated within a very different context, one that puts him into closer dialogue with female authors and with a broader range of artists.

This diverse milieu, however, generated jarring juxtapositions as well as striking complements, discontent as well as satisfaction. While Pound was pleased to be published alongside Joyce, for example, potential advertisers were reluctant to have their ads printed within the same covers as Joyce's work, and many readers (as I discuss below) objected to Joyce's disturbing, corrupting presence within what they viewed as the formerly "admirable" magazine. Quinn, too, disapproved of Joyce's position within this milieu, but he reversed the equation, associating the contamination with the other, less sophisticated works in the magazine—works that he specifically identified as feminine. Suggestive lines in Joyce's *Ulysses* may have offended Quinn, but in his eyes they were not quite as offensive as Anderson's and Heap's lesbianism, or their publication of "inferior" female works. In a letter of October 16, 1920, he complained: "Seriously, it is *wrong* that Joyce's serious work should be published between sheets that are otherwise devoted to such banalities, stupidities and puerilities, paraded as revolutionary, as have made up for the last two years, the remainder of the stupid magazine… Without being personal, I think of female literary excrement."[107] Because Pound had edited "Calypso," Joyce's tendencies to inject "excrement" into his own work may not have been as evident to magazine readers, but "Nausicaa," with its more shocking instances of voyeurism and masturbation, had by this time already appeared. In "Nausicaa," the saturated references to mass culture reinstate the commentary on popular fiction and periodicals that had been lost when Pound deleted the "Calypso" scene in which Bloom wipes himself with *Titbits*.

Hence, Quinn's objections to excremental meditations and literature that is not "serious" are rather mystifying in light of his defense of *Ulysses*, as he articulated it in both his correspondence and the courtroom. Bonnie Kime Scott helps unravel the inconsistency when she explains, "By sleight of pen, […] Quinn places the blame for supposed obscenities, written by Joyce and selected by Pound, upon the publishing of Anderson and Heap."[108] Yet Quinn was off the mark in other places as well. The intermingling to which he so vehemently objects is for Joyce precisely the point: *Ulysses*, itself a text that mixes high with low, destabilizing "any implied opposition between elite and mass cultures,"[109] appropriately appears in a magazine publishing material that, as even its editors admitted, did not always "hold up as art."[110] Furthermore, although Quinn objects to Anderson, Heap, and other "deviant" female authors, these very women were quite frequently Joyce's most avid supporters. Along those lines, Aaron Jaffe tracks two troublesome tendencies in high Modernism: the tendency to subordinate female work to male work; and the parallel tendency (given that women were often editors engaged in collaborative projects) to subordinate collaborative work to singular work. Yet, authors like Joyce were dependent on female editors and collaborative paradigms, and "the very nature of this dependency troubles the brand of aesthetic self-sufficiency long understood to be the dominant message of Modernist form."[111]

When the last installment of *Ulysses* was published in the *Little Review*, it was surrounded by female commentary on the novel. To be sure, Virginia Woolf's comments were more ambivalent than supportive, but the editors' decision to reprint her remarks from the *Times Literary Supplement* nevertheless draws attention to *Ulysses* as an important work of art worthy of debate. Woolf's comments occur as the last article in the September–December 1920 issue, and as such they function as a kind of parting reflection on Joyce's novel while it was still being serialized. Anderson and Heap re-appropriate the article Woolf wrote in the *TLS* for their New York audience, which was not only immersed in Joyce's fiction but also awaiting its fate in the courts. Describing Joyce's "intention" (which, in another context, would become an element in testing literature for pornography), Woolf writes:

> Let us record the atoms as they fall upon the mind [...]. Any one who has read "The Portrait of the Artist as a Young Man" or what promises to be a far more interesting work, "Ulysses," now appearing in the Little Review, will have hazarded some theory of this nature as to Mr. Joyce's intention. On our part it is hazarded rather than affirmed; but whatever the exact intention there can be no question but that it is of the utmost sincerity and that the result, difficult or unpleasant as we may judge it, is undeniably distinct.[112]

Woolf's references to "judging" Joyce's work may carry a more aesthetic than legal register, but her evaluation, floating between praise and blame, captures the sense of uncertainty *Little Review* readers also felt as they waited for the court to decide whether *Ulysses* should be affirmed as a work of art or condemned as a work of pornography.

If Woolf and the Court had not yet made up their minds, Anderson and Heap had already reached their conclusions. Their arrangement of the September–December issue is clearly designed to draw attention to *Ulysses*: not only did they conclude the issue with Woolf's article, but they also began the issue with two of their own essays. Heap's "Art and the Law" asserted that Joyce's work was not obscene while also contemplating the figure of the young girl, and Anderson's "An Obvious Statement" predicted and responded to arguments she believed would be made against *Ulysses* in court. Thus the last installment of Joyce's *Ulysses*—containing the first portion of "Oxen of the Sun," in which Mina Purefoy prepares to give birth at the National Maternity Hospital while the men hold their conversation in a separate room—is prefaced by Anderson's and Heap's editorials and followed by Woolf's commentary, encased by female responses.

When Bonnie Kime Scott argues that recovering female readers' "reactions to Joyce is an invaluable help in reinterpreting Modernism,"[113] she suggests a context for Joyce that is mirrored in miniature by the material positioning of articles in the *Little Review*. In fact, after the final installment of *Ulysses* appeared in 1920, the majority of *Little Review* articles tracing the novel's trajectory was written by women. When a reader named Walter Shaw complained in the January–March 1921 issue that *Ulysses* was not a work of art and did not deserve so many articles, Jane Heap reminded him of the interest Joyce's work had compelled among *Little Review* readers and then concluded:

> If you have not seen him [Joyce] tight-rope-walking the cobweb of the human consciousness, conceiving and executing the rhythms of human thought; if you have not seen Mr. Bloom spring full-fledged from his own brain; if you haven't the carefully organized, masterfully coloured abstract picture of the mind of Dublin; if you have not got the luminosity of his genius, nothing will help you but a work of equal magnitude which no one could write and which you again would not understand.[114]

The same issue also included "Sumner versus James Joyce" by Harriet Monroe and "'Ulysses' in Court'" by Margaret Anderson. Anderson's article is particularly notable for the way that it recasts the *Ulysses* court debates from a female perspective, documenting her silencing by Quinn. Although modern-day anthologies and critical studies have assembled feminist responses to *Ulysses*, many of these reactions were already published and available for consumption in the *Little Review*.

Furthermore, periodical reading could in turn influence periodical writing. As Daniel Ferrer has shown, when Virginia Woolf was preparing her notes on *Ulysses*, she was sidetracked by May Sinclair's article on the novels of Dorothy Richardson (published in the *Little Review* of April 1918). Furthermore, as Ferrer writes, Joyce himself may also have read May Sinclair's review of Richardson's works:

> Superficially at least, Joyce's work was superseded by this essay as the hottest new feature. It is likely that Joyce at least glanced through it and perhaps, consciously or unconsciously, decided to differentiate himself from the kind of stream of consciousness novel that was depicted here (it is in May Sinclair's article that the expression "stream of consciousness" was first used in a literary context).[115]

To Ferrer's account we might also add that, in addition to written text, the placement of advertisements in the *Little Review* further encouraged readers to make a connection between Joyce and Richardson. The December 1919 issue displays an ad for Joyce's works above an ad for Richardson's novels, which quoted May Sinclair. These advertisements, one on top of the other, symbolically convey both the similarities and the tensions between these two authors. In the advertisements, attention is drawn not only to the diversity of Joyce's works, as the genres of fiction, drama, and poetry are displayed, but also to the diversity of publications occurring in the *Little Review*, as different authors are brought together on a single page. Furthermore, Sinclair's April 1918 article itself compares Richardson to Joyce, observing, "Miss Richardson has not plunged deeper than Mr. James Joyce in his *Portrait of the Artist as a Young Man*,"[116] one of the works featured in the December 1919 advertisement.[117]

Sinclair's invitation to compare the two authors is rather vague, but a closer inspection of the two texts reveals stronger points of convergence as well as of divergence. In January 1920, which included the "Cyclops" episode, Richardson's *Interim* also featured a debate about Jews. As Adam McKible shows in a chapter devoted to the *Little Review* and the Jews, the magazine "relied extensively upon the figure of the Jew as a traditionally available" symbol of "uncertainty and rootlessness."[118] McKible discusses Pound, Lewis, Barnes, Mina Loy, Elsa von Freytag-Loringhoven, and Kenneth Burke as *Little Review* contributors who employ the trope of the Jew in their writings. Hence it is curious that McKible does not mention Richardson's Jewish references or Joyce's "Cyclops" dialogue, since the material connection (as opposed to merely ideological or conceptual parallels) is so strong. In Richardson's story, the following dialogue takes place, foregrounding issues of national prejudice that would also be addressed several pages later in *Ulysses*:

> "I have not a scrap of insular prejudice. I like foreigners. They are more intelligent than Englishmen. But there's something they don't know that makes

them all alike. I once heard a wealthy old Jew say that he'd go to Germany for diagnosis and to England for treatment, and he'd had operations and illnesses all over the world. That expresses it."

"You infer that the English have more humanity."

"They don't regard the patient as a case in the way continentals do."

"Well I guess when we're sick we all like to go home."

"You mean the Jew had no home. But he chose the English to go home to when he was ill."[119]

Just a few pages later, the reader was once again confronted by the complex interrelations of Jews, homelessness, and nationality in *Ulysses*, when John Wyse asks, "[W]hy can't a jew love his country like the next fellow?" to which J.J. replies, "Why not? [...] when he's quite sure which country it is."[120] Taken within its original serialized context, this exchange in "Cyclops" becomes more than a localized argument in Barney Kiernan's pub, more than an authorial comment on Jewishness and exile, and more than an abstract depiction of the "double bind" of Irish manhood (as articulated by Joseph Valente); it also becomes part of a larger yet focused interrogation of home and Jewish identity simultaneously being explored by the community of authors and readers formed around the *Little Review*.[121] The subject of Jew as foreigner was one to which the magazine repeatedly returned, thereby situating the fictional debate in "Cyclops" within a discussion already taking place within the periodical's covers.

The Errors of *Ulysses*

It was not just the surrounding context and articles, however, that gave the debates of *Ulysses* a different inflection; in addition, the text of *Ulysses* itself differed in ways that would have given *Little Review* subscribers a substantially different reading experience from readers of later printings. In a novel so invested in errors as portals of discovery, it is significant that the magazine installments contained not only obvious typographical errors but also other, more substantial deviations that could alter the meaning of the text. Even the word "blemish," appropriately enough, cannot escape the pitfalls of imperfection: in Episode XIV, the last chapter to be printed in the magazine (September–December 1920), we are told not of a body "without blemish,"[122] as the phrase is perfectly recorded in Hans Walter Gabler's edition, but rather of a body "without belmish,"[123] as the phrase is imperfectly recorded in the *Little Review*. Here, in the serial printing, the word "blemish" acquires a blemish so that its spelling reflects its meaning.

In revisiting the *Little Review*, we are compelled to reexamine and reinterpret the text as we are confronted with alternatives to familiar passages: Does Bloom suspect Goulding of looking "cute as a rat" or "cute as a cat"? Did Martha Clifford write "I do not like that other word" or "I do not like that other world"? Did Stephen's telegram begin with "Nother" or "Mother"? Did Mr Power ask something "of both windows" or "through both windows"? These are only a few of the many deviations that would have altered the meaning of the text for its initial readers. Or imagine how confused readers in June 1919 would be when they opened what we now know is the beginning of "Wandering Rocks" but, reading the label "IX," found themselves still, ostensibly, in Episode IX ("Scylla and Charybdis").¹²⁴ From the perspective of periodical readers, the style appears to switch in the middle of the episode, with the sudden intrusion of Father Conmee. Only in retrospect does it become clear that the beginning of Episode X was incorrectly labeled "IX," allowing the wandering rocks of Episode X, as it were, to wander into the previous episode.

These errors undoubtedly create confusion, but they are also oddly appropriate to Joyce's technique, at once out of place and in tune with his willingness to incorporate mistakes and misunderstandings into his work. Joyce may have been "irritated by all those printer's errors,"¹²⁵ but he was arguably even more interested in the fertile new meanings these errors would produce. In many ways, *Ulysses* operates as a self-reflexive meditation on the condition of humans in a world of error. The "Nestor" episode, which contains a scene of Mr. Deasy composing a letter, is a good case in point. In this episode that the *Little Review* peppered with frequent typographical errors, there is, coincidentally enough, a direct mention of error in the composition scene:

> He went to the desk near the window, pulled in his chair twice and read off some words from the sheet on the drum of his typewriter. [...] He peered from under his shaggy brows at the manuscript by his elbow and, muttering, began to prod the stiff buttons of the keyboard slowly, sometimes blowing as he screwed up the drum to erase an error.¹²⁶

Whether Joyce intended his readers to think of printers typing up his manuscript is a separate question, but the episode does seem to be acknowledging the likelihood that errors will creep into any document. That Joyce took care to record the "screwed up drum" of the typewriter indicates his recognition of and investment in human error.

Ulysses, I argue, highlights the way Joyce's fascination with scribal errors, misspellings, and linguistic misunderstandings leads into a sustained, theoretical inquiry of circulated errors—mistakes which are also reflected in the correspondence surrounding Joyce's work. In exploring such instances of faulty transcription, I suggest, Joyce offers up Bloom as an ideal reader of errors, a model for generating the sorts of productive meditations that can result from encountering mistakes and negotiating accidents. Bloom's internalization of Martha Clifford's scribal error is particularly telling. Her "corrupted" letter reads, in part: "Dear Henry [...] I called you naughty boy because I do not like that other world."[127] In her phrase "that other world," Martha of course means "word," as her next sentence reveals—"Please tell me what is the real meaning of that word?"[128] Martha's mistake unwittingly unveils an equation between "word" and "world," making a provocative suggestion that one can be substituted for the other. Tim Conley argues that the "'other world' that Martha Clifford mentions and that troubles Bloom is the world of error, the messages that seem scrambled and unreadable and are discarded as unintelligible and thus unintelligent,"[129] but if Martha's error is troubling to Bloom it is also stimulating. Fragments of Martha's letter, and her accidental substitution of "world" for "word," repeatedly infiltrate Bloom's thoughts as he conducts his Odyssean journey—as he attends Paddy Dignam's funeral, as he passes the *Irish Times*, as he reads the *Freeman's Journal*, as he walks along the strand. And, rather than performing the mental correction, Bloom consistently retains Martha's erring substitution, meditating on it and tracing out its consequences. The various "worlds" that are created for Bloom by Martha's accidental transcription suggest that Joyce's text recasts the world of errors as a world of possibilities.

Unlike their twenty-first-century counterparts, however, readers of the *Little Review* would not have been able to trace Martha Clifford's error, because it never existed in the first place. The *Little Review* not only introduced errors into *Ulysses*, but it also corrected errors that were intentional on Joyce's part. Martha Clifford's scribal errors in her "Lotus Eaters" letter are now-famous mistakes that critics have analyzed in detail, but in July 1918, when the episode was first printed, the most widely discussed errors never appeared. The *Little Review*'s Martha was a much more accurate writer, disinclined to insert additional letters into words and less inclined to conjugate her verbs incorrectly. In the *Little Review*, Martha's grammatically incorrect "if you do not wrote"[130] occurs in proper form as "if you do not write."[131] While the latter reading is present in Joyce's manuscript and was only modified by him after serialization, the *Little Review* does falsely correct one of Martha's errors that *was* present in the manuscript, altering the last word of her sentence "I called you naughty boy because I do not like that other world"[132] to the meaning she intends—"word."[133]

Initially, it appears as though these corrections would make the text more understandable and accessible for early readers. But in fact these corrections would only cause greater confusion for readers who opened the January 1919 installment ("Lestrygonians") and encountered Bloom's recapitulation of the letter, in which he retains the error that was never printed: "I called you naughty darling because I do not like that other world."[134] Martha's "word/world" conflation comes only belatedly, and as part of Bloom's thoughts, not the original letter. The introduction of "world" here in Episode VIII would thus be more confusing to readers of 1918/1919, since they would expect to see "word" instead, not only because it makes logical sense, but also because that was how the recited sentence ended in Martha's original letter.

As readers of the *Little Review* themselves recognized, such false corrections and actual typographical errors could result in frustration and cause problems of interpretation. References to error repeatedly surface in the *Little Review*'s correspondence files, as contributors such as Jean de Bosschère, Muriel Ciolkowska, and Dorothy Richardson write in to complain about the typographical errors that littered the magazine. One undated fragmented attributed to Muriel Ciolkowska complains that it had become impossible to know the difference between accidental and intentional deviations.[135] Ciolkowska's point about intentional error is particularly pertinent to *Ulysses*, which includes frequent departures from traditional English punctuation and spelling. Joyce himself anticipated the difficulties that could result from his nonconventional style, and in February 1918—a month before serialization of his novel began—he sent Pound the last episode of the Telemachiad ("Proteus") along with the following instructions: "The spelling and grammatical construction used by me are to be followed by the printer even when words are misspelled and the grammar is at fault."[136] For Joyce, then, errors were an essential part of *Ulysses*. But typographical errors were so frequent that it was often impossible for readers of the *Little Review* to distinguish between accidental mistakes and volitional ones. When Bloom reads the label inside his "Plasto's high grade ha,"[137] with its worn off "t," the word "ha" would be easy to read as a typo, especially given other errors in the episode, including the misspelling of "Gibraltar" as "Gibraltr" on the same page.[138] Here, an intentional error on Joyce's part becomes very tempting to register as a printer's accidental mistake.

To be sure, something is lost in these mistranscriptions, but something is also gained. It is somehow appropriate that a novel about error should appear in a print medium so prone to error itself (here one can also think of the frequent newspaper mistakes recorded in *Ulysses*).[139] Before serialization of *Ulysses* began, a January 1918 promotional ad for Joyce's novel misspelled "Stephen" as "Stephan"; the *Little Review*'s February 1918 ad then perpetuates the same error. As if the novel could not escape extratextual references to its own subject, notices about *Ulysses* were often published next to apologies for error and lists of errata in the *Little Review*. In August 1918 (incidentally, a number devoted to Henry James), under the heading "Announcements," the *Little Review* reported that Episode VI of *Ulysses* would be published in the next number. Further on down the page, under the heading "Errata," the *Little Review* explained that its issues, "through some untraceable mistake," had been misnumbered. It then instructed readers how to assign the correct volume and issue numbers to six previous issues published that year. In December 1918, when Margaret Anderson acknowledged the "typographical errors in the last number,"[140] she included an announcement about Joyce's *Ulysses* on the same page. These suggestive placements, without drawing any direct link between *Ulysses* and the magazine's errata, nevertheless remind readers of the context of error surrounding Joyce's novel. While I do not wish to argue that the editors of the *Little Review* were intentionally pairing announcements for Joyce's work with declarations of error, I do want to argue that the magazine's frequent discussions of error, and the even more frequent typographical mistakes within *Ulysses* itself, would have prompted the novel's first readers to contemplate questions of error and deviation. The announcements and advertisements also suggest that the line between commercial culture and Modernist aestheticism, between the corruption of the marketplace and the purity of art, could not be so easily drawn.

Advertisement and Other Little Magazines

As scholars have often noted, Modernism's "little magazines" were determined to challenge the influence of mass-market periodicals by establishing what Mark Morrisson has termed a "counter-public sphere." In a classic illustration of this opposition, the April 1918 *Little Review* published an article by Pound in which he denounced "profitable periodicals" that "pretended to look after American 'culture'" but actually contributed to the "card-boardizing of the American mind."[141] This disapproving view of profitable periodicals was reflected not only in the *Little Review*'s cover slogan ("making no compromise with the public taste") but also in its editorial columns and article selections. In April 1919, for instance, Margaret Anderson published an article in the *Little Review* that complained bitterly against Chicago periodicals and their pretensions to literary critique, denouncing "their nauseating personal publicity that has served as literary notes."¹⁴² At the same time, the little magazines also recognized that publicity was essential to their own success. In order to further their mission, as Morrisson writes, they also had to adopt the advertising techniques of the successful and profitable mass-market periodicals they opposed.¹⁴³

But the *Little Review* did more than to re-appropriate mass-market features for its own purposes; it also advertised itself alongside these larger magazines. Tellingly, it could be purchased at a reduced rate in combination subscriptions with "popular" periodicals like *Collier's* and *Harper's Monthly*, as evinced by a GRUMIAUX ad occurring in September 1919, among other issues. Furthermore, in March 1918, the *Little Review* relied on citations from other periodicals when it published ads for *A Portrait*, *Dubliners*, and *Exiles* on the page immediately preceding the first episode of *Ulysses*. These blurbs quote the *New Republic*, the *Nation*, and the *New Statesman*, which all praise Joyce's fiction. Although these quotations are directed toward Joyce's earlier works, they serve collectively to promote and introduce *Ulysses*, by acclaiming its author and by praising his character Stephen Dedalus, who also makes an appearance on the first page of *Ulysses*, as if summoned by the ad on the facing page.

Even though the *Little Review* billed itself as "the magazine that is read by those who write the others" (a slogan printed on its title page through March 1919), it also read, reviewed, and advertised other magazines within its covers. The advertisements printed within the *Little Review* reveal the extent to which Modernist magazines, situated in a competitive market, both fought for audiences and formed a complex web of citation and counter-citation that contributed to the mutual strengthening of each periodical network. In April 1918, for example, the *Little Review* ran a full-page ad for the *Egoist*, which also serialized episodes of *Ulysses*. The ad, placed prominently on the inside front cover, describes the *Egoist*'s aims in language that closely mirrors the *Little Review*'s own mission statement:

> This journal is not a chatty literary review: its mission is not to divert and amuse: it is not written for tired and depressed people. Its aim is rather to secure a fit audience, and [...] to present in the making those contemporary literary efforts which ultimately will constitute 20th century literature.

Appropriately enough, Pound's article "Unanism," which attacks frivolous periodicals that divert and amuse readers, is advertised in the *Little Review*'s table of contents on the facing page. Further connections between the *Egoist* advertisement and the *Little Review*'s April 1918 articles may be drawn: In its advertisement, the *Egoist* claims to invest "the novel" with "a new destiny and meaning." On the facing page, the *Little Review* lists "The Novels of Dorothy Richardson" in its table of contents. In its advertisement, the *Egoist* claims to publish writers who are "leaders in pioneering methods radically affecting the allied arts"; on the facing page, the *Little Review* advertises authors known for their pioneering methods, including James Joyce, Ford Madox Hueffer, and Wyndham Lewis. Situated thus, the *Egoist* advertisement and the *Little Review*'s table of contents mutually reinforce each other, together building a mission to promote the artist's freedom, evade the pitfalls of mass-market society,[144] and publish literary works that "ultimately will constitute 20th century literature."

Similarly, advertisements for the *Modernist* and the *Dial* suggest a close, interconnected community of magazines. The *Modernist*, claiming to be "international in scope" in its June 1919 ad, mirrors the ambitions of the *Little Review*, which had both a local office in New York and a foreign office in London, did not hesitate to publish works in German or French, and strove to bring America and Europe into closer intellectual dialogue. Additionally, *The Modernist*'s claim to be "opposed to compromise; pledged to truth" mirrors the *Little Review*'s own motto ("making no compromise with the public taste"). The advertising phrases "A forum for active minds and vital art" and "A better and freer magazine" could easily describe either the *Modernist* or the *Little Review* as they conceived of themselves. But the affinities between the *Little Review* and the *Dial* are even stronger. In an April 1920 ad, the *Dial*, like the *Little Review*, distinguishes itself from mass-circulated newspapers catering to the average mind: It promises "[i]ndependent and competent criticism of everything the intelligent mind cares about, making the Dial a full record not of what the world is doing (read your newspaper) but of what the world is creating." Furthermore, a May–June 1920 ad for the *Dial* prints the table of contents for its July issue and includes Joyce's "A Memory of the Players," not only underscoring how the *Dial* and the *Little Review* shared contributors but also reminding readers that the author of *Ulysses* (of which Episode XIII was being serialized in May–June 1920) published poetry as well as fiction. The ads in the *Little Review*, then, place Joyce and his novel within a broader periodical context; somewhat like a linked hypertext today, the magazine's ads suggest further links that readers can follow if they want to learn more about an author, an artistic movement, or a text.[145]

For some readers, however, the strong similarities between the *Little Review* and the *Dial* pointed not toward unity in mission but toward plagiarism. One reader wrote to express outrage in the September–December 1920 issue of the *Little Review*: "Of course you see the *Dial*? Why in the name of literature do they start a magazine at this date and follow directly in your footsteps? Can't they do any pioneering of their own?"[146] In the same issue, however, Heap responded that she was in fact delighted and not dismayed by the *Dial*'s resemblance to the magazine she edited with Anderson: "Yes, we have had this called to our attention many times. The *Dial*'s contents page often reads like our letter-head; but we don't mind, and they seem to like it. There is room in America for any number of efforts of this kind."[147] While scholars such as Nicholas Joost and Alan Golding have taken the reader's protests as evidence of growing hostility between the two magazines, Heap's response suggests that the *Little Review*, far from endorsing the reader's complaint, was prepared not only to accommodate but also to encourage efforts which closely mirrored its own.

Additionally, the *Little Review* allied its mission with other periodicals by sharing advertising space with them and by offering reduced rates for readers who purchased combined subscriptions. For instance, *Playboy*, edited by Egmont Arens and advertised on the April 1919 back cover, offered readers special subscription prices "If You mention 'The Little Review.'" Furthermore, while early critics like Pound and modern-day scholars like Abby Ann Arthur Johnson have emphasized the antagonistic relation between the *Little Review* and Harriet Monroe's magazine *Poetry*,[148] the advertisements suggest that, whatever the personal animosity, there was nonetheless a strong material relation. In June 1919, the *Little Review* presented a "Special Offer" to readers who purchased both *Poetry* and the *Little Review*. Subscribing to both magazines, the advertisement promised, would give readers not only a discount but also "a complete perspective of the art and letters of to-day." To obtain this complete perspective, the ad implies, one would need to subscribe to both publications. Another ad, presented as an "INVITATION," elaborates upon the virtues of *Poetry*, describing it as an "exhibition" of poems that conveniently came to readers' doors. The ad explains: "POETRY, A MAGAZINE OF VERSE, is not a magazine. Not in the ordinary sense. It is an art gallery. The poet's gallery, where he hangs up his poems." It cultivated not so much "readers" as "poetry spectator[s]" who "*view*[*ed*]" "the gallery" of verse. The advertisement's extended museum metaphor underscores the way many little magazines, including the *Little Review*, were putting themselves "on display" for an audience through acts of publication and advertising. As a visual display itself, the advertisement functions as a synecdoche for the many literary artifacts put on display within the magazine's decorative covers, which were themselves visual modes of advertisement. The *Little Review*'s covers not only enticed readers by listing their featured article(s) of the month, but they also employed a variety of visually appealing designs: solid colors, stripes, and floral, to attract attention. The covers were so distinctive and striking that readers (like Virginia Woolf) would sometimes refer to the magazine not by date or issue number but by color.

Advertising *A Portrait* and *Ulysses*

Within the *Little Review*'s decorative covers, *Ulysses* was itself a regularly advertised item, just as *A Portrait* was a predictable focus of advertisements in the *Egoist*, which began serializing the novel in 1914. I want to take a closer look at advertisements for Joyce's work within these two periodicals—first, because the *Egoist* and the *Little Review* advertised each other, thus demonstrating how little magazines operated in exchanges and networks of mutual support; secondly, because both periodicals embarked on quite striking advertising campaigns for Joyce's work, using a combination of visual and print matter to promote art in ways that trouble the divide between the "counter-public sphere" and the commercial press to which it was ostensibly opposed.

Shortly after serializing *A Portrait of the Artist as a Young Man*, the *Egoist* decided to print a more visual portrait of the author. The portrait interrupted the prose in a February 1917 article by Ezra Pound entitled "James Joyce: At Last the Novel Appears"—an at once exasperated and triumphant reference to the Egoist Press's decision to produce Joyce's work after other English publishers, fearing lawsuits, had refused. "I am very glad that it is now possible for a few hundred people to read Mr. Joyce comfortably from a bound book, instead of from a much-handled file of EGOISTS," Pound writes.[149] Celebrating Joyce's victory over censorship, Pound both applauds the book publication of *A Portrait* and highlights how the physical format a work of art assumes can affect its reception by readers.

Even as Stephen Dedalus becomes more resolutely determined to fly by the nets that constrain him, *A Portrait* itself becomes more closely tied to its surroundings, more firmly rooted in a particular family of Modernist works—a trajectory made apparent when we examine the changing advertisements for Joyce's *Bildungsroman*. In February 1917, the *Egoist* printed an ad with an order form for *A Portrait*, the first book the magazine published.[150] This ad ran until July 1917, when the order form was altered to include space for T.S. Eliot's *Prufrock* as well.[151] Then in December 1917 the form became even more crowded, as Ezra Pound's translation of *The Dialogues of Fontenelle* was also added to the advertisement.[152] Finally, Wyndham Lewis's *Tarr* was placed on the line-up.[153] And if we broaden the view to look at the entire back cover of the

Egoist, we see that the ads for Joyce's work formed part of a larger constellation of advertised products, including Modernist magazines, translations of literary works, book publishers, and the *Egoist* itself.

Tellingly, ads in the *Egoist* direct readers toward the *Little Review*, which in turn directs readers toward Joyce's work. One ad for the *Little Review* (in the *Egoist* of May 1917) announces Joyce's anticipated contribution and adds, "We pay our respects to The Egoist for having published *A Portrait of the Artist as a Young Man*, and for having held its columns open to active and individualist writers."[154] The *Little Review* ad, then, also becomes an ad for Joyce and (coming full circle) an ad for the *Egoist*. And, as the price tags attached to the advertisements reveal, even a novel so deeply concerned with art still found itself sold as commercial merchandise, unveiling a connection between Modernist art and commercialism which is also enacted when Stephen Dedalus composes his villanelle on a cigarette box, the remains of a mass-consumed product.

Before *A Portrait* appeared in book form, however, the *Egoist* deployed Joyce's work as an advertising device to lure readers into buying entire back issues. In the *Egoist* of June 1915, when Stephen Dedalus was expounding his artistic theory to Lynch (making his famous declaration that the artist, like the God of the creation, refines himself out of existence), the *Egoist* had already converted Joyce's work of art into advertisement, declaring in bold type that readers should order back numbers of the magazine because Joyce's novel was "Unobtainable Elsewhere."[155] Notably, the ad highlights both *A Portrait* and Remy de Gourmont's "The Horses of Diomedes," which preceded Joyce's novel as the featured serial story, and it also groups Joyce with other contributors, including Madame Ciolkowska, whose "French chronicles" slip into diary form, anticipating Stephen Dedalus's similar move at the end of *A Portrait*.[156] Serialization, then, both puts *A Portrait* into dialogue with other works and yields commercial advantages, since in order to read the entire work customers would have to purchase twenty-five issues.

When it published *A Portrait* in book form, the *Egoist* also printed several full-page ads promoting the novel. These ads highlight tensions between writers and printers while also reflecting the potential for a symbiotic relationship between periodical culture and the book world. Far from concealing the public's objections to *A Portrait*, the ads emphasize its scandalous history and mixed reception, casting Joyce's novel as the work "for which not only was no British publisher to be found willing to publish, but *no British printer willing to print.*"[157] Culling quotations from reviews in mass-market periodicals as well as little magazines, the *Egoist* ads reprint both overflowing praise and harsh criticism. Alongside such statements as "Sterne himself could not have done it better…

One believes in Stephen Dedalus as one believes in few characters in fiction,"[158] the *Egoist* includes *Everyman*'s denunciation of the work as "Garbage ... We feel that Mr. Joyce would be at his best in a treatise on drains."[159] These ads suggest that *A Portrait* could thrive on scandal as well as on approbation; its reputation for both enticing and offending readers maps out in miniature the trajectory *Ulysses*, serialized in the *Little Review*, would later follow. Across the Atlantic, *Little Review* subscribers encountered yet another portrait of the artist.[160] This photograph of James Joyce, printed as the frontispiece of the July–August 1920 issue, not only marks the magazine's turn toward the visual—its appearance fulfills a (March 1920) promise to publish a contributor's photograph in every issue—but also underscores the way in which technology enabled competing representations of artists, as well as representations of competing artists, to circulate on a mass scale.

The *Little Review* not only used its pages to advertise Joyce's works but also used the scandal of *Ulysses* to promote the magazine. When Sylvia Beach was preparing Joyce's novel for book publication, Anderson and Heap distributed an announcement emphasizing *Ulysses*'s suppression in the *Little Review*. In a letter to Heap, Beach suggests that the magazine's subscribers will make ideal readers of *Ulysses*.[161] But these magazine subscribers were often bewildered readers and even overtly hostile critics. Nevertheless, resistant readers could be spurred to action, and their expressions of outrage served in turn to bring attention to *Ulysses* and the *Little Review*. As Katherine Mullin notes, Anderson and Heap were acutely aware of "Joyce's commercial potential."[162] Because the *Little Review* advertised Joyce's works before, during, and after the serialization of *Ulysses*, original readers were constantly invited to engage more actively with the text and to make further investments: to take advantage of special bargains that combine book purchasing with magazine subscribing, to collect Joyce's works from Huebsch, and to subscribe to the *Little Review* in order to read "Joyce's new novel" (advertised on several back covers leading up to its appearance). Later, in one of the magazine's circulars, original readers were invited to join with editors and artists in protest of *Ulysses*'s suppression. On the reverse side of this 1921 circular, a declaration that "THE LITTLE REVIEW IS IMMORTAL" defies the post office's efforts to stop the magazine.[163] Immortality is also promised to readers themselves: Under the heading "7 reasons why you should subscribe," the *Little Review* lists "if you want to keep eternally young"—a reason it repeats in another brochure, one reminding readers that the *Little Review* has "printed all of James Joyce's 'Ulysses' that the U.S. postal authorities would permit."[164] Prominently advertising the scandal so intimately intertwined with art, the *Little Review* also associates *Ulysses* with its promise of youth. Given these advertisements, Mark

Morrisson writes, "The attacks on it as unfit for the young mind [made during the 'Nausicaa' trials] were perhaps not as irrelevant as Margaret Anderson tried to suggest."[165]

Reader Responses to Joyce

Although it is easy to see how conservative book publishers and governmental authorities would object to *Ulysses*, it may be surprising to learn that many members of the *Little Review*'s target audience—an audience that Alan Golding has described as "already converted and committed"[166]—shared these objections to Joyce. By analyzing letters to the editor that often communicated provocative, shocking responses to *Ulysses* even as it was simultaneously being printed, we can highlight this nascent moment in the novel's reception history to suggest how Joyce's work (not only from postmodern perspectives, but also from its first readers' accounts) fueled and complicated ongoing debates about high and low art—debates showcased in the *Little Review*'s "Reader Critic" columns. In this rich forum of exchange, exuberant praise is counterbalanced by caustic criticism, and Joyce's supporters take arms against the opposition. On the one hand, supportive readers gather together to applaud *Ulysses* and the *Little Review*; on the other hand, resistant readers join forces with government censors to thwart the magazine's collaborative project. This division in the *Little Review*'s relatively narrow audience may have been as surprising as it was troubling, but the conflict also shows how skillfully the magazine editors negotiated disagreement, as they converted negative reviews and judgments into opportunities for promotion and advertisement.[167]

Tellingly, debates in the "Reader Critic" columns anticipate later courtroom arguments about the demographics of Joyce's audience and its susceptibility to corruption. One reader writes, in April 1920 (when the first installment of "Nausicaa" was being printed), "It would seem to me that after all these months he [Joyce] could be accepted, obscenity and all, for surely the post-office authorities should recognize that only a few read him, and those few not just the kind to have their whole moral natures overthrown by frankness about natural functions."[168] To this plea for acceptance a reader labeled as "The Modest Woman" responds (in May–June 1920), "The only cure for the nausea he causes is the thought that 'only a few read him.' [...] You [the *Little Review*] started out to be sincere, unconventional, to refuse to pander to commercialism, etc.: a wonderfully courageous and admirable ambition. But you are a great disappointment to those of us who hoped great things for you."[169] Joyce's novel, then, is attacked not only by the government but also by readers originally devoted to the *Little Review*'s cause. For these readers, the publication of *Ulysses* within the *Little Review* substantially changes the direction and mission of the magazine.

The reactions of "The Modest Woman" are generated by a reader responding to the *Ulysses* question after several episodes—"Lestrygonians," "Scylla and Charybdis," and "Cyclops"—had already been suppressed. But even before the government confiscated episodes of *Ulysses*, the *Little Review*'s own devoted readers expressed anxiety and discontent with Joyce's work. One especially incensed reader from New York writes in July 1918:

> The much bepraised Joyce's "Ulysses" is punk, Lewis' "Imaginary Letters" are punkier and Ezra Pound is punkiest. [...] I cannot see that the drivel that passes for conversation in the Joyce atrocity is improved by the omission of quotation marks. Joyce's pleasing habit of throwing chunks of filth into the midst of incoherent maunderings is not at all interesting and rather disgusting.[170]

The New York reader continues, predicting an early demise for the *Little Review* if it continues to stray from its earlier "beautiful" work: "No freak magazine can hold an audience long. It depends upon shock to taste and convention for its success. And it is always overdone."[171] He urges the editors to purge the magazine's pages of offensive voices: "Why don't you fire Ezra Pound, Joyce and Co., and write in some of yourself?"[172] "What you need," he concludes, "is a literary adviser."[173] At first, it may seem strange that the editors would print such harsh criticism. But as Daniel Gunn notes in another context, "criticism is itself a kind of advertisement,"[174] and the reader-critic reviews of *Ulysses*, even when hostile, draw attention to the novel as a temptingly scandalous work and to the *Little Review* as an important site of controversy.

Yet advertisement itself, as a powerful and suspect medium, prompted many readers to comment on the problematic distinction between commercialism on the one hand and the counter-public sphere of "uncompromised" art represented by little magazines on the other. This was, after all, a magazine that printed its own promotional stationery (including Joyce's name in one sidebar) with decorative envelopes to match, a magazine that collected contributors' signatures to use in a brochure advertising its international gallery of art (including Joyce's name at the top center), a magazine proclaiming itself "devoted entirely to the new movements in the arts" that stamps the lower corners of this declaration with price tags.[175]

Readers as well as writers recognized the tenuous division between commercial activity and artistic activity. Patrick Collier, for example, has discussed how one reader of the *Little Review*—Virginia Woolf—took issue with the kind of professionalism associated with Pound, who used "criticism as a way of disseminating a specialized vocabulary and connecting an ethic of rigor to the creation and appreciation of literature."[176] Woolf, on the other hand, reconfigured traditional binaries, "aligning professionalism with publicity and commercialism" and "positing professionalism as *itself* a market force that threatened to raise obstructions between writers and readers."[177] The concerns Woolf raises were also played out in the "Reader Critic" sections at the end of the *Little Review*, where letters to the editors reveal how troubled readers were about issues of advertising and its relation to the magazine's professed artistic ambitions. In July 1918, for example, a reader from Philadelphia demands, "[W]hy do the magazines that publish this transcendent art push as hard as 'the vulgar sort' for sales?"[178] Denouncing this alleged "inconsistency,"[179] the Philadelphia reader directs the editors toward certain advertising pages in the previous (June) issue. In the same July 1918 issue, however, a reader from Chicago praises the *Little Review*'s June issue as "the best yet," explaining: "It makes a wider appeal. Of course I don't mean that it will reach the multitude—no good stuff does that—but that it will please people who are tired of the commercialized hoakum in the average magazine."[180] Although these two readers at least agree that commerce and art belong to separate spheres, even while disagreeing on where the *Little Review* stands (or falls), other readers boldly brought these opposed spheres together by declaring that certain contributors could have enjoyed success in the mass market. Israel Solon writes, "It [the *Little Review*] is first rate from a purely commercial stand point also. Hueffer, May Sinclair and Joyce ought to be good business getters for any commercial magazine. How in the world did Pound ever get hold of them?"[181]

While Solon suggests that Joyce would be profitable to commercial periodicals, other readers were just as convinced that the mass public would not be able to accept him. *Ulysses* stirred deep anxiety among its early readers, in regard both to its offensive passages and to its literary complexity. One "reader critic" writes (in July 1918), under the heading "The Layman speaks—!!," "The impressionistic prose of James Joyce begins to be a bit bewildering, even to those who believe that he is on the right track."[182] This comment was made while "Lotus Eaters" was being serialized. Two years later (when "Nausicaa" was appearing), readers writing in to the *Little Review* were still at a loss:

> Can you tell me when James Joyce's "Ulysses" will appear in book form? Do you think the public will ever be ready for such a book? I read him each month with

eagerness, but I must confess that I am defeated in my intelligence. Now tell the truth,—do you yourselves know where the story is at the present moment, how much time has elapsed,—just where are we? Have you any clue as to when the story will end?[183]

This is one of the letters Clare Hutton speculates may be made up, since it seems to use an "ignorant reader of *Ulysses*" to set up an editorial rescue by "a rather knowing *jh*."[184] Yet even Jane Heap, who responds affirmatively in her attempts to reorient the lost reader, sprinkles her response with qualifying words and phrases (such as "probably," "it would seem," "perhaps," and "I think") that betray her own uncertainty:

> "Ulysses" will probably appear in book form in America if there is a publisher for it who will have sense enough to avoid the public. [...] We haven't any advance chapters in hand, but it would seem that we are drawing towards the Circe episode and the close of the story. The question of time seems simple and unobscured. [...] [T]he time of the present chapter is about five thirty or six in the evening of the same day on which the story started,—I think Tuesday. Mr. Bloom has had a long day since he cooked his breakfast of kidney, but he has lost no time.[185]

As later readers, with help of Don Gifford's *Ulysses Annotated*, will know, "Nausicaa" takes place at 8:00 p.m., and the day is Thursday. "Circe," the fifteenth episode, never appeared in the *Little Review*.[186] For readers of the *Little Review*, Bloom's day would not see an end and the "close of the story" would never arrive: when the last installment appeared in the September–December 1920 issue, he had made it only to 10:00 p.m. After this first segment of "Episode XIV" was published, the *Little Review*, facing obscenity charges, was forced to cease publication of *Ulysses*. Significantly, the controversy generated by the *Little Review* spawned further periodical publications: not only in other little magazines like the *New Age*, but also in the *New York Times*, the *New York World*, the *New York Tribune*, the *New York Daily News*, and the *New York Herald*. The debate over the "artist's expression" begun in the pages of a little magazine became, in the end, an item of discussion in the commercial sphere of mass-market periodicals.

Conclusion

By the time the final issue of the *Little Review* appeared in 1929, subscribers had access to the conclusion of Joyce's novel in book form, but the magazine editors continued to remind readers that *Ulysses* had serial beginnings. A full-page ad for Anderson's autobiography recalls the "fights" surrounding Joyce in the *Little Review*, and, in a relatively short amount of copy, manages to name Joyce twice. Heap reinforces this focus when she writes in her farewell editorial, "We have not brought forward anything approaching a master-piece except the 'Ulysses' of Mr. Joyce."[187] Although she qualifies this assertion, claiming that *Ulysses* is "too personal, too tortured, too special a document to be a master-piece in the true sense of the word,"[188] Joyce is the only contributor she mentions by name in her final article, which she titles "Lost: A Renaissance." Yet, I want to suggest, this Renaissance, described by Heap as the "revolution in the arts, begun before the war" and perpetuated by the *Little Review*,[189] does not have to be lost for us. By returning to the archive and examining behind-the-scenes correspondence alongside works printed in the *Little Review*, we can uncover the treasures of an ambitiously international little magazine that not only published French works alongside English ones but that also provocatively printed common readers' letters alongside celebrated if controversial literary artifacts. Our own return to the *Little Review* can both give us new perspectives on Joyce's work and allow us to obtain a sharper view of Modernism through the lens of periodicals that forged the transatlantic, cross-cultural connections so essential to the development of early-twentieth-century arts. Only through this patient labor of contextualization, I suggest, can we obtain the full benefits of interpretive work.

Such contextualization also unveils closer material and intellectual ties between high Modernists and their predecessors. As little magazines testify, the emerging generation of avant-garde editors and authors had not forgotten the legacy of proto-Modernists, such as Henry James and Rudyard Kipling. The divisions we make between these authors were perhaps not as stark to their own contemporaries. James may have been the more likely literary progenitor, and the *Little Review* mentions him more frequently than Kipling, but the question of each author's cultural influence was still being worked out during *Ulysses*'s serialization. As late as August 1918, Pound briefly speculated, "one wonders if parts of Kipling by the sheer force of content, of tale to tell, will not outlast most of James's cobwebs."[190] Somewhat surprisingly, an author as commercially popular as Kipling earned a place in an experimental literary magazine. This position is reinforced by several key ads and references in the years leading up to and including *Ulysses*'s serialization. In December 1914, the *Little Review* alluded to *Kim*'s serialization when it ran an ad for S.S. McClure's autobiography. The ad glowingly describes McClure as "the editor who introduced to us Kipling, Stevenson, and others equally famous" and as the "Scotch-Irish boy who came here [to America] to do his best [and] tells of his rise in a simple, fascinating way."[191] The reference is fleeting and understated, but the allusion to Irish hardship under British rule primes readers for the political considerations that would later surface in Joyce's *Ulysses*. The ad and subsequent mentions of Kipling's work, which softly dwindle as *Ulysses*'s serialization picks up, suggest a gradual passing of the literary torch. Kipling's world of British imperial dominance was fading, as Joyce's exploration of Irish colonial identity was coming into focus.

Henry James, who had died some two years before *Ulysses*'s serialization began, was likewise viewed as a member of an older generation, but still a force to be reckoned with. In fact, in August 1918, the *Little Review* published a "Henry James Number," announced in bold black type on a bright red-orange cover: This issue featured commemorations and assessments by Ezra Pound, A.R. Orage, T.S. Eliot, and John Rodker, all prominent editors in the little magazine scene; other contributors to the August 1918 number included the Anglo-Irish writer Ethel Colburn Mayne,[192] who like James had contributed to the *Yellow Book* (a late Victorian predecessor to Modernist little magazines), and James's secretary Theodora Bosanquet, whose memoir *Henry James at Work* would be published by the Woolfs' Hogarth Press in 1924. It was one of the few issues published between March 1918 and December 1920 that did not include an installment of *Ulysses*. Yet its appearance in the midst of *Ulysses*'s serialization—between the episodes now known as "Lotus Eaters" and "Hades"—suggests a kind of literary hand-off.

Albeit with important differences, Joyce continued the narrative of James's "friction with the market," to borrow Michael Anesko's title. Whereas James had fretted about the commercialization of literary work, Joyce faced censorship and printers' fears about obscenity and libel. Prior to the composition of *Ulysses*, his struggle to publish *Dubliners* and *A Portrait* had set an uneasy precedent. Too many English printers feared the legal consequences of publishing his daring work (English law at the time held printers legally responsible for any objectional content), and *Ulysses* upped the ante. As he began writing his epic novel, Joyce would seemingly have solved the problem by turning to an American little magazine that bore the motto "making no compromise with the public taste." Such a move enabled him to evade squeamish publishers and restrictive British printing laws, while the advent of little magazines devoted to art created a coterie space for writers whose works were not primarily commercial.

Yet in making this transatlantic move, Joyce had to cede a certain amount of control and allow for unplanned contingencies. Working with the *Little Review*, he could not choose the font or the color of the cover, as he would insist upon doing when *Ulysses* appeared in book form; he could not proof his text or approve changes before it went to press. As a result, both editorially intended and accidental alterations crept into his novel. "Calypso" was so significantly altered that only the most discerning readers could have detected Bloom's trip to the outhouse. Other problematic scenes were decorated with asterisks—and, in spite of these unauthorized emendations, Joyce ran into the very publishing troubles he was hoping to avoid when the government suppressed the *Little Review*, leading eventually to the ban of *Ulysses*. The dream of an unfettered Modernism in little magazines could not be so easily achieved. As archival evidence has shown, it was not just *Ulysses*, but also surrounding artifacts, that led to the magazine's suppression. Within this periodical milieu, Joyce went from being unable to control the appearance of his text to being unable to publish *Ulysses* in the United States at all—at least not until Judge John Woolsey's landmark decision lifting the ban in 1933.[193] Despite these troubles, the sensation surrounding *Ulysses* ultimately became one of its most promising selling points.

Reflecting on the "Nausicaa" trials, Anderson wrote, "In 1920 we were accused of printing 'obscene literature.' We were tried, and lost our case. But in defending ourselves, and Joyce in the pages of the *Little Review*, we offered some of the best writing about Art and the Artist that has ever been produced in America."[194] As I have argued, an integral part of this discussion about art and the artist involved mastering what the "Aeolus" episode in *Ulysses* calls the "gentle art of advertisement."[195] *Ulysses* was inflected by surrounding advertisements, illustrations, and articles as it influenced them and the magazine's image in turn. In this way, scholars' interpretive arguments about the way Joyce's fictional advertisements provide "internal commentary in *Ulysses*"[196] can be extended to reveal how real-world advertisements surrounding the novel in the *Little Review* also complicate the boundaries between mass-market culture and Modernist aesthetics, locating Joyce's work, from the first moments of its appearance in print, in a medium of advertisement, in an international context, in legal battles about censorship, and in a closely connected community of periodical networks that, for all their resistance to commercialism, nevertheless recognized the growing importance of advertisement to the circulation and dissemination of art.

Notes

1   James Joyce, *Ulysses*, ed. Hans Walter Gabler (New York: Random House, 1986), 8.742–5; *Little Review*, January 1919, 44. In the *Little Review*, "What is home without Plumtree's potted meat?" is italicized. The phrase "All up a plumtree" is

also omitted from the *Little Review*. References to the Gabler edition will be cited as *U* plus episode and line number. As Don Gifford notes, "This advertisement and its position under the obituaries, front page, left column of the *Freeman's Journal*, is a fiction, but a George W. Plumtree was listed as a potted-meat manufacturer at 23 Merchant's Quay in Dublin." See Don Gifford with Robert J. Seidman, *Ulysses Annotated: Notes for James Joyce's Ulysses* (Berkeley: University of California Press, 1988), 87. The fact that the ad did not actually appear in the *Freeman's Journal* not only underscores how Joyce was willing to depart from historical exactitude in his portrayal of 1904 Dublin but also puts Joyce in a position similar to that of an editor who strategically arranges items in a periodical in order to produce certain calculated effects on readers. By placing the meat ad under the obituaries, Joyce lightly parodies editors who unwittingly produce undesired, uncalculated effects on their audience. His distortion of reality also emphasizes how periodical texts, inevitably manipulated by editors' controlling hands, derive meaning and associations not only from authors and editors who are consciously shaping the text but also from readers who make their own independent associations when they encounter the text alongside other artifacts.

2   "during which it becomes a reference first to Paddy Dignam, then to cannibalism, then, after sidetrips into Stephen's parable and other plum and plumtree jokes, to Blazes Boylan and *his* potted meat" (as critics like Jennifer Wicke and Daniel P. Gunn have usefully described). See Daniel P. Gunn, "Beware of Imitations: Advertisement as Reflexive Commentary in *Ulysses*," *Twentieth Century Literature* 42, no. 4 (Winter 1996): 486.

3   Jane Heap's letters have been published in *Dear Tiny Heart: The Letters of Jane Heap and Florence Reynolds*, ed. Holly A. Baggett (New York: New York University Press, 2000). Heap preferred using lowercase initials for her name, though I have followed traditional grammar and mechanics here.

4   See also Clare Hutton's excellent discussion of *Ulysses* in the *Little Review* in her book *Serial Encounters: Ulysses and the Little Review* (Oxford: Oxford University Press, 2019). Periodical contexts are likewise illuminatingly discussed in the Yale edition of Joyce's novel, *The Little Review Ulysses*, edited by Sean Latham, Mark Gaipa, and Robert Scholes (New Haven, CT: Yale University Press, 2015).

5   Qtd. in Mary Reynolds, "Joyce as a Letter Writer," in *A Companion to Joyce Studies*, ed. Zack Bowen and James F. Carens (Westport, CT: Greenwood Press, 1984), 40.

6   Announcement, *Little Review*, March 1918, 60.

7   See Ezra Pound, "Small Magazines," *The English Journal* 19, no. 9 (November 1930): 689–704.

8   Julian Symons, *Makers of the New: The Revolution in Literature, 1912–1939* (London: Deutsch, 1987), 100.

9   Symons, *Makers of the New*, 100.

10 *U* 1.05; *Little Review*, March 1918, 3.

11 *U* 1.78, 80; *Little Review,* March 1918, 5. The phrase "*Thalatta! Thalatta!*" does not appear in the *Little Review.*
12 *U* 1.342; *Little Review,* March 1918, 12.
13 *U* 1.425; *Little Review,* March 1918, 14.
14 *U* 1.638; *Little Review,* March 1918, 20.
15 *U* 1.667; *Little Review,* March 1918, 21.
16 *U* 1.649; *Little Review,* March 1918, 20.
17 *U* 2.377; *Little Review,* April 1918, 43.
18 As Clare Hutton notes, Harriet Shaw Weaver and Ezra Pound had also developed "a plan for the simultaneous dual serialization of *Ulysses* in *The Egoist* in London and the *Little Review* in New York. The US was not, at the time, a signatory to the Berne Convention, and the rationale for printing in New York was compliance with the 'manufacturing clause' of the 1891 International Copyright Act, which would enable the protection of Joyce's copyright in the US" (*Serial Encounters*, 3). However, this plan was not that successful: "During the course of 1919, just three of the chapters were printed in *The Egoist* (2, 3, 6) as well as a portion of chapter 10. In every instance the text had already been printed in the *Little Review*" (*Serial Encounters*, 5).
19 See, for example, Mark Wollaeger, Victor Luftig, and Robert Spoo, eds., *Joyce and the Subject of History* (Ann Arbor: University of Michigan Press, 1996).
20 "A Note to Our Readers," *Little Review,* December 1918, 2.
21 *Little Review* Records, 1914–64, University of Wisconsin-Milwaukee Libraries, Archives Department. Hutton cites this letter in *Serial Encounters*, 51–2.
22 Heap to Reynolds, July 1917, Florence Reynolds Collection related to Jane Heap and *The Little Review*, Manuscript Collection Number 258, Special Collections, University of Delaware; published in *Dear Tiny Heart*, 52.
23 Heap, "The Reader Critic," *Little Review,* August 1917, 25.
24 Heap, "The Reader Critic," *Little Review,* September 1917, 34.
25 John Quinn to Margaret Anderson, November 7, 1917, *Little Review* Records, 1914–64, University of Wisconsin-Milwaukee Libraries, Archives Department.
26 J.K.C., "Art and the War" in "The Reader Critic," *Little Review,* October 1917, 41.
27 Ezra Pound, "The Classics 'Escape,'" *Little Review,* March 1918, 34.
28 Anderson, "To Subscribers Who Did Not Receive Their October Issue," *Little Review,* November 1917, 43.
29 Anderson, "Judicial Opinion," *Little Review,* December 1917, 47.
30 Heap, "Art and the Law," *Little Review,* September–December 1920, 6.
31 Mark Morrisson, *The Public Face of Modernism: Little Magazines, Audiences, and Reception, 1905–1920* (Madison: University of Wisconsin Press, 2001), 159.
32 David Weir, "What Did He Know, and When Did He Know It: The *Little Review*, Joyce, and *Ulysses*," *James Joyce Quarterly* 37, nos. 3–4 (Spring–Summer 2000): 391.

33 Qtd. in Weir, "What Did He Know," 391.
34 Quinn to Anderson, December 5, 1917, *Little Review* Records, 1914–64, University of Wisconsin-Milwaukee Libraries, Archives Department.
35 Abel Sanders, "This Approaches Literature!" in "The Reader Critic," *Little Review*, October 1917, 39.
36 Sanders, "The Reader Critic," 39.
37 Sanders, "The Reader Critic," 39.
38 Sanders, "The Reader Critic," 39.
39 Quinn to W.H. Lamar, November 5, 1917, *Little Review* Records, 1914–64, University of Wisconsin-Milwaukee Libraries, Archives Department.
40 Quinn to Anderson, November 7, 1917, *Little Review* Records, 1914–64, University of Wisconsin-Milwaukee Libraries, Archives Department.
41 See, however, the important studies of the Lewis case conducted by Clare Hutton, Joseph M. Hassett, and David Weir.
42 Quinn to Anderson, June 14, 1919, *Little Review* Records, 1914–64, University of Wisconsin-Milwaukee Libraries, Archives Department.
43 Quinn to Anderson, June 14, 1919, *Little Review* Records, 1914–64, University of Wisconsin-Milwaukee Libraries, Archives Department.
44 Anderson, "Judicial Opinion," *Little Review,* December 1917, 49.
45 Anderson, "Judicial Opinion," *Little Review,* December 1917, 48.
46 Quinn to Anderson, June 14, 1919, *Little Review* Records, 1914–64, University of Wisconsin-Milwaukee Libraries, Archives Department.
47 Quinn to Anderson, November 3, 1917, *Little Review* Records, 1914–64, University of Wisconsin-Milwaukee Libraries, Archives Department.
48 Adam Parkes, "'Literature and instruments for abortion': 'Nausicaa' and the *Little Review* Trial," *James Joyce Quarterly* 34, no. 3 (Spring 1997): 284.
49 Parkes, "'Literature and instruments for abortion,'" 284.
50 Parkes, "'Literature and instruments for abortion,'" 284.
51 Parkes, "'Literature and instruments for abortion,'" 285.
52 Parkes, "'Literature and instruments for abortion,'" 285.
53 Lawrence Rainey, *Institutions of Modernism: Literary Elites and Public Culture* (New Haven: Yale, 1998), 47.
54 Quinn to Heap, August 8, 1917, *Little Review* Records, 1914–64, University of Wisconsin-Milwaukee Libraries, Archives Department.
55 Quinn to Anderson, August 11, 1917, *Little Review* Records, 1914–64, University of Wisconsin-Milwaukee Libraries, Archives Department.
56 See Anderson, *My Thirty Years' War* (New York: Friede, 1930).
57 "Will You Help?" *Little Review,* December 1917, 59.
58 "Will You Help?" 59.
59 These transactions are documented in the *Little Review* Records, 1914–64, University of Wisconsin-Milwaukee Libraries, Archives Department.

60 Bonnie Kime Scott, "'The Young Girl,' Jane Heap, and the Trials of Gender in *Ulysses*," in *Joycean Cultures/Culturing Joyces*, ed. Vincent J. Cheng, Kimberly J. Devlin, and Margot Norris (Newark: University of Delaware Press, 1998), 83.
61 Quinn to Anderson, August 11, 1917, *Little Review* Records, 1914–64, University of Wisconsin-Milwaukee Libraries, Archives Department.
62 Quinn to Anderson, February 2, 1918, *Little Review* Records, 1914–64, University of Wisconsin-Milwaukee Libraries, Archives Department.
63 Quinn to Anderson, December 3, 1918, *Little Review* Records, 1914–64, University of Wisconsin-Milwaukee Libraries, Archives Department.
64 Edward Bishop, "Re:Covering Modernism—Format and Function in the Little Magazines," in *Modernist Writers and the Marketplace*, ed. Ian Willison, Warwick Gould, and Warren Chernaik (London: Macmillan, 1996), 287.
65 Quinn to Heap, August 7, 1917, *Little Review* Records, 1914–64, University of Wisconsin-Milwaukee Libraries, Archives Department.
66 See Weir, "What Did He Know," 394–5; Rainey, *Institutions of Modernism*, 47.
67 Jackson R. Bryer, "Joyce, *Ulysses*, and the *Little Review*," *The South Atlantic Quarterly* 66, no. 2 (Spring 1967): 157.
68 Bryer, "Joyce, *Ulysses*, and the *Little Review*," 162.
69 Scott, "'The Young Girl,'" 82, 84.
70 Bryer, "Joyce, *Ulysses*, and the *Little Review*," 163.
71 Sam Slote, *Ulysses in the Plural: The Variable Editions of Joyce's Novel*, The National Library of Ireland Joyce Studies, no. 05, ed. Luca Crispi and Catherine Fahy (Dublin: The National Library of Ireland, 2004), 8.
72 Although "Quinn argued to Lamar that the magazine was not for or read by the young" (Morrisson, *The Public Face of Modernism*, 160), the judges were ultimately not persuaded.
73 Rainey, *Institutions of Modernism*, 47–8.
74 Qtd. in Bryer, "Joyce, *Ulysses*, and the *Little Review*," 155–6.
75 Bryer, "Joyce, *Ulysses*, and the *Little Review*," 159.
76 *Pound/The Little Review: The Letters of Ezra Pound to Margaret Anderson*, ed. Thomas L. Scott and Melvin J. Friedman (New York: New Directions, 1988), 260.
77 Qtd. in Thomas L. Scott and Melvin J. Friedman, "Introduction," in *Pound/The Little Review*, xxxi.
78 Symons, *Makers of the New*, 91.
79 Bryer, "Joyce, *Ulysses*, and the *Little Review*," 151.
80 Paul Vanderham, "Ezra Pound's Censorship of *Ulysses*," *James Joyce Quarterly* 32, nos. 3–4 (Spring–Summer 1995): 583.
81 Vanderham, "Ezra Pound's Censorship of *Ulysses*," 583, 592.
82 Vanderham, "Ezra Pound's Censorship of *Ulysses*," 586.
83 Vanderham, "Ezra Pound's Censorship of *Ulysses*," 592.
84 Vanderham, "Ezra Pound's Censorship of *Ulysses*," 593.

85 Qtd. in Vanderham, "Ezra Pound's Censorship of *Ulysses*," 593, 595.
86 Vanderham, "Ezra Pound's Censorship of *Ulysses*," 593.
87 Vanderham, "Ezra Pound's Censorship of *Ulysses*," 588.
88 *U* 7.608; *Little Review,* October 1918, 40.
89 *U* 7.605, 607; *Little Review,* October 1918, 40.
90 Bryer, "Joyce, *Ulysses*, and the *Little Review*," 153.
91 See the *Little Review*, May 1919, 20; *U* 9.614–5; and *Little Review*, May 1919, 21; *U* 9.659.
92 *Little Review*, May 1919, 21. In Gabler the missing lines are printed as "when he wants to do for him, and for all other and singular uneared wombs, the holy office an ostler does for the stallion" (*U* 9.663–4).
93 *Little Review*, May 1919, 21. Anderson also placed ellipses and an asterisk after Stephen's reference to "bodily shame so steadfast that the criminal annals of the world, stained with all other incests and bestialities, do not record its breach" (*Little Review*, May 1919, 26; *U* 9.850–2). In the *Little Review,* the quote ends "do not record its breach" instead of "hardly record its breach" in Gabler's edition. In Gabler the following lines replace the ellipses: "Sons with mothers, sires with daughters, lesbic sisters, loves that dare not speak their name, nephews with grandmothers, jailbirds with keyholes, queens with prize bulls" (*U* 9.852–4). The *Little Review* also prints "hell" (*U* 9.846) as "h--l" (*Little Review,* May 1919, 26). In the November 1919 number, passages were also deleted from "Cyclops" to avoid possible suppression.
94 Lamar to Quinn, June 18, 1919, *Little Review* Records, 1914–64, University of Wisconsin-Milwaukee Libraries, Archives Department.
95 *U* 9.1217; *Little Review*, May 1919, 35.
96 Qtd. in *Pound/The Little Review*, xxxi.
97 Editorial Note for "King Adam," *Little Review*, May 1919, 73. The baroness's first name is spelled "Else" in the *Little Review*.
98 Anderson, "To the Book Publishers," *Little Review,* December 1919, 65.
99 Anderson, "To the Book Publishers," 67.
100 Anderson, "To the Book Publishers," 67.
101 Anderson, "To the Book Publishers," 67.
102 "Are There 1000 People in America...?" *Little Review,* April 1920, 62–3.
103 "Are There 1000 People in America...?" 62.
104 "Are There 1000 People in America...?" 62.
105 "Advance in Price," *Little Review*, September–December 1920, n.p.
106 Scott, "'The Young Girl,'" 79.
107 Qtd. in Scott, "'The Young Girl,'" 83.
108 Scott, "'The Young Girl,'" 84.
109 Katherine Mullin, "Joyce through the Little Magazines," in *A Companion to James Joyce*, ed. Richard Brown (Oxford: Blackwell, 2008), 375.

110 Anderson, *My Thirty Years' War*, 134.
111 Aaron Jaffe, *Modernism and the Culture of Celebrity* (Cambridge: Cambridge University Press, 2005), 96.
112 Virginia Woolf, Review of *Ulysses*, *Little Review*, September–December 1920, 93–4.
113 Bonnie Kime Scott, *Refiguring Modernism* (Bloomington: Indiana University Press, 1995), 161.
114 Heap, "The Reader Critic," *Little Review*, January–March 1921, 61.
115 Daniel Ferrer, "The Work of Joyce in the Age of Hypertextual Production," in *Joycemedia: James Joyce, Hypermedia, & Textual Genetics*, ed. Louis Armand (Prague: Litteraria Pragensia, 2004), 101.
116 May Sinclair, "The Novels of Dorothy Richardson," *Little Review*, April 1918, 5.
117 Although William Carlos Williams paired Joyce and Richardson as paragons of artistic virtue in "Four Foreigners" (August 1919), Anderson noted marked differences in their styles. In March 1920, she wrote in response to one reader who complained that "Dorothy Richardson's instalment […] gets more wild, involved, and Joyceish as it goes on" (Subscriber from New York, "The Good Old Days" in "The Reader Critic," *Little Review*, March 1920, 60): "Dorothy Richardson is so unlike Joyce that I can't even begin to argue that with you—though I'm sure there are some five thousand people who will agree with you because Richardson and Joyce have the great soul bond of unconventional punctuation" (Anderson, "The Reader Critic," *Little Review*, March 1920, 61–2).
118 Adam McKible, *The Space and Place of Modernism: The Russian Revolution, Little Magazines, and New York* (New York: Routledge, 2002), 80.
119 Dorothy Richardson, *Interim*, *Little Review*, January 1920, 42.
120 *U* 12.1628–30; *Little Review*, January 1920, 60.
121 The Spring 1923 "Exiles' Number," issued when the *Little Review* had moved to Paris, reflects the way in which the wandering Jew functions as a trope for the exiled artist.
122 *U* 14.310.
123 *Little Review*, September–December 1920, 90.
124 Rather than printing the episode titles we now have today, the *Little Review* printed only episode numbers, further complicating interpretive questions by making the novel's Homeric connections more difficult for its first readers to identify.
125 Qtd. in Hans Walter Gabler, "Foreword," in *Ulysses: A Critical and Synoptic Edition*, ed. Hans Walter Gabler (New York and London: Garland, 1984, Corrected Text, 1986), vii.
126 *U* 2.292–3, 296–8; *Little Review*, April 1918, 40.
127 *U* 5.241, 244–5; *Little Review*, July 1918, 42.
128 *U* 5.245–6; *Little Review*, July 1918, 42.

129 Tim Conley, *Joyces Mistakes: Problems of Intention, Irony, and Interpretation* (Toronto: University of Toronto Press, 2003), 132.
130 *U* 5.253.
131 *Little Review,* July 1918, 43.
132 *U* 5.244–5.
133 *Little Review,* July 1918, 42. Interestingly, the *Little Review* does not correct Martha Clifford's other error, when she uses a plural verb for a singular subject in the line "my patience are exhausted" (*U* 5.254; *Little Review,* July 1918, 43).
134 *U* 8.327–8; *Little Review,* January 1919, 35.
135 *Little Review* Records, 1914–64, University of Wisconsin-Milwaukee Libraries, Archives Department.
136 Qtd. in Philip R. Yannella, "James Joyce to *The Little Review*: Ten Letters," *Journal of Modern Literature* 1, no. 3 (March 1971): 395. The original is found in the *Little Review* Records. The word Yannella transcribes as "mechanical" may actually be "grammatical."
137 *U* 4.7; *Little Review,* June 1918, 40.
138 *U* 4.60; *Little Review,* June 1918, 40. "Gibraltar" is not misspelled in Gabler's edition.
139 In the November 1918 reader-critic column, Marsden Hartley complained, "I should like to ask a little thing. What is the matter with the typesetters of the *Little Review*? So many misprints and omissionss [*sic*] that it makes the reading very restless. In two pages, eight misprints and omissions. Either bad linotype keyboard work, or bad hand work" (Marsden Hartley from Taos, New Mexico, "Breakfast Resume" in "The Reader Critic," *Little Review,* November 1918, 49).
140 Anderson, "An Appeal to Reason," *Little Review,* December 1918, 1.
141 Pound, "Unanism," *Little Review,* April 1918, 26.
142 Anderson, "Notes on Music and the Theatre (and the Critics)," *Little Review,* April 1919, 55.
143 Morrisson, *The Public Face of Modernism*, 6.
144 This mode of championing artistic freedom over popular taste also extended to advertisements for book publishers, including Irving Kaye Davis & Company, which published several ads in the *Little Review*, such as that appearing in September 1919.
145 And if readers did consult the *Dial*, they would have found that it, in turn, advertised the *Little Review* (in April 1920; Golding 45).
146 "A Champion," "Loyalty" in "The Reader Critic," *Little Review,* September–December 1920, 93.
147 Heap, "The Reader Critic," *Little Review,* September–December 1920, 93.
148 Abby Ann Arthur Johnson, "The Personal Magazine: Margaret C. Anderson and the *Little Review*, 1914–1929," *South Atlantic Quarterly* 75 (1976): 357.
149 Pound, "James Joyce: At Last the Novel Appears," *Egoist,* February 1917, 21.
150 Stuart Gilbert, "Introduction," in *Letters of James Joyce* (New York: Viking, 1957), 1:25.

151 Advertisement for *A Portrait* and *Prufrock, Egoist,* July 1917, 96.
152 Advertisement for *A Portrait, Prufrock,* and *The Dialogues of Fontenelle, Egoist,* December 1917, 176.
153 Advertisement for *A Portrait, Prufrock, The Dialogues of Fontenelle,* and *Tarr, Egoist,* June–July 1918, 88.
154 Advertisement for the *Little Review, Egoist,* May 1917, 63.
155 "Back Numbers of *The New Freewoman* and *The Egoist," Egoist,* June 1915, 99.
156 The ad also incorrectly states the dates of *A Portrait*'s serialization, which began February 2, 1914, not March 1, as the ad says; the *Egoist* corrected this error in its October 1, 1915 number.
157 Advertisement for *A Portrait of the Artist as a Young Man, Egoist,* April 1917, 48.
158 Advertisement for *A Portrait of the Artist as a Young Man, Egoist,* April 1917, 48.
159 Advertisement for *A Portrait of the Artist as a Young Man, Egoist,* April 1917, 48.
160 "I am another now and yet the same," Stephen Dedalus tells us in Episode I of *Ulysses,* as he reflects on the way his holding of the shaving bowl marks a departure from the Clongowes Wood altar boy carrying the boat of incense (*U* 1.311–12; *Little Review,* March 1918, 11). Correspondingly, the *Little Review*'s visual portrait of Joyce differs strikingly from the visual image offered in the *Egoist*.
161 Sylvia Beach to Heap, September 20, 1921, *Little Review* Records, 1914–64, University of Wisconsin-Milwaukee Libraries, Archives Department. A portion of this letter is cited in Hutton, *Serial Encounters,* 97.
162 Mullin, "Joyce through the Little Magazines," 383.
163 *Little Review* flyer protesting the suppression of *Ulysses* [1921], *Little Review* Records, 1914–64, University of Wisconsin-Milwaukee Libraries, Archives Department. Morrisson discusses this circular in *The Public Face of Modernism,* 143.
164 *Little Review* Records, 1914–64, University of Wisconsin-Milwaukee Libraries, Archives Department.
165 Morrisson, *The Public Face of* Modernism, 160.
166 Alan C. Golding, "*The Dial, The Little Review,* and the Dialogics of Modernism," *American Periodicals* 15, no. 1 (2005): 44.
167 There are speculations that some of these letters may have been fabricated, as, for example, Hutton notes in *Serial Encounters,* 61.
168 F.E.R., "Obscenity" in "The Reader Critic," *Little Review,* April 1920, 61.
169 Helen Bishop Dennis from Boston, MA, "The Modest Woman" in "The Reader Critic," *Little Review,* May–June 1920, 74.
170 Frank Stuhlman from Vernon, NY, "I have not read much in this number—" in "The Reader Critic," *Little Review,* July 1918, 64.
171 Stuhlman, "The Reader Critic," 64.
172 Stuhlman, "The Reader Critic," 64.
173 Stuhlman, "The Reader Critic," 64.

174 Gunn, "Beware of Imitations," 491.
175 Little Review Gallery [1926], *Little Review* Records, 1914–64, University of Wisconsin-Milwaukee Libraries, Archives Department.
176 Patrick Collier, "Virginia Woolf in the Pay of Booksellers: Commerce, Privacy, Professionalism, *Orlando*," *Twentieth Century Literature* 48, no. 4 (Winter 2002): 376.
177 Collier, "Virginia Woolf in the Pay of Booksellers," 364.
178 T.D. O'B. from Philadelphia, PA, "In Which It Is Left to Us!" in "The Reader Critic," *Little Review,* July 1918, 58.
179 T.D. O'B., "The Reader Critic," 58.
180 Rex Hunter from Chicago, IL, "The Layman Speaks—!!" in "The Reader Critic," *Little Review,* July 1918, 61–2.
181 Israel Solon from New York, "The Reader Critic," *Little Review,* May 1918, 62.
182 Hunter, "The Reader Critic," *Little Review,* July 1918, 62. Questions about Joyce's style multiplied as serialization continued and readers began to feel increasingly lost. The basic setting and plot of the novel was not at all self-explanatory to the first readers of *Ulysses*, as one reader's outburst from June 1918 reveals: "Really now: Joyce! what does he think he is doing? […] I swear I've read his 'Ulysses' and haven't found out yet what it's about, who is who or where" (S.S.B. from Chicago, IL, "What Joyce Is Up Against" in "The Reader Critic," *Little Review,* June 1918, 54).
183 "*Ulysses*" in "The Reader Critic," *Little Review,* May–June 1920, 72.
184 Hutton, *Serial Encounters*, 61n231.
185 Heap, "The Reader Critic," *Little Review,* May–June 1920, 72.
186 Don Gifford, *Ulysses Annotated*, 384. Gifford's guide is based on schema circulated by Joyce.
187 Heap, "Lost: A Renaissance," *Little Review,* May 1929, 5.
188 Heap, "Lost: A Renaissance," 5.
189 Heap, "Lost: A Renaissance," 5.
190 Pound, "A Shake Down," *Little Review*, August 1918, 32.
191 Advertisement for McClure's Autobiography, *Little Review,* December 1914, 74.
192 Her name was spelled "Coburn" in the *Little Review*.
193 "Court Lifts Ban on 'Ulysses' Here," *New York Times*, December 7, 1933: 21, https://archive.nytimes.com/www.nytimes.com/books/00/01/09/specials/joyce-court.html.
194 Anderson, "Greetings to The James Joyce Society from Margaret Anderson," in *A James Joyce Miscellany*, ed. Marvin Magalaner (New York: The Publications Committee of The James Joyce Society, 1957), 77.
195 *U* 7.608; *Little Review,* October 1918, 40.
196 Gunn, "Beware of Imitations," 491.

4

A New Look for Mrs. Dalloway

Consumer Activity and Artistic Production in the *Dial*

Introduction

When Mrs. Dalloway declares that she will "buy the gloves herself,"[1] she immediately marks herself as a consumer. Yet she is a consumer in an artistic work, and when she first appeared in print she was a consumer in a literary magazine that proclaimed its loyalty to art and looked suspiciously upon commerce. The *Dial* published fiction and poetry, according to its own account, "without any intention of making money [or] of truckling to popular prejudice."[2] This declared oppositional stance to commercial culture may well reflect the *Dial*'s editorial mission, but its publication of Modernist literature was nevertheless an "investment in the emerging commodity known as Modernism,"[3] and archival records show just how deeply invested the *Dial* was in marketing and advertising the literary artifacts it collected and distributed. This persistent tension between art and commodity, and the all too easy slippage between these two terms, is—I want to argue—embodied in Clarissa Dalloway, who represents the consumer impulse always hovering behind Modernist production. When Mrs. Dalloway is returned to the little magazine where she first appeared, these conflicting imperatives can be brought into sharper relief and explored in greater depth.

Opening the *Dial* of July 1923, Americans who read "Mrs. Dalloway in Bond Street" encountered a text that both differed substantially from Woolf's full-length novel and appeared in a radically different context, locating Woolf within a larger, interconnected community of little magazines that were deeply anxious about their own commercial investments in art. In the *Dial*, readers saw a text without the shell-shocked Septimus or the climactic party. Exclusively portraying a shopping trip, the short story highlights the tensions between commerce and art—tensions mirrored in the way the *Dial* sought to balance advertising copy with literature. Significantly, this balancing act was also being performed by the

Little Review as it serialized *Ulysses*. When we return Woolf to the periodicals, we receive a sharper image of Woolf's relationship to Joyce and of the *Dial*'s relationship to the *Little Review*; we can locate her ambivalence to the market more concretely; and we can see how the "gift economy" described by Kathryn Simpson fortuitously found its place not only in Woolf's fiction but also in the actual marketing strategies of the magazine that published "Mrs. Dalloway."

As Simpson has noted, the two gifts Clarissa contemplates giving in the short story—the vacation for the shop-girl, and the book *Cranford* for Milly—point toward a feminine economy that seeks to separate itself from patriarchal and capitalist structures. Thus "Mrs. Dalloway" articulates a theory of gift-giving that intersects with the later studies of gift theorists such as Marcel Mauss, Mark Osteen, Lewis Hyde, and Hélène Cixous. Our interpretation of "Mrs. Dalloway" is significantly enriched when we consider the gift as a symbol with important theoretical implications, but there is something more going on here. In the *Dial*, gift-giving was not only a symbolic act in theory and in fiction, but an actual practice being performed by readers. While my work is informed by gift theory, I simultaneously seek to uncover how the *Dial*, as a circulating *material* object, contributes to and complicates the discourse of gifts recorded in its pages. This approach leads us to a more nuanced understanding of Woolf's position in what Jennifer Wicke has aptly termed "market Modernism."[4]

In looking at Woolf's own market strategy, scholars typically, and rightfully, point to Woolf's association with the Hogarth Press, which allowed her to create a publishing arena outside of mainstream commercial culture. But in recent years, scholars researching the Hogarth Press have unearthed evidence suggesting that it in fact operated in much closer dialogue with the mass-market press than previously realized. It may not have been itself a commercial industry, but neither was it divorced from the commercial world. Like the commercial contacts of the Hogarth Press, Woolf's often-sidelined periodical contributions place her in closer contact with the discourses of shopping and consumption that appear prominently in her works.

When scholars do mention Woolf's periodical work, they tend to focus on her early reviews and journalism. Rarely do they mention the *Dial*. But the *Dial*, I argue, played a key role in spreading Woolf's literary reputation to the other side of the Atlantic. In its pages, she is put into dialogue with authors and reporters from Prague, Vienna, Munich, New York, and many other cities, destabilizing the prevalent view of Woolf as a London-centric writer who based her fame in the influential and intimate, yet relatively small, Bloomsbury circle. While the Bloomsbury Group certainly forged many of Woolf's important associations, other constellations in which Woolf was figured deserve greater exploration. These constellations, especially those found in between periodical covers, cast Woolf in a more internationally ambitious light. Although Woolf contributed only three items to the *Dial*—"The Lives of the Obscure," "Miss Ormerod," and "Mrs. Dalloway"—she was frequently mentioned in its pages, and the fruitful combination of works by and about Woolf helped secure her reputation in America. In the pages of the *Dial*, Woolf increased her transatlantic circulation and her literary prestige.

From the *Little Review* to the *Dial*

When the last serialized episode of *Ulysses* appeared in the *Little Review*, Margaret Anderson and Jane Heap published an unattributed reader-critic comment that evaluated Joyce's work:

> [W]e seek to define the element which distinguishes the work of several young writers, among whom Mr. James Joyce is the most notable, from that of their predecessors. It attempts to come closer to life, and to preserve more sincerely and exactly what interests and moves them by discarding most of the conventions which are commonly observed by the novelists. [...] [C]oncerned at all costs to reveal the flickerings of that inermost [sic] flame which flashes its myriad messages through the brain, he disregards with complete courage whatever seems to him adventitious, though it be probability or coherence or any other of the handrails to which we cling for support when we set our imaginations free.[5]

Although unattributed in the *Little Review*, this comment is easily recognized as an excerpt from Virginia Woolf's "Modern Novels," published in the *Times Literary Supplement*. The *Little Review*'s carefully selected excerpt charts the shift from Victorian values to Modernist experimentation, and from conventional narrative forms to the deep explorations of narrative consciousness, "that innermost flame which flashes its myriad messages through the brain."

In addition to charting Modernist developments, the essay puts Woolf into dialogue with Joyce—a connection that was made both by Woolf and by her contemporaries.[6] As she was composing *Mrs. Dalloway*, Woolf was reading *Ulysses*. In her diary entry of August 16, 1922, she remarks, upon having completed 200 pages of Joyce's novel, "An illiterate, underbred book it seems to me: the book of a self taught working man, & we all know how distressing they are, how egoistic, insistent, raw, striking, & ultimately nauseating. [...] For my own part I am laboriously dredging my mind for Mrs. Dalloway & bringing up light buckets." For all her antipathy to Joyce, however, Woolf's critics nevertheless found reason to bring the two together. In the same issue that carried "Mrs. Dalloway," the *Dial* also published a review of *Jacob's Room* that exclaimed, "Jacob's Room and Ulysses! Turn from one to the other and compare them, for both are new departures in literary method."[7] Early reviews of *Mrs. Dalloway* were also keen to make the connection. The *TLS* of May 21, 1925 notes that Woolf's novel, like Joyce's, "describes the passage of a single day. The idea, though new enough to be called an experiment, may not be unique in modern fiction. There was a precedent in *Ulysses*."[8] *The Daily News* also compared Woolf to Joyce,[9] and *The Nation* began its review of *Mrs. Dalloway* by noting, "Mrs Woolf is a sort of decorous James Joyce."[10] Naturally, this comparison of Woolf to Joyce, this pairing of *Ulysses* with *Mrs. Dalloway*, has continued into present scholarship, albeit with ever-varied nuances upon the same theme.

When comparing *Ulysses* to *Mrs. Dalloway*, both early and modern-day critics often note that both novels take place in one day, but these works are also similar for the way that they both begin as truncated periodical pieces in little magazines. In the *Little Review*, legal battles about obscenity brought *Ulysses* to a halt in the middle of "Oxen of the Sun," the fourteenth episode of the novel's eventual eighteen episodes. In the *Dial* of July 1923, the story that would eventually be published in book format as *Mrs. Dalloway* appeared in its embryonic form as "Mrs. Dalloway in Bond Street."[11] As opposed to the solitary book publication of the novel, the periodical publication of "Mrs. Dalloway in Bond Street" repositions Woolf's text, placing it in closer contact with works by Joyce, Yeats, Eliot, Pound, Lawrence, and others who were publishing in the *Dial*. By running David Garnett's review of *Jacob's Room* alongside "Mrs. Dalloway in Bond Street," the *Dial* prompts readers to think of "Mrs. Dalloway" in connection with Woolf's earlier work. While these associations are by now commonplace, what the *Dial* shows is that our routine pairings have a strong material and historical precedent. From the very beginning, readers of the *Dial* were prompted to think of Woolf as part of a larger Modernist milieu, one that came together between periodical pages; and as a writer whose works were evolving within the space that periodicals carved out for them—unfolding in response to reviews and in response to the ever-shifting Modernist scene.

Since critics have often paired *Ulysses* and *Mrs. Dalloway*, it seems only appropriate to compare the periodicals that published the early versions of both these works. Although I refer to their differences at various points below, I want to sketch out briefly here the essential points of convergence and contrast. As Alan Golding notes, the *Dial* "took a more cautious or muted tone" than the *Little Review*, "avoiding political controversy and any evidence of internal debate."[12] Although there were occasional disagreements, the *Dial* in general strove to construct images of harmony and stability, as opposed to the images of competition and discord cultivated by the *Little Review* (as outlined in the previous chapter). This preference for harmony led the *Dial* to exercise a more conservative editorial policy than its more rigorously avant-garde counterpart. Ever eager for controversy, the *Little Review* gladly printed *Ulysses* and defiantly protested its suppression by the government. By contrast, the *Dial* expressed hesitation over publishing Joyce's work, and, though it frequently mentioned him as a contributor in advertisements, it only ever published one poem by him, "A Memory of the Players" (July 1920).

Somewhat surprisingly, given the *Dial*'s fear of scandal, the editors *did* seek out Joyce initially, writing to him proactively in order to ask for contributions. But Scofield Thayer's letter, written shortly after he assumed editorship of the *Dial*, tempers his request with significant qualifications. He cites the censorial Post Office and the *Little Review*'s suppression as reasons for being cautious.[13] Indeed, although Joyce did send *Finnegans Wake* (then *Work in Progress*) to the *Dial*, the editors ultimately decided against publication, in spite of Sylvia Beach's assurance that the censor would not find Joyce's work objectionable.[14] The *Dial* preferred authors like Woolf, who were both innovative and safe.[15] While the *Little Review* heroically fought legal battles over *Ulysses*, the *Dial* "offered encouragement from the sidelines and waited to see what was safe to publish."[16]

The archival record enhances our understanding of this distinction, illuminating why Anderson and Heap embraced scandal while the *Dial* hesitated to publish controversial works. It also highlights the very fraught union between old and new in the *Dial*. The views of its editor are succinctly summed up in an early 1920s letter to T.S. Eliot. Thayer makes it clear that he does not wish to criticize the *Little Review*, but at the same time he cannot take up its mission.[17] Thayer differs from Anderson and Heap for both legal and artistic reasons, in his approach to the government as well as in his approach to authors: Not only does Thayer wish to avoid provoking the authorities, but he also wishes to avoid carving up an author's work, as Pound had done to Joyce's "Calypso" episode before it appeared in the *Little Review*. Finally, Thayer asserts that financial reasons also compel him to avoid taking chances. Precisely because the *Dial* was wealthier, it could not undertake such legal risks; unlike the *Little Review*, Thayer's magazine had too much to lose.

Looking into the archival record, we can add to the accounts given by Alan Golding, Edward Bishop, and other scholars who have compared the financial situations of these two magazines. As Bishop notes, "The *Dial* cost 40 cents a copy when the *Little Review* cost 15 cents; it paid contributors $20 per page for verse; it had a circulation of about 9,000 as opposed to *The Little Review*'s 400; and it was altogether more respectable."[18] And, as Golding and Lawrence Rainey have described, Thayer poured thousands of dollars annually into the production of his magazine, while Anderson and Heap struggled to survive, begged for $5.00 contributions from subscribers, and wildly rejoiced over a gift of $100. But it was not merely that the *Dial* remained financially stable while the *Little Review* narrowly avoided bankruptcy. Another important contrast rests in the financial image each magazine sought to develop. Although John Quinn advised Anderson and Heap to remain reserved about their finances, they rejected his advice and publicly broadcast their precarious financial straits, begging subscribers for money and celebrating each financial success by issuing announcements that they had "survived" difficult seasons (see previous chapter).

By contrast, Thayer sought to promote an image of financial stability. When publishing complications delayed delivery of the *Dial* overseas in late 1922, rumors began to circulate that the *Dial* had gone bankrupt. This crisis of alleged bankruptcy infuriated Thayer, who was in Vienna at the time. Panicked about the reputation of his magazine, he wrote urgently to his staff in New York. He worried that everyone in London believed the *Dial* to be financially ruined and demanded that his staff realize the seriousness of the situation.[19] Although the problem was eventually rectified, Thayer's letter (which is echoed by others) underscores how differently editors of the *Dial* and of the *Little Review* approached financial crises, whether actual or alleged.

These tensions between the *Dial* and the *Little Review* also reflect tensions between Woolf and Joyce, who came from considerably different socioeconomic backgrounds and held different views about "high" and "low" art. Joyce daringly injected his "high" art with "low" scatological references that offended even Pound's sensibilities, and that also caused Woolf to express disgust for the "self taught working man" who appeared to her like "a queasy undergraduate scratching his pimples."[20] But, although Woolf came from a more respectable class background, she also engaged with the "low" arts of commercial culture just as Joyce did. Similarly, although the *Dial* cultivated a self-image of respectability and distinction, it engaged with the commercial sphere even more rigorously than the *Little Review*. Initially, these dual engagements with art and commerce may appear contradictory. But, as I explain below, both Woolf and the *Dial* addressed these apparent contradictions with compelling rationales and innovative strategies that mediated this tension.

Developing Tensions between Art and Commerce

Scholars have long drawn attention to Woolf's vexed relation to the marketplace, but the abundance of scholarship on this topic, far from declaring it a closed issue, underscores just how many nuances and modifications are needed to understand and define that relation. As Kathryn Simpson notes:

> [T]here has been a sustained critical interest in Virginia Woolf's ambivalent engagements with the literary marketplace and commodity culture which has opened up exciting new ways of reading Woolf's writings. [...] As co-owner of The Hogarth Press and as a woman writer intent on making money from her pen, Woolf was interested in markets and profit margins. [...] However, she also felt considerably uncomfortable about her own place in the commercial world (her writing for *Vogue*, for instance, brought anxiety and concern about the debasement that mass production and commercialism can imply).[21]

Indeed, it is quite common to point out the problematic commercial and artistic dynamics implied in Woolf's decision to publish in both mass-market periodicals and elite magazines. In *Reading Virginia Woolf's Essays and Journalism*, for example, Leila Brosnan remarks that Woolf published "in journals which extend from prestigious and highbrow periodicals such as the *Nation and Athenaeum* and *Criterion*, to more popular magazines like *Vogue* and *Good Housekeeping*."[22] But even Woolf's involvement with magazines as literary as the *Criterion* or the *Dial* carried a commercial element. The *Dial* paid Woolf $60 for "Mrs. Dalloway in Bond Street,"[23] and her correspondence with the editors contains frequent references to payment rates, checks, and other business matters.

Of course, one might object that such financially oriented discussions are merely a natural and inevitable part of the business exchange that must take place between any publisher and any author. But an examination of the *Dial*/Thayer Papers at the Beinecke reveals that financial considerations were far from mere formalities that had to be dutifully addressed for record-keeping purposes. On the contrary, financial considerations underwrote the *Dial*'s editorial decisions and advertising policies. Although the *Dial*'s first priority may have been literature, its devotion to art was in constant tension with the commercial demands of the business world in which it operated. Oversized scrapbooks filled with pages of house and exchange ads, detailed financial records, and frantic letters from the treasurer and marketing managers show that the *Dial*'s relation to commercialism was a matter of intense and recurrent editorial debate.

Hence it is necessary to revise the account given by Frederick J. Hoffman, Charles Allen, and Carolyn F. Ulrich in *The Little Magazine*, by now accepted as a standard if outdated bibliography of Modernist magazines.[24] The book is described by Edward Bishop as "indispensable."[25] Yet this indispensable guide, valuable as it may be, leads readers astray when it comes to the *Dial*'s engagement with the commercial sphere. The account given by Hoffman, Allen, and Ulrich emphasizes the artistic ambitions of the *Dial*, ambitions that were certainly present and powerful. But their esteemed bibliography overlooks the commercial considerations that were intimately tied to this artistic endeavor. In describing the origins of the *Dial* under Thayer's leadership, they declare: "Scofield Thayer and Dr. [James Sibley] Watson [...] were both determined to print a magazine for writers and art rather than for circulation and advertising."[26] But then Hoffman, Allen, and Ulrich acknowledge that circulation in fact *did* increase under Thayer's editorship, an admission that problematizes the distinction between little magazines and the mass market: "For the circulation leaped from the 8,000 of the Johnson *Dial* to around 18,000 during the first four years of the Watson-Thayer regime."[27] The figure of 18,000 may seem small in comparison to mass-market periodicals with circulations in the hundreds of thousands, but the leap from 8,000 to 18,000 *is* statistically significant: in the space of four years—that is to say, between the time Thayer assumed editorship and "Mrs. Dalloway in Bond Street" was published—circulation figures had more than doubled.

Instead of linking this increased circulation to advertising strategies or promotional tactics, however, *The Little Magazine* bibliographers turn immediately to the problems that it entailed.[28] Thus the bibliographers leave the *Dial*'s staggering increase in circulation unexplained. This omission is curious, since, as recent scholarship suggests, the figure of 18,000 corresponds to roughly eighteen times the average circulation figures for even the most widely read small magazines.[29] As Katherine Mullin records, "Little magazines were founded to print material appealing to a small group of intellectual readers. Their circulations were rarely more than a thousand: they disseminated work unattractive to commercially run periodicals, often because of its experimental nature, and sometimes because it risked prosecution under obscenity laws."[30] But, I argue, the *Dial* adopted the stance of commercial periodicals when it cautiously and strategically refused to publish works that "risked prosecution under obscenity laws." This evidence, combined with the *Dial*'s peculiar circulation numbers, which are straddled between the typical figures for little magazines and the typical figures for commercial periodicals, reveal that the *Dial* operated as a mediating force between radical experimentalism and conservative tradition.

Another component of this dialectic between the avant-garde and the commercial sphere was, obviously, advertising—a subject that Hoffman, Allen, and Ulrich raise only to dismiss. After noting the *Dial*'s increasing deficit, they explain: "Advertising might have been solicited, but it was apparent, as Dr. Watson points out, that that would have interfered with the magazine's proper function. Though advertisements were accepted, they were not regarded as a sustaining source of income."[31] Yet the archives tell a radically different story. In fact, the *Dial*'s financial records, memos, and letters show that the magazine was deeply engaged in questions of advertising. Far from avoiding the commercial sphere, it actively sought to draw its magazine to the attention of potential advertisers—not just to sympathetic booksellers like Huebsch or other artistic magazines like the *Little Review*, but also to mass-market periodicals like the *New York Times* and large commercial firms like Colgate and Steinway.[32] Since the pathbreaking work of scholars such as Lawrence Rainey and Mark Morrisson, it is not surprising to learn that Modernism's little magazines looked to mass-market advertisements as models. But we still need to investigate the specifics of these complex transactions, which reveal how the *Dial* was extremely preoccupied with advertising, revenue, and promotion in detail.

While the magazine's involvement with commerce is not itself shocking, the extent and intricacy of its involvement should give us pause. Edward Bishop notes that the *Dial* "was supported in part by advertising, but more by massive infusions of Thayer's capital—$220,000 for the three years 1920–2. In editorial policies it borrowed from *The Little Review* but it also leaned towards *Vanity Fair*, stressing publicity and advertising."[33] The implications are important not only for our understanding of the *Dial*'s relationship to art and commerce but also for our understanding of Woolf's positioning within that field. It is important to determine where the *Dial* stands within this spectrum because, as Kathryn Simpson notes, critical assessments of Woolf's relation to the market are still in flux: "Whereas for Abbott in 1992 'Woolf could only be an ambivalent witness to commodity culture,' more recent studies explore Woolf's place *in* the commercial world."[34]

As one of these "more recent studies," Jane Garrity's article on "Selling Culture to the 'Civilized'" explores Bloomsbury's relationship to British *Vogue*, where Woolf published five articles between 1924 and 1926.[35] Hence these articles appeared in *Vogue* just after "Mrs. Dalloway in Bond Street" appeared in the

Dial. In her essay, Garrity makes several observations about British *Vogue* that could be extended to the American *Dial*:

> Although *Vogue* specifically targeted a cultivated upper-class readership [...] it would be inaccurate to assume that the magazine is therefore not a product of mass culture. Although *Vogue* never sold as many copies as some other mass circulation women's magazines, it consistently led all of its competitors in advertising revenue throughout the 1920s. Consistent with the unreliability of statistics for British magazines during this period, Caroline Seebohm documents the magazine's circulation in 1928 as 138,783 (*MV,* 282), and 141,424 (*MV,* 79). Either way, what is conveyed is that—in contrast to the little magazines of the period, which nurtured literary Modernism but whose numbers ranged only from a couple hundred to a high of several thousand subscribers—*Vogue*'s circulation figures and revenues clearly situate the periodical as a formidable market force.[36]

Initially, based on Garrity's evidence, the case for *Vogue* as a mediator between "high" and "low" seems stronger than that for the *Dial*. Certainly, if we look at circulation numbers alone, the roughly 140,000 circulating copies of *Vogue* easily outstrip the *Dial*'s comparatively meager peak at 18,000. And one cannot say for the *Dial*, as Garrity claims for *Vogue*, that it "consistently led all of its competitors in advertising revenue." But just because the *Dial* had smaller circulation numbers does not mean that it was any less interested in market forces, or any less engaged with commercial culture. And just because the *Dial* published fewer advertisements does not mean that it was any less desirous of procuring them. These are differences in quantity of sales, not in seriousness of investment; in numerical statistics, not in guiding ambition; in final results, not in desired outcome.

Thus when Garrity argues that "it becomes possible to read *Vogue* as a mass cultural product even though the magazine explicitly resisted the tactics of universal appeal,"[37] the same could be said for the *Dial*.[38] Thayer's magazine may not have achieved the same commercial success as British *Vogue*, but it was informed by commercial culture in important and revealing ways. Significantly, when Thayer assumed editorship of the *Dial* in 1920, his first task involved increasing subscriptions, as a flurry of letters to lapsed and potential subscribers demonstrates; when the *Dial* developed during the 1920s, it embarked on extensive advertising campaigns, as its numerous house and exchange ads reveal; even more significantly for the purposes of this chapter, the year 1923 saw a crucial re-evaluation of market strategy. Thus when the *Dial* published "Mrs. Dalloway in Bond Street," which Simpson has described as a story "encapsulat[ing] Woolf's ambivalence about consumerism,"[39] the magazine's editors were in the process of seeking answers to the very questions raised by Woolf's fiction. In short, Woolf's story about the anxiety of "consumerism, capitalism, and commodity culture"[40] fictionally embodies the actual anxieties faced by the *Dial*'s editors in 1923, when it became apparent that increasing deficits could not be rectified unless the magazine procured more advertising pages, ads which would encourage readers to purchase commercial products and embark on Clarissa-style shopping trips.

The Emergence of the *Dial*

Woolf begins "Mrs. Dalloway in Bond Street" by sending her character on a shopping trip. Similarly, when Thayer assumed editorship of the *Dial* in January 1920, he began by encouraging customers to go on a shopping trip. Specifically, he sent out circulars to individuals inviting them to subscribe and circulars to businesses inviting them to purchase advertisements. Thus, while both Woolf's fiction and the magazine in which it appears claim to be—and are—artistic media, they also promote the very consumerism from which they seek to distance themselves.

Additionally, both represent a reinvention of prior literary form. Describing the evolution of *Mrs. Dalloway*, Woolf writes, "I adumbrate here a study of insanity & suicide [...] to be more close to the fact than Jacob: but I think Jacob was a necessary step, for me, in working free."[41] Similarly, for Thayer, the previous *Dial* regimes were "necessary steps" for "working free" of past forms. Under the Johnson regime, the magazine had become highly political, much to Thayer's annoyance (at the time, he was an associate editor, and eventually resigned on account of the magazine's propagandist trend). But this unfavorable period in the *Dial*'s history gave Thayer the chance to revive the journal when it came into his hands. Accordingly, he wrote to lapsed subscribers that the *Dial* would abandon politics and devote itself to art.[42]

But aesthetic tastes were far from the only considerations Thayer faced when he became editor. The *Dial* also faced a financial crisis. Thayer found himself in a position similar to that of Robert J. Collier, who faced declining circulation numbers when he succeeded his father as editor of *Collier's*, as discussed in Chapter 1. Thus, although the *Dial* was classed as a little magazine, it nevertheless had to struggle with market forces just like the larger mass-market periodicals. Unlike the *Little Review*, the *Dial* maintained an extensive editorial staff and hired a business manager. This decision to hire a business manager makes it something more than a little magazine—or, perhaps more moderately put, a little magazine with stronger ties than usual to commercial business practices. On January 23, 1920, the *Dial*'s business manager, W.B. Marsh, filed a "Report on the Condition of The Dial Magazine." This report reveals how closely the *Dial* relied upon advertising and market strategy for success. Its careful attention to financial matters shows how deeply concerned the *Dial* was with precise operating calculations, advertising strategy, and business efficiency. It evinces a sophisticated machinery of business practices that a typical small magazine such as the *Little Review* simply could not afford—both because the *Little Review* staff lacked financial expertise and because the magazine literally did not have the funds to hire a business manager.

Like Joyce and many of the other authors it published, the *Little Review* relied rather desperately upon guarantors and benefactors for support. Like Woolf, the *Dial* under Thayer entered existence with the privilege of comparative wealth. But this position of financial privilege does not mean that Woolf and Thayer ignored market pressures or disregarded minor expenses. On the contrary, Virginia and Leonard Woolf frequently worried about finances, and the expenditure records kept by Leonard and reproduced by Quentin Bell show just how "hard up" the Woolfs were.[43] While neither Thayer nor the Woolfs lived in tents on a beach as the *Little Review*'s editors had once done, they nevertheless struggled to balance their budgets. As Bell notes, the Hogarth Press "started on a capital outlay of £41.15s.3d—and this was not easily raised."[44] Similarly, when the *Dial*'s business manager filed his report in January 1920, he expressed deep concern over the precarious financial situation at the start of Thayer's regime.

As Marsh's report reveals, the former management had left behind out-of-date records littered with numerous errors.[45] But this was not all: The previous management also neglected to pursue important advertising opportunities. And this latter complaint lies at the heart of Marsh's report. The previous management's promotional efforts were so severely circumscribed that they were, to Marsh's mind, practically non-existent. This history left the new management with many opportunities for expansion, but also with new challenges. Marsh further notes that the new *Dial*'s change in editorial policy, from a focus on politics to culture, negatively affected circulation numbers, causing many readers to cancel their subscriptions or demand refunds.[46] Rejecting a politically radical past in favor of a literary tradition that balanced conservatism with experimentalism, the *Dial* initially alienated devoted readers. Happily, however, new subscribers outnumbered canceling customers.[47]

But these new subscriptions were not enough to justify higher advertising rates—a major concern for the *Dial*'s business manager. The radical politics of the previous *Dial* had made advertisers nervous, causing them to withdraw their ads and their support. With its departure from this political agenda, Marsh hoped, the new *Dial* could once again attract advertisers and begin earning money. What is interesting about Marsh's report is that, while mentioning the new literary quality of the *Dial*, it nevertheless turns to the marketing logic of commercial periodicals for operational strategy. Publishers of these commercial periodicals, as Mark Morrisson notes, "realized the secret" of market success: "lowering the price of the issue, even below its printing cost (thereby vastly increasing circulation), and then reaping fantastic profits from advertisers."[48] As Marsh's figures show, the printing costs of the revived *Dial* exceeded the subscription income. The former magazine had cost about $1500 per month to produce, but the new *Dial*'s production costs ran up to $2500.[49] This increase created a budget crisis. The solution, Marsh proposes, is not to raise subscription costs, but rather—following sound commercial advice—to increase circulation and advertising revenue.

Marsh's report shows that, from its inception, Thayer's *Dial* looked to revive not only the magazine's literary quality but also its advertising. The *Dial* both sought out advertisers and placed self-promotional ads in other periodicals. In his report, Marsh urges the *Dial* to engage in concentrated acts of self-advertising. But he also urges the *Dial* to launch campaigns that will attract advertisers to its own pages. While noting that advertisers are cautious, he also believes that persuasive tactics can convince commercial enterprises to sign on with the *Dial*, allowing the magazine to fill twenty pages an issue with paid advertisements.[50] Even though twenty advertising pages may have been on the lower end of mass-market expectations, it was considerably high for a little magazine, and it demonstrates the *Dial*'s larger commercial ambitions.[51] In addition to advertising small businesses such as The Brick Row Book Shop of New Haven, Thayer's magazine published ads for large national firms such as Macmillan and the Harper Brothers. The very fact that it had a goal of twenty paid advertising pages unsettles the notion that Thayer's *Dial* divorced art from commercialism. If literary revival was part of the emerging magazine's editorial aims, then so was advertising.

Of course, it is important to keep in mind that Thayer was prepared to run the *Dial* at an annual deficit, that he proclaimed his new periodical devoted to art and literature,[52] and that he continued to promote this agenda for nine years in spite of annual losses. Nevertheless, it is not entirely true that the new

Dial was completely devoted to arts and letters. It would be more accurate to say that it was "primarily" devoted to arts and letters, but that it recognized advertisement and engagement with the commercial sphere as a necessary if paradoxical component of this devotion. In fact, the *Dial* staff consulted experts in the business world to determine how best to run the magazine. As Marsh states in his January 1920 report, these experts regarded the *Dial* not only as an artistic enterprise but also as a good business proposition. Under the right direction, these men believed, the *Dial* could stop relying on infusions of capital and possibly turn a profit.[53] In retrospect, this prediction may appear to have been naïve, akin to John Quinn telling the *Little Review* editors that they should increase circulation numbers enough to become self-supporting, or Ben Hecht predicting that the *Little Review* would eventually attract audiences of the size mass-market periodicals enjoyed.[54] But even if neither magazine achieved commercial success, each considered profit a seriously feasible, if ultimately unrealized, outcome.

As Nicholas Joost records, the *Dial* launched an extensive promotional campaign in the opening years of Thayer's editorship. At the end of 1921, when the new *Dial* had been in operation for two years, the business office of the *Dial* distributed the so-called Peacock Folder, a set of promotional materials "carefully composed as a circular publicizing the taste of *The Dial*."[55] As Joost writes, the editors "were optimistic that the large annual deficit the *Dial* was saddled with might be cut substantially, even, perhaps, eventually eliminated."[56] Joost describes the Peacock Folder in detail, unpacking its "pictures, lists of contents, and advertising matter, together with suitably commendatory passages about the *Dial* selected from periodicals and newspapers ranging from *The New Republic* and *The New York Times* to *The Duluth Herald* and *The New Witness* of London."[57] Analyzing this evidence, Joost writes, "Thayer and Watson were keeping pretty consistently to their original aims, 'without any intention of making money, of truckling to popular prejudice, or of undertaking propaganda for any school of art,' but it is still more interesting because it also shows the publishing achievements that the *Dial* prided itself on and considered important and attractive enough to stand by."[58]

Even more interesting from my standpoint, however, is how the Peacock Folder shows the art of the *Dial* engaging with the art of the marketplace. Here the *Dial*'s contents are praised and validated by mass-market newspapers such as *The New York Times*; here visual material and advertisements are circulated next to declarations about the magazine's literary value. These intermingling portions of the Peacock Folder demonstrate that the *Dial* could draw upon both the advertising techniques and the validating testimonials of mass-market periodicals in order to further its artistic mission. Unfortunately for Watson and Thayer, the elaborately assembled Peacock Folder did not reap the hoped-for benefits. As Joost records, the "total cost of getting out the Peacock Folder was $981, and the money realized [...] was $433."[59] Several other promotional campaigns yielded similar results.[60] From these results Joost concludes, "Thayer and Watson were subsidizing, to a not insignificant extent, American arts and letters."[61] And their contribution must certainly be acknowledged. At the same time, however, financial losses do not necessarily negate commercial ambitions. While it would be inaccurate to say that Thayer and Watson ran the *Dial* with a profit motive, it would be equally misguided to say that they ran their magazine without a commercial strategy. The Peacock Folder may not have been as successful as desired, but it does show how invested the magazine was in the promotional strategies used by its mass-market counterparts.

Indeed, the *Dial* even directly engaged in business with mass-market magazines, as evidenced by a May 20, 1920 "Report on the Situation of the Business Department."[62] In addition to exchanging advertisements with other little magazines, thus building solidarity with the "counterpublic sphere" (as Morrisson terms it), the *Dial* also exchanged ads with large New York magazines and newspapers. Exchange partners included the *New Republic*, the *Little Review*, the *Bookplate Booklet*, the *Unpartizan Review, Good Morning*, the *New York Times*, the *New York Tribune*, and the *New York Evening Post*.[63] Like the *Little Review* mentioned here, the *Dial* extended its advertising pages to include ads for commercial periodicals. Even as these little magazines constructed a "counterpublic sphere," they also stepped outside that sphere in crucial moments to engage directly with the mainstream public.

The May 1920 report underscores this dialogue with the commercial sphere—not only in terms of advertising placement, but also in terms of business management. Here we see that the *Dial* was significantly more engaged in such dialogue than the comparatively amateurish *Little Review*. Notably, the *Dial* even hired an advertising manager, Ruth Stanley-Brown, whose commercial connections and experience in the Macmillan Advertising Department played a significant role in the *Dial*'s decision to hire her. Moreover, the May 1920 report states that the *Dial* has adopted the bookkeeping system of the *New Republic*, a progressive weekly. These decisions—to hire an advertising manager from the commercial ranks, and to adopt the bookkeeping system of another periodical—indicate how persistently Thayer's emergent *Dial* looked outside its own ranks, including to the mass-market sphere, for guidance in its formative years.

Accordingly, Thayer's magazine kept meticulous records of its advertisements and subscriptions, dutifully tracking the effectiveness of the promotional techniques it employed. These careful records demonstrate a serious interest in commercial concerns, even if the aim of the *Dial* was not, primarily, commercial. Its report of May 20, 1920 broke down the source of subscriptions as follows: 300 subscriptions came with the help of agencies, 145 were generated by various advertisements, and 95 arrived at the *Dial* without solicitation. Circulars, by contrast, faired poorly.[64] The most effective way of attracting subscribers, then, seems to come in the form of agencies and advertisement. From its inception, the *Dial* recognized advertisement as a key to its success. Although the circulars did not appear to generate lucrative results, they are nonetheless interesting from a scholarly standpoint. Significantly, the circulars distributed in 1920 cast the *Dial* not only as a cultivated literary magazine but also as an ideal place to advertise consumer products. The circulars also employ some amusing and elaborate metaphors, which were probably designed to attract readers' attention but could have seemed distasteful to some recipients. One such circular, in attempt to make the *Dial*'s small circulation numbers attractive to potential advertisers, compares the *Dial*'s readership to choice red meat.[65] Note here the simultaneous appeal to high culture and the consumer impulse. The *Dial* can satisfy both the reader and the purchaser, bringing the "book" together with the "commercial," the "literary" together with "advertising." For the *Dial*, these were not contradictions, but interdependent and simultaneously interpenetrating agencies.

Another circular letter makes the connection between magazine-reading and product-purchasing even more explicit. Here one may recall that "Mrs. Dalloway in Bond Street," by presenting a shopper as its main character and by appearing as a written story, simultaneously addresses the magazine subscriber's desire to read and to consume. And this was a connection the *Dial* was already eager to capitalize upon in early 1920. Employing sartorial metaphors, the advertising manager announces to prospective advertisers that the *Dial* has, in effect, donned a new garment worthy of notice. The newly decked-out *Dial* will be illustrated, with an enlarged format.[66] These declarations sound suspiciously like *Collier's* claims when it announced plans to become not only more visual but also more highbrow (see Chapter 1). Like mass-market periodicals, the *Dial* emphasizes its magazine's visual elements in order to attract subscribers and, by extension, advertisers. In the next paragraph of the circular, however, the *Dial*'s advertising manager seems to skip back to the literary, emphasizing the magazine's elite, intellectual audience. Importantly, however, this promotion of literary taste does not imply a repudiation of advertisement. Rather, the *Dial* acknowledges that magazine readers are simultaneously consumers. Thus we can extend the point made in the Henry James chapter—where we observed that, in the presence of advertisement, *Collier's* "readers become consumers"— to say that little magazines, too, recognized and even promoted this equation between reader and consumer.

But this equation could be difficult to discern. For part of the *Dial*'s strategy was always to appear highbrow, even in its advertising. An advertisement placed in the *Publisher's Weekly* of September 23, 1922, is especially telling in this regard. "Does Advertising Sell Books?" the ad asks. It then responds:

> Rarely, if ever, alone. Book advertising must be supplemented by reviews and critical appraisal of books to be effective. On the other hand, reviews and comment, rarely if ever, alone sell books. Books sell the best when well advertised in a medium devoted to the stimulation of interest in books, through reviews and critical appreciation. The Dial is such a medium.[67]

Here, then, the *Dial* insists once again that advertisement and literary reading go hand-in-hand. To be effective, advertisements must be paired with scholarly reviews that appeal to the intellect. Interestingly, however, the *Dial* also asserts that the opposite is the case: "reviews and comment, rarely if ever, alone sell books." They need advertisement in order to make their appeals effectively—in order, that is, to convince periodical readers that a reviewed book is stimulating enough to be bought.

From the *Dial*'s collection of letters from readers, it appears as though some readers identified this equation between art and advertisement, but most readers appear to have viewed the magazine as refined and anti-commercial, even a little too high-brow at times. One reader writes to the editors in June 1920, regretting that he cannot renew his subscription because funds are limited and he prefers to support the more radical magazines.[68] But another reader, who did renew her subscription, writes with appreciation for the *Dial*'s artistic tastes, praising the *Dial*'s triumph over commercialism.[69] A different reader, however, sees the *Dial* as more moderate; approving the magazine's new direction, she praises its approach as middle-brow.[70] For her, the *Dial* hovered somewhere in between the little magazines and commercial periodicals. Here she asserts that the *Dial* can be both refined and well-circulated, which most scholarship views as an improbable (though not impossible) combination.

As mentioned, the *Dial*'s relatively widespread circulation was in large part due to its advertisements. Other archival letters to the editor suggest that readers were inclined to view the magazine as attractive, tasteful, and visually appealing—as itself an ad that converted browsers to subscribers—but an ad that was refined and professional, not debased or tawdry.[71] In addition to advertising its attractions within its own pages, the *Dial* exchanged ads with periodicals both at home and abroad. The *Dial* seemed to agree with Richard Aldington, who recommended "judicious advertising."[72] In accord with Aldington's sentiment, Thayer would later himself remark that advertisements should show a certain sophistication and polish.[73] Specifically, Aldington recommended advertising in "literary periodicals." Significantly, however, he regarded certain "larger periodicals" as also being "literary"; thus he recommends that the *Dial* place ads not only in the *Chapbook*, the *London Mercury*, and *Coterie*, but also in the *Athenaeum*, the *Nation*, the *TLS*, and the *Guardian*, among others.

Notably, these "larger periodicals" were also the publications where Virginia Woolf placed her early reviews. As her bibliographer B.J. Kirkpatrick records, Woolf placed her first review with the London *Guardian* in December 1904, landed her first *TLS* review in March 1905,[74] and continued with frequent contributions to both periodicals. Adding several periodicals to her repertoire in subsequent years, she began contributing to the *Athenaeum* in April 1919,[75] and when it merged with the *Nation* in 1921 she remained a regular contributor. Her association with the *Nation and Athenaeum* was further strengthened when Leonard Woolf was appointed literary editor in March 1923.[76] In fact, most of her periodical contributions in 1923 were to that magazine. That year, she also wrote for the *TLS*, the *Literary Review* of the *New York Evening Post*, the *New Statesman*, *Cassell's Weekly*, Eliot's *Criterion*, *Broom*, the *New Republic*, and, obviously, the *Dial*.[77] This mixture represents a blending of American and British periodicals, and of small and large magazines—that is to say, an ambitious flurry of periodical activity that crosses both the Atlantic and the Great Divide. Thus Woolf as well as the *Dial* worked to forge relationships with the mass market. But Aldington's classification of these "larger periodicals" as "literary" also indicates that the traditional equations of large=commercial and small=literary do not hold, either for us or for contemporaneous readers.[78]

The *Dial*, however, went beyond Aldington's recommendations, advertising widely and profusely in multiple papers stretching across America, across the Atlantic, and across Europe. It advertised in New York, Boston, Chicago, Philadelphia, Palo Alto, New Haven, Manchester, London, and Paris; in internationally acclaimed periodicals such as the *New York Times* as well as more obscure publications, such as the questionably titled *Birth Control Review*; in businessmen's newspapers and in college papers alike; in English-language periodicals as well as those published in French and Yiddish. The extensive list of periodicals in which the *Dial* placed ads is at once surprising and impressive. While the *Dial* targeted "the interested, informed general reader,"[79] or, to put it in Aldington's words, "the more intelligent [...] reading public,"[80] the list shows that the *Dial* worked across class, generational, linguistic, and national lines when it placed advertisements and cultivated readerships. When one considers the circulation of these periodicals, news of the *Dial* was circulating to millions of readers worldwide.

Advertisements in the *Dial*

The *Dial*, then, sought to create a broader readership than the *Little Review*, which targeted the "initiate of the avant-garde."[81] As Alan Golding notes, the *Dial* "engaged in dissemination as much as discovery."[82] And the advertisement list testifies to the validity of Golding's statement, which comes almost to look like an understatement. But the *Dial* shared an important overlapping target audience with the *Little Review*. As Morrisson argues, the *Little Review* targeted young readers and "promoted Modernism as a youth movement."[83] His argument could be extended to the *Dial*, which not only courted sophisticated "older" readers but also placed advertisements in dozens of college papers, even attempting to recruit college students as subscription-sellers.

This fraught dialogue between old and new is an important context for "Mrs. Dalloway in Bond Street," since Clarissa in that story worries about the passage of time, the effects of aging, and the intermingling of older and younger people. As she walks to the glove shop, Clarissa contemplates the "mothers of Westminster" who "gave suck to their young. Quite respectable girls lay stretched on the grass. An elderly man, stooping very stiffly, picked up a crumpled paper, spread it out flat and flung it away."[84] These images of young and old figures continue as a motif throughout the story: as Clarissa remembers that Milly Whitbread is "about my age—fifty—fifty-two,"[85] as she recalls a childhood encounter with "the old lady in horned spectacles,"[86] as she concludes that "[m]iddle age is the devil,"[87] as she compares the St. James palace to "a child's game with bricks,"[88] as she mentally retraces the one-hundred-year evolution of Bond Street.[89] Perhaps most memorably, however, the discourse of age and aging emerges when Clarissa enters the glove shop and notices that the shop's assistant has aged considerably— so considerably that Clarissa questions whether she is the same person from her memory: "she looked straight into the shopwoman's face—but this was not the girl she remembered? She looked quite old."[90] Here the slippage between "shopwoman" and "girl" brings out the tension between memory of youth and the reality of age. As the assistant searches for the perfect pair of gloves, Clarissa continues her meditation on the dialectic between young and old: "Yes," she muses, "if it's the girl I remember she's twenty years older."[91] Thus Clarissa muses about age in a periodical that was itself consciously contemplating the diverse ages of *its* audience.

Readers also felt the simultaneous tension and energy that emanated from the *Dial*'s strategy of targeting older and younger generations alike, and archival letters explicitly acknowledge this beneficial intermingling.[92] Thus, it is not so much that the *Dial* rejected the youthful radicalism of the *Little Review*, but rather that it sought to moderate that youthful, revolutionary spirit by simultaneously publishing more traditional works. One ad printed in October 1922 highlights the *Dial*'s investment in youth culture. The ad, which promotes Sherwood Anderson's *Many Marriages* and the *Dial*, presents a "Special Student and Faculty Offer." This ad was circulated in twenty-seven different college newspapers, ranging from the *Daily Californian* at the University of California to the *Daily Maroon* at the University of Chicago, from *Crimson* at Harvard University to *Green and White* at Ohio University.[93] The "Special Student and Faculty Offer!," complete with an exclamation point for visual emphasis, entices readers to subscribe to the *Dial* at reduced rates: "If you will sign this coupon and return to The Dial within ten days, we will make a special subscription rate of $3.50 for a year (regular yearly subscription is $5.00)[.]" This limited-time offer makes use of mass-market advertising techniques that urged consumers to purchase products before time ran out (recall the ads in *Cassell's* urging readers to purchase issues containing *Kim*, which were expected to fly off the shelves). Furthermore, this elaborate advertisement, far more sophisticated than anything the *Little Review* is known to have published, features several cartoon characters with oversized scissors, poised to cut out the subscription "coupon." This added, playful visual element involves readers with the advertisement by pictorially embodying them as scissor-cutting subscribers. The cartoon figures, in short, act both as mirrors of obedient readers and as instructors to skeptical ones. Strikingly, the ad uses both text and image to urge the reader to action.

But the *Dial* also makes a specific offer to students, this time excluding faculty and thereby targeting the youth in particular. In small type next to the coupon, the *Dial* states that it "would like to obtain the services of a number of students to solicit subscriptions. It is ready to pay a very good commission to any student willing to undertake this work." Thus the *Dial* combines promises of literary knowledge with promises of income. The students are at once invited to buy and to sell, to purchase the *Dial* and to earn money soliciting subscriptions.

Simultaneously an invitation to leisurely reading and promotional work, the advertisement underscores the fluidity and reciprocity of financial exchanges. Are students buyers or sellers, readers or workers, consumers or producers? This ad exploits such distinctions by seductively suggesting that a student who invests with the *Dial* can be any or all of these things.

In fact, elsewhere in the ad, the *Dial* uses this "possible selves" rhetoric to persuade students that they must read the magazine in order to cultivate their self-image. Readers are given the option to be "one of the" distinguished readers or to be one of the uninformed, undistinguished mass. Explaining that "The Dial is not satisfied with being caviar to the general—it is caviar to the particular," the ad asks, "Are You One of the Particular?" It then states that "the coupon opposite is the answer," meaning that those who belong to the selective, intelligent group of "particular" readers will purchase a subscription. In explaining what it means to be "caviar to the particular," the *Dial* states that its "sole purpose is to bring the work of the artists who count to the people who care. It is publishing [...] the art and the literature by which our generation, here and abroad, will be remembered by future generations." The *Dial* invites readers to subscribe if they want to become part of an enduring legacy. Although the *Dial* elsewhere rejected any cliquish characterization of its mission,[94] it nevertheless encouraged its readers to think of themselves as part of a selective and largely self-selected community.

Cleverly, the *Dial*'s October 1922 advertisement anticipates what skeptics might say about its approach to literature, beauty, and magazine-reading. Just above the paragraph that explains "Caviar to the Particular," the *Dial* lists and responds to a series of one-word questions that skeptics might pose. Each word represents a perceived fault of which the *Dial* could be accused. The questions begin with "HIGHBROW?" to which the *Dial* responds, "If refusal to compromise with the popular and semi-popular constitutes 'highbrowism,' then we admit the accusation." Other questions ask whether the *Dial* could be considered "QUEER? DULL? MORBID? DEGENERATE? EROTIC?" To the question "DEGENERATE," the *Dial* responds, "Possibly, but wouldn't you like to be associated with the following company of degenerates[?]" and then adumbrates a long list of contributors, including, among others, Joseph Conrad, T.S. Eliot, Thomas Hardy, Amy Lowell, Carl Sandburg, May Sinclair, and William Butler Yeats. To the question "EROTIC," the *Dial* responds, "Well, we never upheld the genteel tradition in American letters and we do publish frequently the work of D.H. Lawrence, Ezra Pound, Arthur Schnitzler, and James Joyce." The fact that the *Dial* published only one poem by Joyce, "A Memory of the Players" (July 1920), does not seem to justify the use of "frequently" here, and unveils how the *Dial* could resort to the exaggeration and hyperbole that characterize so many advertisements. Nevertheless, this series of questions and answers does accurately convey the magazine's sentiment. It is also notable that the *Dial* promotes itself as discriminating enough to be elite and daring enough to be erotic.

In other house advertisements, the *Dial* made use of another mass-market technique—the challenging gimmick or puzzle question—to engage readers' attention. Two ads, labeled "Men of Genius" and "Are You a Judge of Art?," craftily represent how the *Dial* employed this device. The "Men of Genius" ad occurred in the *Yale Daily News* of November 25, 1922. It features pictures of these "men of genius" along the left, top, and right sides of the ad. All of these men are contributors to the *Dial*, which declares, "Men of genius are not born every minute, but most of them born within the past half century are appearing every month in *The Dial*." The ad continues, inviting reader participation:

> Great audiences make for great art. Join THE DIAL's audience, and come into stimulating contact with the foremost creative minds of our generation. A few of the men of genius who contribute to THE DIAL are pictured on this page. How many of them do you know?

This challenge to identify the "men of genius" (one of whom—May Sinclair—is a woman) curiously echoes the question asked by Bovril in its March 1902 ad in *Cassell's*: "How many parts can you name?" (see Chapter 2). While Bovril's question refers to parts of the British Empire that have been creatively rearranged to spell Bovril, the *Dial*'s question refers to portraits of artistic geniuses that have been creatively positioned to frame the ad's artistic declarations. Although I am not positing a direct influence here, the *Dial*'s advertising techniques do indicate that its editors were familiar with the "challenge questions" posed by the mass-market press.

A similar "challenge question" was issued in a February–March 1921 ad placed in *The Arts*. In this ad, the *Dial* reprints two nearly identical woodcuts, one "by the master artist, William Blake; the other a vulgarization of it executed to please the public by a popular engraver." Asking "Are You a Judge of Art?," the *Dial* prompts readers to identify the "true" masterpiece correctly: "Check the cut you think is by Blake; send this card with five dollars to THE DIAL, 152 West 13th Street, New York City. If you are wrong we will send you THE DIAL for one year. If you are right we will send you THE DIAL for one year and Maxim Gorky's Reminiscences of Tolstoy." In this way, the *Dial* entices readers with a competition that has no losers and a special reward for the correct judge. The *Dial*'s competition is meant to separate high art from its "vulgarization."

But in actuality, the close resemblance between the genuine and false engraving highlights the similarities between elite and popular art, rather than accentuating their differences. Furthermore, the use of the puzzle question as an advertising gimmick seems to undermine the *Dial*'s professed commitment to artistic purity. After all, what true expert of art would enter such a frivolous competition? Even as the *Dial* sets up these categories, then, it also (unwittingly in this case) dissolves them.

If the *Dial* could promote itself for the elite reader, it could also promote itself for the national advertiser. To the elite the *Dial* was a magazine for artistic refinement; to the advertiser the *Dial* was an opportunity for commercial profit. An ad for the *Dial* in *Printers' Ink* of March 23, 1922 claims,

> The Dial *has increased 40% in circulation in the past 90 days[.]* This gain is largely attributable to the use of space in the
> New York Times (magazine section)
> Chicago Daily News
> Review of Reviews
> Fifth Avenue Buses
> Atlantic Monthly
> Evening Post (literary review)
> New Republic
> Century
> Bookman
> Smart Set[95]

At the end of this list, the ad flourishingly concludes, "*NATIONAL ADVERTISERS* will get the quickest response from a medium which advertises itself widely." Here, then, the *Dial* suggests a proliferation and reiteration of advertising, as advertising in the *Dial* becomes intertwined with and magnified by the *Dial*'s own advertisements in other periodicals.

Later that same year, in November 1922, the *Dial* placed an ad in *Standard Rate and Data Service* which argued that the "national advertiser" could benefit from the *Dial*'s "8,000 subscribers among wealthy, cultured, intelligent people," its "rapidly increasing circulation," and its "typographical perfection."[96] These factors, the ad insists, make the *Dial* an ideal setting for "quality advertising"—a combination that the editors evidently did not regard as an oxymoron. These ads appear to have been effective in attracting national advertisers, for, according to a February 1923 ad in *Standard Rate and Data Service*, multiple national accounts had placed advertisements with the *Dial*: Dreicer & Co., Colgate &

Co., The French Line, Steinway & Sons, US Shipping Board, American Express Co., Palmer Photoplay Co., and Underwood Typewriter Co.[97] Like the diverse products attracting the window-shopping Clarissa of "Mrs. Dalloway in Bond Street," these ads present reader-consumers with an exciting array of possible purchases.

While the precise parallel between real-world magazine advertisements and fictional ones may be unintended, the similarities nevertheless point to the way ads both within and outside the fiction guided reader-consumers through the same series of emotive responses. Standing outside Hatchard's book shop, Clarissa peers at the books on display, "looking at the frontispiece of some book of memoirs spread wide in the bow window [...]. And there was that absurd book, Soapy Sponge, which Jim used to quote by the yard; and Shakespeare's Sonnets. [...] There must be some little cheap book she could buy for Milly—Cranford of course!"[98] Here, then, the display of books in the shop window prompts Clarissa to contemplate a purchase and decide upon a particular product—precisely the goal of the advertisements in the *Dial*.[99] The consumer impulse in Woolf's fictional world, in other words, reiterates the actual experience of magazine readers, while ads in the *Dial* anticipate the scene of shopping described in "Mrs. Dalloway." Here, advertisement and text become mutually reinforcing, validating readers' acts of consumption. And this mutual reinforcement becomes possible by the coincidence of magazine publication, which removes carefully constructed manuscripts from authors' hands and places them alongside advertising copy completely outside the authors' control. Through suggestive positioning, these disparate ads and stories—now made part of one artifact, the magazine—become interpenetrating texts. It was often accident, not design, that influenced a reader's reception of an artistic work.

In Woolf's full-length novel, of course, there is the airplane with its variously interpreted smoke-advertisement, much discussed by characters and critics alike. The indistinct letters made from the airplane's exhaust smoke are at once a commentary on the delicacy of individual interpretation and on the effectiveness of innovative advertisement as an attention-getting technique. While the airplane does not make an appearance in "Mrs. Dalloway in Bond Street," the discourses of advertising and shopping nevertheless pervade the text. Its geographic and cartographic setting in "commercial London," as Kathryn Simpson points out, very much informs this discourse.[100] Thus the airplane in *Mrs. Dalloway* can be regarded as an extension of the advertising discourse inaugurated in the short story. As Clarissa walks to the glove shop, she passes "club windows full of newspapers,"[101] which not only contain advertisements but also advertise themselves. When "Mrs. Dalloway in Bond Street" is resituated within its original periodical context, the periodicals featured within the story cease to be mere casual references and instead become self-reflexive: here we find reference to periodicals within a periodical, implying a further recursion of embedded advertisement. And when Clarissa passes Hatchard's book shop, the attractive displays prompt her to consider making a purchase. Finally, Clarissa enters the glove shop, where the last words of the story are spoken. Thus the story ends physically within a commercial location, as opposed to the domestic space of Mrs. Dalloway's party in the book. The *Dial* short story, then, devotes a considerably larger percentage of its space to scenes of advertisement and consumption.

And this focus on consumer culture becomes even more significant when we consider that, when the story appeared in the July 1923 *Dial*, the magazine editors had declared that 1923 would be a key year for advertising.[102] This declaration was made as part of a nine-page memo from the *Dial*'s business manager, Samuel Craig. Like the previous business manager, Craig emphasized the importance of advertising income over subscription income. Even if circulation increased to 30,000, the *Dial* still would not be self-supporting, according to his calculations. In fact, the *Dial* was losing money with each issue sold.[103] Like his predecessor, Craig concluded his report by stressing his connections to the business experts who could offer solid commercial advice.

Craig's letter also underscores how concertedly the *Dial*, a nominally anti-commercial magazine, sought to attract the attention of commercial advertisers through extensive campaigns. Craig compares the *Dial* to *Vanity Fair* and draws upon larger, more commercially-oriented periodicals for business advice, producing exact figures to substantiate his claims. Craig then gives a history of the *Dial*'s expenses, noting that the year 1922 saw an increase of $2,400 in advertising expenditures, which he regards as essential. Predictably, when Craig summarizes circulation numbers for the *Dial*, he interprets the data not as indicators of the magazine's successful dissemination of literature, but rather as indicators of future advertising prospects. Because the circulation increased by 86 percent over 1921, the *Dial* could begin to attract more national advertisers.[104] While it may not be surprising to receive this kind of interpretation from a business manager, whose job it is to focus on finances, it is noteworthy that Thayer, too, shared Craig's concerns about advertising. Responding to Craig's letter, he laments that the March issue carried fewer ads than the February issue.[105] Thus it was not only the business manager, but also the editor, who desired increased advertising pages. This evidence means that the *Dial*, so far from resisting commercial intrusions into its magazine, actively courted national advertisers. Craig's letter triumphantly announces contracts with Steinway Pianos, Colgate and Company, Underwood Typewriters, Palmer Photoplay Corporation, and The French Line.

In designing and strategizing self-promotional ads, however, Thayer aimed to attract an elite audience. As the correspondence trail confirms, the editors viewed the commercial value or revenue-generating "pull" of an advertisement as less critical than the ad's ability to affirm literary values. Ultimately, Thayer believed, the *Dial*'s success rested with its ability to win the approval of intelligent, educated people. Thus, while Thayer willingly prints commercial ads in his magazine, he carefully cautions his staff to avoid mass appeals when designing house ads for the *Dial*. Just as the *Dial* drew a distinction between quality art and the "faux bon," so the editor also drew a distinction between "quality advertising" and ignorant, "faux bon" advertising. For Thayer, advertising was not automatically cast underneath the umbrella of "low" culture. On the contrary, advertising, like art, could also be subdivided into the categories of "high" and "low." By claiming that the right kind of advertising could also be considered "high" culture, Thayer was able to legitimize his magazine's dialogue with the commercial sphere. As both Thayer's *Dial* and Woolf's "Mrs. Dalloway" show, consumer activity and artistic production could be intimately intertwined, without any necessary contradiction. Woolf's story and its magazine become part of what Elizabeth Outka has called the "commodified authentic," that paradoxical phenomenon whereby discriminating taste functions as its own marketing appeal and the genuine artifact circulates as a commodity.[106]

The Periodical in Woolf, Woolf in the Periodical: Woolf's Periodical Reverie

Notably, *Mrs. Dalloway* also portrays 1923 as a culminating year, one crystallizing the link between periodicals and commodity culture. The connection may be incidental rather than causal, but it does show how both Woolf's characters and the *Dial* staff pinpointed 1923 as a significant cultural marker, and how each was confronted with a similar set of volatile issues: respectability, commodification, and artistry in print culture. In the full-length novel, Peter Walsh muses:

> [T]he fashions had never been so becoming [...]. [T]here was design, art, everywhere [...]. Those five years—1918 to 1923—had been, he suspected, somehow very important. People looked different. Newspapers seemed

different. Now for instance there was a man writing quite openly in one of the respectable weeklies about water-closets. That you couldn't have done ten years ago—written quite openly about water-closets in a respectable weekly.[107]

Significantly, Woolf chooses periodicals—"newspapers," and "respectable weeklies"—as indices of social change. Stories about water-closets in "respectable weeklies" chart shifting mores, conveying society's willingness to accept references to previously taboo subjects. By using parallel constructions, Woolf reinforces the periodical's role as mirror to humanity: The three-word sentence "Newspapers seemed different" grammatically reflects "People looked different," following the same pattern of subject—linking verb—complement. But if this passage in *Mrs. Dalloway* shows how periodicals reflect society, other passages in Woolf's writing show how they also shaped it.

As her letters and diaries indicate, Woolf's literary ambitions, as well as her literary anxieties, were closely tied to periodicals. Famously, when her books were published, she would anxiously await the reviews, agonizing over anticipated criticism. Yet this was not her only anxiety. She also worried about securing invitations to contribute to respected periodicals on both sides of the Atlantic. From an early point in her career, she desired to appear in the *Dial* and lamented that she had not been invited to write for Thayer's magazine. "I am entreated to write for the T.L.S.," she reports triumphantly in 1920, but mitigates her success by adding, "True, I'm not asked to write for the Dial."[108] Woolf seems to have viewed invitations to contribute to periodicals as strong indicators of artistic merit. Importantly, letters from editors validated her work and affirmed her literary credentials. When Woolf's work appeared under the editorship of someone else, her publications underwent a certain form of credentializing that could not be achieved through self-publication at the Hogarth Press. "No doubt I like getting letters from publishers: even to be asked to preside over Mr [John Davys] Beresford slightly kindles me," Woolf reports, after having been asked to write a review of Beresford's *Revolution* for the *TLS*.[109] But here too Woolf shifts from triumph to defeat, lamenting that Katherine Mansfield's books have been "praised for a column in the Lit Sup—the prelude of paeans to come."[110] In this way Woolf continually looked to periodicals to determine where she stood vis-à-vis her contemporaries.

Her well-known jealousy of Mansfield emerged largely from reading reviews of her contemporaries' work. By allying herself with certain promising periodical projects, however, Woolf could assuage her jealousy and even claim victories over her competitors. In March 1922, she excitedly recorded Eliot's plan to edit the *Criterion*: "He is starting a magazine; to which 20 people are to contribute; & Leonard & I are among them! So what does it matter if K.M. soars in the newspapers, & runs up sales skyhigh?"[111] A crucial element of Woolf's battle against Mansfield, then, was their respective visibility in periodicals. "Ah," Woolf continues, "I have found a fine way of putting her in her place. The more she is praised, the more I am convinced she is bad."[112] Woolf suggests that her association with highly esteemed periodicals elevates her above Mansfield, whom she relegates to the "newspapers." This diary entry captures Woolf in a moment of periodical reverie, when magazine-related opportunities enable her to claim personal victory over literary rivals.

At once anxious to appear in periodicals and anxious to avoid the inevitable criticism that such appearances would entail, Woolf approached journalistic opportunities with marked ambivalence. Woolf's letters and diaries indicate how periodically occupied she was beyond the *Dial* itself: throughout the early months of 1923, she campaigned vigorously to secure Eliot the literary editorship of the *Nation*, a post which was eventually offered to her husband. In her diary, she enthusiastically reports that Leonard's newly acquired position at the *Nation* "opens interesting vistas,"[113] but in her letters she repeatedly stresses the exhaustion and frustration that editing and writing for the *Nation* could entail (see, for example, her letter of April 16 to Roger Fry). Similarly, her letters and diary entries regarding the *Dial* convey a mixture of deflation and elation. In July 1923, after publication of "Mrs. Dalloway," Woolf recorded her meeting with Thayer, describing him somewhat unsympathetically as a "cautious hardheaded American" but then proceeding to transcribe his "good account of flying" in an airplane.[114] Six days later, she attributes her "fame" largely to the *Dial*, writing, "Fame? Is not Clive writing an article on me? Has not Bunny praised me in the Dial? Does not Madame Logé propose to translate The Voyage Out?—But fame 'comes slowly up this way.'"[115] As Anne Olivier Bell notes, the articles by both Clive Bell and "Bunny" (David Garnett) appeared in the *Dial*.[116] Hence Woolf viewed the *Dial* as an important contributor to her steadily growing reputation in the literary marketplace.

But she did not receive consistent praise from Thayer's magazine. Before Woolf appeared in the *Dial*, she first had to suffer the sting of some not entirely complimentary reviews. In her diary of May 15, 1921, she records, "I read 4 pages of sneer & condescending praise of me in the Dial the other day. Oddly enough, I have drawn the sting of it by deciding to print it among my puffs, where it will come in beautifully." As Anne Olivier Bell notes, the May 1921 issue of the *Dial* had just reviewed *Night and Day* alongside *The Voyage Out*; the Woolfs reprinted some of "the more disobliging passages" in the back of *Jacob's Room*.[117] Thus Woolf, recognizing that bad publicity might serve her as well as good publicity, could convert criticism into promotion. Furthermore, Kenneth Burke's negative review did not diminish her respect for the *Dial*, which she continued to regard as "everything honest vigorous & advanced."[118] Throughout her life, Woolf was greatly preoccupied with periodicals, and with obtaining approval from respectable journals like the *Dial* in particular.

Nearly a year later, she was faced with another token of disapproval from the journal whose praise she had long been hoping to receive. "I've just had my dose of phenacetin," she reported on February 17, 1922, "that is to say a mildly unfavourable review of Monday or Tuesday reported by Leonard from the Dial, the more depressing as I had vaguely hoped for approval in that august quarter. It seems as if I succeed nowhere." Reflecting upon the review the next day, however, she decided that it was not completely negative. It had, after all, referred to the "technical superbness" of *The Voyage Out*.[119] The review that depressed her one day could encourage her the next. "[P]erhaps," she wrote, "Night & Day [is] arising—though the Voyage Out seems at the moment most in esteem. That encourages me. After 7 years next April the Dial speaks of its superb artistry. If they say the same of N. & D. in 7 years I shall be content."[120] In these diary entries, Woolf shows how she looked to the *Dial* for approval of her work.

Although most criticism does not draw close ties between Woolf and the *Dial*, choosing instead to emphasize the English periodicals to which she frequently contributed or the popular American periodicals that vigorously pursued her in the 1930s, her diaries and letters show that from the early days she repeatedly looked across the Atlantic for validation. Woolf's periodical reverie, and her dependence upon periodicals for professional validation and personal happiness, is lucidly illustrated in her diary entry of July 8, 1923, when "Mrs. Dalloway" had just been published:

> Anyhow I am content at present, or moderately so. I am alive; rather energetic; asked to write for 2 American papers, & so on & so on. I never said that Vanity Fair has invited me & the Dial & new Broom as well as the Nation & the Times, so that I can't help thinking myself about as successful journalistically as any woman of my day.[121]

Although Woolf follows this triumphant declaration with a characteristic deflation, regretting that she cannot write *The Hours* (what was to become

Mrs. Dalloway) "freely and vigorously," her diary entry nevertheless underscores how she actively cultivated a transatlantic periodical presence and used those periodicals as measures of her own journalistic success.

As Woolf notes, the *Dial* contributed to her gains in "fame & money."[122] She was particularly pleased when the *Dial* paid her £22 for her essay "The Lives of the Obscure," for which J.C. Squire's *London Mercury* had paid only £13.[123] Woolf had requested a payment of £15 from Squire, which he staunchly refused.[124] When he returned her manuscript, Woolf was forced to accept the lower payment. As a result, Woolf felt "snubbed," and reflected in a Jamesian vein "that poverty & the shifts it puts one to is unbecoming."[125] By December 1924, however, she felt more confident, and had gained a greater sense of financial independence: "As for fame & money, Clive's long article on me is out in The Dial. £50, apparently, from Harper. Clearly, as L. said, we are safe to make, both of us, as much as we want by our pens. Never again, I daresay, shall we agitate about getting £15 from Jack Squire."[126] The *Dial* not only gave Woolf higher payment for her own work, but also served as a highly respectable place in which her name could be circulated. In this way it helped free her from the indignities associated with Squire and the *London Mercury*. Although Woolf contributed only three pieces to the *Dial*, the magazine often referred to her work, thereby increasing the transatlantic scope and intellectual prestige of her emerging literary reputation.

Internationalism

"I love walking in London," Mrs. Dalloway tells Hugh Whitbread,[127] in her first line of spoken dialogue. Her first verbalized sentence, and Woolf's preceding references to Westminster and Big Ben,[128] locate us firmly in London. And Woolf's biographical note, on the inside cover of the July 1923 *Dial*, would seem to confirm her own deep entrenchment in the Queen of England's city: "In addition to her fiction, VIRGINIA WOOLF has also contributed a good deal of literary criticism to English reviews. She was born in London (1882) and is still living in that city."[129]

Certainly, in comparison to other contributors' notes, this one appears most geographically rooted. The immediately preceding note, on William Sommer, achieves a much broader geographic scope: "In recent years WILLIAM SOMMER'S paintings have been exhibited in New York and Cleveland. He is a native of Detroit (1867) and has studied in Munich. He is now living near Cleveland."[130] While this biographical note stretches across the Atlantic to encompass both America and Europe, the note following Woolf's own reaches all the way to Asia: "CARL HOFER, a native of Karlsruhe, has studied in Stuttgart, Rome, and Paris. Also, his work has profited by two trips he has made to India. He was born in 1878."[131] In this milieu of internationally ambitious contributors in constant transit, Woolf appears surprisingly localized and geographically static. Next to sentences that tell us other contributors have "painted in various cities of Europe" and published "in various magazines in America," we have Woolf's declaration that she was "born in London" and is "still living in that city."[132]

This image of Woolf's geographic stasis is one that both her early reviewers and later biographers have promoted. In the *Saturday Review of Literature*, Richard Hughes entitles his review of *Mrs. Dalloway* "A Day in London Life," and his article accordingly emphasizes Woolf's evocation of that city.[133] In her biography, Hermione Lee does note that Woolf's "imagination was always at play with continents she had never visited,"[134] but she nevertheless concludes that "the habits and language and tradition of the island define and surround her."[135] England's capital becomes key to both Woolf's fiction and her personal history: "London was her own past, which she traced and retraced, meeting her previous selves as she went."[136] Woolf's own diaries, of course, highlight the city's stimulus to her creative energies: "London itself perpetually attracts, stimulates, gives me a play & a story & a poem, without any trouble, save that of moving my legs through the streets."[137] Thus, when she wrote her contributor's note for the *Dial*, she confirmed a strong, consistent association with London that has been perpetuated by her readers and critics.[138] Accordingly, and with justification, Woolf is often thought of as a counterpoint to figures like Joyce or Eliot, who abandoned their own nations and traveled widely.

But the image of Woolf's geographic stasis can be productively modified by shifting the focus to her widely distributed periodical works, which helped spread her influence on both sides of the Atlantic. Although critics rightly emphasize Woolf's immersion in London, her publication in American periodicals suggests that there is another side to the story that deserves greater attention. Returning to the contributors' notes for July 1923, we see that Woolf, no matter how predictable her city of residence, is nonetheless engaged in dialogue with an international, transatlantic Modernism. In the inside front cover of the July 1923 issue, her contributor's note is sandwiched between notes from Italy, France, Germany, England, and the United States. Here, Woolf becomes part of an international milieu that includes both Americans and Europeans; as readers skim through the contributors' notes, marking the capitalized cities, they jump from Cleveland to London to Karlsruhe, from Detroit to Munich to New York. London becomes one stop on the circuitry of Modernism. At the same time, Woolf's story joins this circuitry as her manuscript physically enacts the transatlantic movements represented on the inside cover. "Mrs. Dalloway in Bond Street" may well be about London, but it is printed and read in New York. The early version of *Mrs. Dalloway*, so far from being a work centered in Britain, is actually a transatlantic text that crosses the ocean to bring England to America.

Here I want to argue, briefly, that I believe Woolf wanted the story to appear first in America. Critics often mention that Woolf had sent the story to T.S. Eliot, hoping that he would publish it in the London-based *Criterion*.[139] Her letter to Eliot is dated June 4, 1923. But on May 21, 1923, she had already received a check of $60 for "Mrs. Dalloway" from the *Dial*; the check had been mailed two weeks earlier, on May 8.[140] And as early as April 19 Thayer reported that he had received and accepted Woolf's story, which had been forwarded to him by Raymond Mortimer.[141] This evidence suggests that Woolf's initial ambition was to publish the story in the *Dial*, across the Atlantic. "Mrs. Dalloway" reached the *Dial* approximately two months before she sent it to Eliot. The *Criterion* was her second choice, not her first. Woolf was undoubtedly hoping for dual publication on both sides of the Atlantic, but it is significant that she initiated negotiations with the *Dial* long before contacting the *Criterion*. While Eliot rejected her story, Thayer praised it as accessible and enjoyable.[142] As Hermione Lee insinuates, Eliot's rejection may have upset her,[143] but she had already received acceptance from Thayer. While Woolf certainly hoped for publication in the *Criterion*, she first envisioned her story in the *Dial*.

It may be even more surprising to learn that the *Dial* presented Woolf as an essential contributor to American culture. In a November 1924 advertisement, the *Dial* displayed Woolf's photograph under the headline "The Dial and American Culture."[144] Curiously, the ad prints the portraits of three other contributors—D.H. Lawrence, Arthur Schnitzler, and George Santayana—none of whom is actually American.[145] But the ad implies that these European authors nonetheless inform and shape American culture. The ad, which occurred in the November 15, 1924 *Saturday Review*, begins with a string of analogies, eventually culminating in an equation between national culture and periodical-reading: "A flower is known by its perfume, a bird by its flight, a wine by its taste, a face by its expression; a nation's culture is known by its magazines." The *Dial*, this ad asserts, defines American culture at its best: "American culture is represented by THE DIAL, the one magazine in America devoted exclusively to art and letters." In the following paragraph, the advertising copy continues to emphasize the particularly

American quality of the magazine. These comments make the *Dial* appear as a magazine that more or less exclusively published and promoted works by American authors.

Hence it seems puzzling that, after making this declaration, the *Dial* should proceed to summon the portraits of European contributors and their works: "The Woman Who Rode Away" by D.H. Lawrence, "Miss Ormerod: A Short Story" by Virginia Woolf, "Lieut. Gustl: A Short Story" by Arthur Schnitzler, and "Self Government" by George Santayana. Yet the pairing of American culture with European heritage is consistent with the *Dial*'s mission to bring the two continents into closer intellectual dialogue. It published a Paris Letter, an Irish Letter, a London Letter, a German Letter, a Vienna Letter, an Italian Letter, even a Prague and a Hungarian Letter,[146] and in general sought to recruit European intellectuals who could report on their native scene to America. Working desperately to forge transatlantic dialogue, the *Dial* sent repeated pleas to Thomas Mann for a German Letter. And Eliot, as an American expatriate, reported on the London literary scene, struggling heroically to produce letters in spite of multiple mental breakdowns.[147] In the *Dial* we not only see the American-born Eliot traveling to London, but we also see Woolf the Englishwoman sending her work across the Atlantic to America.

Collectively, these foreign letters set the stage for Woolf's fiction. They not only situate her internationally, sometimes by direct reference, but also prompt readers to think about the centrality of the city—whether Woolf's London or Hofmannsthal's Vienna—to culture and literature. While each letter focuses on a given city or nationality, the vast array of letters, from both Eastern and Western Europe, collectively creates a collage of intermingling cultures. Within a single year, a *Dial* reader could theoretically become acquainted with the latest cultural developments in England, Germany, Ireland, Hungary, Czechoslovakia, Italy, Austria, and France. Readers would learn that book prices in Germany had become so high as to cause a "consumers' strike,"[148] that Joseph Capek's *The Land of Many Names* and Stanislav Lom's *The Upheaval* were being performed in Czech theaters,[149] and that new literary *salons* were opening every day in France.[150] From Dublin, John Eglinton reports that the Irish Literary Renaissance must account for the "disconcerting new" novel by Joyce,[151] and that Yeats's appointment as poet-senator represents a governmental shift toward the Platonic philosopher-king.[152] Writing from Austria, Hofmannsthal unpacks the musical and dramatic performances of the Salzburg Festival. Writing from Italy, Raffaello Piccoli demystifies the political tensions between Communism and Fascism in his country. These precise descriptions of local events, experienced firsthand by foreign correspondents on the scene, give *Dial* readers privileged access to cultural, political, and literary developments abroad.

When Woolf is mentioned in these letters, she becomes at once a key Londoner and a key figure in this larger international milieu. In his February 1923 London Letter, Raymond Mortimer enumerates the past autumn's literary events, including the publication of *Jacob's Room*:

> It [the autumn] brought from Mr. A.E. Housman [...] his second book of poems [...]. It brought a *virtuoso* translation of the first volume of the incomparable and never sufficiently to be lamented Proust. It brought from Virginia Woolf a new and exciting novel. It brought Lady Into Fox, with which Mr David Garnet [*sic*] has established himself [...]. And it brought The Criterion, a new quarterly, the high qualities of which I presume are already known to readers of THE DIAL. But it did not bring from The London Mercury its long awaited opinion of the merits or faults of Ulysses.[153]

In Mortimer's London Letter, Woolf becomes embedded in a record of international literary activity. Replacing names with nationalities, we see the list announcing a volume of poetry by an English author, a translation of a French author, two novels by members of the Bloomsbury Group, a new quarterly edited by an American expatriate, and an English periodical expected to review the novel of an Irish author. Under London's umbrella, France, Ireland, England, and America make contact and enact complex transactions with each other. Though ostensibly a "London Letter," Mortimer's article reaches beyond the city and the nation of its label.

Additionally, the letters from foreign correspondents inflect Woolf's work by foregrounding the theme of world war, a reminder that international engagements could reap disaster as well as rewards. It is often observed that the shell-shocked Septimus is missing from "Mrs. Dalloway in Bond Street," but readers of the July 1923 *Dial* would have been served with repeated reminders of the Great War's devastation. In terms of emphasis placed on war, their reading experience may not have been quite as different from that of later novel-readers. When we return "Mrs. Dalloway" to the *Dial*, we see, in contradistinction to the usually divergent reading experiences in periodical and book versions of a work, an unexpected convergence between the short story and the novel.

Meditations on the First World War surface not only in "Mrs. Dalloway" but also in surrounding articles. In Woolf's story, Clarissa Dalloway asks the shop-girl, "Do you remember before the war you had gloves with pearl buttons?"[154] When another character splits a glove, the shop-girl apologizes with the explanation, "Gloves have never been quite so reliable since the war."[155] This sense of postwar decline is also taken up several pages later in Raymond Mortimer's London Letter, which begins in the following way:

> It is about a year, as far as I can remember, since any play by Shakespeare has been put on the stage for a "run" in any of the forty-odd theatres in the West End of London. It sometimes seems that the War has reduced England to barbarism: not only by the astonishing, rapid, and almost complete departure of all moral decency and tolerance during the fighting (that was perhaps less marked here than in most of the countries compromised) but by the withering of all public pretense of respect for Art.[156]

Combined, Woolf's short story and Mortimer's Letter create a picture of 1920s London still absorbing the aftershocks of war. Immediately following Mortimer's London Letter, P. Beaumont Wadsworth's Prague Letter begins on a similarly shaken note:

> Living here, right at the centre of Europe, is to feel as though one were lying on the ground, ear pressed to the earth, listening to the slow rumbling which announces the crash of the social structure, and feeling the heavy waves of disintegration which threaten European culture, a disintegration which began in the nineteenth century with Nietzsche, Ibsen, and Strindberg, reaching its highest point during the World War.[157]

Situated alongside these letters, "Mrs. Dalloway" becomes part of the larger seismograph measuring the impact of the war. In the *Dial* of July 1923, readings are taken from England, Germany, and Czechoslovakia, from fiction and from letters, from visual art and the printed word.

Given that *Mrs. Dalloway* has been a key text in defining trauma theory and exploring the phenomenon of shell shock, it seems significant that its early version should have appeared alongside articles that explicitly questioned the impact of war upon art. In the same issue that published "Mrs. Dalloway in Bond Street," an article by Julius Meier-Graefe evaluates, as its title suggests, "German Art After the War." "[N]othing stands out so prominently in the art of the present," he writes, "as the world war."[158] Later in the issue, Edmund Wilson's review essay, "The Anatomy of War," suggests how literature can help readers navigate and recover from the nightmare of warfare.[159] Although Wilson's essay does not mention Woolf, his classification of Siegfried Sassoon's poems as "expressions of madness and despair"[160] resonates with the temperament of Septimus Smith, whom Woolf would later develop as a portrait of "insanity & suicide."[161]

Even without Septimus, however, "Mrs. Dalloway" resonates with Wilson's references to the "nightmare" and "ruin" of war.[162] Clarissa thinks of "Lady Bexborough, who opened the bazaar, they say, with the telegram in her hand—Roden, her favourite, killed."[163] Clarissa's conversation with the shop-girl includes several references to the war, and in the story's penultimate paragraph Clarissa reflects, "Thousands of young men had died that things might go on."[164] Several pages later, Wilson writes of "epitaphs for dead soldiers."[165] Readers thus move from representations of war in fiction to reviews of those fictional representations. And these fictional stories and review articles are tied closely to an immediate historical reality.

Within the *Dial*, then, Mrs. Dalloway becomes part of a larger conversation about the tragedy of war. The story is a fictional medium through which readers may process their own personal losses. Whereas the *Little Review* devoted so little attention to the First World War that readers complained, the *Dial* devoted extensive coverage to the war and its aftermath. Inflected by these surrounding artifacts, "Mrs. Dalloway" becomes not just a shopping story, but a war story.[166] It displays the effects of war on the domestic front: lower-quality goods (never "quite so reliable since the war"),[167] bereaved mothers and widows who must "go on,"[168] the statues that remind civilians of soldiers' heroic acts,[169] the "violent explosion in the street" that causes the shop-woman to "cower behind the counters" as if ducking from aerial raids.[170] These were themes Woolf would later develop in the full-length version of *Mrs. Dalloway*, but their seminal presence here links the tenor of Woolf's story with the prevailing mood of the magazine. Throughout 1923, foreign correspondents continued to comment on the war's reverberations, as further reports were sent in from Vienna, Munich, and Prague.

As important indices of cross-cultural exchange in Modernism, the *Dial*'s pages are full of peripatetic movement of this kind. The editor Scofield Thayer even spent several months in Vienna, during which time he wrote frantic letters back to his staff in New York. These movements could create tensions as well as harmonies, as the *Dial* strove for a balance in coverage that was not always easy to achieve. The 1924 ad for "The Dial and American Culture" (also discussed above) suggests that Woolf was essential not only to the *Dial*'s international scope but also to its efforts to cultivate and refine America. The ad implies that contact with European classics will teach Americans how they can in turn refine their own cultural scene. The ad's portrait of Woolf in profile, with her wide eye looking urbanely off the page, does indeed convey an aura of dignity and refinement. With this portrait-advertisement, we can add to Brenda Silver's assessment of Woolf's early iconic appearances in the 1920s. In *Virginia Woolf Icon*, Silver writes:

> [D]uring the 1920s, while still a rising star, she had made appearances in Britain that extended her visibility beyond literary and intellectual circles. In 1924 she was featured in British *Vogue*'s "Hall of Fame" accompanied by a photograph by Beck and Macgregor, fashionable studio photographers who specialized in the intelligentsia, an appearance that Jane Garrity argues established a split between Virginia Woolf writer and Virginia Woolf beautiful woman and fashionable icon. […] Five years later a more "popular" Virginia Woolf, again accompanied by the Beck and Macgregor portrait, appeared in *Vanity Fair*'s "We Nominate for the Hall of Fame."[171]

Yet, during these same years, in fact as early as 1924, the first date Silver cites above, Woolf's portrait was also being circulated in America. Notably, like *Vogue* and *Vanity Fair* here, the *Dial* promoted Woolf as a cultured writer; in the *Dial*'s 1924 portrait, she appears both beautiful and intellectually refined. This is not to refute Silver's argument about Woolf's iconic circulation in 1920s Britain, but it is to say that this iconic circulation had an American dimension as well. Furthermore, while Silver impressively tracks Woolf's image in multiple American periodicals from the 1930s onward, we can mark an earlier, if less glamorized, beginning to the circulation of Woolf's portrait in America.

Uniting Tradition with Modernity

Even as Woolf was experimenting with new representations of consciousness in London, the *Dial* set out to transform the New York literary scene. Like Woolf, however, the *Dial* desired to preserve tradition even as it sought to revolutionize the artistic world. As Joseph Wood Krutch observes in an early review of *Mrs. Dalloway*, "The method which she uses is the newest and most radical, but the charm which she exploits—the charm of decorum and resignation—is the most conservative thing in the world."[172] The *Dial* thus reflects Woolf's own tendencies to bring traditional Victorian customs and practices into dialogue with innovative and subversive Modernist art.

In the argument that follows, I want to look more closely at the way both Woolf and the *Dial* sought to bridge the divide between old and new forms of art, between traditional conventions and Modernist experiment. As Steve Ellis writes, "If *Night and Day* is a heavily retrospective work, while *Jacob's Room* shows an acute but extremely qualified sense of the contemporary, Woolf's next novel, *Mrs. Dalloway* (1925), aims precisely at combining the worlds of past experience and present receptivity to 'deepen' its sense of the present 'when backed by the past', to the advantage of both.'"[173] The categories Ellis outlines underscore how *Mrs. Dalloway* marked a turning point in Woolf's career. If we accept Ellis's basic premise, then we can say that the vision of Woolf's 1925 novel is shared by the *Dial*'s editors, who also adopted as their technique the merging of past and present.

As an advertisement from July 1920 about "The Philosophy of the New" reveals, this often precarious convergence of tradition and innovation could excite readers' anxieties. While the *Dial* was never as daringly avant-garde as the *Little Review*, its mixture of traditional literary forms with newer artistic experiments unnerved some readers, in some cases proving even more unsettling than the *Little Review*'s outright rejection of tradition. In fact, readers of the *Dial* were so anxious about these newly appearing artistic forms that the *Dial* decided in July 1920 to publish its less traditional works under a separate category designated "Modern Forms." As the ad explained, "The Philosophy of the New sometimes evokes cries of Pain. Therefore its exposition should be guardedly made, and due warning given to protect the uninitiated from being startled."[174] Having come to this recognition, the *Dial* announces a change in policy: "Heretofore it has been the policy of THE DIAL to scatter through its pages unconventional prose, verse, and pictures. Beginning with this number, they are corralled into a department entitled 'Modern Forms.'"[175] Here, then, we witness at once a separation and a union of these two artistic trajectories. Although the "Modern Forms" are "corralled" into a separate department, they nevertheless share the same magazine covers as the more conventional submissions.

By the time "Mrs. Dalloway in Bond Street" appeared in the *Dial*, the "Modern Forms" "corral" had been abandoned, but the *Dial* still continued to advertise itself as a magazine that brought the old into dialogue with the new. Tellingly, Pound instructed Marianne Moore, who would assume editorial responsibilities for the *Dial* in 1925, that she should send to *Exile* any items that seemed too radical for the *Dial*'s use.[176] In light of these declarations, it almost seems surprising that the *Dial* should have published Eliot's *The Waste Land*, a wildly experimental poem that puzzled even Virginia Woolf.[177] "It has great beauty & force of phrase: symmetry; & tensity," she wrote in her diary. "What connects it together, I'm not so sure."[178] But the same October 1922 ad declaring the *Dial* "free" from "eccentricity" also devotes prominent space to *The Waste Land*, slated to appear in the November 1922 issue. Furthermore, the advertising copy pairs *The Waste Land* with *Ulysses*, which by 1922 had emerged in book form after aborted serialization in the *Little Review*: "It is not improbable that the appearance of The Waste Land will rank with that of Ulysses in the degree of interest it will call forth."[179] Critics have pointed to the fact that the *Dial* would not have published *Ulysses*, and archival letters confirm that the *Dial* sought to avoid scandalous works. But its promotion of Joyce and *Ulysses* alongside *The Waste Land* suggests that the *Dial* nevertheless eagerly sought associations with the avant-garde, even while remaining a "more mainstream literary review."[180]

The Economy of Gift Exchange

Yet the equation between art and advertisement is not quite that simple; it was mediated by a third component—the gift economy. In her article "Economies and Desire," Kathryn Simpson argues that, in Woolf's writing, the "gift economy can be read as running counter to, but also contiguous with, capitalist systems and my focus on the gift economy aims, in part, to offer another angle from which to consider the ambivalent relationship to and representation of market economies and consumer culture others have detected in Woolf's writing."[181] Simpson goes on to show how gift-giving features prominently in Woolf's fiction and life: Gifts may take the form of literary texts, erotic exchanges, physical artifacts, letters, or even manuscripts. Simpson specifically mentions the proposed gift of *Cranford* as one such (literary) gift in "Mrs. Dalloway in Bond Street." Simpson usefully proposes the gift economy as a mode of exchange that at once overlaps and provides an alternative to the market economy. While this argument takes an important first step toward modifying our views of Woolf's economics, Simpson's argument can be strengthened by examining "Mrs. Dalloway in Bond Street" as a periodical artifact. When the story is returned to the *Dial*, which advertised itself as "a gift of distinction for people of discrimination," we see how the story itself becomes part of a gift economy—one that extends beyond the fiction to the world of magazine readers. Thus the gift-giving force Simpson identifies in Woolf had long informed the *Dial*'s own market strategy.

In "The Paradox of the Gift," Simpson argues:

> A close reading of Woolf's short story "Mrs. Dalloway in Bond Street" enables the disruptive potential of the intersection of gift and market economies in Woolf's work to be explored. Located in commercial London, this story in many ways encapsulates Woolf's ambivalence about consumerism, capitalism and commodity culture, but also seems to explore the subversive potential of women entering the market place with money to buy and give gifts[.][182]

As Simpson notes, the story is located in "commercial London," but it was being read in America, as the New York-based *Dial* printed it and distributed it to readers across the continent. Thus while the actions of the story take place in London, the story itself (as physical object) is located between the covers of an American periodical in New York. While Simpson's argument illuminatingly unfolds the subversive potential of the gift within London, her argument can be usefully extended across the Atlantic.

By employing clever marketing strategies and describing its magazine more as a gift than as a commercial product, the *Dial* sought to distance itself from the vulgarities of popular promotions. In promoting the "gift economy," the *Dial* in the early 1920s created an alternative to the market economy that Woolf would also highlight in her 1923 short story. As Simpson notes, "'Mrs. Dalloway in Bond Street' explicitly puts the market and gift economies into opposition, but Clarissa's negotiation of and participation in the two economies remains ambiguous" because, while she contemplates giving gifts, she ultimately reneges on those gifts.[183] "In reneging on her gift, Clarissa seems to comply with a masculine" capitalist economy, though in other ways she troubles it.[184] Similarly, brochures distributed by the *Dial* urge readers to consider giving magazine subscriptions as gifts, but this promotion of the *Dial* as a "distinguished gift," distinct from traditional commercial products, still at some level collapses back into the very capitalist system it seeks to escape. For giving a gift still requires making an initial purchase, and the *Dial*'s "gift" advertisements were nonetheless designed to increase circulation and revenue—at bottom they held commercial value.

As gift theorists such as Mark Osteen and Lewis Hyde have noted, objects frequently fluctuate in status: depending on their perceived sentimental or market value, they can function either as commodities or as inalienable gifts. Works of art, as Hyde notes, "exist simultaneously in two 'economies,' a market economy and a gift economy."[185] And, as anthropologists such as Marcel Mauss have documented, gifts confer not only appreciation but also obligation. They can exist (even as prominent elements) in patriarchal societies, yet, as Hélène Cixous notes, when objects are exchanged in masculine economies they are often conceived of in terms of debt, not gifts. The contradictions and problematics of gift-giving are highlighted by three archival artifacts in particular: a late 1921 brochure promoting the *Dial* as "A Gift of Distinction for People of Discrimination," a December 1922 advertisement circulated in twenty-seven college papers, and a brown postcard that folded out into an advertising brochure.

The 1921 brochure establishes the *Dial* as a distinctive gift, and the calligraphic typography used to print this folded brochure underscores the magazine's elitist tone. On the front cover, this pamphlet proclaims:

> The Dial: A Gift of Distinction for People of Discrimination is the one journal in America devoted exclusively to Art and Literature, to beauty and ideas. It brings its readers the finest work of the world's creative artists: fiction, poetry, essays, pictures, reviews of books, exhibitions, concerts, and plays. The Dial does not bother with ephemera. Astonish and delight your friends with The Dial, a gift of charm and distinction.[186]

Using a combination of black-on-white and white-on-black typography, the *Dial* places these statements in a distinguished-looking frame, thereby highlighting artistic value through technological sophistication. Names of contributors are placed in the outer frame, while the text of the *Dial*'s mission statement continues in the inner frame. And here it is worth mentioning that commercial advertisements also succeeded based on *their* technological sophistication, not just on their "vulgar" appeals. In fact, advertisements actually demanded some of the most sophisticated skill and technology to create: the varied typefaces and font sizes, the use of bold and italics to attract readers' attention, the creative alternations of color, and the inconsistent spacing could make ads yet more difficult to set up and print than the regular type used to convey the messages of "higher" arts such as poetry and literature. Hence it is not entirely surprising that the *Dial* saw certain forms of advertisement as belonging to "high" art.

At any rate, its 1921 brochure at once acts as an advertisement and insists upon the *Dial*'s separation from the larger commercial sphere of advertising, buying, and selling. It publishes only the "finest" work, and "does not bother with ephemera." Twice on this cover page, the *Dial* casts itself as a gift. In the headline, it is called "A Gift of Distinction for People of Discrimination," thereby aligning itself with discriminating readers, a move that at once flatters readers and separates them from the masses. Then, in its concluding sentence, the cover text once again reiterates the *Dial*'s distinctive status, calling it "a gift of charm and distinction." But the gift rhetoric does not end there. As readers open the brochure to reveal a two-page spread, they are instructed to buy yet more gifts: "Another gift of merit is one of the books listed below which can be obtained at a greatly reduced price in combination with a subscription to THE DIAL."[187] These books are listed under the categories of fiction (Sherwood Anderson, May Sinclair, Max Beerbohm, John Dos Passos, Padraic Colum), poetry (W.B. Yeats, Ezra Pound, Edwin Arlington Robinson), biography (Anatole France, Wilfred Scawin Blunt), history (Hindrek Willem van Loon), and travel (D.H. Lawrence). Hence, even while the *Dial* claimed to be discriminating and particular, it distributed its discriminating tastes across a broad spectrum of genres. In this way it managed to reach a wide range of readers while simultaneously appealing to an elite audience.

The emphasis on distinction and gift-giving continues on the back cover of this 1921 pamphlet, as the *Dial* announces that it has "once again" been awarded the rating of 100 percent "for short stories of distinction published during the past year."[188] In a small boxed chart to the right of this statement, the *Dial* lists the results of Edward J. O'Brien's annual review of American magazine fiction. In this chart, magazines are ranked "by percentage of distinctive stories." The *Dial* ranks #1, at 100 percent, followed by twenty-two other magazines, including many mass-market periodicals, such as *Harper's*, *Scribner's*, *McClure's*, and *Collier's Weekly*. Although the *Dial* ranks significantly higher than these periodicals (*Collier's* falls at the bottom, with 15 percent distinctive stories, and *McClure's* does not fare too much better, at 17 percent), the chart nevertheless groups the *Dial* with these larger magazines, implying similarity as well as divergence. "Once again" (to borrow the ad's language for another purpose), the *Dial* simultaneously sets itself apart from these other periodicals and implies that it categorically occupies a position alongside these larger mass-market magazines.

After listing these distinguishing statistics, the *Dial* provides a subscription blank for readers to fill in with the names and addresses of gift recipients. Adjusting to readers' versatile needs, the ad promotes the flexibility of its offers: "Both THE DIAL and the book may be sent to different people. If you send THE DIAL, the enclosed card, designed especially for the purpose, may be mailed by you directly to the fortunate recipient of your gift on the date you desire." This "enclosed card" is preserved in the *Dial*/Thayer Papers at the Beinecke Library. The miniature gift card is the same size as a business card, and it displays an image of the August 1921 *Dial* with the following text next to the image: "This card is just to show you what you will receive every month in 1922. With a Merry Christmas and a Happy New Year."[189] This card slips inside a miniature white envelope. The scheme certainly exudes refinement and sophistication in even the most miniature of details, but the cute little gift card that folds neatly into its special envelope is ultimately another form of advertisement, another promotional display of the *Dial* to catch readers' eyes. While the gift strategy does display cultivated taste, it cannot completely escape the discourse of advertising. Just as Woolf was not merely a witness to, but also an actor "*in* the commercial world,"[190] so the *Dial* was also operating *in* that world. And a large part of Woolf's involvement *in* the commercial world stems from her works' placement *in* periodicals. While critics have already pointed to Woolf's commercially based anxiety about her work for mass-circulating periodicals, a close examination of the archival evidence reveals that even the little magazines in which she placed her literary work brought her into deeper dialogue with commercialism.

The *Dial*'s December 1922 advertisement underscores this association. In this advertisement, which was placed in twenty-seven college papers, the *Dial* promotes itself as a distinguished Christmas present far superior to commercial products found in the stores: "The Dial is the easiest gift possible to make. All the time, excitement, worry of Christmas shopping is eliminated," the advertisement reads.[191] The *Dial* may well have been the ideal gift for Virginia Woolf to give, since, as her nephew records, "All through her life Virginia was a vague, undecided and exasperating shopper."[192] Had Virginia Woolf followed the *Dial*'s advice, she might easily have eliminated her frustrating shopping trips. This, at least, is the outcome asserted by the ad, which fits into the genre of advertising that proposes solutions to "instantly curable" problems, as theorized by Richard Ohmann.[193]

The ad also seeks to carve out a professional, educated audience—an audience that most commercial magazines claimed to have. As Ohmann notes, "Most publishers identified their audience as 'the professional class,' for obvious reasons."[194] Only a few claimed to reach "the 'great masses.'"[195] Hence the *Dial* was not actually departing from the marketing practices of commercial periodicals when it courted an audience distinguished by education and intelligence. The December 1922 college ad urges readers to "[a]stonish and delight your discriminating friends with a subscription to THE DIAL—America's leading journal of art and letters."[196] Gift subscriptions are $4.00, one dollar off the regular annual rate of $5.00, and additional gift subscriptions are only $3.00. "Send us your list today," the ad commands, issuing inviting imperatives to college students and faculty. "THE DIAL will do the rest and arrive every month of the year as a source of interest and enjoyment, and a constant reminder of your thoughtfulness."[197] Combining bargain rates with declarations of cultural value, the ad asserts, "THE DIAL is a peculiarly appropriate gift for all those sensitive to beauty and ideas. THE DIAL is not only a gift but a compliment."[198] Giving the *Dial* to a friend, the ad maintains, acknowledges the intelligence and cultural refinement of the recipient. The ad continues, expounding upon the virtues of the *Dial*'s intellectual sophistication while also making an amusing spelling error: "Its selection implies a personal attention, an expenditure of time and thought rather than of money alone, which is distinctly flattering to the intelligence and taste of the receipient."[199] That "receipient" is printed instead of "recipient" ironizes the *Dial*'s claims that it appeals to intelligence. Sometimes the mistakes characterizing "low" art could appear in advertisements for "high" art as well.

But on the whole the *Dial* cultivated a sophisticated, refined image, evident both in the contents of its pages and in their presentation. One advertising scheme proved particularly clever in this regard: a brown envelope that could be sent in the mail opened up and folded out into an advertising brochure of white glossy paper. Moreover, a portion of this brown envelope could be cut by the recipient along a perforated line and sent as a postcard with subscription details back to the *Dial*. The white paper contains notes about individual contributors such as Joseph Conrad, Thomas Hardy, and W.B. Yeats; the brown shell is used to explain the magazine's overarching artistic mission that brings these contributors together. "*The Dial on your library table indicates an alert intelligence and a sophisticated taste*," the ad asserts.[200] The subscription blank urges readers to think of the *Dial* not only as a generic refined artifact, but in particular, as a refined *gift*: "Either THE DIAL or one of these [advertised] books will make a very acceptable Christmas gift," the subscription blank avows. Thus the editors continually instructed readers to view the *Dial* as a gift instead of a commercial product, a strategy in line with Virginia Woolf's own approach to the market economy.

But this strategy could often prove problematic. On the one hand, as Simpson points out, this idea of gift-giving counteracts the normative economic transactions of the commercial sphere (which is concerned with buying and selling for profit, not giving at a loss). But, simultaneously, the *Dial*'s gift-giving strategy also insists upon direct engagement with the very sphere to which it is ostensibly opposed: those who give the gift of the *Dial* must first conduct a commercial transaction and purchase the magazine. For the *Dial*, the idea of the gift was at once a counter-commercial impulse and a calculating marketing strategy.

Conclusion: From Periodical Publication to the Hogarth Press

We often think of Woolf as associated with the Hogarth Press, the alternative form of publishing that brought out her novels in London and allowed her to avoid the struggles and the potential debasement of mass-market publication. As Kathryn Simpson notes, Woolf's ownership of the press "is often seen as being an escape from the taint of the market place and from some of the pressures of publication."[201] But Simpson argues that Woolf's ownership of the Hogarth Press in fact reveals her interest in "markets and profit margins."[202] And Laura Marcus confirms that, as the Woolfs' publication list grew, "they became commercial publishers dependent on commercial printers."[203] More remains to be said, however. One may trace Woolf's development from anonymous periodical reviewer to celebrated self-publisher, but it is worthy of note that, even after the Press was purchased in May 1917, Woolf still continued to place her work in periodicals. B.J. Kirkpatrick's bibliography attributes some 400 periodical contributions to Woolf, roughly 75 percent of them post-1917. "Mrs. Dalloway in Bond Street," published in the July 1923 *Dial*, offers an important case in point. If we return to the periodicals in which Woolf originally published her work, we see that her relationship to commercialism is thrown into yet sharper relief. Far from escaping the demands of commerce through her art, Woolf engaged ever more imaginatively and intensely with it.

As it struggled between artistic purity and commercial necessity, the *Dial* found itself in a similar position to Woolf. As we have seen, the editorial staff engaged in extensive debates about the *Dial*'s position in the mass market, and staff members expressed anxiety over the vexed relationship between the magazine's aesthetic commitments and its advertising goals. The *Dial*, like Woolf, sought to distance itself from commercial culture by promoting a gift economy—but this very act of promotion invariably brought the *Dial* back into commercial transactions and alignments. As Leila Brosnan notes, "When reading the non-fiction [of Woolf], then, we should recognise its grounding in that commercial sphere and consider, for example, the editorial practices and policies of the journals to which Woolf contributed."[204] The same holds true for Woolf's fiction: her short stories in magazines must also be considered in the light of those periodicals' stated editorial missions and actual operating practices. A consideration of the *Dial/Thayer* Papers furthers our understanding of Modernism's relation to commercial culture (extending and modifying the scholarship of Mark Morrisson, Lawrence Rainey, Jennifer Wicke, and others), while also showing how advertisement played a significant role in shaping the vision of Thayer's magazine and in creating dialogue between high and low culture. If Woolf's relationship to consumer culture has been revised in the past decades, it is necessary also to revise the image of the allegedly "anti-commercial" periodical in which she appeared.

Alongside Woolf's relationship to consumer culture, periodicals such as the *Dial* also modify our understanding of her geographic and international positioning. Unlike James Joyce, Rudyard Kipling, and Henry James, who all immigrated to foreign countries, Woolf remained domiciled in the city of her birth, but the *Dial*'s publication of Woolf's work, and its circulation of her portrait in the *Saturday Review*, suggest that we should view her, too, as a well-traveled author. Situating Modernism in a more broadly international context, we can explore not only how the prototypical exile or migrant artist actually travels from country to country, but also how the spread of Modernism is dependent upon the dissemination of its key texts in multiple international journals. Crucially, this dissemination was supported by advertisements and financed by commercial investments. In considering these investments, we can respond resourcefully to Rita Felski's invitation to "view modernity from the standpoint of consumption rather than production."[205] Adding a variation to her formula, I want to say that, when we consider Modernism in this way, we must pay attention to the physical artifacts as well as the ideas they contain. We can analyze "Mrs. Dalloway" as a story about shopping and consumption on its own terms, but our analysis is significantly enriched if we consider the physical artifact—the magazine—that carried this story to readers. It seems only appropriate that we should locate these material concerns—expressed from the moment Mrs. Dalloway says that she would "buy the gloves herself"—in their original material contexts. As Edward Bishop and David Earle have pointed out, we must (not only conceptually, but also quite literally) re-cover Modernism by returning to the original periodical covers that housed these Modernist texts. Only by returning to the early material context of Modernism can we fully understand and recover its highly fraught dances between marketing and gift-giving, production and consumption, advertising and art.

Notes

1   Virginia Woolf, "Mrs. Dalloway in Bond Street," *Dial*, July 1923, 20.
2   Advertisement for the *Dial* in the *Literary Review*, October 28, 1922, 159.
3   Alan C. Golding, "*The Dial, The Little Review*, and the Dialogics of Modernism," *American Periodicals* 15, no.1 (2005): 46.
4   Jennifer Wicke, "Coterie Consumption: Bloomsbury, Keynes, and Modernism as Marketing," in *Marketing Modernisms: Self-Promotion, Canonization, Rereading*, ed. Kevin J.H. Dettmar and Stephen Watt (Ann Arbor: University of Michigan Press, 1996), 120.
5   Margaret Anderson and Jane Heap, "The Reader Critic," *Little Review*, September–December 1920, 93, 94.
6   See Steven Monte, "Ancients and Moderns in Mrs. Dalloway," *Modern Language Quarterly* 61, no. 4 (December 2000): 589n3 for a genealogy of additional comparisons between Woolf and Joyce.

7   Review of *Jacob's Room, Dial*, July 1923, 85. The review of *Jacob's Room* was written by David Garnett.
8   Qtd. in *Virginia Woolf: Critical Assessments*, ed. Eleanor McNees (East Sussex: Helm Information, 1994), 3: 268.
9   Qtd. in *Virginia Woolf: Critical Assessments*, 3:271.
10 Qtd. in *Virginia Woolf: Critical Assessments*, 3:273.
11 See Christine Froula, *Virginia Woolf and the Bloomsbury Avant-Garde* (New York: Columbia University Press, 2005), 354n18 for a succinct summary of the story's origins and titles.
12 Golding, "*The Dial, The Little Review*, and the Dialogics of Modernism," 44.
13 Letter from Scofield Thayer to James Joyce, n.d., probably 1920, *Dial*/Scofield Thayer Papers, Beinecke Rare Book and Manuscript Library, Yale University.
14 Sylvia Beach to Marianne Moore, July 12, 1926, *Dial*/Scofield Thayer Papers, Beinecke Rare Book and Manuscript Library, Yale University; this letter is published in *The Letters of Sylvia Beach*, ed. Keri Walsh (New York: Columbia University Press, 2010), 110–11.
15 David Garnett's review of *Jacob's Room* makes this division explicitly: "Mrs Woolf is incapable of Mr Joyce's offence. She can touch only what will move us aesthetically. She is the kind of butterfly that stoops only at the flowers, Mr Joyce 'a painted lady or peacock that feasts upon bloody entrails dropped by a hawk,' or even on less interesting droppings" (Review of *Jacob's Room, Dial*, July 1923, 85). Garnett objected to *Ulysses* not because it was "obscene," but because its delight in the excremental depleted its "aesthetic value" (85).
16 Edward Bishop, "Re:Covering Modernism—Format and Function in the Little Magazines," in *Modernist Writers and the Marketplace*, ed. Ian Willison, Warwick Gould, and Warren Chernaik (London: Macmillan, 1996), 311. As James Dempsey separately notes, the *Dial* "was exquisitely in touch with both traditional work and the avant-garde" (xi). See Dempsey, *The Tortured Life of Scofield Thayer* (Tallahasse: University of Florida Press, 2014).
17 Letter from Thayer to T.S. Eliot, circa 1920 or 1921, *Dial*/Scofield Thayer Papers, Beinecke Rare Book and Manuscript Library, Yale University.
18 Bishop, "Re:Covering Modernism," 311.
19 Thayer to Kenneth Burke, January 24, 1923, *Dial*/Scofield Thayer Papers, Beinecke Rare Book and Manuscript Library, Yale University.
20 Woolf, *The Diary of Virginia Woolf*, ed. Anne Olivier Bell (London: Hogarth Press, 1978), August 16, 1922. Cited by entry date.
21 Kathryn Simpson, "Economies and Desire: Gifts and the Market in 'Moments of Being': 'Slater's Pins Have No Points,'" *Journal of Modern Literature* 28, no. 2 (2005): 18.
22 Leila Brosnan, *Reading Virginia Woolf's Essays and Journalism: Breaking the Surface of Silence* (Edinburgh: Edinburgh University Press, 1997), 5.

23 Letter from Editorial Department to Woolf, May 8, 1923, *Dial*/Scofield Thayer Papers, Beinecke Rare Book and Manuscript Library, Yale University.
24 It is listed, for example, as a reference source on the Modernist Journals Project (see http://dl.lib.brown.edu/mjp/periodicals.html).
25 Bishop, "Re:Covering Modernism," 315.
26 Frederick J. Hoffman, Charles Allen, and Carolyn F. Ulrich, *The Little Magazine: A History and a Bibliography* (Princeton: Princeton University Press, 1947), 199. Historically, small circulation numbers have been regarded as evidence that a magazine rejected the mass market in favor of art.
27 Hoffman, Allen, and Ulrich, *The Little Magazine*, 199.
28 "But as the circulation grew larger, the yearly deficit increased, reaching $50,000 during two of these years" (Hoffman, Allen, and Ulrich, *The Little Magazine*, 199).
29 Bishop estimates the *Dial*'s average circulation as about 9,000 ("Re:Covering Modernism," 311). But even if we accept his estimate, the figure of 9,000 is still nine times greater than the typical circulation figure for the most widely disseminated little magazines.
30 Katherine Mullin, "Joyce through the Little Magazines," in *A Companion to James Joyce*, ed. Richard Brown (Oxford: Blackwell, 2008), 374.
31 Hoffman, Allen, and Ulrich, *The Little Magazine*, 199.
32 Writing in 1947, *The Little Magazine* bibliographers did not have access to the Beinecke Library's *Dial*/Thayer Papers, purchased in 1987. They themselves admit that, in 1947, "[f]ew persons know much about Dr. Watson" and "[e]ven less of Thayer is known" (Hoffman, Allen, and Ulrich, 199, 200). More recent scholarship has shed light upon the *Dial*'s relationship to advertising and on the life of Scofield Thayer. See, for example, the studies by Nicholas Joost and James Dempsey.
33 Bishop, "Re:Covering Modernism," 311. Joost's works cast the history of the *Dial* as an "editorial search for aesthetic perfection" and "a struggle through which the review was transformed into a work of art" (277). See Nicholas Joost, *Years of Transition: The Dial, 1912–1920* (Barre, MA: Barre Publishers, 1967). But they do hint at another narrative that might be told. As he concludes *Years of Transition*, Joost notes that "Thayer and Watson […] did not aspire to make a profit from *The Dial*, but they did hope that it would cease losing money at the rate of eighty thousand dollars a year. Among the devices to which they and the *Dial* staff resorted in order to attract a wider public than that of *The Little Review* were several used by magazines as diverse as *The Atlantic Monthly*, *The National Geographic*, and *Vanity Fair*" (259). In his sequel, *Scofield Thayer and The Dial*, Joost does address questions of finances and advertising in considerable detail, but not specifically in relationship to Modernism. As its subtitle suggests, his work is an "illustrated history" of the *Dial*, not an argument about the *Dial*'s role in shaping Modernism.
34 Kathryn Simpson, "The Paradox of the Gift: Gift-Giving as a Disruptive Force in 'Mrs. Dalloway in Bond Street,'" *Woolf Studies Annual* 11 (2005): 54.

35 Jane Garrity, "Selling Culture to the 'Civilized': Bloomsbury, British *Vogue*, and the Marketing of National Identity," *Modernism/modernity* 6, no. 2 (1999): 35.
36 Garrity, "Selling Culture," 33.
37 Garrity, "Selling Culture," 33.
38 Here mass culture is defined as "a broad communicative system that posits a single speaking voice and a single audience that seeks to elicit and produce a uniform response" (Garrity, "Selling Culture," 33).
39 Simpson, "The Paradox of the Gift," 59.
40 Simpson, "The Paradox of the Gift," 59.
41 *The Diary of Virginia Woolf*, October 14, 1922. Of course, in the short story, Septimus is not present.
42 Letter from Thayer to lapsed subscribers, February 11, 1920, *Dial*/Scofield Thayer Papers, Beinecke Rare Book and Manuscript Library, Yale University.
43 Quentin Bell, *Virginia Woolf: A Biography* (London: Hogarth Press, 1990), 2:38–40.
44 Bell, *Virginia Woolf*, 2:38.
45 "Report on the Condition of The Dial Magazine," *Dial*/Scofield Thayer Papers, Beinecke Rare Book and Manuscript Library, Yale University.
46 "Report on the Condition," *Dial*/Scofield Thayer Papers, Beinecke Rare Book and Manuscript Library, Yale University.
47 "Report on the Condition," *Dial*/Scofield Thayer Papers, Beinecke Rare Book and Manuscript Library, Yale University.
48 Mark Morrisson, *The Public Face of Modernism: Little Magazines, Audiences, and Reception, 1905–1920* (Madison: University of Wisconsin Press, 2001), 4.
49 "Report on the Condition," *Dial*/Scofield Thayer Papers, Beinecke Rare Book and Manuscript Library, Yale University.
50 "Report on the Condition," *Dial*/Scofield Thayer Papers, Beinecke Rare Book and Manuscript Library, Yale University.
51 Of course, other mass-market periodicals could carry hundreds of advertising pages in a single issue.
52 Letter from Thayer to lapsed subscribers, February 11, 1920, *Dial*/Scofield Thayer Papers, Beinecke Rare Book and Manuscript Library, Yale University.
53 "Report on the Condition," *Dial*/Scofield Thayer Papers, Beinecke Rare Book and Manuscript Library, Yale University.
54 This evidence is found in the *Little Review* Records, 1914–1964, University of Wisconsin-Milwaukee Libraries, Archives Department.
55 Nicholas Joost, *Scofield Thayer and The Dial: An Illustrated History* (Carbondale: Southern Illinois University Press, 1964), 43.
56 Joost, *Scofield Thayer and The Dial*, 43.
57 Joost, *Scofield Thayer and The Dial*, 46.
58 Joost, *Scofield Thayer and The Dial*, 46.
59 Joost, *Scofield Thayer and The Dial*, 41.

60 Joost, *Scofield Thayer and The Dial*, 41.
61 Joost, *Scofield Thayer and The Dial*, 41.
62 "Report on the Situation of the Business Department," May 20, 1920, *Dial*/Scofield Thayer Papers, Beinecke Rare Book and Manuscript Library, Yale University.
63 "Report on the Situation," *Dial*/Scofield Thayer Papers, Beinecke Rare Book and Manuscript Library, Yale University.
64 "Report on the Situation," *Dial*/Scofield Thayer Papers, Beinecke Rare Book and Manuscript Library, Yale University.
65 Generic letter from "Advertising Manager" at the *Dial* to "Gentlemen," January 23, 1920, *Dial*/Scofield Thayer Papers, Beinecke Rare Book and Manuscript Library, Yale University.
66 Generic letter from "Advertising Manager" to "Gentlemen," n.d. [probably January 1920], *Dial*/Scofield Thayer Papers, Beinecke Rare Book and Manuscript Library, Yale University.
67 Advertisement in the *Publisher's Weekly*, September 23, 1922, *Dial*/Scofield Thayer Papers, Beinecke Rare Book and Manuscript Library, Yale University.
68 Letter from Nell M. Todd at 3328 Pleasant Avenue, June 16, 1920, *Dial*/Scofield Thayer Papers, Beinecke Rare Book and Manuscript Library, Yale University.
69 Testimonial from Therese Pottecher of New York City, November 15, 1920, *Dial*/Scofield Thayer Papers, Beinecke Rare Book and Manuscript Library, Yale University.
70 Letter from Blanche Dismoir, May 10, 1920, *Dial*/Scofield Thayer Papers, Beinecke Rare Book and Manuscript Library, Yale University.
71 Testimonial from F.D. Martin of Lake Forest, IL, March 23, 1922, *Dial*/Scofield Thayer Papers, Beinecke Rare Book and Manuscript Library, Yale University.
72 Letter from Aldington to Thayer, May 24, 1920, *Dial*/Scofield Thayer Papers, Beinecke Rare Book and Manuscript Library, Yale University. © Estate of Richard Aldington. Excerpts from Richard Aldington's letter of May 24, 1920 to Scofield Thayer (Beinecke Rare Book and Manuscript Library, Yale University) reproduced by kind permission of the Estate of Richard Aldington c/o Rosica Colin Limited, London.
73 Letter from Thayer to Burke, April 14, 1923, *Dial*/Scofield Thayer Papers, Beinecke Rare Book and Manuscript Library, Yale University.
74 B.J. Kirkpatrick, *A Bibliography of Virginia Woolf*, 3rd ed. (Oxford: Clarendon Press, 1980), 135.
75 Kirkpatrick, *A Bibliography*, 149.
76 See *The Diary of Virginia Woolf*, 2:240.
77 Kirkpatrick, *A Bibliography*, 156–7. Kirkpatrick mistakenly writes "*Dail*" for "*Dial*" here (157), but the index records the title correctly.

78 Here it may be helpful to think of scholarship conducted by Faye Hammill and others on middle-brow magazines. What Hammill says of *Vanity Fair* is true of the *Dial*: "*Vanity Fair*, then, provides a middle space, located between the author-centered production model of the avant-garde magazines and the market-driven arena of the daily papers and mass-circulation weeklies. It addresses a reader who is literate in both high and popular culture, and who possesses or aspires to wit, discriminating tastes, style and current knowledge" (128). See Hammill, "In Good Company: Modernism, Celebrity, and Sophistication in *Vanity Fair*," in *Modernist Star Maps: Celebrity, Modernity, Culture*, ed. Aaron Jaffe and Jonathan Goldman (Farnham, England and Burlington, VT: Ashgate, 2010).
79 Golding, "*The Dial*, *The Little Review*, and the Dialogics of Modernism," 44.
80 Letter from Aldington to Thayer, May 24, 1920, *Dial*/Scofield Thayer Papers, Beinecke Rare Book and Manuscript Library, Yale University. © Estate of Richard Aldington. Excerpts from Richard Aldington's letter of May 24, 1920 to Scofield Thayer (Beinecke Rare Book and Manuscript Library, Yale University) reproduced by kind permission of the Estate of Richard Aldington c/o Rosica Colin Limited, London.
81 Golding, "*The Dial*, *The Little Review*, and the Dialogics of Modernism," 44.
82 Golding, "*The Dial*, *The Little Review*, and the Dialogics of Modernism," 45.
83 Morrisson, *The Public Face of Modernism*, 134.
84 Woolf, "Mrs. Dalloway in Bond Street," *Dial*, 21–2.
85 Woolf, "Mrs. Dalloway in Bond Street," *Dial*, 21.
86 Woolf, "Mrs. Dalloway," *Dial*, 21.
87 Woolf, "Mrs. Dalloway," *Dial*, 22.
88 Woolf, "Mrs. Dalloway," *Dial*, 22.
89 Woolf, "Mrs. Dalloway," *Dial*, 23–4.
90 Woolf, "Mrs. Dalloway," *Dial*, 24.
91 Woolf, "Mrs. Dalloway," *Dial*, 24–5.
92 See, for example, the testimonial from Ada E. Springer of Chicago, March 19, 1922, *Dial*/Scofield Thayer Papers, Beinecke Rare Book and Manuscript Library, Yale University.
93 With the exception of the South, the advertising scheme permeated every major geographic region of the United States.
94 Typescript, "THE DIAL: What it is. What it is Doing," n.d. [circa January 1921], *Dial*/Scofield Thayer Papers, Beinecke Rare Book and Manuscript Library, Yale University.
95 Advertisement in *Printer's Ink*, *Dial*/Scofield Thayer Papers, Beinecke Rare Book and Manuscript Library, Yale University.
96 As seen in the *Dial*/Scofield Thayer Papers, Beinecke Rare Book and Manuscript Library, Yale University.
97 As seen in the *Dial*/Scofield Thayer Papers, Beinecke Rare Book and Manuscript Library, Yale University.

98 Woolf, "Mrs. Dalloway," *Dial*, 23.
99 In the end, however, Clarissa does not buy the book.
100 Kathryn Simpson, *Gifts, Markets and Economies of Desire in Virginia Woolf* (Houndmills, Basingstoke, Hampshire, England: Palgrave Macmillan, 2008), 52.
101 Woolf, "Mrs. Dalloway," *Dial*, 22.
102 Letter from Samuel W. Craig to Thayer, February 23, 1923, *Dial*/Scofield Thayer Papers, Beinecke Rare Book and Manuscript Library, Yale University.
103 Letter from Craig to Thayer, February 23, 1923, *Dial*/Scofield Thayer Papers, Beinecke Rare Book and Manuscript Library, Yale University.
104 Letter from Craig to Thayer, February 23, 1923, *Dial*/Scofield Thayer Papers, Beinecke Rare Book and Manuscript Library, Yale University.
105 Letter from Thayer to Craig, March 21, 1923, *Dial*/Scofield Thayer Papers, Beinecke Rare Book and Manuscript Library, Yale University.
106 See Elizabeth Outka, *Consuming Traditions: Modernity, Modernism, and the Commodified Authentic* (New York: Oxford University Press, 2009).
107 Woolf, *Mrs. Dalloway* (London: Hogarth Press, 1925), rpt. in *The Mrs. Dalloway Reader*, ed. Francine Prose (Orlando: Harcourt, 2003), 228.
108 *The Diary of Virginia Woolf*, December 19, 1920.
109 *The Diary of Virginia Woolf*, December 19, 1920.
110 *The Diary of Virginia Woolf*, December 19, 1920.
111 *The Diary of Virginia Woolf*, March 12, 1922.
112 *The Diary of Virginia Woolf*, March 12, 1922.
113 *The Diary of Virginia Woolf*, March 23, 1923.
114 *The Diary of Virginia Woolf*, July 22, 1923.
115 *The Diary of Virginia Woolf*, July 28, 1923.
116 Anne Olivier Bell, ed., *The Diary of Virginia Woolf*, 2:259.
117 Bell, ed., *The Diary of Virginia Woolf*, 2:118. See also Hermione Lee, *Virginia Woolf* (New York: Knopf, 1997), 450, for a discussion of Woolf's response to criticism, and her use of it in *Jacob's Room*.
118 *The Diary of Virginia Woolf*, May 15, 1921.
119 "Briefer Mention," *Dial*, February 1922, 215.
120 *The Diary of Virginia Woolf*, February 18, 1922.
121 *The Diary of Virginia Woolf*, July 8, 1923.
122 *The Diary of Virginia Woolf*, December 21, 1924.
123 *The Diary of Virginia Woolf*, March 17, 1923 and January 23, 1924. "The Lives of the Obscure" appeared in the *Dial* of May 1925.
124 *The Diary of Virginia Woolf*, March 17, 1923.
125 *The Diary of Virginia Woolf*, March 17, 1923.
126 *The Diary of Virginia Woolf*, December 21, 1924.
127 Woolf, "Mrs. Dalloway," *Dial*, 21.
128 Woolf, "Mrs. Dalloway," *Dial*, 20.

129 *Dial*, July 1923, n.p.
130 *Dial*, July 1923, n.p.
131 *Dial*, July 1923, n.p.
132 *Dial*, July 1923, n.p.
133 Richard Hughes, "A Day in London Life," *Saturday Review of Literature*, 16 May 1925, 755, rpt. in *Virginia Woolf: Critical Assessments*, 3:266.
134 Lee, *Virginia Woolf*, 547.
135 Lee, *Virginia Woolf*, 547.
136 Lee, *Virginia Woolf*, 545.
137 Qtd. in Lee, *Virginia Woolf*, 545.
138 Correspondence in the *Dial*/Thayer Papers suggests that Woolf herself provided the contributor's note.
139 Froula, *Virginia Woolf and the Bloomsbury Avant-Garde*, 354; Lee, *Virginia Woolf*, 438; Woolf, *The Letters of Virginia Woolf*, ed. Nigel Nicolson and Joanne Trautmann (New York and London: Harcourt Brace Jovanovich, 1977), 3:45.
140 Letter from Woolf to *Dial*, May 21, 1923, *Dial*/Scofield Thayer Papers, Beinecke Rare Book and Manuscript Library, Yale University; Letter from "Editorial Department" of *Dial* to Woolf, May 8, 1923, *Dial*/Scofield Thayer Papers, Beinecke Rare Book and Manuscript Library, Yale University.
141 Letter from Thayer to Burke, April 19, 1923, *Dial*/Scofield Thayer Papers, Beinecke Rare Book and Manuscript Library, Yale University.
142 Letter from Thayer to Burke, April 19, 1923, *Dial*/Scofield Thayer Papers, Beinecke Rare Book and Manuscript Library, Yale University.
143 Lee, *Virginia Woolf*, 438.
144 As seen in the *Dial*/Scofield Thayer Papers, Beinecke Rare Book and Manuscript Library, Yale University.
145 Santayana, to be sure, was Spanish-American, but he was born in Madrid, he died in Rome, and in 1924 he was living in Europe. As someone who retained his Spanish citizenship throughout life and who never became a US citizen, Santayana was hardly more American than Woolf. See the *Stanford Encyclopedia of Philosophy* for further biographical details.
146 In 1923, the *Dial* ran letters from all of these locations. It is not entirely clear why the *Dial* sometimes referred to these letters by the city, and other times by the nation. These letters appeared in English.
147 These exchanges are documented in the *Dial*/Scofield Thayer Papers, Beinecke Rare Book and Manuscript Library, Yale University.
148 Thomas Mann, "German Letter," *Dial*, June 1923, 610.
149 P. Beaumont Wadsworth, "Prague Letter," *Dial*, July 1923.
150 Paul Morand, "Paris Letter," *Dial*, August 1923. I give the dates of publication of these letters—that is to say, the date of the journal issue in which they appeared. However, the date of composition often precedes the date of publication by one

month. Acknowledging this discrepancy, the *Dial* included datelines for these letters.
151 "Dublin Letter," *Dial*, February 1923, 188.
152 "Dublin Letter," *Dial*, 191.
153 Raymond Mortimer, "London Letter," *Dial*, February 1923, 186–7.
154 Woolf, "Mrs. Dalloway," *Dial*, 25.
155 Woolf, "Mrs. Dalloway," *Dial*, 26. See also Froula, *Virginia Woolf and the Bloomsbury Avant-Garde*, 91–2, for a discussion of war and elegy in "Mrs. Dalloway."
156 Mortimer, "London Letter," *Dial*, July 1923, 73.
157 Wadsworth, "Prague Letter," *Dial*, July 1923, 79.
158 Julius Meier-Graefe, "German Art After the War," *Dial*, July 1923, 1.
159 "The Anatomy of War" is a review of Thomas Boyd's *Through the Wheat*, but it conducts a trans-historic account of war, art, and literature.
160 Edmund Wilson, "The Anatomy of War," *Dial*, July 1923, 95.
161 *The Diary of Virginia Woolf*, October 14, 1922.
162 Wilson, "The Anatomy of War," 93.
163 Woolf, "Mrs. Dalloway," *Dial*, 26.
164 Woolf, "Mrs. Dalloway," *Dial*, 27.
165 Wilson, "The Anatomy of War," 95.
166 In addition to the Great War, the South African War is also explicitly mentioned (21).
167 Woolf, "Mrs. Dalloway," *Dial*, 26.
168 Woolf, "Mrs. Dalloway," *Dial*, 26.
169 Woolf, "Mrs. Dalloway," *Dial*, 21.
170 Woolf, "Mrs. Dalloway," *Dial*, 27. In the novel, the explosion is explained as a car backfiring, but the explosion is left unexplained in the short story. For readers of the novel, the explosion is an instance of delayed decoding; for readers of the short story, there is no decoding. For the novel's rendition of this scene, see Woolf, *Mrs. Dalloway* (London: Hogarth Press, 1925), rpt. in *The Mrs. Dalloway Reader*, ed. Francine Prose (Orlando: Harcourt, 2003), 205.
171 Brenda Silver, *Virginia Woolf Icon* (Chicago: University of Chicago Press, 1999), 91, 92.
172 Joseph Wood Krutch, "The Stream of Consciousness," *The Nation*, 3 June 1925, 631–2, rpt. in *Virginia Woolf: Critical Assessments*, 3:275.
173 Steve Ellis, *Virginia Woolf and the Victorians* (Cambridge: Cambridge University Press, 2007), 52.
174 "Modern Forms," *Dial*, July 1920, III.
175 "Modern Forms," *Dial*, III.
176 Letter from Pound to Marianne Moore, July 27, 1928, *Dial*/Scofield Thayer Papers, Beinecke Rare Book and Manuscript Library, Yale University.

177 It may also be significant that Pound made these comments in 1928, when the *Dial* was already well-established, at least in terms of the relatively short life spans of little magazines. When viewed collectively, the archival letters suggest that as it aged the *Dial* moved along a continuum from radicalism toward traditionalism, without ever actually hitting upon either extreme.
178 *The Diary of Virginia Woolf*, June 23, 1922.
179 Advertisement for the *Dial*, *The Literary Review,* October 28, 1922, *Dial*/Scofield Thayer Papers, Beinecke Rare Book and Manuscript Library, Yale University.
180 Golding, "*The Dial, The Little Review*, and the Dialogics of Modernism," 46.
181 Simpson, "Economies and Desire," 20.
182 Simpson, "The Paradox of the Gift," 59.
183 Simpson, "The Paradox of the Gift," 66; Simpson, *Gifts, Markets and Economies of Desire*, 57.
184 Simpson, "The Paradox of the Gift," 66.
185 Lewis Hyde, *The Gift: Imagination and the Erotic Life of Property* (New York: Random House, 1983), xi.
186 1921 brochure, *Dial*/Scofield Thayer Papers, Beinecke Rare Book and Manuscript Library, Yale University.
187 1921 brochure, *Dial*/Scofield Thayer Papers, Beinecke Rare Book and Manuscript Library, Yale University.
188 1921 brochure, *Dial*/Scofield Thayer Papers, Beinecke Rare Book and Manuscript Library, Yale University.
189 As seen in the *Dial*/Scofield Thayer Papers, Beinecke Rare Book and Manuscript Library, Yale University.
190 Simpson, "The Paradox of the Gift," 54.
191 Advertisement for the *Dial,* December 1922, *Dial*/Scofield Thayer Papers, Beinecke Rare Book and Manuscript Library, Yale University.
192 Bell, *Virginia Woolf*, 1:149.
193 Richard Ohmann, *Selling Culture: Magazines, Markets, and Class at the Turn of the Century* (London: Verso, 1996), 210.
194 Ohmann, *Selling Culture*, 114.
195 Ohmann, *Selling Culture*, 114.
196 Advertisement for the *Dial,* December 1922, *Dial*/Scofield Thayer Papers, Beinecke Rare Book and Manuscript Library, Yale University.
197 Advertisement for the *Dial,* December 1922, *Dial*/Scofield Thayer Papers, Beinecke Rare Book and Manuscript Library, Yale University.
198 Advertisement for the *Dial,* December 1922, *Dial*/Scofield Thayer Papers, Beinecke Rare Book and Manuscript Library, Yale University.
199 Advertisement for the *Dial,* December 1922, *Dial*/Scofield Thayer Papers, Beinecke Rare Book and Manuscript Library, Yale University.

200 Advertisement for the *Dial,* December 1922, *Dial*/Scofield Thayer Papers, Beinecke Rare Book and Manuscript Library, Yale University.
201 Simpson, "The Paradox of the Gift," 54.
202 Simpson, "The Paradox of the Gift," 54.
203 Laura Marcus, "Virginia Woolf and the Hogarth Press," in *Modernist Writers and the Marketplace*, ed. Ian Willison, Warwick Gould, and Warren Chernaik (London: Macmillan, 1996), 126.
204 Leila Brosnan, *Reading Virginia Woolf's Essays and Journalism: Breaking the Surface of Silence* (Edinburgh: Edinburgh University Press, 1997), 41.
205 Rita Felski, *The Gender of Modernity* (Cambridge: Harvard University Press, 1995), 61.

Coda

"What Had He Done?" the headline asks. "Why did she recoil with fear?" To the right, a girl is pictured clutching her throat with one hand and reaching desperately toward a basket with the other. Her eyes widen with terror as shadows build up ominously in the background. "It was only a basket of delicious fruit," the text explains, before inserting a dramatic dash and adding, tantalizingly, "—from her lover." Then the story begins to unravel in rapid-fire paragraphs, as the dramatic dashes multiply:

> Yet she seized it feverishly. And there—at the bottom—was the thing she dreaded.
> She clutched it and fled to her room. But her husband was there. On she fled—
> But it is too tense—too vivid and human—to be told in any words but those of[1]

And here the paragraph ends. As it turns out, the ad is for the works of Gustave Flaubert, and the scene one depicting Madame Bovary as she realizes that her lover, Rodolphe Boulanger, has abandoned her, leaving her with only a basket of fruit to conceal an insincere apology. Readers of French literature will easily recognize this scene, but they may be surprised to find the story represented this way, as a sensational and suspenseful thriller, a romance that here appears to address a popular audience. Yet this was the way the publishers Wm. H. Wise & Company elected to portray Flaubert's fiction. And indeed it was quite common for advertisers in early-twentieth-century magazines to cast fiction in sensational terms. After all, advertisers are selling a product, and they want to cast it in the most urgent and appealing light possible. Hence publishers could make canonical literature, even novels that were supposed to be "pure style" (as articulated by Flaubert in multiple letters), appear plot-driven, suspenseful, and popular.

What may surprise us, however, is the location of this ad. It is found in the June 1923 issue of the *Dial*, a little magazine that actively recruited an elite audience of intellectuals and believed in art for art's sake. Indeed, if we were to look only at the official contents of the *Dial* (in many versions of the *Dial* today, that is all that is left to us), we would not suspect it of running such advertisements, which seem to be at odds with its artistic mission. Nor does the category of "little magazine" conjure images of suspense and breath-taking action, which are typically reserved for the sensational fiction of mass-market periodicals that had dominated the nineteenth century and continued to exercise considerable influence in the twentieth century.

The *Dial*'s ad for Flaubert's works offers a good case in point, highlighting several key concerns addressed by my book. First, it shows that elite artistic works could be repackaged and marketed to a popular audience. Second, it shows that this kind of packaging often departed from authorial intention, generating interpretations beyond the writer's control. Third, the ad registers the shock value of daring literary works. Flaubert's 1857 novel was not merely telling a sensational story, but also assaulting prevailing morals in the manner of its telling, anticipating the censorship trials that *Ulysses* and other Modernist works would later face. "The Novel that Shocked Paris," the ad declares, is "Now in Every Cultured Home."[2] When this ad was printed, in June 1923, *Ulysses* was considered obscene by the US government, but over the course of the twentieth century it too would make the passage from banned book to celebrated classic, a marker of intellectual sophistication to be found in every "cultured home." It is fitting, then, that Ezra Pound should have described Joyce's work as approximating "Flaubertian prose" (even if this judgment was based on Joyce's earlier work).[3] The ad for Flaubert's works, located in an American magazine, also gestures toward the increasingly international scope of Modernist journals, as editors scrambled to include both translated and untranslated foreign works in their issues.

The authors addressed in my book—Henry James, Rudyard Kipling, James Joyce, and Virginia Woolf—all took part in this transatlantic flurry of activity. They published in periodicals on both sides of the Atlantic for a variety of reasons: to secure copyright; to generate additional income; to increase their work's visibility and circulation; and to engage in dialogue with a community of artists and intellectuals who were similarly contributing to an emerging international conversation. In agreeing to publish their works in journals, these authors ceded control that they elsewhere enjoyed. As much as we extol the self-fashioned Modernist author, we must recognize that many works of this time period reached early readers through magazines—enterprises that were at once collaborative and subject to chance. Proto-Modernists such as James and Kipling, who wrote many of their serialized works in the nineteenth century, were intimately familiar with the mass-market periodicals that dominated the Victorian era. They knew that their literary works would be positioned alongside a kaleidoscopic array of articles, illustrations, and advertisements beyond their purview. While a given magazine's character and mission might be readily identifiable, the precise contents in any issue would be unpredictable. In other words, Victorians and proto-Modernists were long accustomed to letting editors and a certain amount of serendipity situate their literary works within the rather expansive parameters of commercial periodicals. But randomness did not vanish when high Modernists and their beloved little magazines arrived on the scene. Just as pioneers of the stream-of-consciousness technique including Joyce and Woolf constructed characters who embarked on seemingly random flights of thought, so they placed their works in periodicals that allowed for free-flowing associations between frequently disparate items.

I want to conclude by proposing some applications to our pedagogy. What if, instead of constructing syllabi with cherry-picked authors, we instead designed our courses around periodicals and asked students to read issues of magazines? One version of this set-up could require students to read complete issues, thus bringing Modernist authors (or authors from other time periods for that matter) into more intimate dialogue with the full slate of their original counterparts. Another, more conservative version of this approach could involve asking students to focus on particular literary works in magazines—something like the *Little Review Ulysses* or the *Collier's Weekly Version of The Turn of the Screw* (and indeed, scholars have published editions with these titles, inviting a return to the magazine versions). What I am hinting at, though, is a little more radical than simply consulting a text in its magazine version. I am proposing a more expansive and democratic approach to syllabi, one that would give students greater agency and more opportunities to make their own discoveries. Even if it's just one day out of the semester, there would be value in re-creating the experience of early-twentieth-century readers who stood in front of a news stand or bookshop window, with a choice of periodicals to read.

Although courses in periodical studies certainly exist, the predominant practice is still to use a collection of professor-picked novels, poems, plays, or other literary and cultural works; in survey courses, the practice is very often to use anthologies, which rely on expert editors to decide on a list of works to include. While anthologies, like periodicals, have editors who place literary works in context with other works (e.g., by strategically grouping several Modernist texts together), they tend to be more homogeneous and organized than magazines. For example, anthologies typically do not include such disparate elements as advertisements, breaking news articles, letters to the editor, or pleas for financial contributions (though a few isolated items of this nature may make an appearance from time to time); and illustrations tend to be sparse. Anthologies, even while providing context, fundamentally alter the reading experience and pace since they do not serialize literary works across several issues. Their groupings are as retrospective as they are valuable, enabled by the time-lapsed, panoramic lens of a later historical moment. Read reductively, anthologies could be taken to imply greater intention and coherence to literary-historical periods than actually existed. In reality, the typically canonical—or marginalized and rediscovered—authors in anthologies were initially published amidst a much wider and dizzying array of contemporaneous authors and media. Original readers had to "fish" to find the key authors and pairings that modern anthologies seemingly so effortlessly and predictably bring together. In other words, anthologists are performing a function distinct from that of periodicals. They are organizing what was originally a much more chaotic and chance-driven field.

While I am not proposing that we abandon anthologies (though I know colleagues who have for reasons other than those I have articulated here), I am suggesting that we, like the experimental Modernists many of us teach, consider entertaining greater risks—or at least indulge in a thought experiment. What if we allowed students to choose which magazine items they read, and which they skimmed or skipped, thus introducing an element of chance into the course's reading list? Would we be terrified if students assigned to the *Little Review* casually sidelined *Ulysses* and instead fell in love with ads for chocolates, pianos, and typewriters, even as they also dabbled in the prose of some eccentric authors with less cultural stature than Joyce? What if students who read magazines that serialized Kipling's fiction managed to keep the pedagogically significant imperial context in their peripheral vision and instead gravitated toward the cheap romantic stories? What if student readers of *Collier's* became so wrapped up in photos of the *Maine* wreckage that they began debating about political issues instead of James's literary ghosts? And, since Woolf's "Mrs. Dalloway in Bond Street" was published in just a single issue of the *Dial*, rather than being serialized across several issues, would students miss it altogether?

Part of our job as professors is to tell students what they are "supposed" to notice. We should not abandon this function. And yet, there is something to be said for the felicitous pairings and unexpected discoveries that we, or our students, might stumble across when encouraged to read more freely, with less direction—like original readers 100 years ago. I once gave my students an assignment to choose any advertisement they found in a magazine that had been digitized by the Modernist Journals Project. In the next class, they would deliver a one-minute report on their chosen ad. To be sure, this was not a completely directionless assignment; I limited the periodicals to those on a particular site (which I knew would be in the time frame of my course), and I instructed my students to ask reflective questions similar to those posed by Robert Scholes and Clifford Wulfman in *Modernism in the Magazines*. But, within those parameters, they were given a free range of magazines and ads to choose from, and, judging by their enthusiasm (which sometimes required a bit of restraint), I would venture to say this set-up produced a much more engaged discussion about early-twentieth-century culture than if I had assigned each student to a particular ad. Other times I have been more intentional—telling students, for example, to read selected *Ulysses* episodes in the *Little Review*. Even then, however, they tend to fall most heavily for the letters to the editor in the back, and then again for their classmates' own creatively re-imagined letters to the editor (I allow them to adopt personas and "write in" on discussion boards; their favorite persona is the outraged reader). As a committed Joycean, I am not sure how I feel about these letters stealing the show, yet it is the everyday people, not the stars, whom Joyce celebrated in *Ulysses*. From that perspective, I think poetic justice is served when students-turned-magazine-consumers discover the value of the pedestrian response, the amateur reader, the seemingly quotidian writer, or the shy flower that was, perhaps, not really born to blush unseen.

Modernist Authorship and Transatlantic Periodical Culture asks what happens when we return the authors we think we know so well—Henry James, Rudyard Kipling, James Joyce, and Virginia Woolf—to the periodicals that originally brought their works to the public. It is, essentially, an act of historical recovery. The other side of the coin, of course, would be to ask what happens when we zoom out from canonical celebrities, soften our focus, and examine these same magazines in a way that would give equal or perhaps greater weight to less recognized authors and texts. That, too, would be a project of historical recovery. And it is one I encourage us to take up with our students.

Notes

1 Advertisement for Flaubert's Works, *Dial,* June 1923, III.
2 Advertisement for Flaubert's Works, *Dial,* June 1923, III.

3   See, for example, the advertisement B.W. Huebsch published in the *Little Review* of December 1919, which quotes Pound's assessment of Joyce. This ad was published in the midst of *Ulysses*'s serialization.

Bibliography

Adams, Henry. "The Mind of John La Farge." In *John La Farge*. New York: Abbeville Press, 1987.
Anderson, Margaret. *The Fiery Fountains*. New York: Hermitage House, 1951.
Anderson, Margaret. *My Thirty Years' War*. New York: Covici, Friede, 1930.
Anesko, Michael. *"Friction with the Market": Henry James and the Profession of Authorship*. New York: Oxford University Press, 1986.
Ardis, Ann, and Patrick Collier, eds. *Transatlantic Print Culture, 1880–1940: Emerging Media, Emerging Modernisms*. Basingstoke: Palgrave Macmillan, 2008.
Baggett, Holly A., ed. *Dear Tiny Heart: The Letters of Jane Heap and Florence Reynolds*. New York: New York University Press, 2000.
Banta, Martha. *Barbaric Intercourse: Caricature and the Culture of Conduct, 1841–1936*. Chicago: University of Chicago Press, 2003.
Bates, Charles Austin. *Short Talks on Advertising*. New York: Press of Charles Austin Bates, 1898.
Beach, Sylvia. *The Letters of Sylvia Beach*, edited by Keri Walsh. New York: Columbia University Press, 2010.
Beidler, Peter G., ed. *The Collier's Weekly Version of Henry James's The Turn of the Screw*. Seattle: Coffeetown Press, 2010.
Beidler, Peter G. *Ghosts, Demons, and Henry James*. Columbia: University of Missouri Press, 1989.
Bell, Quentin. *Virginia Woolf: A Biography*. London: Hogarth Press, 1990.
Bénézit, Emmanuel, ed. *Dictionary of Artists*. English ed. 14 vols. Paris: Gründ, 2006.
Birkenhead, Lord. *Rudyard Kipling*. New York: Random House, 1978.
Booth, Alison. *Greatness Engendered: George Eliot and Virginia Woolf*. Ithaca, NY: Cornell University Press, 1993.
Booth, Wayne C. *The Rhetoric of Fiction*. Chicago: University of Chicago Press, 1961.
Bornstein, George. *Material Modernism: The Politics of the Page*. Cambridge: Cambridge University Press, 2001.
Brooker, Peter, and Andrew Thacker, eds. *The Oxford Critical and Cultural History of Modernist Magazines, Volume I: Britain and Ireland, 1880–1955*. Oxford: Oxford University Press, 2009.
Brooker, Peter, and Andrew Thacker, eds. *The Oxford Critical and Cultural History of Modernist Magazines, Volume II: North America, 1894–1960*. Oxford: Oxford University Press, 2012.
Brooker, Peter, Sascha Bru, Andrew Thacker, and Christian Weikop, eds. *The Oxford Critical and Cultural History of Modernist Magazines, Volume III: Europe, 1880–1940*. Oxford: Oxford University Press, 2013.

Brosnan, Leila. *Reading Virginia Woolf's Essays and Journalism: Breaking the Surface of Silence*. Edinburgh: Edinburgh University Press, 1997.

Bryer, Jackson R. "Joyce, *Ulysses*, and the *Little Review*." *The South Atlantic Quarterly* 66, no. 2 (Spring 1967): 148–64.

Budgen, Frank. *James Joyce and the Making of Ulysses*. London: Grayson and Grayson, 1934.

Bulson, Eric. *Little Magazine, World Form*. New York: Columbia, 2016.

Calkins, Earnest Elmo, and Ralph Holden. *Modern Advertising*. New York: D. Appleton, 1907.

Carrington, Charles. *Rudyard Kipling: His Life and Work*. London: Macmillan, 1955.

Chasar, Mike. "The Business of Rhyming: Burma-Shave Poetry and Popular Culture." *PMLA* 125, no. 1 (January 2010): 29–47.

Churchill, Suzanne W., and Adam McKible, eds. *Little Magazines and Modernism: New Approaches*. Aldershot: Ashgate, 2007.

Cixous, Hélène. "Castration or Decapitation?" *Signs* 7, no. 1 (Autumn 1981): 41–55.

Cixous, Hélène. "The Laugh of the Medusa." *Signs* 1, no. 4 (Summer 1976): 875–93.

Cole, Jean Lee. "The Hideous Obscure of Henry James." *American Periodicals* 20, no. 2 (2010): 190–215.

Collier, Patrick. "Virginia Woolf in the Pay of Booksellers: Commerce, Privacy, Professionalism, *Orlando*." *Twentieth Century Literature* 48, no. 4 (Winter 2002): 363–92.

Conley, Tim. *Joyces Mistakes: Problems of Intention, Irony, and Interpretation*. Toronto: University of Toronto Press, 2003.

Cornwell, Neil, and Maggie Malone, eds. *The Turn of the Screw and What Maisie Knew*. New York: St. Martin's, 1998.

Culleton, Claire A. *Joyce and the G-Men: J. Edgar Hoover's Manipulation of Modernism*. New York: Macmillan, 2004.

Dawson, Melanie. "The Literature of Reassessment: James's *Collier's* Fiction." *Henry James Review* 19 (1998): 230–8.

Dempsey, James. *The Tortured Life of Scofield Thayer*. Gainesville, FL: University of Florida Press, 2014.

Dettmar, Kevin, and Stephen Watt, eds. *Marketing Modernisms: Self-Promotion, Canonization, Rereading*. Ann Arbor: University of Michigan Press, 1996.

Dial/Scofield Thayer Papers. Beinecke Rare Book and Manuscript Library, Yale University.

Dick, Susan, ed. *The Complete Shorter Fiction of Virginia Woolf*. Orlando: Harcourt, 1989.

Drucker, Johanna. *The Visible Word: Experimental Typography and Modern Art, 1909–1923*. Chicago and London: University of Chicago Press, 1994.

Earle, David. *Re-Covering Modernism: Pulps, Paperbacks, and the Prejudice of Form*. Burlington, VT: Ashgate, 2009.

Edel, Leon, ed. *Henry James: Stories of the Supernatural*. New York: Taplinger, 1980.

Edel, Leon. *Henry James: The Treacherous Years*. Philadelphia: Lippincott, 1969.

Eliot, T.S. *A Choice of Kipling's Verse*. New York: Doubleday, 1962.
Ellis, Steve. *Virginia Woolf and the Victorians*. Cambridge: Cambridge University Press, 2007.
Felman, Shoshana. "Turning the Screw of Interpretation." *Yale French Studies* 55/56 (1977): 94–207.
Felski, Rita. *The Gender of Modernity*. Cambridge: Harvard University Press, 1995.
Ferrer, Daniel. "The Work of Joyce in the Age of Hypertextual Production." In *Joycemedia: James Joyce, Hypermedia, & Textual Genetics*, edited by Louis Armand, 86–104. Prague: Litteraria Pragensia, 2004.
Florence Reynolds Collection related to Jane Heap and the *Little Review*. Manuscript Collection Number 258. Special Collections. University of Delaware.
Froula, Christine. *Virginia Woolf and the Bloomsbury Avant-Garde*. New York: Columbia University Press, 2005.
Gabler, Hans Walter. Foreword to *Ulysses: A Critical and Synoptic Edition*. New York and London: Garland, 1984. Corrected Text, 1986.
Gaipa, Mark, Sean Latham, and Robert Scholes, eds. *The Little Review Ulysses*. New Haven, CT: Yale University Press, 2015.
Garrity, Jane. "Selling Culture to the 'Civilized': Bloomsbury, British *Vogue*, and the Marketing of National Identity." *Modernism/modernity* 6, no. 2 (1999): 29–58.
Genette, Gérard. *Paratexts: Thresholds of Interpretation*, translated by Jane E. Lewin. Cambridge: Cambridge University Press, 1997.
Gifford, Don, with Robert J. Seidman. *Ulysses Annotated*. Berkeley: University of California Press, 1988.
Gilbert, Elliot L., ed. *Kipling and the Critics*. New York: New York University Press, 1965.
Gilmour, David. *The Long Recessional: The Imperial Life of Rudyard Kipling*. London: John Murray, 2002.
Glass, Loren. *Authors, Inc.: Literary Celebrity in the Modern United States, 1880–1980*. New York and London: New York University Press, 2004.
Golding, Alan C. "*The Dial*, *The Little Review*, and the Dialogics of Modernism." *American Periodicals* 15, no. 1 (2005): 42–55.
Goldman, Jonathan. *Modernism Is the Literature of Celebrity*. Austin: University of Texas Press, 2011.
Goldman, Jonathan, and Aaron Jaffe, eds. *Modernist Star Maps: Celebrity, Modernity, Culture*. Farnham, England and Burlington, VT: Ashgate, 2010.
Gunn, Daniel P. "Beware of Imitations: Advertisement as Reflexive Commentary in *Ulysses*." *Twentieth Century Literature* 42, no. 4 (Winter 1996): 481–93.
Hamilton, Richard F. *President McKinley, War and Empire*. Vol. 1. New Brunswick: Transaction Publishers, 2006.
Hassett, Joseph M. *The Ulysses Trials: Beauty and Truth Meet the Law*. Dublin: The Lilliput Press, 2016.
Hayes, Kevin J., ed. *Henry James: The Contemporary Reviews*. Cambridge: Cambridge University Press, 1996.

Heller, Terry. *The Turn of the Screw: Bewildered Vision*. Boston: Twayne, 1989.
Hoffman, Frederick J., Charles Allen, and Carolyn F. Ulrich. *The Little Magazine: A History and a Bibliography*. Princeton: Princeton University Press, 1947.
Howard, June. *Publishing the Family*. Durham: Duke University Press, 2001.
Hughes, Linda, and Michael Lund. *The Victorian Serial*. Charlottesville: University Press of Virginia, 1991.
Hutton, Clare. *Serial Encounters: Ulysses and The Little Review*. Oxford: Oxford University Press, 2019.
Huyssen, Andreas. *After the Great Divide: Modernism, Mass Culture, Postmodernism*. Bloomington: Indiana University Press, 1986.
Hyde, Lewis. *The Gift: Imagination and the Erotic Life of Property*. New York: Random House, 1983.
Jacobson, Marcia. *Henry James and the Mass Market*. Alabama: University of Alabama Press, 1983.
Jaffe, Aaron. *Modernism and the Culture of Celebrity*. Cambridge: Cambridge University Press, 2005.
James, Henry. "American Magazines; John Jay Chapman." In *Henry James: The American Essays*, edited by Leon Edel, 233–41. Princeton: Princeton University Press, 1989.
James, Henry. *The Art of the Novel*. New York: Charles Scribner's Sons, 1962.
James, Henry. *Henry James Letters*, edited by Leon Edel. Vol. 4. Cambridge: Harvard University Press, 1984.
James, Henry. *The Letters of Henry James*, edited by Percy Lubbock. Vol. 1. New York: Charles Scribner's Sons, 1920.
James, Henry. *The Notebooks of Henry James*, edited by F.O. Matthiessen and Kenneth B. Murdock. New York: Oxford University Press, 1970.
James, Henry. *Notes of a Son and Brother*. New York: Charles Scribner's Sons, 1914.
James, Henry. "Preface to the New York Edition." In *The Turn of the Screw*, edited by Deborah Esch and Jonathan Warren, 123–9. New York: Norton, 1999.
James, Henry. *The Turn of the Screw*, edited by Deborah Esch and Jonathan Warren. New York: Norton, 1999.
Johnson, Abby Ann Arthur. "The Personal Magazine: Margaret C. Anderson and the *Little Review*, 1914–1929." *South Atlantic Quarterly* 75 (1976): 351–63.
Joost, Nicholas. *Scofield Thayer and The Dial: An Illustrated History*. Carbondale: Southern Illinois University Press, 1964.
Joost, Nicholas. *Years of Transition: The Dial, 1912–1920*. Barre, MA: Barre Publishers, 1967.
Joyce, James. *A Portrait of the Artist as a Young Man*. New York: Penguin, 1993.
Joyce, James. *Letters of James Joyce*. Vol. 1, edited by Stuart Gilbert. New York: Viking, 1957.
Joyce, James. *Selected Letters of James Joyce*, edited by Richard Ellmann. New York: Viking Press, 1966.
Joyce, James. *Ulysses*, edited by Hans Walter Gabler. New York: Random House, 1986. Cited as *U* plus episode and line number.

Kendrick, Walter. "The Corruption of Gerty MacDowell." *James Joyce Quarterly* 37, nos. 3–4 (Spring–Summer 2000): 413–23.

Kern, Stephen. "Changing Concepts and Experiences of Time and Space." In *The Fin-de-Siècle World*, edited by Michael Saler, 74–89. London and New York: Routledge, 2015.

Kipling, Rudyard. *Kim*. London: Penguin, 1989.

Kipling, Rudyard. *The Letters of Rudyard Kipling: 1890–1900*, edited by Thomas Pinney. Vol. 2. London: Macmillan, 1990.

Kipling, Rudyard. "Recessional." *The London Times*, July 17, 1897, 13.

Kipling, Rudyard. *Rudyard Kipling's Definitive Edition*. New York: Doubleday, 1940.

Kipling, Rudyard. *Something of Myself and Other Autobiographical Writings*, edited by Thomas Pinney. Cambridge: Cambridge University Press, 1990.

Kipling, Rudyard. "The White Man's Burden." *The Five Nations*, 79–81. New York: Doubleday, 1903.

Kipling, Rudyard. "The White Man's Burden." *The London Times*, February 4, 1899, 14.

Kipling, Rudyard. "The White Man's Burden." *McClure's Magazine* 12, no. 4 (1899): 290–1. Unless otherwise stated, the line numbers parenthetically cited refer to the poem as it appeared in *McClure's*. Because I read "The White Man's Burden" as a statement of Kipling's views, I have not differentiated between the speaker of the poem and its author.

Kirkpatrick, B.J. *A Bibliography of Virginia Woolf*. 3rd ed. Oxford: Clarendon Press, 1980.

La Farge, Henry. *John La Farge*. New York: Kennedy Galleries, 1968.

Landers, James. "Island Empire: Discourse on U.S. Imperialism in *Century, Cosmopolitan, McClure's*—1893–1900." *American Journalism* 23, no. 1 (Winter 2006): 95–124.

Latham, Sean, and Robert Scholes. "The Rise of Periodical Studies." *PMLA* 121 (2006): 517–31.

Ledger, Sally, and Roger Luckhurst, eds. *The Fin de Siècle: A Reader in Cultural History, c. 1880–1900*. Oxford: Oxford University Press, 2000.

Lee, Hermione. *Virginia Woolf*. New York: Knopf, 1997.

Little Review Records, 1914–1964. UWM Manuscript Collection 1. University of Wisconsin-Milwaukee Libraries, Archives Department.

Livingston, Flora V. *Bibliography of the Works of Rudyard Kipling*. New York: Burt Franklin, 1927.

Livingston, Flora V. *Supplement to Bibliography of Rudyard Kipling*. New York: Burt Franklin, 1968.

Lycett, Andrew. *Rudyard Kipling*. London: Weidenfeld & Nicolson, 1999.

MacLeod, Kirsten. "Material Turns of the Screw: The *Collier's Weekly* Serialization of *The Turn of the Screw* (1898)." *Cahiers Victoriens et Eduoardiens* 84 (2016): 1–18. https://doi.org/10.4000/cve.2986.

Mallett, Phillip. *Rudyard Kipling: A Literary Life*. New York: Palgrave Macmillan, 2003.

Margaret C. Anderson Papers, 1930–1973. UWM Manuscript Collection 12. University Manuscript Collections. University of Wisconsin-Milwaukee Libraries, Archives Department.

Margolis, Anne T. *Henry James and the Problem of Audience*. Ann Arbor: UMI Research Press, 1985.

Mauss, Marcel. *The Gift: The Form and Reason for Exchange in Archaic Societies*, translated by W.D. Halls. London: Routledge, 1990. Originally published 1925.

McKible, Adam. *The Space and Place of Modernism: The Russian Revolution, Little Magazines, and New York*. New York: Routledge, 2002.

McNees, Eleanor, ed. *Virginia Woolf: Critical Assessments*. Vol. 3. East Sussex: Helm Information, 1994.

Miller, David, and Richard Price. *British Poetry Magazines, 1914–2000: A History and Bibliography of "Little Magazines."* London: Oak Knoll Press, 2006.

Monte, Steven. "Ancients and Moderns in Mrs. Dalloway." *Modern Language Quarterly* 61, no. 4 (December 2000): 587–616.

Morrisson, Mark. *The Public Face of Modernism: Little Magazines, Audiences, and Reception, 1905–1920*. Madison: University of Wisconsin Press, 2001.

Mott, Frank Luther. *A History of American Magazines*. 5 Vols. Cambridge: Harvard University Press, 1938–68.

Mullin, Katherine. "Joyce through the Little Magazines." In *A Companion to James Joyce*, edited by Richard Brown, 374–89. Oxford: Blackwell, 2008.

Murphy, Gretchen. *Shadowing the White Man's Burden: U.S. Imperialism and the Problem of the Color Line*. New York: New York University Press, 2010.

Nagai, Kaori. *Empire of Analogies: Kipling, India and Ireland*. Cork, Ireland: Cork University Press, 2006.

Norris, Margot. *Virgin and Veteran Readings of Ulysses*. New York: Palgrave Macmillan, 2011.

North, Michael. *Reading 1922: A Return to the Scene of the Modern*. New York: Oxford University Press, 1999.

Ohmann, Richard. "The New Discourse of Mass Culture: Magazines in the 1890s." *Studies in Literature* 16, no. 2 (1984): 16–35.

Ohmann, Richard. *Selling Culture: Magazines, Markets, and Class at the Turn of the Century*. London: Verso, 1996.

Osteen, Mark, ed. *The Question of the Gift*. London and New York: Routledge, 2002.

Outka, Elizabeth. *Consuming Traditions: Modernity, Modernism, and the Commodified Authentic*. Oxford: Oxford University Press, 2009.

Paffard, Mark. *Kipling's Indian Fiction*. New York: St. Martin's Press, 1989.

Parkes, Adam. "'Literature and instruments for abortion': 'Nausicaa' and the *Little Review* Trial." *James Joyce Quarterly* 34, no. 3 (Spring 1997): 283–301.

Parry, Ann. *The Poetry of Rudyard Kipling*. Buckingham: Open University Press, 1992.

Poe, Edgar Allan. "The Man of the Crowd." In the *Norton Anthology of American Literature*, Vol. B, edited by Nina Baym, 1561–7. New York: Norton, 2003.

Pound, Ezra. "Small Magazines." *The English Journal* 19, no. 9 (November 1930): 689–704.

Pound/The Little Review: The Letters of Ezra Pound to Margaret Anderson, edited by Thomas L. Scott and Melvin J. Friedman. New York: New Directions, 1988.

Rainey, Lawrence. *Institutions of Modernism: Literary Elites and Public Culture*. New Haven: Yale, 1998.

Reynolds, Mary T. "Joyce as a Letter Writer." In *A Companion to Joyce Studies*, edited by Zack Bowen and James F. Carens, 39–70. Westport, CT: Greenwood Press, 1984.

Reynolds, Paige. "'Chaos Invading Concept': Blast as a Native Theory of Promotional Culture." *Twentieth Century Literature* 46, no. 2 (Summer 2000): 238–68.

Ricketts, Harry. *The Unforgiving Minute: A Life of Rudyard Kipling*. London: Chatto and Windus, 1999.

Rickover, H.G. *How the Battleship Maine Was Destroyed*. Washington, DC: Naval History Division, Dept. of the Navy, 1976.

Rosenbaum, S.P. "A Note on John La Farge's Illustration for Henry James's *The Turn of the Screw*." In *The Turn of the Screw*, by Henry James, edited by Robert Kimbrough, 254–9. New York: Norton, 1966.

Rutherford, Andrew. "Some Aspects of Kipling's Verse." In *Critical Essays on Rudyard Kipling*, edited by Harold Orel, 21–45. Boston: G.K. Hall, 1989.

S.S. McClure Company. *Concerning McClure's, Being a Little Book about a Big Magazine*. New York: S.S. McClure Company, 1901.

Said, Edward W. *Culture and Imperialism*. New York: Vintage Books, 1993.

Scholes, Robert, and Clifford Wulfman. *Modernism in the Magazines: An Introduction*. New Haven and London: Yale University Press, 2010.

Scott, Bonnie Kime. *Refiguring Modernism*. Bloomington: Indiana University Press, 1995.

Scott, Bonnie Kime. "'The Young Girl,' Jane Heap, and the Trials of Gender in *Ulysses*." In *Joycean Cultures/Culturing Joyces*, edited by Vincent J. Cheng, Kimberly J. Devlin, and Margot Norris, 78–94. Newark: University of Delaware Press, 1998.

Silver, Brenda. *Virginia Woolf Icon*. Chicago: University of Chicago Press, 1999.

Simpson, Kathryn. "Economies and Desire: Gifts and the Market in 'Moments of Being': 'Slater's Pins Have No Points.'" *Journal of Modern Literature* 28, no. 2 (2005): 18–37.

Simpson, Kathryn. *Gifts, Markets and Economies of Desire in Virginia Woolf*. Basingstoke, England: Palgrave Macmillan, 2008.

Simpson, Kathryn. "The Paradox of the Gift: Gift-Giving as a Disruptive Force in 'Mrs. Dalloway in Bond Street.'" *Woolf Studies Annual* 11 (2005): 52–75.

Slote, Sam. *Ulysses in the Plural: The Variable Editions of Joyce's Novel*. The National Library of Ireland Joyce Studies, no. 05, edited by Luca Crispi and Catherine Fahy. [Dublin]: The National Library of Ireland, 2004.

Sonstegard, Adam. "'A Merely *Pictorial* Subject': *The Turn of the Screw*." *Studies in American Fiction* 33 (2005): 59–85.

Spoo, Robert. "'Nestor' and the Nightmare: The Presence of the Great War in *Ulysses*." In *Joyce and the Subject of History*, edited by Mark A. Wollaeger, Victor Luftig, and Robert Spoo, 105–24. Ann Arbor: University of Michigan Press, 1996.

Stewart, J.I.M. *Rudyard Kipling*. New York: Dodd, Mead, 1966.

Stewart, James McGregor. *Rudyard Kipling: A Bibliographical Catalogue*, edited by A.W. Yeats. Toronto: Dalhousie University Press, 1959.

Sullivan, Zohreh T., ed. *Kim*, by Rudyard Kipling. New York: Norton, 2002.

Sullivan, Zohreh T. *Narratives of Empire: The Fictions of Rudyard Kipling*. Cambridge: Cambridge University Press, 1993.

Symons, Julian. *Makers of the New: The Revolution in Literature, 1912–1939*. London: Deutsch, 1987.

Tintner, Adeline R. *The Museum World of Henry James*. Ann Arbor: UMI Research Press, 1986.

Vanderham, Paul. "Ezra Pound's Censorship of *Ulysses*." *James Joyce Quarterly* 32, nos. 3–4 (Spring–Summer 1995): 583–95.

Wasserstrom, William. *The Time of The Dial*. Syracuse: Syracuse University Press, 1963.

Weir, David. "What Did He Know, and When Did He Know It: The *Little Review*, Joyce, and *Ulysses*." *James Joyce Quarterly* 37, nos. 3–4 (Spring–Summer 2000): 389–412.

Wicke, Jennifer. *Advertising Fictions: Literature, Advertisement, and Social Reading*. New York: Columbia University Press, 1988.

Willison, Ian, Warwick Gould, and Warren Chernaik, eds. *Modernist Writers and the Marketplace*. London: Macmillan, 1996.

Wilson, Angus. *The Strange Ride of Rudyard Kipling: His Life and Works*. London: Secker and Warburg, 1977.

Wilson, Edmund. "The Ambiguity of Henry James." In *The Turn of the Screw*, edited by Deborah Esch and Jonathan Warren, 170–3. New York: Norton, 1999.

Wilson, Harold S. *McClure's Magazine and the Muckrakers*. Princeton: Princeton University Press, 1970.

Wollaeger, Mark. *Modernism, Media, and Propaganda: British Narrative from 1900 to 1945*. Princeton: Princeton University Press, 2006.

Woolf, Virginia. *The Diary of Virginia Woolf*, edited by Anne Olivier Bell. 5 vols. London: Hogarth Press, 1978. Cited by entry date.

Woolf, Virginia. *The Letters of Virginia Woolf*, edited by Nigel Nicolson and Joanne Trautmann. 6 vols. New York and London: Harcourt Brace Jovanovich, 1977.

Woolf, Virginia. *To the Lighthouse*. 1927. San Diego: Harcourt, 1981.

Woolf, Virginia. *Mrs. Dalloway*. 1925. *The Mrs. Dalloway Reader*, edited by Francine Prose, 195–371. Orlando: Harcourt, 2003.

Woolf, Virginia. "Mrs. Dalloway in Bond Street." *Dial*, July 1923, 20–7.

Yannella, Philip R. "James Joyce to *The Little Review*: Ten Letters." *Journal of Modern Literature* 1, no. 3 (March 1971): 393–8.

Index

A
Adams, Henry 26, 58
advertising. *See also* commercial magazines
   for Aitchison Patent Eyeglasses 85
   as ambiguous genre 46–47
   for Berlitz School of Languages 129
   for Bovril 80, 200
   in *Cassell's* magazine 77–85, 200
   for *Cassell's Standard Library* 115–116
   for Cerebos Table Salt 77–79
   in *Collier's* magazine 21–22, 43–52
   for Dexter Brothers' English Shingle Stains 66, 123n175
   in and for *Dial* magazine 2, 80, 158, 185–204 *passim*, 210–211, 214, 216, 219–222, 235–236
   for *Dubliners* (Joyce) 116, 157
   for *Egoist* magazine 157–158
   for Eliot, T.S., in *Dial* magazine 199
   for Epps's Cocoa 97–98
   for *Exiles* (Joyce) 116, 157
   for GRUMIAUX 157
   imperialism and 77–85, 108–112
   for James, Henry 21–22, 46
   for Joyce, James 115–117, 151, 156–157, 160–162, 199, 216–217, 240n3
   near *Kim* (Kipling) installments 65–66, 77–85
   for Kipling, Rudyard and *Kim* 11, 67, 69–71, 80–83, 85, 94, 110–111, 115–116
   Kipling, Rudyard used to promote consumer products 118n45, 123n175; *see also* Pears' Soap
   in *Little Review* 2, 44–45, 68, 115–117, 138, 145–147, 151, 156–160, 162, 167–168, 169n1, 176nn144–145, 240n3
   for *Madame Bovary* (Flaubert) 235–236
   mass-market techniques appropriated by Modernism 1–2, 21, 65, 115–117, 157, 187, 191–204 *passim*, 237
   for McClure's autobiography 167–168
   in *McClure's* magazine 97–98, 103, 108–112
   for *Modernist* magazine 158
   for Multiplex Hammond Writing Machine (typewriter) 129
   national advertisers 14, 191, 201, 203–204
   for Pears' Soap 43, 103, 109–111
   for Plumtree's Potted Meat 125, 169n1
   for *Portrait of the Artist as a Young Man, A* (Joyce) 116, 151, 157, 160–162
   for *Poetry* magazine 159
   for Pound, Ezra, in *Dial* magazine 199, 219
   for Ripans Tabules 43, 47–51
   sensational, in *Dial* magazine 235–236
   subscription prices and 46, 159, 191, 198, 219–222
   for Swan Fountain Pen 84–85
   for *Turn of the Screw, The* (James) in *Collier's* magazine 21–22
   near *Turn of the Screw, The* (James) installments 43–52
   for *Ulysses* (Joyce) 116, 156–157, 160, 162, 216–217
   near *Ulysses* (Joyce) installments 156–160, 169, 238
   for *Waste Land, The* (Eliot) 216–217
   "White Man's Burden, The" (Kipling) and 97–98, 103, 109–111
   for Woolf, Virginia 12, 65, 210–212, 214–215
Advertising Fictions (Wicke) 13
Aitchison Patent Eyeglasses, advertising for 85
Aldington, Richard 131, 196–197
Allen, Charles 186–187

ambiguity
  in advertisement 46–47
  in *Collier's* coverage of U.S.S. *Maine* disaster 28; *see also* U.S.S. *Maine*
  in James, Henry, work of 7, 10, 18–19, 23–31, 36, 38, 40, 49, 51–53, 66
  in Joyce, James, work of 149, 153, 166; *see also Ulysses*, errors and misprints in
  in Kipling, Lockwood, work of 7, 11, 66, 69, 94, 100; *see also Kim*, illustrations of
  Modernist 7, 10–11, 18–19, 38, 44, 52, 66
  in New Criticism debates 31
  in Woolf, Virginia, work of 218
American Scene, The (James) 26
"Anatomy of War, The" (Wilson) 213, 232n159
Andersen, Hans Christian 30
Anderson, Margaret. *See also* censorship; *Little Review*
  autobiography of 167
  on "Cantleman's Spring-Mate" (Lewis) 133
  commercial culture and 2; *see also Little Review*, advertising in
  comparisons of Joyce, James and Richardson, Dorothy by 175n117
  on errors in *Ulysses* (Joyce) 156
  "Obvious Statement, An" 150
  Quinn, John, and 127, 134–139, 148–150
Anderson, Sherwood 147, 198, 219
Anesko, Michael 26, 45–46, 55, 168
anthologies, reading experience of 237–238
Ardis, Ann 12–13
Arens, Egmont 159
"Art and the Law" (Heap) 150
artistic culture, tension with commodity culture. *See* commodity/commercial culture
"Art of Fiction, The" (James) 46
Ascension, The (La Farge) 26
Athenaeum, The 12, 185, 196
Atlantic Monthly 26, 201, 226n33
Austen, Jane 116
authorial control, versus outside factors. *See also* authorship; chance
  in James, Henry 2–7, 10, 13, 18–19, 26, 37, 51, 53–55, 236–237
  in Joyce, James 2–6, 11, 13, 126, 144, 168–169, 170n1, 236–237
  in Kipling, Rudyard 2–6, 11, 13, 66, 236–237
  in Woolf, Virginia 2–6, 11–12, 202, 236–237; *see also* gift economy; Hogarth Press
authorship. *See also* authorial control; chance
  artistic autonomy 2–3
  concept defined 2–6
  editorial control versus 2–3, 13, 18–19, 51, 54, 170n1, 236–237
  governmental control versus 143, 145
  Hogarth Press and Woolf's 2, 12, 180, 185, 205, 222
  paratextual issues versus 5–6, 18
autonomy, artistic 2–3
Awkward Age, The (James) 15n16

B

Banta, Martha 41–42
Barnes, Djuna 147–148, 151
Barr, Robert 76, 113
Bates, Charles Austin 118n45
"Battle of Forty Fort, The" (Crane) 76–77
Beach, Sylvia 162, 183
Bearns, George F. 102
Beidler, Peter G. 9, 13, 26, 33, 60nn100–101
Bell, Anne Olivier 206
Bell, Clive 206
Bell, Quentin 190
Belloc, Marie A. 73–74
Benfey, Christopher 7, 8, 15n17
Benson, E.F. 45
Beresford, John 205
Berlitz School of Languages, advertising for 129
Besant, Sir Walter 20, 98
Bible, The 122nn143–144
Bigelow, Poultney 110
Birkenhead, Frederick W. 66–67
Birth Control Review 196
Bishop, Edward 139, 183–184, 186–187, 224, 226n29
Blake, William 200

Blast magazine 1
Bloomsbury Group 180, 187, 212
Boer War 77
Bookman magazine 36, 201
Bookplate Booklet 193
Booth, Wayne C. 22
Bosanquet, Theodora 168
Bosschère, Jean de 155
Bovril, advertising for 80, 200
British superiority claims. *See*
    imperialism; *Kim* (Kipling)
Brontë, Charlotte 116
Brooklyn, Pat 83–84
Broom magazine 12, 196, 207
Brosnan, Leila 185, 223
Bryant, Sara Cone 113
Bryer, Jackson R. 139, 142
Buchanan, Robert 98, 101
Bulson, Eric 13
Burke, Kenneth 151, 207
Burne-Jones, Philip 81
Burnett, Frances Hodgson 45

C
"Cantleman's Spring-Mate" (Lewis)
    132–136, 139, 144–145
Capek, Joseph 211
Captains Courageous (Kipling) 68
Carlsen, Emil 30
Carrington, Charles 68
Cassell's magazine 65–117 *passim*. *See also*
    Kim (Kipling)
  advertisements in 77–85, 200
  circulation of 82
  eighteenth and nineteenth-century
    authors promoted by 116
  imperialist context in 11, 67, 69–85, 93,
    110, 112
  Kim (Kipling) serialized in 6, 11,
    65–117 *passim*
  McClure's compared to 96, 104, 110,
    112, 115
  synopses to promote *Kim* (Kipling) in
    82–83
  Woolf, Virginia published in 196
Cassell's Standard Library 116
censorship
  of *Little Review* and "Cantleman's
    Spring-Mate" (Lewis) 132–136, 139,
    144–145
  of *Little Review* and *Ulysses* (Joyce) 4,
    11, 126, 132–142, 149–150, 160,
    162–163, 168–169, 183, 236
  Modernist debates on 9, 236
  of *Ulysses* (Joyce), by *Little Review*
    editors 142–147
Cerebos Table Salt, advertising for 77–79
Chambers, Robert W. 20
chance. *See also* authorship
  in competition with authorial control
    and intent 5–6, 11–13, 15, 18–19,
    37, 51, 53–55, 66, 168–169, 202
  of connection between Cerebos Salt
    and *Kim* (Kipling) 79
  errors and misprints in *Ulysses* (Joyce)
    126–127, 152–156
  geographical factors impacting
    Kipling's reception 10–11, 66
  of gifts in Woolf's work and *Dial* 12,
    180; *see also* gift economy
  inherent to periodical production 5,
    13, 202, 236–238
  Modernism dependent upon 2, 6, 9,
    14, 54–55
  parallels between real-world
    advertisements and fictional ones
    125, 202
  in periodicals versus anthologies 238
  of U.S.S. *Maine* explosion during
    serialization of *Turn of the Screw,
    The* (James) 7, 10, 19, 37, 41, 51, 55;
    see also U.S.S. *Maine*
Chapbook magazine 196
chapters, overview of 10–12
Children of the Nations, The (Bigelow) 110
Churchill, Suzanne W. 12
Ciolkowska, Muriel 155, 161
Cixous, Hélène 180, 218
Collier, Patrick 12–13, 164
Collier, Robert J. 17, 21, 52, 189
Collier's magazine 17–55 *passim*. *See also*
    Turn of the Screw, The (James)
  advertising in 21, 43–51, 54–55
  Cassell's and 85–86, 94
  circulation of 17, 189
  Dial and 194–195, 220
  highbrow art and 116, 194
  illustrations of *Turn of the Screw, The*
    (James) in 19, 23–37, 60n100,
    60n101

Little Review in combination subscription with 157
"picture coverage" of U.S.S. *Maine* and Spanish-American War 22, 37–43, 52–54
Turn of the Screw, The (James) serialized in 6, 8, 10, 17–55 *passim*
Collier's Weekly Version of Henry James's The Turn of the Screw, The (Beidler) 9, 13, 33, 60nn100–101, 237
commercial magazines. *See also Cassell's; Collier's; McClure's; entries for other individual magazines*; commodity/commercial culture; little magazines
   advertising-heavy 1, 46, 191, 227n51
   advertising techniques of 198, 200, 219
   circulation of 46, 62n143, 186, 191
   in Edward J. O'Brien's annual review 220
   illustration-heavy 29, 65, 85
   literature-advertisement interplay in 14
   little magazines versus 1, 8, 65, 115–117, 140, 156–157, 186–187, 220
   pedagogical approaches to 9, 237–239
   proliferation of 62n137, 236–237
   represented in *Dial's* Peacock Folder 192–193
commodity/commercial culture (mass-market culture). *See also* advertising; commercial magazines; elite versus popular culture; *and entries for individual authors, texts, and magazines*
   artistic culture's tension with 65–66, 115–117, 126, 140, 156, 179–180, 184–189, 223, 229n78, 236
   counter-public sphere's engagement with, *see* counter-public sphere
   Hogarth Press's connections with 180
   little magazines' impact on 140, 166; *see also* little magazines
   Modernism's interactions with 1–2, 14, 44, 65, 115–117, 126, 169, 223–224
Concerning McClure's, Being a Little Book about a Big Magazine 121nn114–115
Conley, Tim 127, 154
Conrad, Joseph 8, 23, 199, 222

consumerism. *See* advertising; commercial magazines; commodity/commercial culture; elite versus popular culture; "Mrs. Dalloway in Bond Street" (Woolf)
Cook, George Cram 76
Cosmopolitan magazine 62n143
Coterie magazine 196
counter-public sphere
   concurrent mass-market engagement 44–45, 156–157, 193
   constructed by little magazines 8, 116, 132, 156, 164, 193
   divide from popular culture 115–117, 156, 160, 164
Covering End (James) 53
Craig, Samuel 203–204
Crane, Stephen 20, 76–77, 97
Crawford, F. Marion 45
Crimson (Harvard University) 198
Criterion magazine 12, 185, 196, 206, 210, 212
"Curious Corpse, The" (Zangwill) 20

D
Daily Californian (University of California) 198
Daily Maroon (University of Chicago) 198
Daily News, The 182
Dawson, Melanie 40–41, 53
Dear Tiny Heart: The Letters of Jane Heap and Florence Reynolds (Baggett) 170n3
Definitive Edition of Kipling's verse 101
Dempsey, James 225n16
Demuth, Charles (illustrator) 55n4
Dettmar, Kevin 45
Dexter Brothers' English Shingle Stains, advertisement for 123n175
Dial magazine 179–224 *passim*. *See also* "Mrs. Dalloway in Bond Street" (Woolf); Woolf, Virginia
   advertising in and for 2, 80, 158, 185–204 *passim*, 210–211, 214, 216, 219–222, 235–236
   circulation of 184, 186, 188–192, 194–195, 201, 203, 218, 226nn28–29
   early years of 189–197

First World War's impact on 8–9, 212–214
gift economy in 11–12, 180, 217–222
internationalism in 196, 208–215, 223–224
Little Review versus 181–184, 187, 189–190, 192–193, 197–198
as mediator between experimentalism and tradition 215–217, 225n16, 233n177
"Mrs. Dalloway in Bond Street" (Woolf) published in 6, 12, 179–224 *passim*, 238
Peacock Folder 192–193
tensions between art and commerce in 2, 185–196, 203–204, 218–223, 226n33, 229n78
text-heavy content in 65
Waste Land, The (Eliot) in 216–217
Woolf's literary reputation impacted by 180–182, 205–208
Dick, Susan 12
Dowling, Richard 20
Doyle, Arthur Conan (Sir) 96
Duluth Herald, The 192

E
Eagleton, Terry 38
Earle, David 224
"Eat Not Thy Heart" (Gordon) 20
"Ebb-Tide, The" (Stevenson) 96
Edel, Leon 58n42
editorial control 2–3, 13, 19, 51, 54, 170n1, 236–237
Eglinton, John 143, 211
Egoist magazine
advertising for, in *Little Review* 157–158
counter-public sphere created by 132
Joyce, James promoted by 115–116, 160–163
mission statement of 157–158
Portrait of the Artist as a Young Man, A (Joyce) serialized in 116, 160–162, 177n156
Ulysses (Joyce) serialized in 171n18
"Elephant Hunting in Africa" (Henley) 112, 124n188
Eliot, George 116

Eliot, T.S.
advertising and promotion of 116, 131, 160, 199, 216–217
as *Criterion* editor 196, 206, 210–211
as *Dial* contributor 182, 211
Dial's publication of *Waste Land, The* 216
First World War focus in *Waste Land, The* 7
James, Henry commemorated by 168
as *Little Review* contributor 131, 141, 147, 168
elite versus popular culture
advertising and 14, 51, 65, 115–116, 169, 187, 191–195, 200–204, 217–222, 236
artistic pursuits versus mass-market dynamics 44–45, 139–140, 166, 185
counter-public versus commercial sphere 115–117, 156–157, 160, 164
high literature in mass-market magazines 21, 44, 116, 185
mixing of high and low culture in *Ulysses* (Joyce) 142–143, 148, 184
in news distribution networks 140, 166
representation of, in James, Henry versus Kipling, Rudyard 7
Ellis, Steve 215–216
Esch, Deborah 55n4, 56n4, 56n6
Espionage Act 134
Exile magazine 216

F
Faulkner, William 38
Felman, Shoshana 22
Felski, Rita 62n137, 83, 224
feminism
aberrations from traditional standards of 137
attacks on 148
in gift theory 9, 180
in responses to *Ulysses* 139, 150
Ferrer, Daniel 150–151
Finnegans Wake (Joyce) 130, 183
First World War
as defining military conflict of Modernism 10, 38, 126
Conrad, Joseph and 23

Dial magazine affected by 8–9, 212–214
　Joyce, James and 8, 11, 128, 130–131, 134
　Little Review affected by 8, 126, 128–132, 134–135, 141, 146
　propaganda 23
　Woolf, Virginia and 7–9, 212–214
Fish, Stanley 54
Fitzgerald, F. Scott 38
Five Nations, The 101
Flaubert, Gustave 235–236
Flynt, Josiah 104–107, 113
Ford, Ford Madox (Hueffer) 38, 147, 158, 165
"Four Foreigners" (Williams) 175n117
Freedman, Samuel 20
Freytag-Loringhoven, Elsa von 151
Friction with the Market (Anesko) 26
"From Sunset to Sunrise" (Spender) 76–77
"Frontenac the Savior of Canada" (Henley) 124n188
Froula, Christine 225n11, 232n155

G
Gabler, Hans Walter 152
Gaipa, Mark 9, 13
Garnett, David 182, 206, 212, 225n7, 225n15
Garrity, Jane 187–188, 215
Gender of Modernity, The (Felski) 62n137
Genette, Gérard 5, 18, 19, 54, 66
"German Art After the War" (Meier-Graefe) 213
Gifford, Don 166, 170n1
gift economy 9, 11–12, 180–181, 217–223
Gilmour, David 68, 99, 102
Gissing, George 20
Golden Bowl, The (James) 29
Golding, Alan 159, 163, 182–184, 197
Goldman, Jonathan 3
Good Housekeeping magazine 185
Good Morning 193
Gordon, Julien 20, 22
Grand, Sarah 20
"Greatest in the World, The" (Brooklyn) 83–84
Great War. *See* First World War
"Green Flag, The" (Doyle) 96
Green and White (Ohio University) 198

GRUMIAUX, advertising for 157
Guardian 196
Gunn, Daniel 164, 170n2

H
Hammill, Faye 229n78
Hand, Learned 133
Hannah, Daniel 15n16
Hardy, Thomas 199, 222
Hare, Jimmy 17
Harper's Monthly 157
Harper's Weekly 15n16
Hartley, Marsden 176n139
Heap, Jane. *See also* Little Review
　"Art and the Law" 150
　disagreements with Quinn, John 137–143, 148–149
　farewell editorial for *Little Review* 167
　First World War's impact on 131
　Joyce's work evaluated by 181
　on *Little Review*'s finances 137–138, 184
　"Nausicaa" trials and 134
　public letters in *Little Review* of 131–132, 170n3
　on resemblances between *Dial* and *Little Review* 159
　on suppression of *Ulysses* (Joyce) in *Little Review* 162, 166, 183
Heart of Darkness (Conrad) 23
Hecht, Ben 147, 192
Heller, Terry 31, 33, 60n96
Henley, W.E. 124n188
Henry James at Work (Bosanquet) 168
historical recovery 5, 14, 239
History of American Magazines, A (Mott) 17, 62n143
Hofer, Carl 209
Hoffman, Frederick J. 186–187
Hofmannsthal, Hugo von 211
Hogarth Press
　financial matters of 185, 190
　Henry James at Work (Bosanquet) published by 168
　mass-market connections of 180
　Mrs. Dalloway (Woolf) published by 232n170
　Woolf's artistic self-fashioning through 2, 12, 180, 185, 205, 222
Hope, Anthony 96

Housman, A.E. 212
Howard, June 21
Howells, William Dean 98, 102, 122n150
Hughes, Linda K. 20
Hughes, Richard 209
Hutton, Clare 3, 13, 166, 170n4, 171n18, 177n167
Huyssen, Andreas 116, 142
Hyde, Lewis 180, 218

I

Illustrated London News 67
illustrations. *See also named illustrators*
  author frustrations with 29
  for *Kim* (Kipling) 11, 65, 69, 85–94, 109, 111, 114, 120n84, 120n94, 120n96, 120n98
  for *Kim* (Kipling) compared to *Turn of the Screw, The* (James) 86, 94
  for *Turn of the Screw, The* (James) 10, 17–37 *passim*, 47, 51–52, 55–56n4, 57n33, 60n96, 60nn100–101
imperialism. *See also Cassell's; Kim* (Kipling); *McClure's*
  advertising's support of 77–79
  British superiority claims 74–77
  in *Cassell's* 11, 67, 69–85, 93, 104, 110, 112
  Collier's magazine and 37–38
  Kipling and 8, 10–11, 66–112 *passim*
  in *McClure's* 11, 67, 69–70, 103–104, 108–112, 115, 123n175
  narratives on 70–71
  soap advertising linked to 109–110
  "White Man's Burden, The" (Kipling) and 97–103
imprimatur, authorial 3, 19
India 6, 11, 65–113 *passim*, 209
"In Memory of Robert Gregory" (Yeats) 147
Inness, George 27
Institutions of Modernism (Rainey) 13
internationalism. *See also* little magazines, transatlantic perspectives of; *and entries for individual texts and authors*
  Modernist magazines' engagement with 6–7, 26, 117, 158, 224, 236; *see also individual magazines listed by title*

transatlantic periodical culture defined 6–10
"In the World of Graft" (Flynt) 104–107
Ireland/Irish
  "double bind" of Irish manhood 152
  Ireland's colonial legacy 130, 168
  Irish Letter in *Dial* 211
  Irish Literary Renaissance 211
  Joyce as Irish author 6
  Kipling's Irish heritage 65, 82
  Kim's Irish heritage in *Kim* (Kipling) 77, 85, 86–88
  McClure's Irish heritage 167–168

J

Jacobson, Marcia 55
Jacob's Room (Woolf) 182, 207, 212, 215, 225n15
Jaffe, Aaron 3, 149
James, Henry 17–55 *passim. See also* authorial control; *Turn of the Screw, The* (James); *and other works listed by title*
  advertising and promotion of 21–22, 46
  Archbishop of Canterbury and 36
  artistic ambiguity of 7, 10, 18–19, 23–31, 36, 38, 40, 49, 51–53, 66; *see also* narrative reliability
  on copyright 46
  dislike of periodical illustrations 29, 36
  friendship with La Farge, John 26–27
  journal versus book publications of 4
  Kipling, Rudyard and 7–8, 45, 66, 167
  Little Review issue devoted to 168
  mass-market appeal of 45–46
  New York Edition design and 2
  opposed to nationalism and war 19, 39, 55, 112
  as proto-Modernist 14, 167, 237
  stylistic trademarks of 7
  as transatlantic 6–8, 27, 223, 236
  on *Turn of the Screw, The* as ghost story and potboiler 36, 55
  vexed relationship to marketplace 17, 45, 55
  well-established reputation of 81
James, William 27, 39

Jefferson, Thomas 108
Jepson, Edgar 147
Johnson, Abby Ann Arthur 159
Joost, Nicholas 159, 192–193, 226n33
Joyce, James 125–169 *passim*. *See also* authorial control; *Ulysses* (Joyce); *and other works listed by title*
    advertising and promotion of 115–117, 151, 156–157, 160–162, 199, 216–217, 240n3
    errors of *Ulysses* and 153–155
    female authors and editors, dialogue with 147–151, 175n117
    First World War and 128–129
    "Flaubertian prose" of 236
    as high Modernist 8, 14, 65
    James, Henry and 168
    Kipling, Rudyard and 167–168
    mass-market appeal of 162, 165
    "Memory of the Players, A," in *Dial* 158, 183, 199
    Modernist authors' objections to 142–143
    reader responses to 163–166
    stylistic innovations of 3, 129–130
    as teacher at Berlitz School 129
    as transatlantic 6, 8, 236
    willing to depart from historical exactitude 170n1
    Woolf, Virginia, and 8, 142, 147, 149–150, 165, 180–184, 209, 223, 225n15, 237

K

Kern, Stephen 38
Kim (Kipling) 65–117 *passim*. *See also Cassell's* magazine; Kipling, Rudyard; *McClure's* magazine
    advertising near installments of 65–66, 77–80, 84–85
    advertising and promotion of 11, 67, 69–71, 80–83, 85, 94, 110–111, 115–116
    American independence from England and 11, 69, 107–108, 112, 115
    British superiority claims in 74–77
    Cassell's synopses of 82–83
    games as metaphor in 71–72
    illustrations of 11, 85–94

    muckraking and 104–107
    railways in 95–96
    serialization of 6, 11, 65–117 *passim*
    technology and Empire linked in 73, 83–85
    transatlantic reach of 71, 94, 96
"King's Visit, The" (Barr) 113
Kipling, John Lockwood (illustrator)
    as father of Kipling, Rudyard 67
    images of *Kim* (Kipling) by 11, 69, 86, 88, 90–94, 111, 114
Kipling, Rudyard 65–117 *passim*. *See also* authorial control; *Kim* (Kipling); "White Man's Burden, The" (Kipling); *and other works listed by title*
    advertising and promotion of 11, 67, 69–71, 80–83, 85, 94, 110–111, 115–116
    as celebrity 65, 70
    featured in ad for shingle stains 123n175
    featured in advertising guide 118n45
    as imperialist 8, 10–11, 66–112 *passim*
    James, Henry and 7–8, 45, 66, 167
    lawsuit 2
    Little Review and 167–168
    magazine serializations versus books of 4
    mass-market appeal of 2, 7–8, 45, 66, 81–82, 115, 118n45, 123n175
    Nobel Prize 7
    political impact of 7–8
    portrait of 81
    as proto-Modernist 7, 14, 167, 237
    as transatlantic 6–7, 123n175, 223, 236
Kirkpatrick, B.J. 196, 223
Krutch, Joseph Wood 215

L

La Farge, John (illustrator) 17, 19, 22–27, 29–30, 52, 55–56n4, 58n42, 58n57
Lamar, W.H. 135, 144–145
"Lament of the Country, A" (Henley) 124n188
Land of Many Names, The (Capek) 211
"Landscape Painter, A" (James) 26
Latham, Sean 1, 9, 13, 18, 47

Lawrence, D.H. 142, 182, 199, 210–211, 219
Lee, Hermione 209–210
Lewis, Wyndham
  advertising and promotion of 158, 160
  "Cantleman's Spring-Mate," suppression of 132–136, 139, 144–145
  on First World War's impact 131
  "Imaginary Letters" 164
  Jewish tropes used in writing by 151
  on Joyce, James 147
  Pound's comments on 141
  Tarr 160
"L'Homme Moyen Sensuel" (Pound) 132
"Lieut. Gustl: A Short Story" (Schnitzler) 211
Life magazine 36–37
Light, James (illustrator) 144
Lincoln, Abraham 97
Literary Review, New York Evening Post 196, 201
Literary World magazine 36–37
Little Magazine, The (Hoffman, Allen, and Ulrich) 186
Little Magazine, World Form (Bulson) 13
little magazines. *See also Dial; Little Review; and other magazines listed by title*
  adopting mass-market advertising techniques 2, 14, 21, 65, 115–117, 157, 186–189, 236
  affiliation with high Modernism 1–2, 8, 14, 21, 65, 115–117, 132, 156–157, 167–168, 236–237
  Cassell's versus 115–116
  circulation of 1, 139, 186, 188, 226n26
  commercial magazines versus, *see* commercial magazines; commodity/commercial culture
  counter-public sphere constructed by 8, 116, 132, 156, 164, 193
  defined 1, 139, 186
  devotion to art 1, 139, 164, 168, 236
  financial affairs of 137, 139
  First World War, approaches to 8–9; *see also* First World War
  governmental agencies' competition with 133
  literature-advertisement interplay in 14
  military conflict opposed by 132
  monochromatic covers of 65
  in networks of mutual support 157–161
  pedagogical approaches to 9, 237–239
  proliferation of 21
  transatlantic perspectives of 7–8, 146–147, 167–168, 196, 209, 224
Little Magazines and Modernism: New Approaches (Churchill) 12
Little Review (Anderson and Heap) 125–169 *passim*. *See also Ulysses* (Joyce)
  advertising in 2, 44–45, 68, 115–117, 138, 145–147, 151, 156–160, 162, 167–168, 169n1, 176nn144–145, 240n3
  censoring and suppression of 4, 11, 126, 132–150 *passim*, 160, 162–163, 168–169, 183, 236
  circulation of 139, 184, 192
  commitment to internationalism 126–132, 146–147, 158
  Dial magazine versus 181–184, 187, 189–190, 192–193, 197–198
  errors of *Ulysses* in 152–156, 176n139
  financial difficulties of 146–147, 190
  First World War's impact on 8, 126, 128–132, 134–135, 141, 146
  Henry James Number 168
  joint subscriptions with commercial magazines 2, 157
  Reader Critic column in 163–166, 176n139, 178n182
  text-heavy content in 65
  transatlantic operations of 131–132, 146–147, 158
  Ulysses (Joyce) serialized in 3–4, 6, 8–9, 11, 68, 125–169 *passim*, 171n18, 180–181, 183, 238–239
Little Review Ulysses, The (Gaipa, Latham, and Scholes) 9, 13, 237
"Lives of the Obscure, The" (Woolf) 181, 208
Lom, Stanislav 211
London Mercury magazine 12, 196, 208, 212

Longman magazine 46
Lowell, Amy 142, 147, 199
Loy, Mina 147, 151
Luftig, Victor 130
Lund, Michael 20
Lustig, T.S. 20
Lycett, Andrew 68

M
Macmillan's Magazine 67
Madame Bovary (Flaubert) 235
Mahan, Alfred T. 97
Mann, Thomas 211
Mansfield, Katherine 205–206
Many Marriages (Anderson) 198
Margolis, Anne T. 21
"Marines Signaling under Fire at Guantanamo" (Crane) 97
Marketing Modernisms (Dettmar and Watt) 45, 224n4
Marsh, W.B. 190–192
"Marvels of Modern Production" (Waldron) 95
Masses magazine 132
mass-market culture. *See* commodity/commercial culture; elite versus popular culture
masthead illustrations
  for *Kim* (Kipling) 86–87
  for *Turn of the Screw, The* (James) 17, 19, 23–27, 29
Mauss, Marcel 180, 218
Mayne, Ethel Colburn 168
McCarthy, Patrick 127
McClure, Samuel Sidney 68, 96, 167
McClure's magazine 65–117 *passim*. *See also Kim* (Kipling)
  advertising in 108–112
  Cassell's compared to 96, 104, 110, 112, 115
  circulation of 121n115
  critiquing authority in 104–108
  in Edward J. O'Brien's annual review 220
  imperialism in 11, 67, 69–70, 103–104, 107–112, 115
  Kim serialized in 6, 11, 65–117 *passim*
  literary and technological innovation in 94–96

  October 1901 issue 113–115
  "Recessional" (Kipling) published by 99
  "White Man's Burden, The" (Kipling) published by 68–69, 97–99, 103
McKible, Adam 12, 151
Meier-Graefe, Julius 213
"Memory of the Players, A" (Joyce) 138, 158, 199
"M.I." (Kipling) 113
Millar, H.R. (illustrator) 11, 69, 86–90, 93, 109, 111, 120n84, 120n94
"Mill on the Kop, The" (Barr) 76
"Miss Ormerod" (Woolf) 181, 211
Modernism in the Magazines (Scholes and Wulfman) 13, 239
Modernist authorship. *See* authorship
Modernist Journals Project (Brown University and University of Tulsa) 1, 13, 239
Modernist magazine 158
Modernist novel, characteristics of 38
"Modern Novels" (Woolf) 181
Monroe, Harriet 150, 159
"Monseigneur: Unfolded in Eleven Mysteries" (Freedman) 20
Moore, Marianne 216
Morgan, J. Pierpont 113
Morning Post, The 67
Morris, Clara 113
Morrisson, Mark
  on advertising 46, 62n137, 187, 191
  on combining literature with advertising 51
  on counter-public sphere in Modernism 132, 156–157
  on Lewis trial 134
  on *Little Review*'s targeting young readers 139, 163, 173n72, 197
  on Modernism in commercial sphere 1–2
  Public Face of Modernism, The 12, 62n137
Mortimer, Raymond 210, 212–213
Mott, Frank Luther 17, 95, 104, 108–109
"Mrs. Dalloway in Bond Street" (Woolf) 179–224 *passim*. *See also Dial* magazine; Woolf, Virginia
  advertising and 202–203

art and commodity tension in 11–12, 179–180, 204, 217–218, 223
Criterion and 210
Dial's payment to Woolf for 185, 210
Dial's publication of 6, 12, 179–224 *passim*, 238
First World War in 7–9, 212–214
gift economy in 12, 180, 217–218
Mrs. Dalloway (novel) versus 179, 182, 202, 204–205, 207–208, 212–216
shopping in 11, 179, 189, 202–203, 224
as transatlantic 12, 181, 210, 217–218
youth and age in 197–198
muckraking movement in journalism 11, 69, 97, 103–104
Mullin, Katherine 162, 186
Multiplex Hammond Writing Machine (typewriter), advertising for 129

N

narrative ambiguity. *See* ambiguity
narrative reliability
  Kim (Kipling) and 94
  Modernism and 7, 18–19
  Turn of the Screw, The (James), and U.S.S. *Maine* crisis 22–23, 28, 37–43, 51–53
Nation, The 157, 182, 185, 196, 206–207
"Nausicaa" episode of *Ulysses* (Joyce). *See also Ulysses* (Joyce)
  accusations of reader corruption and 133–134, 163
  Anderson, Margaret on 169
  mass culture references in 148
  New York Society for the Suppression of Vice on 127, 140
  occurrence in *Ulysses* 142, 165–166
  Quinn's approach to trial of 127, 136–137, 139–140
  suppression of 139
New Age magazine 166
New Criticism, school of 31
New Republic, The 157, 192–193, 196, 201
New Statesman 157, 196
New Witness, The (London) 192
New York Daily News 166
New York Edition (James) 2, 18, 56n6, 60n102
New York Evening Post 27, 50, 193, 196

New York Herald 166
New York Society for the Suppression of Vice 127, 139
New York Times 166, 187, 192–193, 196, 201
New York Tribune 27, 140, 166, 193
New York World 27, 166
Night and Day (Woolf) 207, 215
Nobel Prize of 1907 (to Kipling) 7
Norris, Margot 4, 113
Novels and Tales of Henry James, The (James) 18

O

O'Brien, Edward J. 220
"Obvious Statement, An" (Anderson) 150
Ohmann, Richard 46, 49–50, 109, 221
"Old Corcoran's Money" (Dowling) 20
Orage, A.R. 168
Orientalism 69, 86, 90, 93, 111
Osteen, Mark 180, 218
"Other Man, The" (Bryant) 113
Oxford Critical and Cultural History of Modernist Magazines, The 13

P

Paffard, Mark 88, 95
Pall Mall Gazette 67
Pape, Eric (illustrator) 10, 17, 19, 22, 24, 29–37, 47, 51–52, 55–56n4, 57n33, 60n96, 60nn100–101
Paratexts: Thresholds of Interpretation (Genette) 5, 19
paratextual elements 3, 5, 18–19, 26, 54, 66
Parkes, Adam 136–137, 172nn48–52
Parry, Ann 100
Pears' Soap, advertising for 43, 103, 109–111
Pemberton, Max 96
periodical studies 9, 12–14, 237–238
Piccoli, Raffaello 211
Playboy (1919) 159
Plumtree's Potted Meat 125, 169n1
Poetry magazine 159
Portrait of the Artist as a Young Man, A (Joyce) 116, 149, 151, 157, 160–162, 177n156
Pound, Ezra
  advertising and promotion of 199, 219
  "Classics Escape, The" 133

Dial and 182, 199, 216, 219
Egoist and 160
on "Flaubertian prose" of Joyce, James 236
on James, Henry 167–168
on Kipling, Rudyard 167
"L'Homme Moyen Sensuel" 132
Little Review and 127, 129, 131, 133, 141–168 *passim*, 183
Quinn, John and 137, 139, 141
"Small Magazines" essay 1
Ulysses (Joyce) and 131, 134, 141–145, 148, 155, 171n18, 183
"Unanism" 157
Woolf, Virginia and 165, 182, 184
Princeton Blue Mountain Project 13
Printer's Ink 108, 201
propaganda in First World War 23
Public Face of Modernism, The (Morrisson) 12, 62n137
Publisher's Weekly 195

Q
Quinn, John
concerns about government attention 132, 134–135
disagreements with *Little Review* editors 127, 135–137, 145, 148–150
financial advice to *Little Review* editors 137–142, 184, 192
on First World War's impacts 131
gender stereotypes of 137
Lamar, W.H., communication with 144

R
racial purity, soap advertising links to 109–111
Rainey, Lawrence 13–14, 44, 184, 187, 223
"reader response" theory 54
Reading Virginia Woolf's Essays and Journalism (Brosnan) 185
"Recessional" (Kipling) 98–99, 102
Red Badge of Courage, The (Crane) 132
Revolution (Beresford) 205
Richardson, Dorothy 150–151, 155, 158, 175n117
Ricketts, Harry 68–69
Rickover, H.G. 57nn23–24, 61n129

Ripans Tabules, advertising for 47–51
Rodker, John 147, 168
Roosevelt, Theodore 96, 104
Rosenbaum, S.P. 26–27, 30
Rupert of the Hentzau (Hope) 96

S
Said, Edward 66, 71, 74, 86, 93, 112
Sandburg, Carl 199
Santayana, George 210–211, 231n145
Sassoon, Siegfried 213
Saturday Evening Post 23
Saturday Review of Literature 209–210
Schnitzler, Arthur 199, 210–211
Scholes, Robert 1, 9, 13, 18, 47, 239
Scofield Thayer and The Dial (Joost) 226n33
Scott, Bonnie Kime 136, 139, 147–148, 150
Scott, Walter 116
Seebohm, Caroline 188
"Self Government" (Santayana) 211
Selling Culture (Ohmann) 63nn154–160, 109, 233nn193–195
Serial Encounters: Ulysses and the Little Review (Hutton) 13, 171n18, 177n167
Shaw, Walter 150
Short Talks on Advertising (Bates) 118n45
Silver, Brenda 12, 214–215
Simpson, Kathryn 180, 185, 188–189, 202, 217–218, 222
Sinclair, May 150–151, 165, 199–200, 219
"Small Magazines" (Pound) 1
"Solid Objects" (Woolf) 12
Sommer, William 208
Sonstegard, Adam 25, 29–33, 37, 53
Spanish-American War. *See also* U.S.S. Maine
Awkward Age, The (James) and 15n16
as "newspaper-made war" 23
Turn of the Screw, The (James) and 7, 18, 23, 37–42
as ushering in Modernist era 38
Spender, E. 76–77
Spoo, Robert 130
Squire, J.C. 208
"Staging 'Miss Mutton'" (Morris) 113
Standard Rate and Data Service 201

Stanley-Brown, Ruth 193
Stein, Gertrude 44
Stevenson, Robert Louis 45, 96, 167
Stewart, J.I.M. 67
St. James's Gazette 67
"Story of the Declaration of Independence, The" (Tarbell) 107–108
Strand Magazine 67, 78–79
Sullivan, Zohreh T. 66, 93
Sumner, John 139, 146, 150
"Sumner versus James Joyce" (Monroe) 150
Swan Fountain Pen, advertising for 84–85

T
"Tammany Commandment, The" (Flynt) 113
Tarbell, Ida M. 107–108, 115
Tatar, Maria 30
technology
  in advertisements' layout 219
  linked to Empire in *Kim* (Kipling) 73, 83–85
  in *McClure's* 94–96
  in printing press 62n137, 95
Thayer, Scofield. *See also Dial* magazine
  advertising strategies of 186, 188–196, 203–204
  contacting Joyce, James for contributions 183
  financial support of *Dial* 184, 190–191, 193, 226n33
  as founder of *Dial* 186
  goals for *Dial* 183, 186, 188–189, 192
  Woolf, Virginia, interactions with 206, 210
Ticknor, Benjamin 46
Times Literary Supplement 149, 181–182, 196, 205
Times (London) 97–98
Tintner, Adeline R. 25
transatlantic periodical culture. *See* internationalism; periodical studies
Transatlantic Print Culture, 1880–1940 (Ardis and Collier) 12–13
Translation Bureau 134
Trollope, Anthony 20
Turn of the Screw, The (James) 17–55 *passim. See also Collier's* magazine; James, Henry
  advertising and promotion of 21–22
  Collier's revitalization and 17–18
  Collier's serialization of 6, 8, 10, 17–55 *passim*
  illustrations by Demuth, Charles, of 54–55n4
  illustrations by Pape, Eric, of 10, 29–37, 52
  Kim (Kipling) compared to 66, 86, 94
  masthead illustration for 17, 19, 23–27, 29
  narrative reliability in 22–23, 28, 37–43, 51–53
  revisions to 56n6
  Ripans Tabules advertisements and 47–51
  serialization's impact on organization of 20–23
  speculations versus truth in 28–29, 52–54
  as transatlantic text 37
  "unreliable governess" as emblem in 38
  U.S.S. *Maine* and, *see* Spanish-American War; U.S.S. *Maine*
Turn of the Screw, The: Bewildered Vision (Heller) 33
Two Magics, The (James) 18, 56n6, 60n104

U
Ulrich, Carolyn F. 186
Ulysses (Joyce) 125–169 *passim. See also* Joyce, James; *Little Review*; "Nausicaa" episode of *Ulysses* (Joyce)
  advertisements in 125
  advertisements near installments of 156–160, 169, 238
  advertising and promotion of 115–117, 151, 199, 216–217
  book design for 2
  censoring by *Little Review* editors 142–147
  censoring of *Little Review* by government 4, 11, 126, 132–142, 149–150, 160, 162–163, 168–169, 183, 236
  errors and misprints in 126–127, 152–156

First World War and 8, 11, 128, 130–132, 134
internationalism in 125, 129–132
Jews and 151–152
Joyce's struggles to publish 168–169
mixing of high and low culture in 142–143, 148, 184
Mrs. Dalloway (Woolf) compared to 8, 182–183
other items in *Little Review* and 68, 147–152, 167–169
Portrait of the Artist as a Young Man, A (Joyce) and 116, 149, 151, 157, 160–163
reader responses to 163–166, 178n182
serialization in *Little Review* 3–4, 6, 8–9, 11, 68, 125–169 *passim*, 171n18, 180–181, 183, 238–239
stylistic innovation in 3, 129–130
Waste Land, The (Eliot) and 216–217
Ulysses Annotated (Gifford) 166, 170n1
"Unanism" (Pound) 157
Unpartizan Review 193
unreliable narrative. *See* narrative reliability
"Unwritten Novel, An" (Woolf) 12
Upheaval, The (Lom) 211
U.S. Post Office 11, 127, 135, 139, 143–145, 162–163, 183
U.S.S. *Maine*. *See also* Spanish-American War; *Turn of the Screw, The* (James)
ambiguity of reports on 10, 28, 37–41, 52–54, 61n129, 129n61
Collier's "picture coverage" of 22, 37–43, 52–54
Turn of the Screw, The (James) and 7, 10, 17–18, 22–23, 28, 37–43, 49–55, 61n121, 238

V
Vanderham, Paul 142, 173nn80–87
Vanity Fair magazine 44, 187, 203, 207, 215, 226n33, 229n78
Victorian era 7, 20, 38, 66, 103, 181, 215, 237
Victorian Serial, The (Hughes and Lund) 20
Virginia Woolf and the Bloomsbury Avant-Garde (Froula) 225n11, 232n155

Virginia Woolf Icon (Silver) 215
Vogue magazine 185, 187–188, 215
Voyage Out, The (Woolf) 206–207

W
Wadsworth, P. Beaumont 213
Waldron, George B. 95
Waldstein, Louis 36
war. *See* Boer War; First World War; Spanish-American War
Ward, Mrs. Humphrey 45
"War on the Sea and its Lessons, The" (Mahan) 97
Warren, Jonathan 55n4, 56n6
Waste Land, The (Eliot) 7, 216–217
Watson, James Sibley 186–187, 192–193
Watt, Stephen 45
Weeks, E.L. (illustrator) 11, 86–88, 90, 92–94, 111, 120n84, 120n98
Weir, David 4, 134
"White Man's Burden, The" (Kipling)
Empire and 69, 77, 103
impact on American politics 7
McClure's publication of 68, 97, 109
Pears' Soap ads and 103, 111
publication history of 97–103
"Recessional" as sister poem of 98–99
Wicke, Jennifer 1, 13, 180, 223
Williams, William Carlos 175n117
Wilson, Angus 68
Wilson, Edmund 30, 48, 213–214
Wilson, Harold 104
Windsor Magazine 67
Wm. H. Wise & Company 235
Wollaeger, Mark 23, 130
"Woman Who Rode Away, The" (Lawrence) 211
Woolf, Leonard 2, 190, 196, 206, 207
Woolf, Virginia 179–224 *passim*. *See also* authorial control; "Mrs. Dalloway in Bond Street" (Woolf); *and other works listed by title*
advertising and promotion of 12, 65, 210–212, 214–215
in American press 12, 214–215
artistic self-fashioning of 2, 12
book versus periodical publications of 4
financial worries of 190, 208

as high Modernist 14, 65
Hogarth Press set up by 2, 12, 180, 205, 222
internationalism of 6–9, 12, 180–181, 196, 208–215, 223–224, 236
Joyce, James, and 8, 142, 147, 149–150, 165, 180–184, 209, 223, 225n15, 237
Mansfield, Katherine, and 205–206
mass-market appeal of 185, 187–188, 220–221
periodical culture and 12, 185, 187, 204–208, 237, 239
on professionalism as market force 165
on tensions between art and commerce 185, 187, 189, 220–224
on tradition and modernity 215–217

World War I. *See* First World War
Wulfman, Clifford 13, 239

Y

Yannella, Philip R. 176n136
Years of Transition (Joost) 226n33
Yeats, William Butler 131, 147, 182, 199, 211, 219, 222
Yellow Book magazine 168
youth culture
    Cassell's and 76
    Dial and 197–198
    Little Review and 162–163, 197

Z

Zangwill, Louis 20, 22
Zipes, Jack 30

www.ingramcontent.com/pod-product-compliance
Lightning Source LLC
Chambersburg PA
CBHW062122300426
44115CB00012BA/1776